MONDAY NIGHT AT NARSAI'S

AN INTERNATIONAL MENU COOKBOOK FROM THE LEGENDARY RESTAURANT

NARSAI M. DAVID
&
DORIS MUSCATINE

Illustrations by Susan Mattmann

SIMON AND SCHUSTER   New York

Copyright © 1987 by Narsai M. David and
Doris Muscatine
All rights reserved
including the right of reproduction
in whole or in part in any form
Published by Simon and Schuster
A Division of Simon & Schuster, Inc.
Simon & Schuster Building
Rockefeller Center
1230 Avenue of the Americas
New York, New York 10020
SIMON AND SCHUSTER and colophon are
registered trademarks of Simon & Schuster, Inc.

Designed by Levavi & Levavi
Manufactured in the United States of America

10 9 8 7 6 5 4 3 2 1
Library of Congress Cataloging-in-Publication Data
David, Narsai.
   Monday night at Narsai's.

   Bibliography: p.
   Includes index.
   1. Cookery, International.   2. Menus.   3. Narsai's
Restaurant.   I. Muscatine, Doris.   II. Title.
TX725.A1D28   1986   641.5'09794'63   86-26296
ISBN: 0-671-53011-9

The authors wish to thank the following for permission to
use the recipes.

Columbia University Press: Martha Washington's
Booke of Cookery by Karen Hess. Copyright © 1981
Columbia University Press. By permission.
   Shirley Sarvis: A Taste of Portugal by Shirley Sar-
vis. Copyright 1967 by Shirley Sarvis. Published by
Charles Scribner's Sons. Reprinted by permission of
the author.
   Simon & Schuster: Jacques Pépin: A French Chef
Cooks at Home. Copyright © 1975 by Jacques Pépin.
Reprinted by permission of Simon & Schuster.
   Time-Life Books: Foods of the World/The Cooking
of the Caribbean Islands © 1970 Time-Life Books,
Inc.

To Shulamith, Michael, Veni, and Danny:
my mother, father, wife, and son—N.M.D.
For Charles, Jeff, Neen, Lissa, and Naomi—D.M.

ACKNOWLEDGMENTS

Our warmest thanks to Venus David and Maggie Mah, who researched and developed the original menus and recipes for the Monday Night dinners—Veni for the first year, and Maggie for the duration—and to Samuel Scopiola David, whose sense of style set the tone for the dining room at Narsai's and helped shape the restaurant itself. We also owe special thanks to M. Abdelli and M. M. Mohaba of Meskerem Restaurant in Washington, D.C., Robert Boyle, Daniel N. David, Carol Field, Rachel Harris, Erik Housh, Ludwig Immergluck, Christopher Lee, the late Theodore Meng-fei Lee, from whom we learned so much about Chinese culture, Susan and Robert Lescher, Gordon (Don) Link, Charles Muscatine, Grace O'Connell, Claire Harrison Reed, William Reinhard, and Josef Maximilian Strasser. Our particular gratitude goes to our editor, Carole Lalli, for her extraordinary expertise, patience, and good humor. We also give thanks to her very capable assistant, Nancy Kalish.

Contents

�

Foreword

❖

I met Narsai and Doris a dozen or so years ago on the West Coast and we became friends, as lovers of food do, around a table sharing wine and food. These are two of my favorite people in the food world and they are well paired to produce a superlative cookbook.

For two years Doris took my classes in San Francisco. Her varied and eclectic background and her knowledge of the cultural history of food and wine—especially her knowledge of the West Coast—had already led her to write three books: *A Cook's Tour of San Francisco; A Cook's Tour of Rome*, depicting vividly the beauty of the Italian capital; and *Old San Francisco —The Biography of a City*. She recently edited *The University of California/Sotheby Book of California Wine*. That background and knowledge she brings to *Monday Night at Narsai's*; it is a great asset to the book and complements Narsai's cooking.

Narsai is, before anything else, a generous man, ready to cook for friends, to feed friends, to give. Although his restaurant, Narsai's, in Kensington (next to Berkeley in California), was serving his brand of classic French cuisine, his background took him to other types of cooking and his open-mindedness made him experiment with types of cooking that most people had never heard of. Narsai's cooking is a creation of the West. A talented and versatile man, involved not only in the professional world of cooking but in catering, he created an innovative and exciting food market, as well as starred in his own PBS-TV series, *Over Easy*.

For eleven years, Helene and Stan Schwartz, friends in common from Danville, California, have done a food party each year that coincides with my teaching on the West Coast. Year after year, Narsai has officiated over the grill, creating new, interesting, and exciting concoctions. I have great memories of his restaurant and the eclectic cooking featured on the menu, especially dishes in the Assyrian style— particularly his lamb prepared in the Assyrian manner. His knowledge, however, goes beyond the preparation of meat and, perhaps because he had no formal training in cooking, he has kept an open mind with food—from his rich Chocolate Decadence sert and the beautiful French bread he served at the market, to his little goat cheeses in oil, homemade jam, praline, homemade caviar, and smoked salmon. There is no part of food or any type of ethnic cooking that doesn't attract him in one way or the other.

For many years—and before such specialized set menus were fashionable—he presented "Monday Night at Narsai's" at his restaurant. Here, he would investigate a different type of ethnic food each week, and those special evenings, which made the restaurant famous, exemplified the distinctive cooking philosophy of a friend who is a restaurateur, caterer, television chef, *charcutier*, and a great wine connoisseur, having a cellar of more than 60,000 bottles. These fifty-three menus take you around the world. From a simple *gado gado* (a spicy vegetable and peanut dip from Indonesia), to a carpetbagger's steak from Australia, a braised duck with peanut and lime sauce from West Africa or such all-American dishes as sausage cooked in cider and hazelnut cake with rose water frosting —his menus will make you discover new, exciting worlds of cooking and fascinating dishes, accompanied by wine suggestions, from all over the world.

With the plethora of cookbooks that appear on the market every year, it would seem that everything has been said about food. This is not the case. There is always room for an intelligently presented, well-constructed book incorporating serious and delectable recipes, and this is what this book is all about. Above all, it is a book to use when cooking with friends.

I remember little quail and duck hearts cooked on the barbecue at the Schwartzes' and a delectable roast of lamb that Narsai's did at Trefethen winery in the Napa Valley for a lunch, as well as an incredible dinner that reproduced the famous $4,000 dinner that Craig Claiborne and Pierre Franey enjoyed years ago at Chez Denis in Paris and that Narsai produced using the food and wine of the West Coast. His cooking shows progression, a sense of adventure, but, more than anything, advocates fun and friendship. In my opinion this is how cooking should be enjoyed—with the conviviality of the people you feel comfortable with, are happy to be with, and want to drink wine and share food with.

—JACQUES PÉPIN

Introduction

✤

From the beginning, San Francisco has been an eating town. During the Gold Rush of the 1850s, the instant city suddenly overflowed with a vast population from all over the world. To accommodate this homeless, predominantly male, and diversely ethnic group, boardinghouses and restaurants proliferated, serving their food in tents, hastily assembled shacks, and even in ships deserted in the harbor. At first, there were imported provisions but few knowledgeable cooks. As the city grew, its lusty eating habits became more refined and complex. By the 1870s, Eastern investors were coming by private railcar, bringing their own French chefs, many of whom deserted to mine their fortunes in kitchens and restaurants catering to the wealthy population.

The newly rich Californians, furthermore, were taking up culture, traveling to the Continent, and acquiring more sophisticated culinary tastes. They were now eating dinners of a dozen or more courses, of great ethnic variety, and drinking wines from abroad as well as from their own burgeoning vineyards. By the last decade of the century, only forty years after the discovery of gold, San Francisco had earned a worldwide reputation for great cooking and great eating.

The city has maintained its gastronomic style over the years, continuing to synthesize its inheritance of foreign flavors with its tradition of high-spirited enthusiasm at the table. Today the San Francisco area has more restaurants per capita than any other city in the world except Paris, and its cooking represents a much greater variety of styles and cuisines than most. The current population of the metropolitan area has an ethnic diversity, according to the last U.S. census, seen nowhere else in the country. And each successive immigrant group—from Europe, Africa, the Orient, the Middle East, Mexico, and Latin America—contributes to and continues to change the city's culinary direction. Able to combine exotic imports with the fresh products of nearby farms and ranches, seafood from the Pacific, and wines from the state's wineries, the San Francisco area has continued to draw the attention of the country to its innovative culinary tradition.

People who come to this kind of place,

for whatever reasons, can be powerfully, sometimes irrevocably, inspired by it, even to taking up careers in food and cooking. The authors of this book are cases in point.

When Doris Muscatine moved to the Bay Area from the East Coast in 1948, her fascination with the area's culinary tradition led to her work as a writer and cultural historian focused on wine, food, and regional history. Her first book was about the restaurants of San Francisco, their history and ethnic diversity. She later wrote a history of the city that included long sections on the development of the area's restaurant and wine industries and the cultural contributions of its various ethnic populations. Her most recent book is about California wine.

During the two years she lived in Paris and one in Rome, Doris studied cooking at the Cordon Bleu, wrote articles about wine and food for U.S. and foreign journals, and completed a book on the restaurants and cooking of Rome. Like Narsai David, she travels frequently, which gives her, as it does Narsai, the opportunity to sample a great many of the cuisines described in this book in their native habitats. And, also like Narsai, she owns a vineyard in the Napa Valley.

Narsai David has been involved with food in one way or another ever since he came to California from Chicago when he was still a young boy. In Turlock, in the Central Valley, he worked in the fields harvesting produce, put up peaches and prunes in the local canneries, learned

about dehydrating garlic, and, by the time he was in high school, worked part-time as an assistant butcher in a supermarket. As a student at the University of California, he supplemented two scholarships by working as a soda jerk at a Berkeley drive-in, supervising the kitchen of his 300-student co-op, and becoming chairman of central food services for all of the seven student co-op houses. At the end of Narsai's freshman year, he opened his first "restaurant," the Tri-Valley Huddler, a sandwich and soup wagon at the Turlock Farmer's Market.

While still a student at Berkeley, he spent some time as relief bartender at the Pot Luck Restaurant, then became its manager, and eventually a partner. The place was famous for its casual bistro atmosphere, bottomless bowls of homemade soups, and such dinner specialties as sweetbreads and a standard dessert of apples and cheese—quite sophisticated at the time. The Pot Luck also held to a belief in California wines when it was more fashionable to serve French ones. The Pot Luck partnership later included interests in two other restaurants, the Black Sheep and Cruchon's. People still talk about the Black Sheep's coconut cream pie made with fresh coconut—they used to hack away at the coconuts in the basement— and the chocolate fudge and lemon cream cheese pies from Cruchon's. You could buy those to take out, which Doris fondly remembers doing.

Narsai left the Pot Luck in 1970 to start his own catering business and look into the possibilities of opening a restaurant. He found a property in Kensington, a quiet neighborhood in north Berkeley, and got things started on mostly borrowed funds and unrestrained enthusiasm. After a lengthy search, he finally obtained an affordable liquor license. He bought a 200,000-gallon redwood tank, the old Beacon Hill Reservoir, made of clear vertical-grained heartwood, 18 feet high and 45 feet across. The 15,000 board feet of lumber produced from its staves and floorboards surfaced the restaurant walls and the building's exterior. Douglas fir roof supports, submerged under water during the tank's life as a reservoir, became the supporting posts in the restaurant's entrance hall. The rods and castings went into wall sconces and massive metal sculptures, designed and produced by the artist Martin Metal. The bar top, a 21-foot-long solid piece of black walnut carved by Miles Karpilow, came from a tree on a friend's Napa Valley property. And the antique back bar came out of the old Moose Lodge in Oakland.

The restaurant opened for business on April 3, 1972. It was the real start of, and inspiration for, Narsai's wide-ranging career in the food world. Within just a few years, he had become a prominent restaurateur, *charcutier*, caterer, and vineyardist; the operator of specialty food markets and the producer of a line of fancy food products; a familiar figure nationwide as the resident chef for six years on the PBS television show "Over Easy," and as the host of the weekly radio program, the KCBS "Saturday Kitchen," and the daily program, "Narsai & Company."

Narsai's Restaurant at once became an East Bay gathering place for serious diners. The audience of the PBS television station KQED, polled on their restaurant preferences, voted it among the top five restaurants in the entire Bay Area. Narsai's even had its own bakery, which produced breads appropriate to each meal—many years before the current vogue of restaurants' baking their own bread. Over the years, Narsai commissioned such artists as Harold Paris, Raymond Saunders, and Tom Holland to execute annual commemorative posters for the restaurant's celebrations.

During its thirteen-year existence, the restaurant also developed one of the greatest wine lists in the country: the regular card listed 400 bottles, the special reserve list another 1,100; the cellars held 60,000 bottles. A few years ago, Frank Prial, the wine writer for the *New York Times*, included Narsai's wine card (duplicated on page 311) as among the ten best restaurant lists in the world. For years, the Berkeley Wine and Food Society held its monthly tastings in the Back Room at Narsai's. When the restaurant announced that it would close in June of 1984, the society took over the dining room for its last meeting, a great dinner to honor Narsai and bid the restaurant farewell. On closing night, the crowd, which jammed the rooms and spilled onto the rainy sidewalks outside, was treated to caviar and champagne.

Narsai closed the restaurant as well as the adjacent market to devote more time to his catering business and the manufacture and international distribution of his own line of products—mustards, preserves, chocolate sauces, seasoned salts, and so on. Among Narsai's most challenging catering assignments have been serving hot dogs backstage at celebrity rock concerts; breakfast for 6,000 after an all-night New Year's Eve concert; dinner for a black-tie event staged in a tent on a bluff overlooking a quarry; and 1,000 hot outdoor lunches delivered in nine minutes to guests at the annual Napa Valley Wine Auction by using a flotilla of golf carts.

The idea for the Monday Night dinners at Narsai's—presenting a different ethnic dinner every week—had started on a less ambitious scale when Narsai was a partner at the Pot Luck. When he opened his own restaurant, he resurrected the idea and for more than ten years served a weekly five-course ethnic menu, complete with the appropriate breads and wines.

Monday Night at Narsai's is fondly dedicated to the memory of those splendid celebrations of foods from all around the world and to the exuberant interest of Americans in a variety of ethnic cuisines.

The fifty-six dinner menus collected here represent the best of the dishes from over the years. Some cuisines were presented on more than one occasion. In order to provide balance and a variety of recipes, we have in some cases combined courses from different original menus devoted to the same cuisine. One special menu—Duck Liver Pâté with Port Aspic; Mushroom-Clam Velouté; Rack of Lamb Assyrian; Rice and Rye Pilaf; Vegetable Mélange; Romaine Hearts with Fresh Herbs and Citronnade Dressing; Strass Rye Bread; and Chocolate Decadence—a selection of perennial favorites from the regular menu—celebrates the flavor of every night at Narsai's.

A Word About Wine

Because there are so many wines currently on the market—there are now over 650 bonded wineries in California alone—it would be impossible to suggest any particular recent bottling, domestic or foreign, let alone any particular wine drunk in the past, with any assurance that the reader would be able to find it. Therefore, we have provided nearly all of the menus with the historic record of the actual wines drunk, as a way of suggesting styles and types, and names of typical makers. This will give a sense of the specific wine characteristics that are compatible with each dish; if not the same wine, then one with similar characteristics can be sought. We have also reproduced the basic wine list from the restaurant (see page 311). It is particularly useful in identifying specific wines and vintages that impressed us.

About matching wines and foods: Because they are a natural combination, most wines can be drunk with most foods. In red wine–producing districts in Europe, for example, no one would ever think "white wine with fish; red wine with meat." They would simply drink the local red wine with everything. The same would apply in white wine–producing areas. And it would all taste fine. What is appropriate with every-day food, however, might not be as enjoy-able with a more elaborate menu. There, one might choose wines of greater variety, complexity, and elegance. Conversely, the nuances of a Château Lafite would be lost with a pepperoni pizza.

Another factor, besides appropriate-ness, is contrast. Some wines harmonize with the flavors of a dish, others provide a counterpoint to it. One effect is not better than the other, simply different than the other; but while one combination might be agreeable, another might be outstanding. We have tried throughout to make these distinctions by discussing the rationale of the wines chosen.

Wine drunk by itself tastes different than when accompanied by food. The same wine tastes different when drunk with different foods. Even the same food often tastes different when paired with different wines. The best rule is to drink whatever wine you most enjoy with what you are eating.

Africa (East and West)

❖

Tropical Fruit Salad

Sautéed Mushrooms on Yam Slices

Braised Duck with Peanut and Lime Sauce
Okra and Fig Casserole
Steamed Rice

Millet Bread

Banana and Coconut Pudding

Wines:
Mark West Vineyards Johannisberg Riesling
Mazis-Chambertin, Clerget

TROPICAL FRUIT SALAD

(SERVES 6)

1 small ripe pineapple
1 large mango
1 papaya
juice of 1 lemon
juice of 1 lime
¼ teaspoon salt
1 tablespoon sugar
¼–½ teaspoon red pepper flakes or
*   cayenne pepper*
6 sprigs mint

Peel the pineapple, cut it into 6 wedges, and remove the cores. Peel and seed the mango and papaya and cut them each into 6 wedges. Put all the fruit into a large bowl.

Mix the lemon and lime juices, salt, and sugar in a small bowl. Pour the juice mixture over the fruit, tossing gently to coat the wedges with the dressing.

To serve, arrange the fruit on individual serving plates and very carefully sprinkle a whisper of red pepper flakes or cayenne over it. Garnish each portion with a mint sprig.

SAUTÉED MUSHROOMS ON YAM SLICES

Melt some butter in a skillet and sauté 1 pound small button mushrooms with a few chopped green onions, a small amount of chopped green pepper, and a very small amount of fresh chili pepper. Season with salt and pepper and a little lemon juice. Reserve. Peel some yams and slice them diagonally into ovals about 2 inches long by 3 inches wide. Deep-fry them in vegetable oil until they are golden brown and tender. Drain on paper towels. Top them with the sautéed mushrooms.

BRAISED DUCK WITH PEANUT AND LIME SAUCE

(SERVES 6 TO 8)

Some of the preparation of the duck, as well as the sauce, can be done a day in advance. This dish is traditionally made by partially roasting, then braising, the whole duck. When we prepared it for the restaurant dinner, however, we treated it like a salmi of duck, boning it off the carcass after roasting and making a natural stock of the bones. This made for an easier service than carving the duck at the table, yet retained the original seasonings and flavors. It is this method that we give here.

If you do all of the advance preparation of duck and sauce the day before, cover them tightly with foil or plastic wrap and refrigerate. When ready to cook, increase the baking time to 50 or 60 minutes.

2 4-pound ducks
paprika
salt and pepper
2 cups water
12 allspice
½ teaspoon grated nutmeg

1 small chili pepper, halved, or ½ teaspoon
  cayenne pepper
2 tablespoons flour
½ cup peanut butter
juice of 2–3 limes

Preheat the oven to 450°F.

Prepare the ducks first: Pull off and discard any pockets of fat. Season the ducks with paprika and salt and pepper. Place ducks, necks, hearts, and gizzards on a rack in a roasting pan and roast until the skin is brown but the meat is still very rare, about 30 minutes. Lower the oven temperature to 350°F.

Remove the ducks and parts from the roasting pan and let them cool until you can handle them. Cut away the leg and thigh in one piece. Lay it skin side down and cut between the leg and thigh bone to separate the cartilage, but do not disjoint. Remove each half breast from the carcass with the wing still attached. Remove the second and third joints of the wing, leaving the meaty first joint still attached to the breast (see illustration, page 213). Arrange the meat in a casserole and set aside.

Discard the fat in the roasting pan and deglaze the pan drippings with the 2 cups water. Transfer the deglazed pan juices to a large soup pot or Dutch oven. Add the duck carcasses and any bone and trimmings of skin. Cover with fresh water. Add the allspice, nutmeg, and chili pepper or cayenne. Simmer for 1 to 1½ hours to make a stock. Strain into a sauce pot, skimming off and reserving any fat.

Bring the stock to a rapid boil. Mix 1 tablespoon of the reserved fat with the flour and add it to the stock. Add the peanut butter and cook, uncovered, until the stock has reduced to 4 cups. Add the lime juice to taste and adjust the seasoning with salt and pepper. Simmer just long enough to blend.

Pour the sauce over the duck pieces. Cover and bake at 350°F for about 30 minutes, or until the duck has heated through (see Note). If the sauce seems too thin, remove the cover while baking.

NOTE: If the duck has been refrigerated overnight, increase the baking time to 50 or 60 minutes.

OKRA AND FIG CASSEROLE
(SERVES 6)

3 tablespoons butter
1 large onion, thinly sliced
1 pound okra, stems cut off
juice of 1 lemon
1 cup water
1 tablespoon honey
salt and pepper
10–12 small fresh green figs (or black, if
  green not available)

Melt the butter in a large skillet, add the onion, and sauté until it is translucent. Add the okra and stir until it is well coated with the butter. Add the lemon juice, water, and honey and season with salt and pepper. Cook, covered, for 5 to

10 minutes, or until the okra is almost tender.

Preheat the oven to 350°F.

While the okra is cooking, remove the stems from the figs and arrange the fruit on the bottom of an ovenproof casserole. Pour the cooked okra mixture over the figs and bake, uncovered, until heated through, 10 to 15 minutes.

STEAMED RICE

A simple steamed rice should accompany the duck and the okra-fig casserole. Use the basic recipe in the menu for China.

MILLET BREAD

Use the recipe for Granny Wheat Bread in the Sweden menu, substituting 1 cup whole millet seeds, untoasted, for the cup of toasted wheat flakes.

BANANA AND COCONUT PUDDING
(SERVES 6)

Allow for time to chill before serving this lovely dessert.

> 1 tablespoon butter, melted
> 4 eggs
> 3 tablespoons brown sugar
> ½ cup half and half
> ¾ cup coconut cream, bottled or
>   homemade (page 61)
> 2 ripe bananas
> 1 teaspoon pumpkin pie spice or ground
>   cinnamon
> meat of 1 small coconut, shredded, or 1½
>   cups canned shredded coconut

Preheat the oven to 350°F.

Cover a 1½-quart casserole or 6 to 8 individual custard cups with the melted butter. Set aside.

In a blender or food processor mix the eggs, sugar, half and half, coconut cream, bananas, and spice until smooth. Stir in all but ¼ cup of the shredded coconut. Pour into the casserole and sprinkle the remaining coconut on top.

Bake the large casserole for 40 to 50 minutes, the individual custard molds for 30 to 35 minutes, or until a small knife inserted near the center comes out clean. Chill in the refrigerator for 2 to 3 hours or overnight.

A Note on the Wines

Our choice to harmonize with the fruits and vegetables that make up the first part of this African dinner would be a delicate white Johannisberg Riesling, light of body, and quite fruity, such as a bottle from Mark West Vineyards.

A rich, full-bodied red wine, with the kind of lingering aftertaste often found in regal French Burgundies, would be a good match with the richness of the duck. An example is a Mazis-Chambertin by Clerget, from the Côte de Nuits.

Armenia

✻

Lentil Soup with Lemon and Fresh Tarragon

Phyllo Pastry with Spinach-Cheese Filling

Stuffed Lamb and Wheat Balls with Minted Yogurt Sauce
Fried Zucchini

Lavash

Poached Stuffed Apples in Honey

Wines:
Kenwood Vineyards Chenin Blanc
Edna Valley Pinot Noir

LENTIL SOUP WITH LEMON AND FRESH TARRAGON
(SERVES 6)

¼ cup olive oil
2 medium onions, thinly sliced
*4 cups beef broth (see recipe below) or
    water*
¾ cup lentils, picked over and washed
½ teaspoon salt
¼ teaspoon pepper
1 tablespoon lemon juice
*1 tablespoon chopped fresh tarragon or
    1 teaspoon dried*

Heat the olive oil in a 4-quart Dutch oven or stewpot. Add the onions and sauté until golden brown. Add the beef broth or water, lentils, salt, and pepper. Bring to a boil and skim off any froth that forms. Lower the heat to a simmer, cover, and cook until tender, about 45 minutes to 1 hour. Stir in the lemon juice, sprinkle with the tarragon, and serve immediately.

Brown Meat Stock
(MAKES 5 TO 6 CUPS)

This meat stock can be used in all recipes calling for a meat stock, broth, or consommé.

2½–3 pounds beef, veal, or lamb bones
2 quarts water
1 carrot, or peelings from 3–4 carrots
1 medium onion, unpeeled, chopped

*3–4 large sprigs parsley, or stems from
    1 bunch parsley*
1 stalk celery, or leaves from 1 head celery
2 bay leaves
½ teaspoon thyme
4 cloves
12 black peppercorns
*a small piece of bacon rind, or 2 ounces
    ham*
*2 medium tomatoes, or 1 cup canned
    tomatoes*
1 cup dry red wine

Roast the bones in a baking pan at 350°F for 1 hour, or until lightly browned. Transfer to a heavy stockpot or Dutch oven with a spoon in order to avoid the rendered fat in the roasting pan. Discard the fat. Add all remaining ingredients. Bring to a boil, then lower to the slowest possible simmer. Simmer for at least 6 hours, or overnight. At no time should there be less than 6 cups of liquid. Add more water if necessary. Remove from the heat and cool until it is safe to handle. Strain through a fine sieve. Discard the bones and vegetables. Skim the excess fat. Any fat that remains will solidify on the surface and can be discarded before using the stock. Refrigerate or freeze in containers of a size most suitable to your uses. If this stock is to be used for a sauce or glace de viande (page 298), strain it through a cloth.

NOTE: Since veal has so much more gelatin than beef or lamb bones, the best results are obtained by using beef and veal or lamb and veal together.

PHYLLO PASTRY WITH SPINACH-CHEESE FILLING
(MAKES 6 TO 8 APPETIZERS)

FILLING:
  ¼ *bunch spinach (about 1 cup)*
  ¼ *cup pine nuts*
  4 ounces feta cheese
  4 ounces cream cheese
  1 egg
  ½ *teaspoon grated nutmeg*
  ⅛ *teaspoon cayenne pepper*
  1 tablespoon chopped fresh parsley

DOUGH:
  ½ *cup (1 stick) butter*
  7 or 8 sheets of packaged phyllo dough

DO AHEAD:
Defrost the phyllo dough and return remainder to the freezer. If a very hot day, cover the sheets with wax paper and a damp cloth to keep them from drying out.

Melt the butter and remove from the heat.

To prepare the filling, wash the spinach and dry it thoroughly; this is very important (a lettuce spinner works well). Chop the spinach. Toast the pine nuts lightly. Blend the cheeses with the egg, nutmeg, and cayenne. Add the spinach, toasted pine nuts, and parsley. Set aside.

The sheets of packaged phyllo dough measure about 12 x 17 inches. Cut them in half the short way, giving you two pieces approximately 12 x 8½ inches from each single sheet. Cut the sheets again to make one piece about 8 inches square, and a sec-

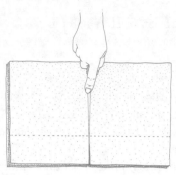

ond piece about 4 x 8 inches for each cut sheet. (See illustration.) You can stack the uncut sheets on top of each other and cut them all at once.

Brush an 8-x-8-inch square baking pan with some of the melted butter. Lay one 8-inch square or two half-squares of dough in the pan. Brush with the butter. Stack a total of 8 to 10 layers, brushing each sheet with butter. Spread the filling evenly over the layers of dough. Layer the remaining phyllo sheets on top, brushing each with butter. Chill in the refrigerator for an hour or more, covered with plastic wrap.

Preheat the oven to 350°F.

Cut the pastry into 2-inch diagonal serving pieces *before* baking. Bake for about 30 minutes or until puffed up and golden brown.

STUFFED LAMB AND WHEAT BALLS WITH MINTED YOGURT SAUCE
(SERVES 6)

WALNUT BUTTER STUFFING:
  ½ *cup (1 stick) butter, softened*
  ½ *teaspoon ground cinnamon*

¼ teaspoon black pepper
½ cup chopped walnuts or pistachio nuts

LAMB AND WHEAT BALLS:
¾ cup fine cracked bulgur wheat
½ cup water
1½ pounds lean lamb, very finely ground
1 medium onion, ground or minced
2 teaspoons paprika
1 teaspoon salt
¼ teaspoon cayenne pepper
4 cups meat broth (page 23) or water

SAUCE:
2 tablespoons butter
1 medium onion, finely chopped
1 cup broth from cooking the meatballs
1 cup plain yogurt
1 egg
3–4 tablespoons chopped fresh mint, or
1 tablespoon dried

DO AHEAD:
Soak the cracked wheat in the ½ cup water
for 10 minutes.

Blend together the butter and seasonings.
Mix in the chopped nuts. Chill. Divide
into 18 lumps and form into tiny balls,
using butter paddles or the palms of your
hands. Refrigerate.

Mix the cracked wheat with the lamb,
onion, paprika, salt, and cayenne. Use a
paddle, or knead by hand, until smooth.
Shape into 18 balls. Press a lump of the
walnut butter stuffing into the center of
each ball. Roll between your palms until
smooth and round. Simmer the meatballs
in the broth or water for 6 to 8 minutes.

To make the sauce, melt the butter in a
saucepan. Add the onion and sauté until
golden brown. Add the broth. In a bowl
whisk together the yogurt and egg. Add
the yogurt mixture to the broth all at once
and whisk just until heated through. Keep
the heat below a simmer or the sauce will
curdle. Stir in the mint.

Turn the meatballs onto a serving platter or divide among individual shallow
soup plates and pour the sauce over.

FRIED ZUCCHINI

Slice 3 or 4 thin zucchini into rounds
⅜ inch thick. Put some flour, salt, and
pepper in a paper bag, add the zucchini
pieces several at a time, close the bag, and
shake back and forth to coat the slices
evenly. Heat some olive oil or clarified butter in a skillet, add the zucchini, and fry
until brown on both sides. The zucchini
will brown more quickly if they are not
crowded in the pan.

LAVASH

With this dinner we served lavash, the flat
bread used so frequently in the Middle
East. For instructions on how to moisten
it, see the Assyrian menu.

✳

POACHED STUFFED APPLES IN HONEY
(SERVES 6)

6 medium tart cooking apples

FILLING:
*⅓ cup chopped currants or seedless raisins
  (see Note)
4 tablespoons chopped dried apricots
2 teaspoons sugar
½ teaspoon ground cinnamon
¼ teaspoon grated nutmeg*

SYRUP:
*1 cup water
1 tablespoon lemon juice
⅓ cup sugar
⅓ cup honey
1 cinnamon stick, or ½ teaspoon ground
  cinnamon
1 teaspoon orange-flower water*

GARNISH:
½ cup heavy cream, whipped

Wash the apples well and cut out the cores.

Make the filling by mixing the currants or raisins and apricots with the sugar, cinnamon, and nutmeg. Stuff the apples with the apricot mixture.

Put the water and lemon juice to cook over medium heat in a pot large enough to hold the apples side by side. Stir in the sugar and honey. When the sugar has dissolved, add the cinnamon and cook until the mixture becomes syrupy. Place the apples in the syrup, lower the heat, and cover the pot. Simmer for about 15 minutes, or until the apples are tender, basting with the syrup a few times during the cooking.

Remove the apples to individual dessert plates. Stir the orange-flower water into the syrup, then spoon the syrup over the apples. Garnish with a dollop of whipped cream just before taking to the table. Serve warm or chilled.

NOTE: If you are not serving this dessert in a dinner that includes the meatball entrée above, ⅓ cup chopped walnuts may be substituted for the currants or seedless raisins.

A Note on the Wine

The fresh taste of lemon and tarragon in the soup, and the delicate, creamy, spinach-cheese filling baked between layers of flaky phyllo pastry, suggested a white wine that would echo the light, crisp textures and subtle flavors. For the original dinner we selected a dry, pleasantly fruity Chenin Blanc 1983 from Kenwood in Sonoma.

We matched the meatballs with an Edna Valley Pinot Noir 1981, a dry red wine of medium body and lots of character, complex enough to stand up to the flavors of nuts, lamb, wheat, mint, and yogurt.

Assyria

✤

Cabbage Borscht

Grape Leaf Dolma

Rack of Lamb Assyrian
Rice Pilaf with Lentils, Dried Apricots, and Onions
Grilled Tomatoes and Peppers

Romaine Hearts with Dipping Sauce

Lawasha (Lavash)

Kahda with Fruits and Walnuts

Wines:
Freemark Abbey Chardonnay
Fretter Cellars Merlot, Narsai David Vineyards

Ancient Assyria, the land of Narsai's heritage, lay in the valley between the Tigris and Euphrates rivers in the area that was once also called Sumeria, Babylonia, and Mesopotamia, and is today a part of Iran and Iraq. On May 15, 1985, the *New York Times* reported that a French Assyriologist had deciphered some cuneiform tablets from that region inscribed around 1700 B.C. To everyone's surprise—for they had expected records of ancient pharmacopeia—they turned out instead to be cookbooks, by far the oldest recorded recipes in the world. They described, according to the translator, "a cuisine of striking richness, refinement, sophistication and artistry, which is surprising from such an early period. Previously we would not have dared to think a cuisine 4,000 years old was so advanced." Master chefs had turned out exotically spiced dishes of game, fish, and fowl, and more than 300 different breadstuffs. Many familiar Middle Eastern seasonings, such as onions and garlic, cumin and coriander, mint and pomegranates, were in wide use then. The dishes described in the ancient menu were much different than the modern cuisine in that part of the world, yet there remains a 4,000-year-old thread from the past through many of the foods and flavorings.

Narsai's parents grew up in the land that was ancient Assyria, the birthplace of haute cuisine and the first recorded recipes. It was in his mother's kitchen that Narsai learned the dishes from modern-day Assyrian cooking that are given here.

CABBAGE BORSCHT
(SERVES 6)

> 6 cups beef broth (page 23) (see Note)
> 1 8-ounce can tomato sauce
> 3 cups chopped cabbage (about ⅓ medium cabbage)
> 1 cup diced beets (about 2 small beets)
> 1 stalk celery, chopped
> 1 carrot, diced
> 1 small onion, chopped
> 2 cloves garlic, minced
> 1 bay leaf
> 4 tablespoons wine vinegar
> 1½ teaspoons Worcestershire sauce
> 3 tablespoons brown sugar
> juice of ½ lemon
> salt
> pepper
> sour cream (optional)

Simmer together all but the last 4 ingredients. When the vegetables are tender, add the lemon juice. Adjust the seasoning with salt and pepper. Serve with a dollop of sour cream on each portion, if desired.

NOTE: On a cold winter day my mother occasionally made this borscht with a piece of beef and served it as the main course, along with dried French bread for dunking. If you want to make this heartier, main-course version, use beef neck bones or short ribs (about 1½ pounds meat with bones). Simmer the meat in water or beef broth until almost tender, about 1 to 1½ hours, skimming off any froth that forms during the cooking. Use the liquid from cooking the beef for the 6 cups broth called for, with the other ingredients, and proceed as above.—N.D.

GRAPE LEAF DOLMA
MAKES 50 (6 TO 8 ENTRÉE PORTIONS, 12 TO 16 APPETIZER PORTIONS)

½ cup (1 stick) butter
3 pounds lean lamb, coarsely diced into ½-inch cubes
1¼ cups raw pearl rice
1½ cups chopped whole leeks
2 medium onions, chopped
½ large bunch parsley, stemmed and chopped
4 tablespoons dried dill
½ green pepper, seeded, deribbed, and minced
4–6 cloves garlic, finely minced
salt and pepper
1 pint grape leaves, rinsed and spread open
lettuce or cabbage leaves
¾ cup water or lamb broth (page 23)
juice of 1 lemon
plain yogurt
Tomato Butter Sauce (see recipe below)

Melt the butter in a large skillet. Braise the lamb cubes until they begin to brown—about 10 to 15 minutes. Remove from the heat and add the rice, leeks, onions, parsley, dill, green pepper, garlic, and salt and pepper to taste.

Preheat the oven to 350°F.

Place approximately 2 tablespoons of the filling mixture on each prepared grape leaf and roll into cylinders. Fold the sides in like an envelope as you roll.

Line a baking dish with lettuce or cabbage leaves and arrange the dolmas on them neatly side by side. Add the water or lamb broth and the lemon juice. Cover with a layer of lettuce or cabbage leaves. Then cover tightly with a layer of foil. Bake for 1¼ to 1½ hours.

These dolmas are traditionally served hot. Spoon yogurt over each portion and top with a bit of Tomato Butter Sauce.

NOTE: If using this recipe as an appetizer course, cut the ingredients in half.

Tomato Butter Sauce

¼ cup (½ stick) butter
1 small onion, minced
2 cloves garlic, minced
1 6-ounce can tomato paste
2 tablespoons water

Melt the butter in a small saucepan. Sauté the onion and garlic until they are transparent. Add the tomato paste and water. Whisk vigorously. It does not matter if the butter separates from the sauce, since it is not meant to be emulsified.

RACK OF LAMB ASSYRIAN
(SERVES 6)

MARINADE:
    1 large onion
    2–3 cloves garlic
    1 teaspoon dried basil leaves
    ½ cup pomegranate juice (or less of
        concentrate)
    ¼ cup dry red wine
    ½ teaspoon salt
    ½ teaspoon pepper

    2½ lamb racks, each with 8 to 9 ribs
        (see Note)

DO AHEAD:
Marinate the meat overnight in the refrigerator, or for 6 to 8 hours at room temperature (see instructions).

In a blender or food processor puree the marinade ingredients. Rub the marinade well into the racks. Place the racks in a shallow glass or enameled pan and pour the remaining marinade over them. Marinate in the refrigerator overnight or at cool room temperature for 6 to 8 hours.

If it has been kept in the refrigerator, let the meat come to room temperature— about 45 minutes—before roasting. Preheat the oven to 450°F.

When ready to cook, wipe off any excess marinade and roast the racks for 15 to 20 minutes for medium rare, longer if you like lamb done to a greater degree.

NOTE: Ask the butcher to remove the chine bone and the lifter meat and to French-cut the rib bones.

RICE PILAF WITH LENTILS, DRIED APRICOTS, AND ONIONS
(SERVES 6)

    salt
    1 cup converted rice
    ⅓ cup lentils
    5 tablespoons butter
    ½ small onion, chopped
    ⅓ cup coarsely diced dried apricots
    6 tablespoons water

Bring a pot of salted water to a boil. Add the converted rice and cook until almost tender. Drain and rinse with hot water. Set the rice aside.

Refill the pot with salted water and bring to a boil. Add the lentils and cook until almost tender, about 30 minutes. Drain and reserve.

Melt 1 tablespoon butter in a small pot or skillet. Sauté the onion in the butter until transparent. Add the dried apricots and 2 tablespoons water. Simmer until the water is absorbed. Remove from the heat and reserve.

Preheat the oven to 350°F.

Layer the reserved rice, lentils, and apricot mixture in a small (1½-quart) round casserole in the following order:

Spread one-third of the rice on the bottom. Cover the rice with the apricot-onion mixture. Spread another one-third of the rice over the apricot mixture. Cover with a layer of the lentils. Cover the lentils with the remaining rice. Dot the top with the remaining 4 tablespoons butter cut into small pieces. Add the remaining 4 tablespoons water. Cover the casserole tightly. Bake for 20 to 25 minutes, until heated through.

VARIATION: Substitute dates, white raisins, or a mixture of dried fruits for the apricots.

GRILLED TOMATOES AND PEPPERS

Over charcoal, roast small whole tomatoes and small yellow wax peppers (both hot and mild varieties), turning until they have started to char on all sides. Serve without peeling.

ROMAINE HEARTS WITH DIPPING SAUCE

Use only the yellow, crunchy center romaine leaves that are not very large. The original Assyrian dipping sauce is simply a grape "molasses" with sherry vinegar added —sweet and sour and refreshingly pungent. To obtain a somewhat similar flavor, puree in a blender or food processor ½ cup raisins, ½ cup honey, and ½ cup sherry vinegar or balsamic vinegar. Strain the

mixture through a tea strainer. Adjust the flavors with more honey or vinegar. If too thick, dilute with apple juice or water.

LAWASHA (LAVASH)
(MAKES EIGHT 12-x-15-INCH BREADS)

The bread in the Middle East is traditionally a type of cracker bread called lavash (*lawasha* in Assyrian). This flat leavened bread is available in grocery stores and specialty markets and can be eaten as a cracker in the dry, crisp form in which it comes. However, to serve along with a meal, it is preferable to dampen it so that it becomes more breadlike:

Moisten the lavash, one cracker at a time, under cold running water, making sure that both sides are completely wet; place in a plastic bag for 3 hours, at the end of which time the bread will be pliable and chewy. Lavash prepared in this fashion is also used for Aram sandwiches, the filling spread over a whole dampened lavash, the entire bread then rolled up like a jelly roll and cut into sandwiches about 3 inches thick. The filling makes an attractive spiral pattern. Some popular combinations are cream cheese, thinly sliced onions, tomatoes, and lettuce with thin slices of rare roast beef, turkey, or smoked salmon.

To make your own lawasha or lavash, here is an Assyrian recipe. In the old country, a lawasha bread would bake in a clay-bottomed oven in 2 to 3 minutes. You can get much the same result baking on a ceramic baking tile or directly on the floor of a gas oven.

> 1 package of yeast, or 1 tablespoon dry
>   yeast
> 2 cups warm water
> 2 tablespoons sugar
> 5½ cups all-purpose flour
> 2 teaspoons salt

DO AHEAD:
Lightly oil a bowl for the dough.

Mix the yeast, water, and sugar in a large mixing bowl. Add the flour and salt and mix until it forms a well-blended but somewhat soft dough. (Resist the temptation to work in any more flour than absolutely necessary!)

Knead the dough by hand or machine. If by hand, turn it out on a floured board and work it until it is smooth and elastic, approximately 10 minutes. If using a dough hook on an electric mixer, knead the dough at the slowest speed for about 5 minutes.

Pat the dough into a ball and put it in the oiled bowl. Cover the dough with a kitchen towel and set it in a warm, draft-free place to rise until the dough has doubled in bulk, about 30 to 40 minutes. (A perfect place is a gas oven with its slight heat given off by the pilot light; an electric oven, turned on low for no more than 2 minutes, then turned off, works equally well.)

When the dough has doubled, turn it out on a floured board, punch it down, and knead it again until there is no air left in it. Divide the dough into 8 rough mounds, place them on the board, cover again with a towel, and let rise until almost doubled, about 30 minutes.

While the dough is rising, preheat the oven to 450°F. Position a rack as close as possible to the oven bottom. Flour a 12-x-15-inch baking sheet.

When the 8 mounds of dough have risen, roll them out, one piece at a time, into rectangles about 12 x 15 inches (the size of a standard sheet pan) and about as thin as for a pizza. Puncture the entire surface at ½-inch intervals with the tines of a roasting fork.

Bake the breads, one at a time, for 6 to 8 minutes, or until the tops are lightly browned. Remove each finished bread to a wire rack to cool and continue baking the remaining breads until all 8 are finished. During the baking, if any large bubbles start to puff up, puncture them immediately with the fork.

KAHDA
(SERVES 6 OR MORE)

Kahda is a very dense, very rich pastry, somewhat like shortbread in its texture. Some families make the dough layers much thicker than this one. Sometimes the roux is sweetened with honey or sugar. At the time of Lent, a popular filling is made of lentils, onions, and ground walnuts. My favorite as a child was ground walnuts and honey. Because the basic recipe (given here) is not sweet, it is equally good at breakfast or dinner. Kahda is usually served, as in this menu, with fresh or dried fruits (as in my parents' house), walnuts, and sweet tea—N.D.

DOUGH:

1 tablespoon sugar
½ cup lukewarm milk
½ package of yeast, or 1½ teaspoons dry yeast
6 tablespoons butter, melted and cooled
2 eggs, beaten separately
1¾ cups all-purpose flour
sesame seeds

FILLING (ROUX):

¾ cup (1½ sticks) butter
⅞ cup all-purpose flour

DO AHEAD:

Oil a mixing bowl for the dough to rise in.

Stir the sugar into the milk, sprinkle the yeast on top, and let stand for 5 minutes. (If using fresh yeast, mash it with a fork into the sweetened milk.)

To the yeast add the cooled butter and 1 beaten egg. Blend in the flour until smooth. Work with the dough hook or knead very gently by hand just until the dough comes together and forms a smooth surface. The consistency will be softer than bread dough. Place in the oiled mixing bowl, cover, and let rise in a warm, draft-free place until doubled in volume. Punch down, return to the bowl, cover, and let rise again until doubled. Each rising will take about 40 minutes. Butter and flour a baking sheet. Meanwhile prepare the filling:

In a thick-bottomed skillet, melt the butter, add the flour, and cook, stirring constantly, until the mixture is a hazelnut-brown color. Cool to room temperature before spreading on the dough. This roux can also be made in the oven (350°F) by mixing the butter and flour and baking on a sheet pan, stirring occasionally. I prefer to cook it on the stove because it is easier to stir and to judge the color. A roux that does not brown evenly will taste a bit floury.

Preheat the oven to 350° F.

Turn the dough onto a floured board, punch down, and form the dough into a smooth round ball. Roll out into a circle about 18 inches in diameter. Position the dough so that one-half of it is draped over the prepared baking sheet (the other half will later fold over it, making a giant turnover). Spread the filling over the half of the dough circle that is on the baking sheet, stopping within ½ inch from the outside edge. Moisten the edge with water and fold the other half of the dough over the first so that the entire turnover is on the baking sheet. Seal the edges with a fork. Brush with the other beaten egg and sprinkle with sesame seeds. Prick the surface all over with a fork. Bake for about 20 to 25 minutes, until the kahda is a uniform golden brown. Cool and cut into pie-shaped wedges to serve.

A Note on the Wines

A rich, full, oaky white wine is a good accompaniment to dolma. We would choose a Chardonnay by Freemark Abbey of Napa Valley.

With the rack of lamb, we suggest a Merlot, a full-bodied dry red in the style of Fretter Cellars, particularly its bottlings of 1978 and 1980 through 1984, from the Narsai David Vineyards in Napa Valley. (Narsai blended the 1979 grapes as a non-vintage wine under his own label.)

Australia

❖

Carrot Soup

Mussels Broiled with Garlic and Nuts

Carpetbagger Steak (Fillet of Beef Stuffed with Oysters)
Buttered String Beans
Roasted Pumpkin

Salad with Egg Dressing

Baguettes

Pavlova (Meringue Topped with
Whipped Cream and Fruit)

Wines:
Hardy's Sauvignon Blanc (Australia)
Kaiser Stuhl Cabernet Sauvignon Reserve (Australia)

CARROT SOUP
(SERVES 6)

1 bunch leeks, green tops and roots
    discarded
¼ cup (½ stick) butter
2 stalks celery, chopped
1 bunch carrots, peeled and chopped
1 potato, peeled and coarsely chopped
1 parsnip, peeled and coarsely chopped
1 turnip, peeled and coarsely chopped
1 quart chicken broth (see recipe below)
salt and pepper
chopped fresh chives

Split the leeks lengthwise, wash very carefully, and cut into 1-inch pieces. Melt the butter in a soup pot and sauté all the vegetables until the leeks are transparent but not brown. Immediately add the chicken broth and salt and pepper to taste, and blend in well. Simmer for 20 to 30 minutes, or until the vegetables are very tender.

Puree the soup in a blender or food processor. Adjust the seasoning. Serve with chopped chives sprinkled on top.

Chicken Stock
(MAKES 5 TO 6 CUPS)

This stock can be used in any recipe calling for chicken broth or stock.

2½–3 pounds chicken bones
2 quarts water
1 carrot, or peelings from 3–4 carrots
1 medium onion, unpeeled, chopped
3–4 large sprigs parsley, or stems from
    1 bunch parsley
1 bay leaf
3 cloves
12 black peppercorns

Place all the ingredients into a heavy stockpot or Dutch oven. Bring to a boil, then lower to the slowest possible simmer. Simmer for at least 2 hours, or overnight. Remove from the heat and cool until it is safe to handle. Strain through a fine sieve. Discard the bones and vegetables. Skim the excess fat. Any fat that remains will solidify on the surface and can be discarded before using the stock. Refrigerate or freeze in containers of a size most suitable to your uses. If this stock is to be used for a sauce or glace de viande (page 298), strain it through a cloth.

MUSSELS BROILED WITH GARLIC AND NUTS
(SERVES 6)

36 mussels in the shell
3 cloves garlic, finely minced
1 sprig parsley, finely minced
½ cup (1 stick) butter, softened to room
    temperature
salt and pepper
½ cup finely ground macadamia nuts
2 tablespoons dry bread crumbs
rock salt

DO AHEAD:
Scrub and beard the mussels.

Work the finely minced garlic and parsley into the softened butter. Season with salt and pepper.

Mix the macadamia nuts with the bread crumbs.

Place the cleaned mussels in a skillet with just enough water to keep the bottom from burning. Cover and heat over a very high flame until the shells just start to crack open. Discard any that do not open. Remove from the heat and finish opening the shells with a knife or by hand. Discard the top shells, leaving the meat in the bottom.

Make a bed of rock salt in a large baking dish or 6 individual baking dishes. Cover each mussel on the half shell with some of the garlic butter and sprinkle with the ground nuts and bread crumbs. As each mussel is prepared, nestle it into the rock salt so that the shell is level and steady. Place the baking dish or dishes under a hot broiler for 4 to 5 minutes, or until the mussels are plump and cooked through and the nut mixture has turned golden. If using one baking dish, remove the mussels carefully with tongs or a large spoon to individual serving dishes; otherwise place each individual baking dish on a folded napkin on a large service plate.

NOTE: An alternative to broiling the mussels is to remove them from the shells along with their liquor, place them in a low, flat baking dish, cover with the softened garlic butter, sprinkle with the nut mixture, and bake in a 400°F oven until hot, bubbly, and browned on top, about 10 to 15 minutes. Serve spooned over squares of toast.

CARPETBAGGER STEAK
(Fillet of Beef Stuffed with Oysters)
(SERVES 6)

> 6 5-ounce beef tournedos, cut from the center eye and trimmed of all fat and gristle
> 12 small to medium oysters
> cracked black pepper
> salt
> 2 tablespoons butter
> 1 tablespoon oil

SAUCE:
> 6 tablespoons butter, melted
> 2 tablespoons chopped fresh parsley

Lay the trimmed tournedos flat on a cutting board. With a small sharp knife, slit a pocket from one side of each piece into the center, being careful not to puncture the sides.

Grind a bit of the cracked pepper over the oysters and place 2 oysters in each tournedos' pocket. Skewer the opening closed with 2 large toothpicks. Season with salt and additional cracked black pepper.

Heat the butter and oil in a sauté pan and brown the tournedos very quickly over high heat. Cook for only 2 or 3 minutes on each side for rare. Serve with a sauce made of the melted butter to which the chopped parsley has been added.

NOTES: It will take a 6- to 7-pound filet mignon to yield 6 tournedos. If you buy the whole filet and cut the tournedos yourself, you will have a lot of trim left over that will be suitable for grenadines and paillards. An alternative is to keep the piece whole, make a pocket in the center, stuff with the oysters, and skewer or sew closed. Grill the meat over charcoal or roast it in a hot oven (400°F) for 20 minutes or until done to the degree of rareness you prefer. To ensure browning, baste with melted butter before putting the meat in the oven. Another possibility is to cook 6 strips of bacon partially, wrap them around the individual tournedos or the whole piece of meat, skewer them with a toothpick, and proceed to broil or roast the meat as above.

There are also variations on the oyster stuffing: Sauté the oysters quickly with some sliced fresh mushrooms and bread crumbs, or add other seasonings, such as chopped parsley or grated lemon rind.

BUTTERED STRING BEANS

Boil small trimmed string beans whole in salted water until just tender. Drain and toss lightly with melted butter, salt, and pepper.

ROASTED PUMPKIN

Split a small (3- to 4-pound) pumpkin into 6 portions, removing all of the seeds and fibrous strings. Place the portions in a baking pan, skin side down, dot with butter, sprinkle with salt and pepper, and bake in a 350° to 375°F oven for 45 minutes to 1 hour, or until tender when pierced with the tip of a knife. If covered with foil for the first half hour, the cooking time will be slightly shorter. If pumpkin is not available, substitute a winter squash, such as acorn or hubbard.

SALAD WITH EGG DRESSING
(SERVES 6)

2 eggs, hard-cooked and chopped
½ cup chopped pimiento-stuffed green olives
salt and pepper to taste
½ cup light vinaigrette dressing, made with part lemon juice, part white wine vinegar (see Glossary)
1 small head butter lettuce, washed and dried

Mix together the hard-cooked eggs, olives, salt and pepper, and vinaigrette.

Arrange the leaves of butter lettuce on 6 salad plates and spoon the egg vinaigrette over them.

BAGUETTES

A good bread for this meal would be a simple baguette. The recipe can be found in the first French menu, page 119.

PAVLOVA
(Meringue Topped with Whipped Cream and Fruit)
(SERVES 6)

In Australia, as in New Zealand where it originated, the Pavlova is a favorite dessert. The light airy meringue cake came into the culinary repertory in the wake of the ballet star Pavlova's successful 1920 dance tour of New Zealand. There is a continuous argument over whether the centers should be soft or crisp, and each side has its staunch advocates. However, the meringues are always garnished with whipped cream, no matter the condition of the centers, and any of a wide variety of fruits, usually tropical. The most popular are passion fruit, raspberries, kiwis, pineapple, papaya, and mango. Although the recipe given here is the basic, classic version, we have also seen Pavlova made of coffee-flavored meringues garnished with whipped cream and toasted macadamia nuts.

 5 egg whites
 1 cup sugar
 1 cup heavy cream, whipped
 4–6 kiwis, peeled and sliced into rounds
   about the thickness of a 50-cent piece

DO AHEAD:
Line a baking sheet with parchment or oiled heavy brown paper.

In a pot large enough to accommodate the bowl of a mixer, bring enough water to a boil so that the pot can sit over it without touching it.

Place the egg whites and sugar in a metal mixer bowl over the pot of boiling water, taking care that the bowl does not touch the water. Beat with a whisk or hand beater until the mixture reaches a temperature of 120°F on a candy or jelly thermometer. Remove from the heat and continue to beat with the mixer until very stiff, about 8 to 10 minutes. Meanwhile, preheat the oven to 225°F.

Spoon the egg whites into a pastry bag fitted with a plain round tip. Pipe 6 rounds of meringue (about 3 inches in diameter) onto the parchment-lined baking sheet, shaping them higher on the sides to make cases or shells. (If you do not have a pastry bag, use a cooking spoon.)

Bake for 50 to 60 minutes. The meringues should be dry and crisp outside, yet still soft inside, like marshmallows. Cool. (As an alternative, the meringues will keep for a few days if baked crisp all the way through and stored, after cooling, in an airtight container. Keep the meringues in the oven with the door closed for an hour after baking to dry out the centers.)

Garnish the meringue cases by spooning or piping them full of whipped cream, then decorating the top and edges with the kiwi rounds. If kiwis are not available, use raspberries or any fruit of your choice.

A Note on the Wines

For the Australian dinner, we suggest trying some of the excellent wines from that country. With the garlicky mussels we recommend a young, assertive dry white, such as a Hardy's Sauvignon Blanc.

To accompany the rich carpetbagger steak, we would open a well-aged, mature dry red, such as an older Cabernet Sauvignon Reserve from Kaiser Stuhl.

Austria

❁

Beef Consommé with Liver Dumplings

Bass Baked with Paprika and Sour Cream

Stuffed Loin of Veal
Oven-Roasted Potatoes
Sweet-Sour Green Beans

Marinated Celery Root Salad

Light Corn Rye Bread

Sachertorte

Wines:
Ockfener Herrenberg Moselle
Bachelet-Morey Santenay

BEEF CONSOMMÉ WITH LIVER DUMPLINGS
(SERVES 6 TO 8)

1 cup milk
2 slices of bread, toasted and cut into
½-inch cubes (1 cup)
1 egg, beaten
1 teaspoon grated onion
1 tablespoon capers, drained
rind of ½ lemon, grated
salt and pepper
grated nutmeg
½ teaspoon dried marjoram
½ pound chicken or calf's liver, ground or
finely chopped
6 cups or more strong beef broth or
consommé (page 23)
chopped fresh parsley

Put the milk in a small saucepan, stir in the bread cubes, and cook over moderate heat just until the mixture is smooth. Beat together the egg, onion, capers, lemon rind, salt and pepper, a grating of nutmeg, and the marjoram in a large mixing bowl. Stir in the bread-milk mixture. When it is thoroughly blended, add the liver and mix well. Form into 16 small balls by rolling between the palms of the hands. (Dipping the hands in cold water makes this easier.) Reserve.

Bring the beef broth or consommé to a boil. Add the dumplings, cover, and simmer until they are firm, about 20 minutes. Ladle the broth into individual bowls and serve 2 to 3 dumplings in each, garnished with chopped parsley.

NOTE: The dumplings, napped with sauce instead of served in broth, make a fine appetizer, or by doubling the recipe, a light main course for lunch or dinner. Poach the dumplings in a pot of salted boiling water, drain them, and serve with a sauce made by sautéing in butter 2 to 3 slices of bacon, diced, with ½ a small onion, minced. When the onion and bacon start to brown, add 2 cups of the water in which the dumplings poached, and a beurre manié (1 tablespoon butter worked into 2 tablespoons flour to make a smooth paste). Whisking gently, continue to cook for several minutes over low heat, until the sauce is smooth and has thickened. Serve over the dumplings and garnish with chopped parsley. An alternative is to eliminate the capers from the dumpling mixture and substitute ¼ to ½ cup of them for the bacon in the sauce recipe.

BASS BAKED WITH PAPRIKA AND SOUR CREAM
(SERVES 6)

2 tablespoons butter
1 onion, thinly sliced
1–1½ pounds bass fillets
1 cup sour cream
2 teaspoons paprika
salt and pepper
caraway seeds

Preheat the oven to 375°F.

Melt the butter in a skillet, add the onion, and sauté until limp and beginning to turn golden, about 10 minutes over moderate heat. Spread it over the bottom of a low baking dish. Place the fish fillets on top.

In a small bowl mix together the sour cream, paprika, and salt and pepper. Pour the seasoned sour cream over the fish. Bake for about 20 minutes, or until the fish is cooked and the flesh is opaque all the way through. Divide evenly into 6 portions and spoon any remaining sauce from the pan over the fish. Sprinkle with caraway seeds.

STUFFED LOIN OF VEAL
(SERVES 6)

There are at least three distinct types of veal generally available on the market. If the modern "Dutch Process" or "Provimi" milk-fed veal is available and you have the budget to go with it, it is surely the best. It has enough fat to remain moist when it is oven roasted, and is at its best roasted medium rare or slightly pink.

The second type of veal is baby beef (7 to 10 months old), also known in some regions as "kip." Fairly red in color, it is much more like young beef than true veal. It, too, can be roasted in the oven and is best cooked only until pink.

Finally, there is "drop calf." Butchered usually at 2 weeks of age, the calf has no fat and its meat has very little configuration. It is best used for braising or stewing. This recipe can be made with a drop calf

loin, if it is available, but the meat should be roasted with 1 or 2 cups of veal or chicken stock in a large covered pot such as a Dutch oven, rather than in the oven.

Ask your butcher's advice on the size of the roast since it will vary with the type of veal.

> 1 5- to 6-pound veal roast (including bone)

STUFFING:
> 4 slices of bread, toasted and cut into ½-inch cubes (2 cups)
> ½ teaspoon dried thyme
> 10–12 mushrooms, chopped
> rind of 1 lemon, grated
> 4 ounces ham, finely chopped
> 4–6 anchovy fillets, minced
> 2 eggs, beaten
> salt and pepper
> ¼ cup (½ stick) butter
> 2 cups veal or chicken stock (see below or pages 23 and 36)

Remove the bone and any pockets of fat from the roast, or ask the butcher to do it. Use the bone to make stock by boiling in water for 1 to 1½ hours.

Preheat the oven to 350°F.

Mix together the bread cubes, thyme, mushrooms, lemon rind, ham, anchovies, and eggs. Adjust the seasonings with salt and pepper. If it seems too dry, moisten with a bit of water or stock. Place the stuffing in the butterflied cavity left by the bone. Roll up the meat, being careful to keep the stuffing in the center, rather than spread out like the filling in a jelly roll. Tie the meat with string or skewer it together to create a long roll.

Melt the butter in a large Dutch oven and brown the meat on all sides. When it is well colored, put it in the oven and roast until it is medium rare, 45 to 60 minutes. Remove the veal from the pan to a carving board or service platter. Allow to rest in a warm place for 15 to 20 minutes before carving.

To make a light sauce, add 2 cups veal or chicken stock to the roasting pan and boil vigorously until reduced by one-third.

OVEN-ROASTED POTATOES

Peel 2 small new potatoes or red potatoes per person and roast alongside the veal loin in the same roasting pan.

SWEET-SOUR GREEN BEANS

Cook trimmed green beans until just tender in water seasoned with some sliced onion, garlic, salt, pepper, and a bay leaf. Remove the beans, strain the liquid, and reduce it over high heat to about ¾ cup. Flavor the reduced liquid with 2 tablespoons vinegar, 2 tablespoons sugar, 3 tablespoons butter, and a pinch of nutmeg. Pour over the beans and garnish with chopped fresh parsley.

MARINATED CELERY ROOT SALAD

Cut peeled celery root into slices and cook in salted water until barely tender. Drain the slices, cool, and marinate in a dressing of 2 parts olive oil to 1 part white wine vinegar, a dash of sugar, coarsely ground black pepper, a few drops of Worcestershire sauce, and a sprinkling of coriander seeds. Serve chilled on butter lettuce leaves.

LIGHT CORN RYE BREAD

An appropriate bread for this dinner is a light rye without seeds. (Use the recipe for Jewish Corn Rye in the menu for Poland and omit the caraway seeds.)

SACHERTORTE
(SERVES 6)

According to the best information, Franz Sacher, chef to the Viennese prince Klemens von Metternich and patriarch of the Sacher clan, created the Sachertorte in 1832 in the royal kitchens. Eduard Sacher, Franz's son, was the first to introduce the torte to the public when he served it at the Hotel Sacher, of which he and his wife, Frau Anna, were proprietors. Neither the Hotel Sacher nor Demel's, a pastry shop that later acquired legal rights to the name "Sachertorte" from one of Franz Sacher's descendants—most probably grandson Eduard—agrees on what is the "authentic" recipe.

In order to prepare the closest version possible when we made our Austrian dinner at the restaurant, we ordered a Sachertorte from the hotel in Vienna, the version which the Austrian courts had earlier declared the original. Packed handsomely in a wooden box, it turned out to be a somewhat dry but intensely chocolate cake filled with apricot preserves and glazed with a firm chocolate topping. The large dollop of whipped cream traditionally served alongside really is necessary to cut through the intensity of the chocolate. Demel's version, in spite of its acquisition of the name, is a one-layer cake topped by the apricot preserves before being glazed. Some recipes substitute ground almonds and corn flour for all-purpose flour. Here is the Hotel Sacher version.

CAKE:

6 ounces dark sweet chocolate (such as
  semisweet or bittersweet)
6 tablespoons sweet butter
6 egg yolks
1 teaspoon vanilla extract
8 egg whites
½ cup granulated sugar
¾ cup all-purpose flour
½ cup apricot preserves, sieved

ICING:

8 ounces dark sweet chocolate (such as
  semisweet or bittersweet)
½ cup heavy cream
2 tablespoons light corn syrup

WHIPPED CREAM GARNISH:

1 cup heavy cream
2 tablespoons confectioners' sugar (if
  lumpy, put through a sieve)
½ teaspoon vanilla extract

DO AHEAD:

Butter and flour two 8-x-1½-inch cake pans, or line them with a circle of buttered and floured parchment or wax paper. Line a cookie sheet with wax paper.

Preheat the oven to 350°F.

To make the cake, melt the chocolate and butter in the top of a double boiler and remove from the heat. Allow to cool slightly. Stir in the egg yolks, slightly beaten, and vanilla and set aside.

Beat the egg whites just until they begin to show white froth. Add the sugar slowly, a tablespoon at a time, still whipping, until the whites are stiff enough to hold firm peaks; they should hold their shape.

Mix one-third of the beaten whites into the chocolate mixture to lighten it, then pour the lightened chocolate back over the egg whites. Sprinkle the flour over all and fold it in gently using a wide spatula and an over-and-under motion.

When the chocolate is reasonably well incorporated—it is all right if some white streaks remain—divide the batter evenly between the 2 pans. Tap the pans gently to level the batter.

Bake for 40 to 50 minutes, or until a toothpick inserted in the center comes out clean. When done, cool for 10 to 15 minutes, then turn the cakes out of the pans onto racks. Remove the parchment or wax paper, if used, and allow the cakes to cool completely.

The cakes can be prepared ahead to this point and frozen until ready to fill and glaze. Take out of the freezer several hours before the final preparation.

To make the icing, melt the chocolate, cream, and corn syrup in a small saucepan or the top of a double boiler. Remove from the heat and cool slightly.

When the cakes have cooled, place one of them, still on the cake rack, over the cookie sheet. Heat the apricot jam and, using a knife blade or long spatula, spread the jam over the top of the cake. Invert the second layer over the first. Pour the slightly cooled chocolate icing over the cake. It should be runny enough to spread smoothly but not so warm that it flows too quickly and runs off the cake. If necessary allow the icing to cool until it reaches a slightly thicker, more spreadable consistency. Smooth the icing carefully with a long spatula, taking up any excess from the wax paper and returning it to the top.

To serve, whip the cream with the confectioners' sugar and vanilla. Pass at the table or spoon a large dollop alongside each slice of cake.

A Note on the Wines

For the bass dish, with its rich sauce of onions and sour cream, a fruity, crisp Moselle would contrast well. A good choice would be an Ockfener Herrenberg from Germany.

With the stuffed veal loin, we suggest an older, dry red Burgundy of medium body, such as a Bachelet-Morey Santenay from Beaune.

Basque

❊

Snails and Prosciutto in Onion-Tomato Sauce

Pipérade

Lamb Sauté with Garlic and Lemon
Green Rice
Carrots in Sauce

Mixed Salad

Country Bread (Pain au Levain, Poilâne)

Walnut and Raisin Tart (Pastel)

Wines:
Saint-Aubin Clerget Burgundy
Château Nenin Claret or Fretter Cellars Merlot

SNAILS AND PROSCIUTTO IN ONION-TOMATO SAUCE

(SERVES 6)

3 tablespoons olive oil
1 medium onion, chopped
2–3 garlic cloves, minced
1 large tomato, chopped
½ cup white wine
¼ cup chopped fresh parsley
12 snails, drained, rinsed, and chopped
   (reserve shells)
8 slices of prosciutto, chopped
1 tablespoon fresh basil, or 1 teaspoon
   dried

Heat the olive oil in a skillet. Add the onion, garlic, and tomato and sauté until the vegetables are tender. Add the wine and simmer for about 10 minutes. Stir in the parsley and remove the pan from the heat. Reserve.

Mix the snails, prosciutto, and basil with 2 tablespoons of the sauce. Pack into the snail shells.

Place the stuffed snail shells in the pan of reserved sauce and simmer for about 10 minutes, or until heated through.

PIPÉRADE

(SERVES 6)

4 tablespoons olive oil
2 green peppers, thinly sliced
1 red pepper, thinly sliced
1 onion, thinly sliced
2 cloves garlic, minced

3 tomatoes, peeled (see Glossary), seeded,
   and coarsely chopped
¼ teaspoon dried oregano
salt and pepper
8 eggs, beaten

Heat the olive oil in a skillet. Add the peppers and onion and sauté slowly until they are soft. Add the garlic, tomatoes, oregano, and salt and pepper. As soon as they have heated through, add the beaten eggs and stir quickly, as you would for scrambled eggs, cooking until they are barely set. The consistency should be moist and loose rather than firm like a standard omelet. Serve immediately.

LAMB SAUTÉ WITH GARLIC AND LEMON

Heat some olive oil in a skillet and sauté single, thick lamb chops. Top with onions and garlic that have been sautéed until golden brown, then finished with paprika and the juice of a lemon.

GREEN RICE

(SERVES 6)

2 tablespoons olive oil
1½ cups converted long-grain rice
2 cloves garlic, minced
2 cups chicken stock (page 36) or hot
   water

¼ cup dry white wine
2 tablespoons minced fresh parsley
pinch of saffron (about .2 gram)
salt and pepper

Heat the olive oil in a 1- to 2-quart pot. Add the rice and garlic and sauté until they begin to sizzle. Stir in the remaining ingredients. As soon as the mixture comes to a boil, turn the heat to the lowest setting, cover the pot, and simmer for 18 to 20 minutes. When the rice is done, turn it into a bowl and serve with the lamb.

CARROTS IN SAUCE
(SERVES 6)

1 tablespoon olive oil
6 carrots, peeled and cut into ¼-inch-thick
    slices
2 tablespoons chopped onion
2 cloves garlic, minced
¼ teaspoon paprika
pinch of ground allspice
½ cup water
1 teaspoon sugar
salt and pepper

Heat the olive oil in a pot or skillet and add the carrots, onion, and garlic. Sauté until the onion is translucent. Add the paprika and allspice and stir for a minute. Add the water, sugar, and salt and pepper. Cover and simmer until the carrots are tender.

MIXED SALAD

Toss a mixture of romaine, Boston, or Bibb lettuces, curly endive, sliced radishes, sliced celery, and black olives with a simple vinaigrette dressing (see Glossary). Top with hard-cooked egg yolk rubbed through a sieve.

COUNTRY BREAD
(Pain au Levain, Poilâne)
(MAKES ONE 3-POUND LOAF)

This comes from Doris's good friend Lionel Poilâne, whom many consider to be the best baker in Paris. Over the years, he has shared with her many baking tricks, invited her to spend some time baking in his shop on the rue du Cherche Midi, and has given her many of his recipes, including this one for the miche, or large country loaf, called pain au levain. We have adapted it slightly to account for the differences between French and American flours and between equipment and facilities in a bakery and a home. Even so, there are differences for which a recipe cannot account: the humidity and temperature on the day of baking, how long the flour has been stored, and how much moisture it has absorbed. Lionel offers this advice: "Do not confuse the baker with the pharmacist. The pharmacist weighs the ingredients, but the baker really doesn't; he uses measures only as guidelines. In my opinion, the best way to succeed in bread making is to do things as empirically as possible and trust one's senses." In any case, this is good bread for this flavorful Basque dinner.

  2 packages of yeast, or 2 tablespoons dry
     yeast
  2 cups warm water
  2 tablespoons sugar
  ¾ cup whole-wheat flour
  5 cups (approximately) white bread or all-
     purpose flour
  2½ teaspoons salt

DO AHEAD:
The starter used in this recipe needs 2 or 3 days to develop (see instructions below).

To make the starter, mix 1 package of yeast with 1 cup warm water, 1 tablespoon sugar, the whole-wheat flour, and ½ cup white flour. Cover the mixture loosely with plastic wrap and leave it on the kitchen counter to develop for 2 to 3 days. It should smell distinctly sour. If the temperature is warm, the process may go more quickly; if cool, it may take longer—as much as 4 days. The starter will keep in the refrigerator for up to a week before using; if replenished regularly—ideally after a week but up to 3 or 4 weeks will work—it will last indefinitely.

To keep a starter going, add 1 cup water and 1 cup flour to 1 cup of the original. Allow to ferment at room temperature for a day, then store again in the refrigerator.

To make the bread, place the starter in a mixing bowl. Add the remaining cup of warm water, 1 tablespoon sugar, and package of yeast. Stir well, then add the remaining 4½ cups white flour and the salt. Mix until the liquid is completely absorbed, adding a bit more flour as necessary if the dough is too moist.

Knead the dough by hand or machine. If by hand, turn it out on a floured board and work it until it is smooth and elastic, approximately 10 minutes. If using a dough hook on an electric mixer, knead the dough at the slowest speed for about 5 minutes.

Lightly oil a bowl, pat the dough into a ball, and put it in the bowl. Cover the bowl with a kitchen towel and set it in a warm, draft-free place to rise until the dough has doubled in bulk, about 60 to 75 minutes. (A perfect place is a gas oven with its slight heat given off by the pilot light; an electric oven, turned on low for no more than 2 minutes, then turned off, works equally well.)

When the dough has doubled, turn it out on a floured board, punch it down, and knead it again until there is no air left in it. Shape it into a large round loaf. Cover it again with a towel, and let it rise until almost doubled, about 30 minutes.

When it has risen, cut 5 gashes with a razor blade on the top edge of the loaf, following the circumference and at a slight angle to it. Then cut 4 gashes in a tic-tac-toe pattern in the center of the loaf. Cover it with a towel and let it rise for another 15 minutes.

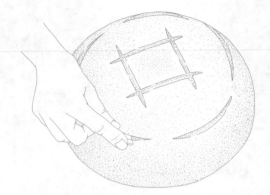

While the loaf is rising, preheat the oven to 375°F. Place a pie tin half filled with water on the bottom shelf. Position an oven rack just above the bottom rack. Flour a baking sheet or large pan.

Gently pick up the loaf and transfer it to the baking sheet or pan and place it in the oven on the rack just above the bottom rack. Bake for 50 to 60 minutes. The crust should be golden brown. Test the doneness by rapping the top with your knuckle. The loaf should feel firm and make a hollow sound. Cool on a wire rack.

WALNUT AND RAISIN TART (Pastel)

(SERVES 8)

*enough rich sweet pastry dough to line a
    9-inch pie tin (see Note)*
½ cup (1 stick) butter
⅔ cup sugar
4 eggs
1 cup chopped toasted walnuts
⅔ cup raisins

⅓ cup currants
zest of 1 orange, grated

Preheat the oven to 375°F.

Roll the dough thin and line a 9-x-1½-inch pie tin. Flute the edges or decorate by depressing with the tines of a fork.

Cream the butter and sugar in a mixer. Add the eggs one at a time and continue beating until the mixture is light and fluffy. Stir in the remaining ingredients. Pour the mixture into the prepared pastry shell. Bake for 25 to 30 minutes, or until the custard sets and the crust is well browned.

NOTE: Use any favorite rich sweet pastry such as pâté sablé or short pastry or the recipe for Danish Waffle dough, page 95, which makes the best possible tart dough.

A Note on the Wines

The Saint-Aubin Clerget is the kind of light, elegant Burgundy from the Côte de Beaune that makes a fine counterpart to the snails and prosciutto.

Our choice to go along with the lamb sautéed with garlic and lemon would be a red claret that has the earthy and intense qualities found in the wines of Château Nenin. This claret from the Pomerol is made predominantly from Merlot grapes, and an alternative would be a California Merlot, such as one from Fretter Cellars.

Belgium

❊

Asparagus with Brown Butter

Steamed Mussels

Braised Chicken Breasts and Sweetbreads in Cream
Belgian Endive with Mustard Dressing

Baguettes

Flemish Waffles with Strawberries

Wines:
Pouilly-Fuissé, Jaboulet-Vercherre
Meursault Genevrières, Lafon

ASPARAGUS WITH BROWN BUTTER

Drop trimmed asparagus spears into rapidly boiling salted water. Be sure they are totally immersed. Do not cover the pot as that will cause the loss of the bright green color. When the asparagus are just tender, add a dash of cold water to stop the boiling, drain immediately, and dress with butter heated until it starts to brown.

STEAMED MUSSELS

These mussels are made exactly the same way as the French Mussels Steamed in Wine, so use that recipe (page 123).

BRAISED CHICKEN BREASTS AND SWEETBREADS IN CREAM

(SERVES 6)

> 1½ pounds veal sweetbreads
> ½ lemon
> 1 tablespoon pickling spice
> 2 carrots, cut diagonally into 2-inch-long pieces
> 2 leeks, cut into ½-inch pieces (white part and 1 inch of green)
> 12 pearl onions, peeled
> 6 small new potatoes, peeled
> ½ cup white wine
> 1½ cups chicken or veal broth (page 36 or 23)
> 2 whole chicken breasts, skinned
> salt and pepper

> ½ teaspoon dried thyme
> 1 cup heavy cream
> 1 tablespoon flour
> 2 egg yolks
> 2 tablespoons chopped fresh parsley

DO AHEAD:

Prepare the sweetbreads (see instructions).

Wash the sweetbreads in cold water. Place them in a pot and cover them with fresh cold water. Squeeze the juice of the half lemon directly into the pot, then drop in the rind. Add the pickling spice and bring the mixture to a boil. Turn down to a simmer and cook, uncovered, for 20 minutes. Remove from the heat and leave the sweetbreads in the poaching liquid for 30 minutes to cool.

Remove the cooled sweetbreads from the liquid and trim them carefully of any membranes, skin, or fat. Cut or break them into 6 or 8 pieces.

Place the carrots, leeks, pearl onions, new potatoes, and sweetbreads in a large skillet or Dutch oven with a cover. Add the white wine and broth, leave uncovered, and bring the mixture to a boil. Reduce the heat to a simmer, cover, and cook for 20 minutes.

While the sweetbreads and vegetables are simmering, prepare the chicken breasts. Cut each breast in half. Gently pull away the "fillet" from each half. (Illustrations follow, steps 5–9.) Cut the remaining half-breasts into 2 or 3 strips lengthwise, about the same size as the fillets.

STEP 1

STEP 2

STEP 3

STEP 4

STEP 5

STEP 6

STEP 7

STEP 8

STEP 9

DISJOINTING A WHOLE CHICKEN AND FILLETING THE BREASTS

STEP 1: *Remove wings.*

STEP 2: *Remove whole legs and thighs.*

STEPS 3 AND 4: *Cut through the rib cage to separate breasts from backbone.*

STEP 5: *Cut through the cartilage behind the breastbone.*

STEP 6: *Remove the keel-shaped breastbones and cartilage.*

STEP 7: *Carefully slide a knife under the ribs and cut them away.*

STEP 8: *Gently pull the fillet away from each half.*

STEP 9: *Cut the remaining half-breasts into 2 or 3 strips lengthwise, about the same size as the fillets.*

Put all of the chicken into the pot. Season with salt, pepper, and thyme. Make a mixture of the cream and flour and add it to the pot. Cover again and cook only until the chicken is tender, about 10 minutes.

In a small bowl whisk the egg yolks with 1 cup of sauce from the pot. Pour the egg-sauce mixture back into the pot and stir gently. Continue to cook long enough to heat through without allowing the sauce to boil. Remove the pot from the heat. Turn the braised chicken mixture into a large serving bowl and sprinkle with the chopped parsley.

BELGIAN ENDIVE WITH MUSTARD DRESSING

Wash, trim, and cut off the bottom ends of several small heads of Belgian endive. Toss the leaves in a bowl with a vinaigrette dressing (see Glossary) made with the addition of 1 tablespoon Dijon mustard.

BAGUETTES

The basic recipe for the baguettes called for with this menu is on page 119.

FLEMISH WAFFLES WITH STRAWBERRIES

(SERVES 6)

¾ cup heavy cream, plus enough to whip
  for garnish
3 tablespoons butter
½ cup granulated sugar
1 package of yeast, or 1 tablespoon dry
  yeast
6 eggs, beaten
¼ cup brandy
3 cups all-purpose flour
2 pints strawberries, washed, hulled, and
  halved
confectioners' sugar

Warm the cream and butter in a small saucepan just until the butter melts. Remove from the heat and cool to lukewarm.

Put 1 tablespoon sugar, the yeast, eggs, and brandy into a bowl. Stir in the cooled cream and butter mixture. Add the flour and mix for 2 to 3 minutes, or until all the ingredients are well blended and the mixture is very smooth. Cover the bowl and set it in a warm place to rise until the batter has doubled, about 30 to 40 minutes.

Mix the strawberries with the remaining granulated sugar and set aside.

Preheat a waffle iron to medium hot. Spoon the batter onto the heated waffle iron and bake each waffle until it is golden brown. (The steam stops escaping about the time the waffle is done.) Sprinkle the finished waffles with confectioners' sugar and top with the reserved sugared strawberries and fresh whipped cream. Serve immediately.

A Note on the Wines

For the dish of steamed mussels, we recommend a crisp Chardonnay of good acidity, such as the Pouilly-Fuissé from Jaboulet-Vercherre.

For the richer dish of chicken breasts and sweetbreads in cream, we would serve another Chardonnay, this one a full-bodied, slightly oaky wine, such as the Meursault Genevrières, Lafon, which gets its toasty bread aroma from the oak barrels in which it ages.

Brazil

❖

Chicken and Rice Soup

Onions Stuffed with Shrimp

Feijoada Completa (Black Bean Casserole)
Accompaniments:
Collard Greens
Rice
Orange Slices
Toasted Manioc

Rolls

Coconut Pudding

Wines:
Pine Ridge Chardonnay
Sutter Home Special Selection Zinfandel

CHICKEN AND RICE SOUP

(SERVES 6)

6 cups chicken broth (page 36)
½ chicken, cut into 3 or 4 pieces
1 onion, chopped
2 medium tomatoes, peeled (see Glossary)
    and coarsely chopped
2 carrots, peeled and diced
2 small turnips, peeled and diced
¼ cup rice
salt and pepper
2 tablespoons chopped fresh parsley

Put the broth in a 3- to 4-quart pot. Add the chicken pieces, onion, tomatoes, carrots, turnips, and rice and simmer for 15 to 20 minutes. Remove the chicken pieces to a plate or bowl. When they are cool enough to handle, remove and discard the skin and bones. Cut or tear the meat into long narrow strips and add them to the pot. Season with salt and pepper to taste. Simmer for 5 minutes more and serve piping hot, garnished with the chopped parsley.

ONIONS STUFFED WITH SHRIMP

(SERVES 6)

6 medium red onions
2 tablespoons olive oil
1 green bell pepper, chopped
1 small green hot pepper, ribbed, seeded,
    and minced
2 garlic cloves, minced
3 tomatoes, peeled (see Glossary) and
    coarsely chopped
½ pound tiny or small shrimp (raw best,
    but cooked and frozen also acceptable)
2 tablespoons roughly chopped coriander
    leaves (cilantro)
salt and pepper
3 tablespoons butter
2 tablespoons flour
¼ cup dry white wine
¾ cup water from cooking the onions
1 8-ounce can tomato sauce
¼ cup dry bread crumbs

Peel the onions and boil in water for 15 to 20 minutes. Remove and cool. Reserve the cooking water. When the onions are cool enough to handle, scoop out the centers, leaving a shell about ¼ inch thick. Set aside the shells and pulp.

Heat the olive oil and sauté the bell pepper with the hot pepper until they are soft. Add the garlic and cook for only a minute or two before adding the tomatoes. Continue cooking until most of the juice evaporates. Stir in the shrimp, coriander, and salt and pepper and remove from the heat. Stuff the shrimp mixture into the onion shells and place them in a small ovenproof casserole.

Preheat oven to 350°F.

Heat 2 tablespoons butter and sauté 1 cup of the reserved onion pulp until the onions are translucent. Sprinkle with the flour and stir until the mixture browns uniformly. Immediately add the wine, the reserved water from the onions, and the tomato sauce. Simmer for about 5 minutes, or until the sauce thickens.

Pour the sauce over the stuffed onions. Sprinkle with the bread crumbs and dot with the remaining tablespoon of butter broken into bits. Bake at 350°F for 15 to 20 minutes, or until nicely browned.

FEIJOADA COMPLETA
(Black Bean Casserole)
(SERVES 6 TO 8)

Feijoada Completa is the Brazilian national dish. Like paella in Spain, the variations are endless, ranging from a simple peasant bean casserole with little meat to a festive holiday extravaganza incorporating as many as 10 varieties of beef and pork. Smoked beef tongue and beef jerky are invariably included along with fresh or smoked pork, a variety of pork sausages, and fresh pig's feet. If you like the idea of family service at the table, cut the meat into serving-sized pieces and place artfully on a platter, with the beans presented in a separate casserole.

3 cups dried black beans, picked over and
  washed
1 1½-pound smoked beef tongue
2½ quarts fresh water
1 large ham hock
2 pounds fresh center-cut pork loin, boned
  (reserve the bones)
1 pound linguiça or other pork sausage
2 pounds smoked or corned pork spare
  ribs, cut in half, making pieces about 3
  inches long

1 large onion, chopped
3–4 cloves garlic, minced
3 medium tomatoes, peeled (see Glossary)
  and chopped
1 small hot pepper (such as jalapeño),
  seeded, ribbed, and chopped
black pepper

Put the beans in a pot. Cover the beans with 3 times their volume of water. Bring to a rapid boil and boil for 2 minutes. Remove from the heat, cover, and let stand for exactly 1 hour. Drain the beans and discard the soaking liquid.

While the beans are soaking, cover the smoked tongue with water, bring it to a boil, and simmer it, covered, for 2 hours.

Transfer the drained beans to a 10- to 12-quart kettle. Cover them with the 2½ quarts fresh water. Add the ham hock and pork bones and bring to a boil. Reduce the heat and simmer slowly for 1½ hours.

Meanwhile brown the sausages in a heavy skillet, remove from the pan, and set them aside. Trim and discard the fat from the pork loin and, using the pan in which the sausages cooked, brown the loin on all sides. Set it aside. Discard all but 1 tablespoon of the fat in the pan and set the pan aside.

When the tongue has simmered for 2 hours, discard the liquid and cool the tongue to a temperature for handling. Peel away the skin and cut away any fat and bones. When the beans have simmered for 1½ hours, add the tongue, browned pork loin and sausages, and the spare ribs. Continue to cook, adding water as necessary so that the beans remain juicy. Cook for 30 minutes more or until the meat is tender.

Meanwhile, return the skillet to the heat and sauté the onion in the remaining tablespoon of fat until the onion is transparent and starting to brown. Add the garlic, stir for a minute, then add the tomatoes and hot pepper, 2 cups of beans, and the liquid from the pot. Mash gently with a potato masher. Cook the mixture slowly, stirring, until it makes a thick sauce.

When the meats are tender, remove them from the bean pot. Stir the sauce into the beans. Adjust the seasoning with the black pepper.

To serve, slice the meats into neat, uniform slices. For family-style service, arrange the meats on a platter and serve the beans separately. If serving individual plates, arrange a portion of each kind of meat around a central portion of beans.

ACCOMPANIMENTS FOR THE FEIJOADA

Collard Greens

Wash 3 bunches collard greens. Cut in half lengthwise, then into ½-inch strips. Chop 2 to 3 slices of bacon. Fry in a skillet until the fat is rendered but the bacon is still soft. Add the greens and stir-fry until barely tender. Season with black pepper and serve immediately.

Rice

Make a basic Rice Pilaf (see Perennial Favorites menu), adding the raw rice to a thinly sliced onion sautéed in olive oil. Add 2 medium tomatoes, peeled and chopped, to the broth before adding it to the rice.

Orange Slices

Peel 2 oranges with a knife, removing the layer of tissue under the rind. Slice the oranges into circles and arrange them on a small plate to be passed at the table.

Toasted Manioc

Manioc is the tuberous root from which tapioca is made. Coarsely ground (the way it is sold), dried, and toasted, it is used as a garnish on many Brazilian dishes. To prepare manioc, toast it on a cookie sheet in a hot oven. Stir constantly and watch carefully to avoid burning. It is used much in the way fried bread crumbs are used in Spanish cooking, and can, in fact, be lightly fried in butter or olive oil instead of being toasted in the oven.

ROLLS

The crusty rolls for this menu should be made from the basic dough for Baguettes (p. 119.)

COCONUT PUDDING
(SERVES 6)

1 cup brown sugar
5 tablespoons unsalted butter, cold from
  the refrigerator
1 cup coconut cream made from 2 fresh
  coconuts (see Note), or 1 cup bottled
  coconut cream
6 egg yolks
zest of 1 orange, grated
2 baskets of strawberries
1/3 cup granulated sugar

Preheat the oven to 350°F.

Whisk the sugar, butter, and coconut cream together. Whisk in the egg yolks and orange zest. Divide the mixture among 6 ramekins and place them in a baking pan filled with hot water almost to the level of the custard. Bake for 30 minutes, or until the custard firms up. Remove the ramekins from the pan and allow them to cool before putting them to chill in the refrigerator.

Meanwhile wash and stem the berries, picking out and reserving 5 or 6 perfect ones to garnish each portion. Puree the remaining berries with the sugar. Unmold the custards on dessert plates, garnish with the whole berries, and pour the sauce over all.

NOTE: To make the coconut cream, peel and grate 2 fresh coconuts. Steep the meat in 2 cups boiling water and let it stand for 30 minutes. Press the mixture through a sieve, discarding the shreds. Let the liquid stand until the water settles to the bottom. Skim off the cream, which will rise to the top.

A Note on the Wines

For the dish of onions stuffed with shrimp, we suggest a wine of medium body, a good flavor of varietal fruit, and only a light overtone of oak, typical of the Pine Ridge Chardonnays.

The complex, robust flavors of the feijoada go well with a rich, intense, full-bodied Zinfandel, one with the taste of berries and earthy overtones found in such wines from Amador County as the Sutter Home Special Selections.

Bulgaria

✱

Troushia I Syrene
(Relish Plate and Cheese)

Bonitza
(Cheese-Filled Pastry)

Tchorba
(Sour Soup of Lettuce and Spinach)
Tvitchki
(Stuffed Cabbage Rolls)
Oroz
(Fluffy Steamed Rice)

Bulgarian White Bread

Kompot
(Fruit Compote of Fresh Apricots and Plums)

Wines:
Chateau Montelena Chardonnay
Monopol Vinimpex Cabernet Sauvignon (Bulgaria)

My wife, Venus, was born in the United States to Bulgarian parents, Martin and Ruth Petcoff, who reared her in Glen Ellyn, a suburb of Chicago. These recipes are her mother's, carefully recorded and tested, and represent the food of her childhood. The Bulgarian cuisine, although it may sound heavy with its emphasis on potatoes, cheese, and sturdy bread, has in fact an austere quality as there is very little fat used. —N.D.

TROUSHIA I SYRENE
(Relish Plate and Cheese)

The relish and cheese plate, which stays on the table throughout the meal, generally contains fresh dill, pickled peppers, green tomatoes, cucumbers, and green onions. The cheese, always made from sheep's milk, is usually feta, sometimes kashkaval or kasseri. The pickles are always homemade and change with the season. The green onions and fresh herbs come from the garden.

BONITZA
(Cheese-Filled Pastry)
(SERVES 6)

FILLING:
  3 eggs, whipped
  ½ cup large-curd cottage cheese
  ½ pound feta cheese, crumbled
  ½ teaspoon sugar

DOUGH:
  ½ cup (1 stick) butter
  7 or 8 sheets of packaged phyllo dough

DO AHEAD:
Defrost the phyllo dough and return the remaining sheets to the freezer. If it is a very hot day, cover the sheets with wax paper to prevent them from drying out.

Melt the butter and remove it from the heat.

Preheat the oven to 350°F.

Mix the filling ingredients together and set aside.

Sheets of packaged phyllo dough measure about 12 x 17 inches. Cut them in half the short way, giving you two pieces approximately 12 x 8½ inches from each single sheet. Cut the sheets again to make one piece about 8 inches square, and a second piece about 4 x 8 inches for each cut sheet. (See illustration, page 24.) You can stack the uncut sheets on top of each other and cut them all at once.

Brush an 8-x-8-inch square baking pan with some of the melted butter. Lay one 8-inch square of dough in the pan and brush it with butter. Scatter about 1½ tablespoons filling over the pastry. Continue stacking one layer of dough, brushing it with melted butter, and sprinkling with cheese mixture, ending with a top layer of dough brushed with butter.

Bake for about 30 minutes, or until puffed up and golden brown.

NOTE: This pastry is not crunchy like an Armenian boereg or baklava, but rather is soft and moist except for the flaky top. Normally served warm, it can be reheated if baked ahead, or eaten at room temperature.

TCHORBA
(Sour Soup of Lettuce and Spinach)
(SERVES 6 TO 8)

Tchorba simply means "soup" and has endless variations. In summer months, it is invariably made with fresh spinach and garden lettuce, usually the red-blushed leaves. In winter, the spinach has to be store-bought and once in a while a potato is chopped and added. Although the original recipe calls for water, chicken broth really adds a nice dimension and so we have included it as an alternate ingredient. The final dish seems almost a cross between the French printanier and the Greek avgolemono.

> 1 medium potato, peeled and diced into ½-inch cubes
> 5 cups water or chicken broth (page 36)
> 1 bunch green onions, chopped, including all the green tops
> 3–4 cloves garlic, minced
> ½ bunch spinach, washed and chopped, including the stems
> ½ head red lettuce, washed, cored, and chopped
> 2–3 tablespoons lemon juice
> salt and pepper
> 2 egg yolks
> ½ cup sour cream

Simmer the diced potatoes in water or broth for 5 minutes. Add the green onions,

garlic, spinach, and lettuce and simmer for 10 minutes, until the vegetables are tender. Add the lemon juice to taste. Adjust the seasoning with salt and pepper.

In a small bowl whisk the egg yolks into the cream. Remove the soup from the heat and whisk in the egg yolk and cream mixture. Serve immediately.

TVITCHKI
(Stuffed Cabbage Rolls)
(SERVES 6)

> 1 large cabbage (about 3 pounds)
> 2 tablespoons oil
> 2 onions, chopped
> ½ cup rice
> 3–4 cloves garlic
> 2 teaspoons paprika
> 2 teaspoons fresh dill
> 1 tablespoon fresh mint leaves
> 1 teaspon salt
> ¼ teaspoon cayenne pepper
> ½ cup water
> 1 pound pork, ground
> ½ pound veal, ground
> 2 cups tomato sauce
> 2 eggs, beaten
> 1 cup plain yogurt

Carefully cut the core from the cabbage but keep the head together. Simmer the cabbage head slowly in water to cover for 10 to 15 minutes. Remove it from the pan and drain. Pull the leaves apart gently. Cut the large leaves in half, away from the thick central rib, and set the leaves aside.

Heat the oil in a skillet, add the onions, and sauté until golden brown. Add the rice and garlic and stir until the rice is coated with oil and starting to sizzle. Stir in the paprika, dill, mint, salt, and cayenne. Add the ½ cup water and stir the mixture until the liquid is absorbed. Remove from the heat and stir in the ground meat.

Preheat the oven to 375°F.

To assemble, line a 5-quart Dutch oven with the small inner cabbage leaves that are too small to stuff. Reserve the coarse outer leaves and spread the remaining leaves flat. Spoon 3 to 4 tablespoons of filling in the center of each flat leaf. Roll the leaves starting from the stem end, leaving both side ends open. The finished rolls should be about 3 to 4 inches long. Line them up neatly in the Dutch oven in 2 layers. Pour the tomato sauce over them and cover with the reserved coarse outer leaves. Cover the pan with a lid or with foil and bake for 1 hour. Remove the cover and the topping of coarse cabbage leaves. Spread the beaten eggs over the top of the cabbage rolls and bake the casserole, uncovered, for 15 minutes, or until the egg has browned. Serve hot and pass the yogurt at the table.

OROZ
(Fluffy Steamed Rice)

Make a simple buttered Steamed Rice, as in the menu of China.

BULGARIAN WHITE BREAD
(MAKES 18 BUNS OR 2 LOAVES)

1 cup milk
2 teaspoons salt
1 teaspoon sugar
2 tablespoons butter
1 cup cold water
1 package of yeast, or 1 tablespoon dry yeast, dissolved in ¼ cup water
5½–5¾ cups all-purpose flour

DO AHEAD:
Lightly butter a bowl for the dough.

Put the milk, salt, sugar, and butter in a small saucepan and heat until the butter melts. Pour the mixture into a large bowl or the bowl of a mixer, add the cold water, and let stand until the mixture cools to lukewarm. Stir in the dissolved yeast.

Add about 5 cups flour, blending it into the milk mixture, then as much more flour as needed to make a dough that is firm enough to hold together but soft enough to work. If you are using a mixing machine with a dough hook, knead the dough for 4 to 5 minutes. If you are kneading by hand, turn the dough out onto a floured counter or pastry board and work it for 6 to 8 minutes. The dough should be smooth and soft.

Place the dough in the buttered bowl, cover it with a towel, and put it in a warm place to rise. (An ideal place is the oven. The pilot light of a gas oven provides the perfect source of heat, but an electric oven is comparable if turned on low for a minute or two, then shut off, before the dough is put in.)

When the dough has doubled in volume —1 to 2 hours—turn it out onto a floured surface and punch it down to get out the air that has inflated it. Kneading a few times also helps in this step. Shape the deflated dough into a ball, return it to the bowl (it is not necessary to butter it again), cover it, and let it rise a second time. When it has doubled, which should take only about half the time of the first rise, turn it out and cut it into 2 pieces.

If you are baking loaves, butter two 5-x-9-inch loaf pans; if you are making buns, butter a cookie sheet.

To form the loaves, work the dough with your hands into 2 elongated balls, smoothing from the top down the sides and tucking the dough under. Place the loaves in the pans, smooth side up, and correct the shape to make it even. Cover and let rise again until doubled, about the same time as the second rise. If you are making buns, cut each half of the dough into 3 equal pieces, then each piece into 3 pieces again. Using the same smoothing, tucking technique, shape the dough into 18 round balls, place them on the cookie sheet, cover, and let rise until doubled.

About halfway through the rising, preheat the oven to 375°F.

When the loaves or buns have doubled, make a cross on the top of each by slashing with the blade of a single-edged razor, a sharp knife, or kitchen scissors. Place in the oven to bake: The loaves will take about 45 minutes, the buns 20 to 25 minutes. They are done when they produce a hollow, thumping sound when rapped on the bottom with a knuckle. Remove to a rack to cool.

NOTE: You can make up a batch of dough and freeze it after the second rising. Punch it down, wrap it well in plastic wrap, and seal it. To thaw before using, leave at room temperature for at least half a day, or in the refrigerator for at least 24 hours (you will have to adjust the time depending on the temperature of your refrigerator). Proceed as above.

KOMPOT
(Fruit Compote of Fresh Apricots and Plums)

Place 1 cup water, ½ cup sugar, and a thinly sliced lemon in a saucepan. Add fresh apricots and plums and simmer until tender. Serve chilled, along with some of the syrup. (In winter, dried prunes and apricots are frequently simmered in the same way.)

A Note on the Wines

A full-bodied white wine is a fine accompaniment to the rich phyllo pastry filled with savory cheese. Our choice would be a Chardonnay made in the style of the Napa Valley winery, Chateau Montelena.

The robust cabbage rolls stuffed with pork and veal call for a young and assertive red. To go with this Bulgarian dish, we would pick a Bulgarian wine, such as a Cabernet Sauvignon from Monopol Vinimpex.

Chile

✿

Escabeche
(Pickled Chicken)

Sea Bass Soup

Beef and Vegetable Stew

Rolls

Almond Meringues with Fresh Fruit

Wines:
Concha y Toro, Marqués de Casa Concha Chilean Riesling
Cousiño Macul, Don Matias Cabernet

ESCABECHE
(Pickled Chicken)
(SERVES 6)

This dish needs a day to marinate before serving.

2 tablespoons oil
6 fryer chicken thighs
salt and pepper
1 red pepper, thinly sliced
1 large onion, sliced
1 stalk celery, sliced
1 cup dry white wine
½ cup white wine vinegar
juice of 1 lemon
2 bay leaves
½ teaspoon ground mace
¼ teaspoon ground allspice
scant ¼ teaspoon red pepper flakes

Heat the oil in a skillet. Salt and pepper the chicken and brown until the skin side of the thighs is well colored. Add the remaining ingredients. Cover the pan and simmer for about 25 minutes, or until the chicken is tender. Transfer the thighs, vegetables, and liquid to a serving casserole and marinate overnight in the refrigerator. Serve chilled.

SEA BASS SOUP
(SERVES 6)

In recent years 2 or 3 different kinds of fresh sea bass have been imported, flown in fresh from Chile. No matter the particular variety, it is always called Chilean sea bass in the market, and has a sweet, firm, white flesh that is so tender it seems to melt in the mouth. If Chilean sea bass is not available, any white-fleshed fish will make a good substitute in this recipe.

7 cups water
1 cup white wine
1 pound fish trimmings (any fish but salmon)
2 teaspoons pickling spice
2 tablespoons oil
1 large onion, chopped
2–3 cloves garlic, minced
1 medium potato, cut in ½-inch dice
1 small hot pepper, seeded and deveined, or ¼ teaspoon red pepper flakes
2 medium tomatoes, peeled (see Glossary) and chopped
½–¾ pound sea bass or other firm white-fleshed fish fillets, cut into ½-inch cubes
salt
2 tablespoons chopped fresh coriander leaves (cilantro)

DO AHEAD:

First make the fish stock: Simmer the water, wine, fish trimmings, and pickling spice in a soup kettle for about 30 to 40 minutes.

Heat the oil in a separate 2- to 3-quart pot, add the onion and garlic, and sauté without browning until translucent. Strain the finished soup stock from the soup kettle directly into the pot of onion and garlic. Add the potato and hot pepper and simmer for about 10 minutes, or until the potato cubes are tender. Add the tomatoes and fish. Bring back to a boil over high heat, then immediately lower the temperature to a simmer, and cook for 3 to 4 minutes more, just until the fish becomes white and opaque. Add salt to taste. Serve immediately sprinkled with the coriander leaves.

BEEF AND VEGETABLE STEW
(SERVES 6)

2 tablespoons oil
2 pounds beef stew meat
2 large onions, chopped
2–3 cloves garlic, minced
2 teaspoons cuminseed, preferably whole but ground also acceptable
2 teaspoons paprika
1 small green chili pepper, seeded and deveined, or 1/4–1/2 teaspoon crushed red pepper flakes
1/2 cup white wine
2 cups chicken or meat broth (page 36 or 23)
1 1/2 teaspoons salt
3 tablespoons rice
1 1/2 cups pumpkin or squash, peeled and cut in 3/4-inch dice
1/2 cup frozen or cooked peas
1 cup fresh or canned corn kernels
2 egg yolks
2 tablespoons chopped fresh parsley

Heat the oil in a heavy Dutch oven, add the meat and onions, and brown them well. Add the garlic, cumin, paprika, and hot pepper, and stir until the mixture is sizzling. Add the wine, broth, and salt, and bring to a boil. Reduce the heat to a slow simmer, cover the pot, and cook the stew for 1 hour. If the liquid evaporates too quickly during the cooking, add water to replace it.

After an hour, stir in the rice and pumpkin or squash, cover the pot again, and simmer for 20 to 30 minutes, or until the meat is tender. Add the peas and corn and simmer, uncovered, for another 2 to 3 minutes.

Whisk the egg yolks in a small bowl. Add 1 cup of broth from the pot and whisk it into the eggs until the mixture is well blended. Pour the egg mixture back into the stew pot and stir in gently. Garnish the stew with the chopped parsley and serve immediately.

ROLLS

In Latin American countries, the breadstuffs before colonial times were made of ground cooked cornmeal, the same as modern-day tortillas and arepas, the Venezuelan variation. The colonials introduced rolls. Our Latin American menus call for either tortillas or rolls, and sometimes both.

To make the rolls for this dinner, use the recipe for Baguette dough (page 119).

ALMOND MERINGUES WITH FRESH FRUIT
(SERVES 6)

>4 egg whites
>1 cup sugar
>½ cup water
>¾ cup almond meal or finely chopped
>   toasted almonds
>fresh fruit, such as pineapple, papaya, or
>   berries

DO AHEAD:
Line a sheet pan with parchment paper.

Preheat the oven to 300°F.

Beat the egg whites until stiff.

In a small saucepan dissolve the sugar in the water and heat it to the soft-ball stage (240°F on a candy thermometer). Pour the sugar syrup slowly over the stiff egg whites, beating continuously. This will make a heavy meringue, somewhat like an Italian meringue. Stir in the almond meal or almonds.

Using a pastry bag, pipe six 3-inch circles about ¾ inch thick onto the lined sheet pan. Bake at 300°F for 20 to 25 minutes. The meringues should be just starting to brown but still soft in the center. Cool. Meanwhile, clean and peel the fruit and cut into dice or slices appropriate for topping the meringues.

When ready to serve, place the meringues on individual plates. At the last possible moment before serving, top the meringues with the fresh fruit.

A Note on the Wines

To go along with the pickled chicken and the sea bass soup, we would suggest a light-bodied, refreshing Chilean Riesling, one of the country's most popular white wines. A typical example would be from the Concha y Toro firm under their Marqués de Casa Concha label.

For the substantial beef and vegetable stew, we would choose one of the barrel-aged Cabernets, perhaps the country's most successful red wine, rich, dark, and full-bodied. The well-made Don Matias Cabernets from Cousiño Macul are in that style.

China

❁

Chicken Soup with Green Noodles, Sichuan-Style

Cantonese Barbecued Pork

Chinese New Year's Salad of Raw Fish
(or Cooked Fish or Chicken)

Whole Steamed Rock Cod
Steamed Rice
Asparagus, Shantung-Style

Fresh Lichee Nuts, Mandarin Oranges,
Tangerines, or Pomelos

Wines:
Chardonnay
Cabernet Sauvignon or Zinfandel

A few years ago, when tourists were still a curiosity in the People's Republic of China, I had the good fortune to travel for more than a month on the mainland with a group of Chinese friends. We tasted regional specialties, modest country cooking, and banquet dishes, and although there were similarities, never was the same dish prepared the same way. Chinese recipes are sets of basic instructions from which each chef interprets, embellishes, and creates. The Monday Night menu given here is in that spirit. If you have some leftover bits of chicken or a few leaves of spinach, or you love snow peas, by all means, throw them in the soup!

Except at banquets, the Chinese do not serve meals in courses. Even the soup is often eaten throughout the meal. For Western tastes, we have served the soup as a first course, followed by all of the other dishes together except the fruit. Save the soup bowls for the rice, then put a little of this, a little of that atop it. In China, diners use their chopsticks as serving tools, turning them around—that is, using the broad, noneating handle end—for dipping foods out of communal serving dishes.—D.M.

CHICKEN SOUP WITH GREEN NOODLES, SICHUAN-STYLE
(SERVES 6)

Sichuan Province is famous for its smoked foods, its green noodles, and its fiery dishes, as this soup demonstrates.

6 dried black Chinese mushrooms, or
  6 fresh shiitake mushrooms
6 cups unsalted chicken stock (page 36)
a few drops of oil
4 ounces green egg noodles (spinach
  fettuccine)
3–4 slices smoked ham with the fat left on,
  sliced in julienne strips or cut into small
  chunks
1/4 teaspoon or more to taste of hot pepper
  oil (available in Chinese markets, or see
  recipe below)
1/2 teaspoon soy sauce
1/2 teaspoon Chinese sesame oil
2–3 whole green onions, finely sliced
a few sprigs coriander (Chinese parsley)

DO AHEAD:

Soak the dried mushrooms for about 20 minutes in enough warm water to cover. Drain and rinse thoroughly, saving the soaking liquid and making sure all the sand is washed away. Strain the soaking liquid through a sieve lined with a towel or fine cheesecloth and reserve.

Trim off the hard stems from the mushrooms and slice the caps into long slivers about as thick as a 50-cent piece; reserve. If using fresh mushrooms, clean them well with a brush or damp cloth, trim off the stems, and slice as above.

Put the stock in a large pot over medium heat. While it is heating, fill a second pot with salted water and bring it to a boil. Add a few drops of oil (to keep the noodles from sticking together), add the noodles, and cook briefly until just tender, 3 to 5 minutes. Immediately add a glass of cold water to the pot to stop the cooking, and drain the noodles in a colander. Reserve.

When the soup is just at the boiling point, add the ham, mushrooms, reserved mushroom liquor, hot pepper oil, soy sauce, and sesame oil. Simmer just long enough to heat through and blend the flavors. Taste and adjust the seasoning. Add the green onions and noodles and garnish with sprigs of coriander. Heat another minute, then spoon out into individual bowls or serve in a large tureen on the table.

Hot Pepper Oil

Heat 1 cup peanut oil or ¾ cup peanut oil mixed with ¼ cup sesame oil until very hot. Remove from the heat and add 1 to 2 tablespoons dried red chili flakes or 2 tablespoons powdered cayenne pepper. Let the oil sit until it is completely cool. Remove the flakes by straining the oil through a sieve lined with fine cheesecloth. Store in a glass jar or bottle with a tight lid.

CANTONESE BARBECUED PORK
(SERVES 6)

A version of this recipe, Char Siew, first appeared in *A Cook's Tour of San Francisco*, by Doris Muscatine. Any leftover barbecued pork is good in soups and salads.

2 1-pound pork tenderloins (see Note)

MARINADE:
  ½ cup soy sauce
  ½ cup sugar or honey
  2 cloves garlic, mashed
  2 tablespoons ketchup

GARNISH:
  toasted sesame seeds (see Glossary)

DIPPING:
  dry Chinese mustard powder
  water
  ketchup

DO AHEAD:
If you are barbecuing over charcoal, build your fire 30 to 45 minutes before you are ready to cook.

Marinate the pork for at least 3 hours (see instructions).

Although the pork tenderloin is often cut into 2 long strips, I prefer to leave it whole. It stays more juicy, though it is more difficult to cook without burning the outside before the inside is done.

In a large mixing bowl combine the marinade ingredients. Add the pork, turning it in the marinade so that it is coated all over. Marinate for at least 3 hours at room temperature, or overnight in the refrigerator. Turn the meat from time to time so that it marinates evenly.

When ready to cook, drain the meat well, scraping off most of the marinade (the sugars will burn during long cooking), and barbecue it over a charcoal fire or under the oven broiler, turning frequently so that it browns evenly. If the meat has been left whole, it should take approximately 20 to 25 minutes to reach the safe internal temperature of 137°F on a meat thermometer. If it has been cut into strips, test by cutting into one piece at the thickest part: It is done when the meat is almost entirely white with just the lightest blush of pink in the center. Just before the meat is done, brush it with marinade, turning it so that all sides get an even coating.

Remove to a carving platter and let rest for several minutes before slicing. Cut the meat into ¼-inch pieces and arrange them in an overlapping pattern on a service platter. Sprinkle with toasted sesame seeds.

To make the dipping sauce, mix Chinese mustard powder with enough water to make a paste. It is very strong; each diner will need only a small amount. Serve each diner individual dishes of mustard and ketchup for dipping.

NOTE: Pork tenderloins are available in Chinese markets but are sometimes hard to find in Western butcher shops. Pork shoulder is an acceptable substitute.

CHINESE NEW YEAR'S SALAD OF RAW FISH
(or Cooked Fish or Chicken)
(SERVES 6)

The Chinese always use raw fish for this recipe, but cooked fish or poached chicken combine equally well with the other ingredients.

1 pound cod, salmon, hardhead, or smelt, or 1 whole chicken breast (2 sides)
1 carrot (optional)
1 stalk celery (optional)
1 onion (optional)
black peppercorns (optional)
slice of gingerroot (optional)
vegetable or peanut oil
¼ pound transparent rice noodles
12 won ton skins (see Notes)

DRESSING:
½ cup salad oil
2 tablespoons Chinese sesame oil
juice of 1 lemon
1 teaspoon 5-spice powder (a mixture of 5 to 7 spices, including ground fennel seeds, ginger, cloves, cinnamon, Sichuan peppercorns, and star anise); if unavailable, use individual spices or substitute allspice
1 tablespoon sugar
1 teaspoon salt
2 teaspoons sumak (see Notes)
½ teaspoon white pepper

GARNISHES:
3 green onions, cut into 2-inch-long julienne strips
15 pickled scallions or shallots, sliced (see Notes)
3 tablespoons preserved red ginger
1 small carrot, shredded
2 small bunches coriander (Chinese parsley), or 1 large bunch
½ cup chopped toasted peanuts
1 tablespoon toasted sesame seeds (see Glossary)

Prepare the salad ingredients:

Raw fish: Skin the fish, remove the bones, and cut the meat into very thin julienne slices (or have the fish market skin and fillet the fish for you). Reserve.

Cooked fish: Poach the fish in water flavored with the optional ingredients. When it is just cooked through (the flesh should be opaque and firm), remove from the heat and cool in the stock. When cool, skin the fish, flake the meat off the bones, and reserve.

Cooked chicken: Halve the chicken breast. Poach for 20 to 25 minutes, or until cooked through, in water flavored as for the cooked fish above. Cool. Remove the skin and shred the meat by hand from the bones; reserve. Strain and reserve the stock (use for the soup in this menu or freeze for later use).

Noodles and won ton skins: Pour oil to a depth of about ¼ to ½ inch into a wok or deep-sided pot and heat until very hot. Add the dried noodles a few at a time as they expand dramatically. If they are too hard to pull apart, cut with kitchen shears. Remove each fried batch and drain on brown paper or paper towels. There should be about 6 cups of crisp brown noodles. Fry the won ton skins in the same oil until they are brown and crisp. Remove with tongs or a slotted spoon and drain on brown paper or paper towels.

Mix together all the dressing ingredients.

To assemble, arrange the noodles on a large platter. Break up the won ton skins over the noodles. Toss the raw or cooked fish or the poached chicken with the dressing and, when well mixed, distribute it evenly over the noodle–won ton layer. Sprinkle each garnish over the top.

NOTES: Won ton skins are available packaged in the refrigerator section of Chinese grocery stores.

Sumak is a berry with a somewhat sour flavor frequently found in Middle Eastern cooking. If you can't locate it, substitute an extra squeeze of lemon juice.

Pickled scallions or shallots are found in jars in Chinese markets.

WHOLE STEAMED ROCK COD
(SERVES 6)

> 1 whole 2–2½-pound fresh rock cod (or any fish of a similar type), cleaned, with head and skin left on
> ½ teaspoon salt
> 1 teaspoon shredded fresh gingerroot
> 2 green onions
> ¼ cup vegetable oil
> ¼ cup light soy sauce
> a few coriander leaves (Chinese parsley)

Put the fish on a large plate, sprinkle it with salt, and spread the gingerroot evenly over it. Place 1 whole green onion on top.

Bring some water in a steamer to a rapid boil. Place the fish platter on the steamer rack or trivet, cover, and steam over high enough heat to keep the water at a slow boil for about 25 minutes, or until the fish is opaque and cooked through. (Test with a fork.) Remove the fish as soon as it is done so that it will not overcook.

While the fish is steaming, heat the vegetable oil with the soy sauce. Prepare the remaining green onion by cutting off and discarding the green ends and finely shredding the white top.

When ready to serve, pour the hot oil-soy mixture over the fish and garnish it with the shredded green onion and coriander leaves.

STEAMED RICE
(SERVES 6)

> 1 cup rice
> 1½ cups water
> ¼ teaspoon salt

Place the rice in a large, fine-meshed strainer and rinse under cold running water. Set aside.

Put the water and salt in a 2-quart saucepan with a tight-fitting lid and bring to a boil. Add the rice, stirring occasionally, until the water boils again. Reduce the heat to the lowest setting and simmer the rice, covered, for 15 to 16 minutes, or until all the liquid is absorbed.

ASPARAGUS, SHANTUNG-STYLE

Wash and trim 1 bunch of asparagus, breaking off the root end by hand at the point where it gives naturally. Drain well, slice the stalks on the diagonal into 2-inch pieces (hold the knife at a 45-degree angle as you cut). In a wok or skillet, heat 1 to 2 tablespoons of vegetable oil with ½ to 1 teaspoon Chinese sesame oil. When it is very hot, add the asparagus and toss it in the oil. Add a few splashes of soy sauce and continue to toss-cook the asparagus until they are just tender but still retain their crispness—a few minutes at most.

FRESH LICHEE NUTS, MANDARIN ORANGES, TANGERINES, OR POMELOS

Except at banquets, sweet desserts are not a normal part of a Chinese meal, although fruit often comes to the table to finish things off. Serve a large bowl of fresh lichee nuts, mandarin oranges, or tangerines, or one of the large, football-shaped grapefruits called pomelos, depending on the season and availability. Slight chilling makes all of these fruits more refreshing—serve them unshelled and unskinned. Fresh lichee nuts and pomelos are available in Chinese markets or fancy produce stores though they have limited seasons. If fresh fruits are not available, use canned lichee nuts or mandarin oranges.

A Note on Bread

The Chinese do not normally eat bread as such with their meals, and none is specified here. Dumplings, breakfast doughnuts, steamed buns, sweetened cakelike "breads," and various kinds of pancakes all take their appropriate places as part of many meals.

A Note on the Wines

Tea is the ubiquitous Chinese drink. It is offered hospitably at every stop. Hotel rooms are always supplied with tea leaves, lidded cups, and thermos bottles of hot water, instantly replenished by the staff. Although, during my trip, tea was automatically served with all the meals, for the Chinese it is a drink that is consumed more often between meals. Alcohol is for festive occasions or get-togethers and is not drunk as a normal beverage with meals. Grape wine, now making its appearance in China, was a rarity during my travels. "Wine" frequently refers to rice wine, served warm in thimble-sized glasses; it has a baked, sherrylike taste. Kaoliang, a colorless liquor made from sorghum, turns up at banquets and other festive occasions. Chinese beer is generally excellent and a good choice to drink with this meal. The Tsing Tao brand that was served at Narsai's is available in the United States.

Matching wine with a Chinese meal where many dishes and flavors are consumed at the same time is a different challenge than pairing one specific food with wine, as we do in the West. A Chinese meal requires a wine that at once harmonizes, contrasts, and stands up to strong spices, sweet and sour flavors, hot peppers, garlic, and ginger. Cold, crisp, dry white wine—a Sauvignon Blanc or Chablis—will certainly be fine with this Chinese menu, but it is not a very imaginative choice. My own recommendation would be for a rich, full-bodied Chardonnay, which has the kind of complexity to equal the variety of tastes in the cooking; or for a Cabernet Sauvignon or a claret-style Zinfandel, which go surprisingly well with fish and chicken prepared as these are, with enough sprightly seasonings to overcome any delicacy and impart the much more solid character of meat.—D.M.

Creole

❖

Mirlitons (Chayotes) Stuffed with Shrimp

Oyster and Sausage Gumbo

Green Tossed Salad

Charlie's Mother's Cloud Biscuits

Pecan Molasses Pie

Wines:
St. Andrews Winery Sauvignon Blanc
Louis Martini Special Selection Zinfandel

MIRLITONS (CHAYOTES) STUFFED WITH SHRIMP

(SERVES 6)

3 small mirlitons (chayote squash)
¼ cup (½ stick) butter
1 small onion, chopped
2 cloves garlic, minced
1 medium tomato, peeled (see Glossary) and chopped
3 tablespoons chopped fresh parsley
¼ teaspoon dried thyme
6 ounces prawns, peeled, deveined, and chopped
1 teaspoon Worcestershire sauce
salt
hot sauce
¼ cup olive oil
½ cup coarse fresh bread crumbs

Simmer the unpeeled mirlitons in water to cover in an open pot for 30 minutes, or until almost tender. Drain and cool, then cut them in half lengthwise. Scoop out and discard the seeds. Scoop out the pulp, leaving a shell about ¼ inch thick. Chop the pulp and set it aside.

Preheat the oven to 400°F.

Melt the butter in a thick sauté pan. Add the onion and sauté until it starts to brown. Add the garlic, tomato, parsley, and thyme. Stir for a minute or two, then add the chopped squash. Cook, stirring, until most of the liquid released by the squash has evaporated. Stir in the prawns. Adjust the seasoning to your taste by adding the Worcestershire sauce, salt, and hot sauce. Set aside.

Spoon the stuffing into the squash shells. Arrange them side by side in a 9-inch casserole. Place in the oven.

While the squash are baking, heat the olive oil in a small skillet, add the bread crumbs, and fry until golden. Set aside. After the squash have baked for 15 minutes, remove them from the oven. Sprinkle the fried bread crumbs over the top and return the squash to the oven. Continue baking for another 5 to 10 minutes, or until brown.

OYSTER AND SAUSAGE GUMBO

(SERVES 6)

1 tablespoon oil
1½ pounds smoked andouille sausage (Creole-style pork sausage; if unavailable, substitute any other smoked pork sausage such as kielbasa; don't use the French-style andouille, which is tripe sausage), cut into ½-inch pieces
1 large onion, chopped
1 tablespoon flour
4–5 cloves garlic, minced
½ teaspoon dried thyme
½ teaspoon black pepper
¼–½ teaspoon cayenne pepper
4 large tomatoes, peeled (see Glossary) and chopped
6 cups seafood stock (page 113), canned clam broth, or chicken broth (page 36)
½ bunch green onions, including green tops, chopped
salt and pepper

3 tablespoons filé powder (powdered
  sassafras leaves)
24 medium oysters, shucked (about 1
  quart shucked oysters)
1 recipe Steamed Rice (page 76)(see
  Notes)

In a heavy soup pot or Dutch oven, heat
the oil, add the sausage and onion, and
sauté until the onion is well browned. Stir
in the flour and cook until lightly browned.
Then add the garlic, thyme, black pepper,
and cayenne, cooking only a minute or two
before adding the tomatoes and stock.
Cover and simmer for about 30 minutes.
Add the green onions.

When the mixture has finished cooking,
adjust the seasoning with salt and pepper
and set aside. When ready to serve, bring
the gumbo to a boil and stir in the filé and
oysters. Return to the boil, then remove
from the heat and serve immediately over
plain steamed rice.

NOTES: Start the rice cooking approximately 30 minutes before you serve. If
making your own fish stock, strain it and
reserve any little bits of fish to add to the
gumbo with the oysters.

GREEN TOSSED SALAD
(SERVES 6)

1 head iceberg lettuce, cut into bite-sized
  pieces
1 bunch radishes, trimmed and sliced

1 bunch green onions, chopped
½ bunch parsley, chopped
1 green pepper, chopped coarsely
1 large tomato, cut into 6 wedges

DRESSING:
½ cup salad oil
¼ cup wine vinegar
1 clove garlic, crushed
1 teaspoon Worcestershire sauce
juice of ½ lemon
1 tablespoon ketchup
½ teaspoon dry mustard
2 tablespoons capers
4 anchovy fillets, mashed or minced

Chill the cleaned, cut vegetables in the
refrigerator. Mix the dressing ingredients. Toss with the vegetables just before
serving.

CHARLIE'S MOTHER'S CLOUD BISCUITS
(MAKES 12)

2 cups all-purpose flour
1 tablespoon sugar
4 teaspoons baking powder
½ teaspoon salt
½ cup (1 stick) butter
1 egg
⅔ cup milk

Preheat the oven to 450°F.

In a large bowl mix the flour, sugar, baking powder, salt, and butter until they are
crumbly. Mix in the egg and milk until
they are barely incorporated.

Pat or roll out the dough lightly on a floured board to about ½-inch thickness. With a floured biscuit cutter or the rim of a glass, cut the dough into 12 biscuits. Place them on an ungreased cookie sheet with space between them and bake for 15 to 20 minutes, or until golden and fluffy.

NOTE: To use this recipe for shortcake, increase the sugar to 2 tablespoons and proceed as above. Spread the finished dough evenly in a cake pan. If using a 9-inch pan, bake for 20 minutes; an 8-inch pan, for 25 minutes. When the cake has cooled, cut it into 2 layers. Fill with strawberries or other fruit of your choice mixed with a bit of sugar to taste. Top with whipped cream and more of the fruit.

PECAN MOLASSES PIE
(SERVES 8)

½ cup sugar
¾ cup light corn syrup
¼ cup molasses
3 eggs
1 teaspoon vanilla
¼ teaspoon ground cinnamon
½ cup (1 stick) butter, melted and cooled
1½ cups pecans
1 9-inch unbaked piecrust (see Danish
   Waffle dough, page 95)

Preheat oven to 375°F.

Mix together the sugar, corn syrup, molasses, eggs, vanilla, and cinnamon. Stir in the melted butter and pecans.

Pour the filling into the piecrust and bake for 45 to 50 minutes, or until the crust is quite brown. The center of the pie will still be soft. Cool and serve at room temperature.

A Note on the Wines

A California Sauvignon Blanc, a good fruity white wine with herbaceous overtones, seemed just the right choice to go with the shrimp-stuffed mirlitons. We selected one from the Napa Valley, the St. Andrews Winery 1983.

A solid Zinfandel was our choice to stand up to the rich oyster and sausage gumbo. We picked one that had enough fruit to complement the spices, a Louis Martini Special Selection 1974.

Cuba

❖

Scallop Seviche

Corn Soup

Spicy Beef Hash
(Picadillo)
Black Beans and Rice
(Moros y Cristianos)

Cucumber Salad

Rolls

Cheese Custard

Wines:
Hacienda Cellars Gewürztraminer
Conn Creek Zinfandel

SCALLOP SEVICHE

Conch is abundant in the Caribbean. It is commonly sliced thin, pounded, and quickly sautéed, much as we would prepare abalone in California. It is most succulent, however, marinated in lime juice as a seviche. If you are fortunate enough to find conch fresh—it is occasionally available in specialty fish markets in Chinese, Spanish, or Italian neighborhoods—use it to make this seviche. Otherwise, use fresh scallops, which also make an excellent seviche. Leave tiny bay scallops whole; slice large ocean scallops into "coins" about ¼ inch thick. Discard the tiny muscle sometimes atttached to one side of the scallop; it is so tough that eating it is like chewing on a string. Use the recipe for Clemente's Seviche in the Nicaragua menu, substituting scallops for the fish.

CORN SOUP
(SERVES 6)

> 2 tablespoons butter
> 1 large onion, chopped
> 4 cups chicken broth (page 36)
> 1 large red bell pepper, roasted (see Glossary), seeded, and peeled
> 1 medium potato, peeled and sliced
> 2 cups fresh or canned corn
> salt and pepper
> 1 cup heavy cream
> 2 tablespoons chopped fresh parsley

Melt the butter in a 3- to 4- quart pot, add the onion, and sauté until it is translucent.

Add the broth, red pepper, potato, and corn. Bring to a boil, lower to a simmer, and cook for 20 to 25 minutes, or until the vegetables are tender. Transfer to a blender or food processor and puree until smooth. Return the mixture to the pot and season with salt and pepper. Stir in the cream and heat the soup without boiling it. Serve with parsley sprinkled on top.

SPICY BEEF HASH
(Picadillo)
(SERVES 6)

Almost a national dish in Cuba, picadillo is a very elegant beef hash served with a wide variety of accompaniments. At Narsai's, we made the basic ingredients into a sauce, eliminating the meat, and spooned it over medallions of beef fillet for a more lavish presentation. Here we present the traditional recipe, which is at its best made from the trimmings of a beef roast.

> 3 tablespoons oil
> 1 large onion, chopped
> 3–4 cloves garlic, minced
> 3 cups coarsely chopped cooked beef (see Note)
> 2 red bell peppers, seeded and chopped
> 1 small green chili pepper, seeded, deveined, and chopped, or ¼ teaspoon crushed red pepper flakes
> ¼ teaspoon ground allspice
> 3 tomatoes, peeled (see Glossary) and chopped

½ cup slivered blanched almonds
½ cup raisins
2 tablespoons capers, with their liquid
12 green olives, pitted and quartered
½ cup sherry

Heat the oil in a large heavy skillet or a Dutch oven. Add the onion, and sauté until it starts to brown. Add the garlic, beef, bell peppers, hot pepper, and allspice. Stir well and cook until the mixture is sizzling and starting to stick at the edges. Add the remaining ingredients. Simmer the mixture until the sherry has almost evaporated and the consistency is somewhat like hash.

NOTE: If you don't have beef roast trimmings, use 2 pounds raw skirt steak or beef stew meat, season with salt and pepper, and brown it in a heavy Dutch oven in its own fat. Add 1 cup beef broth (page 23) or water and braise the meat for 1 hour or more, adding liquid, if necessary, until it is tender. Let the meat cool, and chop it coarsely. Reserve.

BLACK BEANS AND RICE
(Moros y Cristianos)

(SERVES 6 AS A MAIN COURSE,
10 TO 12 AS A SIDE DISH)

Picadillo is served with a variety of accompaniments, almost always including fried eggs, but that seemed more a breakfast or lunch dish than one for dinner, so we eliminated them. The other most common embellishments are rice, fried bananas or plantains, stewed okra, and marinated cucumbers. We chose black beans and rice, called locally Moros y Cristianos, because we like that traditional Caribbean combination.

Black beans and rice are usually cooked together, the beans partially cooked first, the rice and additional liquid added for the final 20 minutes. This recipe calls for cooking the beans and rice separately, then serving by spooning the cooked beans over the rice, or mixing it in.

2 cups (1 pound) black beans, picked over and washed
6–8 cups water
1 bay leaf
6 cloves garlic (2 whole, 4 minced)
4 tablespoons oil
2 onions, chopped
1 green pepper, chopped
¼ cup wine vinegar
¼ teaspoon dried thyme
salt and pepper
1 recipe Steamed Rice (page 76)

DO AHEAD:
Put the beans in a pot, then cover with 3 times their volume of water. Bring to a rapid boil and boil for 2 minutes. Remove from the heat, cover, and let stand for exactly 1 hour. Drain the beans and discard the soaking liquid.

The beans will take about 2 hours to cook, but can be made ahead and reheated.

The rice will take about 20 minutes to steam, and should be prepared enough ahead to be ready when the meal is to be served.

Put the beans in a large pot, cover them with the water, and add the bay leaf and 2 whole garlic cloves. Cover the pot and simmer the beans very slowly until they are tender, about 2 hours.

While the beans are simmering, prepare the sauce. Heat the oil in a skillet, add the onions, and sauté until they start to brown. Add the 4 minced garlic cloves and the bell pepper, lower the heat, and continue to cook until the vegetables are sizzling. Stir in the vinegar and thyme.

Spoon out about 1½ cups of beans and liquid from the pot into the skillet of onions and garlic. Gently mash the mixture with a potato masher. Stir the mashed bean mixture back into the bean pot. Adjust the seasoning with salt and pepper. Spoon the beans over the steamed rice, or mix them into the rice, and serve as a side dish with the picadillo.

CUCUMBER SALAD

Although we are serving this salad as a separate course, in the Cuban meal it would more likely take its place as an additional item on the picadillo plate. The traditional dressing of fresh lime juice, crushed garlic, salt and pepper, and a cautious pinch or two of red pepper flakes, echoes the flavors of the seviche served as the first course of this menu, so we would toss the cucumbers for a salad course with a simple vinaigrette

(see Glossary) instead. However, if you use the cucumbers as an accompaniment to the picadillo, you might prefer to use the spicy-tart lime dressing.

If you use regular cucumbers, which are tough-skinned, peel and seed them; if you use the long "European" type, there is no need to do this, as they are usually quite tender. Cut the cucumber into thin slices and toss with the dressing of your choice.

ROLLS

Use the recipe for Baguette dough (page 119) and make into rolls.

CHEESE CUSTARD
(SERVES 6 TO 7)

My wife and I first ate this dessert in a Mexican restaurant where it was called Cuban Flan. The cream cheese gives it a dense texture somewhat like cheesecake. We tried making it with fresh cream instead of evaporated milk, but the texture never seemed right. This recipe is the only one in which we ever used evaporated milk at the restaurant, but the results make it clear that here it is preferable to fresh cream.—N.D.

6 ounces cream cheese
½ cup sugar
4 eggs
2¼ cups evaporated milk
1½ teaspoons vanilla extract

Preheat the oven to 350°F.

Beat the cream cheese and sugar together until blended. Add the eggs and continue beating until smooth. Mix in the milk and vanilla.

Pour the mixture into 6 or 7 custard cups. Place them in a baking pan and put it into the oven. Using a pitcher, carefully pour very hot water into the pan until it comes halfway up the sides of the custard cups. Bake for about 35 minutes, or until set. Test by inserting a small knife blade halfway between the center and the edge of a custard cup. The blade should come out clean. It is all right if the custard remains just a bit runny in the very center of the cup. Do not let the custards dry out.

A Note on the Wines

A perfumy, crisp white wine seems a good choice to pair with the seviche and corn soup, and we would pick a Gewürztraminer from Hacienda Cellars.

The spicy picadillo needs a robust partner, a rich, intense, oaky Zinfandel, a style of wine that Conn Creek makes so well.

Czechoslovakia

❖

Chicken Consommé with Parsnips

Bass Baked with Nuts and Prunes

Veal Braised with Sour Cream, Mushrooms, and Caraway
Buttered Spinach Leaves
Egg Noodles with Bread Crumbs

Green Pepper and Tomato Salad

Strass Rye Bread

Chestnut Cake

Wines:
Brander Sauvignon Blanc
Carneros Creek Pinot Noir

CHICKEN CONSOMMÉ WITH PARSNIPS
(SERVES 6 TO 8)

Heat 6 to 8 cups of chicken consommé (page 36) in a soup pot. Peel and thinly slice 1 medium-large parsnip. When the soup is hot, add the parsnip slices and cook them in the consommé for a few minutes, or enough to cook them through. Serve each portion of soup garnished with a few slices of parsnip.

BASS BAKED WITH NUTS AND PRUNES
(SERVES 6)

2 tablespoons sugar
1 cup water
½ cup red wine vinegar
*½ lemon, juice reserved and the zest finely
    chopped or grated*
1 carrot, sliced
1 small onion, sliced
½ teaspoon dried tarragon
8 whole allspice
1 tablespoon sliced fresh ginger
½ cup chopped pitted prunes
6 2–2½-ounce bass fillets
salt and pepper
6 tablespoons butter
2 tablespoons slivered toasted almonds
2 tablespoons chopped toasted walnuts

In a heavy saucepan, mix the sugar with 1 tablespoon of the water and place over high heat. The water will evaporate and the sugar will dissolve, melt, and caramelize. To avoid burning the sugar, watch it carefully: Just as soon as it becomes a rich brown color, add the vinegar and the remainder of the water and stir until the caramelized sugar dissolves. Add the lemon juice and zest, the carrot, onion, tarragon, allspice, and ginger. Cover the pot and simmer for 20 to 30 minutes, or until the vegetables are tender. Strain the sauce through a sieve, pressing the vegetables with a wooden spoon to get out all of the juice. Stir in the prunes and set aside.

Put the fish in a large frying pan or Dutch oven and season with salt and pepper. Pour the reserved sauce over the fish and heat it to boiling. Reduce the heat to a simmer, cover, and cook for 5 to 10 minutes, or until the fish just starts to flake but is not dried out. Using a slotted spoon, transfer the fish to service plates. Boil the sauce rapidly. When it has reduced slightly —it should be of a light, slightly runny consistency—remove it from the heat and whisk in the butter. Pour the sauce over the fish and sprinkle with the toasted almonds and walnuts.

VEAL BRAISED WITH SOUR CREAM, MUSHROOMS, AND CARAWAY
(SERVES 6)

1 cup white wine
*½ cup dried Boletus edulis mushrooms
    (cepes in French, porcini in Italian)*

3 pounds boneless veal stew, cut into cubes
salt and pepper
2 tablespoons oil
1 medium onion, chopped
1½ tablespoons caraway seeds
2 tablespoons flour
2 tablespoons tomato paste
2 cups veal or chicken stock (page 23 or
   36)
½ cup sour cream

DO AHEAD:

Put the white wine in a mixing bowl, add the mushrooms, and soak them for 30 minutes.

Season the meat with salt and pepper. Heat the oil in a heavy pot such as a Dutch oven, add the onion and meat, and cook over a medium-high heat until the meat is lightly browned. Add the caraway seeds and flour, stirring well until the flour is incorporated. Add the tomato paste and stock and bring to a boil. Lower the heat, cover, and simmer for 30 minutes more.

Meanwhile, gently stir the mushrooms soaking in the wine, rub them gently with your fingers to loosen any sand, and allow them to rest so that the sand will settle to the bottom.

Remove the mushrooms with a slotted spoon and add them to the stewpot. Carefully "decant" the mushroom liquor into the pot, leaving behind any sediment. (A good way to do this is to line a sieve with a towel and strain the liquor through it.) Continue braising the stew until the veal is tender. The total cooking time should be

about 1¼ to 1½ hours. If, during the cooking, the sauce looks too thin, cook the stew uncovered; if too thick, add a bit of stock or water. Just before serving, stir in the sour cream and continue to cook just enough to heat it through.

BUTTERED SPINACH LEAVES

Wash and trim 2 bunches of spinach (about 2 pounds). Put the leaves in a large skillet with just the washing water that clings to them, and cook, covered, over high heat for only a minute or two, or until steam begins to escape and the leaves are wilted. Drain immediately and serve dotted with butter and seasoned to taste with salt and pepper.

EGG NOODLES WITH BREAD CRUMBS

Cook wide egg noodles until just tender in a large pot of boiling water. While the noodles are cooking, prepare a bread-crumb garnish: Heat 2 tablespoons butter in a small saucepan, add ½ cup dry bread crumbs, and cook over moderately high heat, stirring rapidly, until they are lightly browned. Remove from the heat and transfer immediately to another container to prevent burning. When the noodles are cooked, drain and toss lightly with a large dab of butter, then sprinkle with the browned, buttered bread crumbs.

GREEN PEPPER AND TOMATO SALAD

Toast 3 green peppers in the oven or under the broiler, rotating them so that the skins blacken all around. Put them into a paper bag for a few minutes so that they will steam and the skins will loosen. When they are cool enough to handle, remove the skins and seeds and cut the peppers into wide slices.

Blanch 3 large tomatoes for 1 minute in boiling water. Their skins should peel off easily under cold running water. Cut the tomatoes into wedges.

Peel 1 large red onion and cut it into thin slices.

Mix the peppers, tomatoes, and onions in a large bowl with ½ cup of dressing made with 3 parts olive oil to 1 part wine vinegar. Season with salt and pepper and a good quantity of chopped fresh dill and parsley. Mix thoroughly before serving.

STRASS RYE BREAD

See the recipe in the menu for Germany.

CHESTNUT CAKE
(SERVES 8 TO 10)

 ¼ cup dry bread crumbs
 2 cups canned chestnut puree (see Note)
 2 cups milk
 6 tablespoons butter
 1 cup sugar
 6 eggs, separated
 1 teaspoon vanilla extract
 ½ cup all-purpose flour
 1½ cups heavy cream, whipped

DO AHEAD:
Butter a springform pan and dust it with bread crumbs. Rotate the pan so that the crumbs cover the surface evenly, then pour off any excess crumbs.

Preheat the oven to 350°F.

To make the batter, blend the pureed chestnuts with the milk in a food processor. Cream the butter and sugar. Add the egg yolks and beat the mixture until smooth and fluffly. Mix in the chestnut puree. Then mix in the vanilla and flour. In a separate bowl beat the egg whites until stiff. Add one-third of the egg whites to the chestnut mixture. Then fold the mixture into the remaining egg whites.

Turn the batter into the prepared springform pan and bake for 60 to 70 minutes, or until a toothpick inserted in the center comes out clean. Remove the side of the springform. Cool on a rack.

Remove the cake from the pan bottom and put it on a cake dish. Whip the cream until it is stiff enough to spread like a frosting. Using a knife blade or spatula, spread the cream generously over the top and sides of the cake as you would to frost with icing.

NOTE: If you prefer to make your own chestnut puree, you will need about 1 pound raw chestnuts in the shell. Make a slit in each shell. Roast in the oven until the chestnuts begin to brown and open slightly; or simmer in water for 15 to 20 minutes. Peel carefully, removing all the brown tissue under the shell. Cook the chestnut meat in 2 cups of milk until tender, about 30 minutes. Turn the mixture into a blender or food processor and puree. Proceed as above.

A Note on the Wines

For the bass with its lively mixture of ginger, prunes, nuts, and sweet and sour flavors, we selected a dry Sauvignon Blanc, a full-bodied white wine with strong herbal and grassy overtones. We chose a Brander 1982, one of the best examples of Sauvignon Blanc made in this style, and particularly typical of those wines from the San Luis Obispo area.

A well-balanced, medium-bodied Pinot Noir was our choice to accompany the veal with its distinctive flavors of wild mushrooms and caraway. We picked a 1981 Carneros Creek from the cool northern regions of Napa Valley, one of the areas in California where the Pinot Noir grape seems to do well.

Denmark

❖

Gravlax
(Salmon Marinated in Dill and Aquavit)
Mustard Dill Sauce

Pork Loin Stuffed with Prunes
and Garnished with
Oven-Browned Potatoes, Carrots, and Pearl Onions

Pickled Cucumber Salad

Strass Rye Bread

Danish Waffles
(Flaky Short Pastry Filled with Buttercream)

Wines:
Schramsberg Blanc de Blancs
Schramsberg Blanc de Noirs

GRAVLAX
(Salmon Marinated in Dill and Aquavit)
(SERVES 8 TO 12 AS A FIRST COURSE, 4 TO 6 AS A MAIN COURSE)

I am grateful to the great restaurateur Kenneth Hansen, of Scandia in Hollywood, for putting me on the track of the perfect gravlax. Each time I visited him I ate a large portion of gravlax and each time he promised to send me the recipe. Well, the recipe never came—he was probably just too busy to commit it to paper. However, each time I went to Scandia during the next couple of years, we discussed the recipe and I was finally able to duplicate the wonderful subtlety of flavors of Scandia's gravlax. Hansen used to do something special that added to the dish. After carving the salmon, he would send the skin back to the kitchen to be cut into strips and deep-fried until crisp. Those salmon "cracklings" were used to garnish the gravlax along with the mustard dill sauce.—N.D.

You will need 2 days to marinate the salmon.

> 1 teaspoon each dried dillweed and dillseed,
>   or 1 tablespoon chopped fresh dill
> 2 pounds salmon fillet with skin
> 2 tablespoons coarse salt
> 4 tablespoons sugar
> ¼ teaspoon each freshly ground black
>   pepper and allspice
> ¼ cup aquavit

Mix the dillweed and dillseed and sprinkle half of them in the bottom of a flat pan or dish that just fits the salmon comfortably. Slash the skin side 3 or 4 times with a sharp knife. Set the salmon skin side down in the pan. Sprinkle with the remaining dill. Blend the salt, sugar, pepper, and allspice and distribute them evenly over the salmon, patting lightly into the flesh. Pour the aquavit over the fish.

Cover the pan with clear plastic wrap and place a weight on top—a couple of large cans of juice or soup (or anything else) works well. Refrigerate for at least 2 days; occasionally spoon the juices over the fish during this time. After the first day, remove the weights. The salmon will keep as long as 5 days. After that it becomes too salty.

Thinly slice the fish across the grain on a diagonal to the skin, cutting away from the skin.

NOTE: You can fry or broil the fish skin for a delicious, traditionally Danish garnish.

MUSTARD DILL SAUCE
(MAKES 1 CUP)

> ¼ cup Dijon-style mustard
> 1 teaspoon mustard powder
> 3 tablespoons sugar
> 2 tablespoons white wine vinegar
> ⅓ cup olive oil
> ¼ cup chopped fresh dill or 2 tablespoons
>   dried

Mix the mustards, sugar, and vinegar. Drizzle in the oil slowly, whipping constantly to make a light mayonnaiselike consistency. Add the dill.

PORK LOIN STUFFED WITH PRUNES AND GARNISHED WITH OVEN-BROWNED POTATOES, CARROTS, AND PEARL ONIONS
(SERVES 6)

24 pitted prunes, cut in halves
½ cup hot apple juice
2 teaspoons lemon juice
rind of 1 lemon, grated
1 5-pound pork loin, center cut, chine
   bone removed (see Note)
salt and pepper
2 tablespoons oil
1 cup dry white wine
6 small potatoes
6 large carrots, or 12 small
18–24 pearl onions
2 tablespoons currant jelly

DO AHEAD:

Put the prunes in a bowl, pour the hot apple juice, lemon juice, and grated lemon rind over them, and set aside to soak.

Preheat the oven to 350°F.

Lay the prepared meat flat and straight on a worktable. Carefully push a clean sharpening steel through the length of the loin (or ask your butcher to do it for you). You will have a hole or "tube" about ½ inch in diameter. Enlarge it by jiggling the steel around, first from one side, then from the other.

Fill the cavity, pushing prunes in from each side, leaving at least 1 inch of space at each end. This will avoid the fruit being forced out as the roast shrinks during cooking. Season with salt and pepper.

In a heavy ovenproof pot with a cover, heat the oil and brown the roast well on all sides. Pour in the wine. Cover the pot, and roast the pork for 30 minutes.

While the pork is roasting, peel the potatoes, carrots, and pearl onions. (Make a slit in the root end of each onion, and put the onions to boil for a few minutes. The skins will then slip off easily.) Cut large carrots into 2 or 3 pieces.

When the roast has cooked for 30 minutes, arrange the potatoes, carrots, and onions around it, cover, and continue to roast for another 30 minutes. Remove the cover and cook uncovered for another 30 minutes so that the vegetables will brown. The roast should cook for a total of 1½ hours, or until tender. Remove it to a warm platter and allow it to rest. Remove the vegetables to a bowl and keep them warm.

Skim off and discard the fat from the roasting pan. Add the jelly to the remaining pan juices and boil them vigorously until reduced to about 1 cup of sauce. Adjust the seasoning.

Carve the pork into ¾-inch slices and serve 2 slices per person, accompanied by the sauce. Garnish each plate with the reserved vegetables.

NOTE: Ask the butcher to cut away the chine bone and to trim the excess fat from the pork loin.

PICKLED CUCUMBER SALAD

If using the traditional tough-skinned cucumber, peel and seed 2 of them; if the modern "European" type, leave both skin and seeds, as they are quite tender; one such cucumber will be sufficient. Slice the cucumbers as thin as possible so that the pieces are almost transparent. Dress them with a mixture of ¾ cup white wine vinegar, 1 tablespoon sugar, ½ teaspoon salt, ¼ teaspoon white pepper, and 2 tablespoons chopped fresh dill (or 1 tablespoon dried). After marinating for 1 hour, strain off all of the liquid, mix the cucumbers with 1 cup sour cream, and garnish with a sprinkle of dill leaves.

STRASS RYE BREAD

See the recipe in the Germany menu.

DANISH WAFFLES
(Flaky Short Pastry Filled with Buttercream)
(MAKES 6—OR ENOUGH DOUGH FOR A DOUBLE-CRUST 9-INCH PIE)

WAFFLE DOUGH:
1 cup (2 sticks) sweet butter
2 cups all-purpose flour
7 tablespoons heavy cream
sugar

FILLING:
4 egg yolks
6 tablespoons granulated sugar
1 tablespoon water
¾ cup (1½ sticks) sweet butter, softened
1¼ cups heavy cream, whipped
1 teaspoon vanilla extract

confectioners' sugar

DO AHEAD:
Line a baking sheet with parchment, or butter and flour a pan.

Cut the butter into the flour. When there are no large pieces of butter left, add the cream and mix only until smooth. Turn out onto a floured board. Working very quickly, roll out the dough into a large rectangle. Fold it into thirds. Roll out and fold the dough 2 more times, reversing the direction each time. (See illustration.)

Chill the dough in the refrigerator for 20 minutes.

Preheat the oven to 425°F.

Roll out a fourth time into a rectangle ¼ inch thick. Using a cookie cutter, cut out 3-inch rounds. Sprinkle the board and the circles of dough with sugar. Roll out the circles gently to make 3-x-5-inch ovals. Place the ovals on the parchment-lined baking sheet. Bake until they are puffed up and lightly browned—about 15 to 20 minutes.

Beat the egg yolks until they are light and fluffy. Cook the sugar and water in a small saucepan to the small-ball stage (236°F on a candy or jelly thermometer). Pour the sugar syrup in a steady stream into the egg yolks, whipping continuously. Continue whipping until the mixture is cool. Add the butter and whip it in until smooth. Fold in the whipped cream and vanilla.

Spread the filling on half of the baked Danish waffles. Top with the remaining half of the waffles, as if making sandwiches. Dust with the confectioners' sugar.

A Note on the Wines

Gravlax is marvelously well suited to sparkling wines; it is, perhaps, the very best of matches, and since many white wines are not good partners at all with this dish of cured salmon, we chose a fine California champagne, a Schramsberg Blanc de Blancs 1973.

The festive, bubbly beginning suggested a harmonious follow-up to accompany the pork stuffed with prunes: a Schramsberg Blanc de Noirs 1974. This dry, salmon-pink, sparkling wine is a fine example of those white or tinted wines made from black grapes using white-wine techniques, their pastel hues achieved by separating juice from skins quickly, before much color is extracted, and by pressing little or not at all.

Ecuador

✺

Potato Soup

Fried Snapper with Cumin Sauce

Chicken Braised with Peanuts and Annatto Seeds
Grated Corn Steamed in Its Husk
(Choclotandas)
Black Beans

Avocado Salad

Corn Tortillas

Caramelized Bananas

Wines:
Stony Hill Gewürztraminer
Kenwood Vineyards Zinfandel

POTATO SOUP
(SERVES 6)

¼ cup (½ stick) butter
2 medium onions, coarsely chopped
2 potatoes, peeled and cut into ½-inch dice
2 cups water
salt and pepper
2 bay leaves
¼ teaspoon ground allspice
6 ounces Monterey Jack or Swiss cheese, grated
3 cups milk (see Note)
2 tablespoons chopped fresh parsley

In a soup pot melt the butter and sauté the onions slowly until they are translucent. Add the potatoes and water, and season lightly with salt, pepper, bay leaves, and allspice. Simmer until the potatoes are tender, about 15 to 20 minutes. Stir in the grated cheese and additional salt and pepper to taste. Remove from the heat.

Stir the milk into the soup, a little at a time. Return the soup to the heat and cook it without allowing it to boil. When the soup has heated through, remove the bay leaves and serve the soup immediately with a sprinkle of chopped parsley on top.

NOTE: Traditionally the soup is enriched and further thickened by the addition of an egg to the milk. To prepare the richer version, whisk an egg into the milk before adding it to the soup, stirring it in a little at a time, as above.

FRIED SNAPPER WITH CUMIN SAUCE
(SERVES 6)

SAUCE:

2 teaspoons cuminseed
3 cloves garlic, crushed
½ teaspoon red pepper flakes
¾ cup white wine vinegar
3 medium tomatoes, peeled (see Glossary) and chopped
1 tablespoon chopped fresh parsley
salt

FISH:

6 2–2½-ounce red snapper fillets (or substitute sea bass)
salt and pepper
flour
¼ cup (½ stick) butter
2 tablespoons oil
6 large sprigs parsley

Heat the cuminseed in a dry skillet for 2 or 3 minutes, or until they start to sizzle and release aroma. Add the garlic, red pepper flakes, vinegar, and tomatoes and sauté until the tomatoes are soft and the flavors blended, about 10 minutes. Add the parsley and salt to taste. Pour the finished sauce into a large shallow bowl and set aside.

Season the fish with salt and pepper and dust with flour. Heat the butter and oil in a skillet until quite hot. Add the fish and fry until brown on all sides. Remove from the pan and place it immediately in the sauce, turning so that each piece is completely coated. Arrange the fish on individual plates and serve immediately with a spoonful of sauce over each portion and a parsley sprig alongside.

CHICKEN BRAISED WITH PEANUTS AND ANNATTO SEEDS
(SERVES 6 TO 8)

The subtle flavors of the sauce give this delicate dish a gentle, suave, smooth character rather than one that is robust or spicy.

> 2 teaspoons annatto seeds (achiote),
>   powdered in a blender (or substitute 1
>   teaspoon paprika—see Note)
> 6 tablespoons butter, softened
> 2 3–3½-pound frying chickens, disjointed
>   (page 54; steps 1–6)
> 1 tablespoon oil
> 2 medium onions, chopped
> 2 large green peppers, chopped
> 2 teaspoons paprika
> salt and coarse black pepper
> 1 cup milk
> 3 tablespoons peanut butter
> 2 large tomatoes, peeled (see Glossary)
>   and chopped

Mix the annatto or paprika with the softened butter. Rub the disjointed pieces of chicken all over with the mixture and set them aside. In a large frying pan heat the oil until it is hot, add the onions and green peppers, and sauté until the onions are transparent and starting to brown. Add 2 teaspoons paprika, salt, and coarse black pepper, stirring until the vegetables are thoroughly coated with the spice mixture.

Add the chicken pieces to the pot in 2 stages to ensure that all the pieces will be cooked to the same degree of doneness. First, arrange the legs, wings, and thighs over the sautéed vegetables; add the milk, cover, and simmer for 15 minutes. Next, add the chicken breasts, skin side up. Replace the cover and simmer for 15 to 20 minutes more, or until all the chicken is cooked through and tender.

Remove the finished chicken pieces to a platter and keep warm. Add the peanut butter and chopped tomatoes to the pan. Cook, stirring, over enough heat to keep the sauce bubbling, until it is smooth. If it becomes too thick, thin it with chicken stock or water. Adjust the seasoning. Spoon the sauce over the chicken and serve immediately.

NOTE: If annatto seed is unavailable, 1 teaspoon paprika will give the dish a similar color.

GRATED CORN STEAMED IN ITS HUSK
(Choclotandas)
(SERVES 6)

Ecuadoran choclotandas are a wonderfully simple sort of tamale, easy to make, and an unusual alternative at any meal to an ear of corn. If fresh corn is not available, canned or frozen kernels, ½ cup per person, are an excellent substitute, corn being one of the few canned vegetables that retains its quality. If using canned or frozen kernels, you will need 12 whole dried corn husks to substitute for the husks from the fresh ears of corn. Dried husks are available from Latin groceries the year round and need only be moistened in warm water to prepare them for use.

> 6 ears of corn in the husk, or 3 cups
>   canned or frozen kernels plus 12 whole
>   dried corn husks
> ¼ cup (½ stick) butter
> 2 large onions, chopped
> 2 green bell peppers, seeded and chopped
> 1 small hot pepper, seeded and chopped, or
>   ¼ teaspoon cayenne pepper
> 1 teaspoon dried basil leaves
> ½ teaspoon salt

Carefully cut the husks away from the ears of corn, keeping the pieces as large as possible. Place them in a pan of warm water to keep them soft. (If using dried husks, place them in a pan of warm water to moisten.) Grate the corn into a bowl and set aside. Reserve the cobs. If using canned or frozen kernels, chop them as finely as possible to resemble corn grated from the cob. A few pulsing motions in a food processor fitted with a metal chopping blade will do the job.

Heat the butter in a skillet, add the onions, and sauté until they are just starting to brown. Stir in the green peppers, hot pepper, basil, and salt. Remove the mixture from the heat and stir it into the grated corn.

Select the 12 largest leaves of corn husks. For each choclotanda, use 2 leaves, overlapping them about 2 inches. They should form a rectangle of about 5 x 8 inches. (See illustration.)

Divide the corn mixture into 6 equal portions, placing one portion in the center of each of the rectangles. Roll each rectangle carefully into a long cylinder, leaving each end free of the corn stuffing. Tie off the unstuffed ends using a strip of corn husk or string. It should look much like a birthday party "snapper." Tie once loosely also in the middle. (See illustration.)

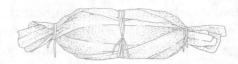

Arrange the cobs side by side in the bottom of a heavy Dutch oven or soup pot. Add ½ inch of hot water. Place the choclotandas over the cobs. (If you are using canned or frozen corn and have no cobs, use a small rack instead, or place them in a colander inside a large soup pot.) Cover the pot and steam the choclotandas for about 30 minutes, or until they are heated through. Check the water after 15 minutes; replenish, if necessary, with boiling water to keep the pot steaming.

To serve, cut the ties before serving to make it easier to open the husks at the table.

BLACK BEANS

Put 1 cup black beans in a pot and cover with 3 times their volume of water. Bring to a rapid boil and boil for 2 minutes. Remove from the heat, cover, and let stand for exactly 1 hour. Drain the beans and discard the soaking liquid.

Cook the beans in water to cover until they are tender, about 1½ to 2 hours. Heat 2 tablespoons oil in a skillet. Add 1 to 2 chopped garlic cloves, 1 chopped onion, 1 chopped green pepper, and some chopped fresh coriander (cilantro). Sauté until the onions are transparent. Flavor the cooked beans by stirring in the sautéed vegetables and salt to taste.

*

AVOCADO SALAD

Place a large slice of peeled tomato on each salad plate. Top it with a wedge of peeled avocado. Dress with a tablespoon or two of a vinaigrette flavored with garlic, chives, capers, parsley, and a pinch of sugar. You will need about ¾ cup of basic vinaigrette (see Glossary).

CORN TORTILLAS

The best bread to accompany this meal would be corn tortillas, one of the traditional breadstuffs of the region.

CARAMELIZED BANANAS
(SERVES 6)

> ¼ cup (½ stick) butter
> ½ cup brown sugar
> ½ cup sherry
> 6 bananas, peeled, halved lengthwise, then halved again crosswise
> 1 cup heavy cream, whipped

In a skillet large enough to hold all of the bananas heat the butter and brown sugar until the sugar melts and starts to bubble. Immediately add the sherry and stir until the sugar has dissolved, about 2 to 3 minutes. The sauce will have thickened into a rich caramel. Gently place the bananas in the sauce, spooning it over them until they are well coated. Heat for 2 to 3 minutes, just enough to warm the bananas through.

To serve, arrange 4 pieces of banana on

each plate, spoon the caramel sauce over them, and top with a dollop of whipped cream.

A Note on the Wines

To complement the peppery cumin sauce of the snapper, we would select a dry white wine that was at the same time rich, fragrant, and spicy, such as a Stony Hill Gewürztraminer.

The annatto-red chicken braised with onions, peppers, and peanut butter needs a medium-bodied dry red wine of some complexity, such as a Kenwood Vineyards Zinfandel.

England

❖

Oxtail Soup

Finnan Haddie with Egg Sauce

Prime Rib with Yorkshire Pudding
Brussels Sprouts

Watercress and Mushroom Salad

Baguette

Tipsy Lady

Wines:
Spring Mountain Sauvignon Blanc
Spring Mountain Cabernet Sauvignon Trois Cuvées

OXTAIL SOUP

(SERVES 6)

1 tablespoon oil
2 pounds oxtails, cut into 1-inch pieces
1 onion, chopped
2 tablespoons flour
2 quarts water
1 leek, chopped (the white part plus 1 inch
   of the green)
1 stalk celery, chopped
stems from 1 bunch parsley, chopped
1 teaspoon dried thyme
1 bay leaf
salt and pepper
2 carrots, peeled and diced
2 small turnips, peeled and diced
2 tablespoons port

Heat the oil in a soup pot or Dutch oven. Add the oxtails and onion and cook over moderately high heat until they are brown. Sprinkle with the flour and stir well until it is absorbed. Add the water, leek, celery, parsley stems, thyme, and bay leaf. Bring to a boil, then lower the heat to a simmer, cover, and cook about 1½ hours, or until the meat is tender.

Remove the pieces of oxtail from the pot with a slotted spoon and set aside. Strain the soup through a colander and return to the pot. Boil rapidly to reduce the soup to about 6 cups. Adjust the seasoning with salt and pepper. Add the carrots, turnips, and port. Return the oxtails to the pot. Simmer for about 10 minutes, or until the vegetables are tender. Skim any fat from the surface before serving.

FINNAN HADDIE WITH EGG SAUCE

(SERVES 6)

2 tablespoons butter
2 tablespoons flour
1 cup heavy cream
1 cup milk
1 cup dry white wine
1 teaspoon mustard powder
½ teaspoon Worcestershire sauce
salt and white pepper
½ teaspoon ground allspice
1 onion, thinly sliced
2 eggs, hard-cooked and coarsely chopped
1 pound smoked haddock, cut into 6 pieces
a few sprigs parsley, chopped

In a pot large enough to hold the fish and sauce, melt the butter and stir in the flour. Cook, stirring constantly, for 2 or 3 minutes, until the flour is all absorbed but not browned. Add the cream, milk, wine, mustard, Worcestershire sauce, a spare amount of salt and white pepper, and the allspice, and whisk until thoroughly blended. Add the onion and the fish. Cover the pot, lower the heat, and simmer for 10 minutes, or until the fish is heated through.

Using a slotted spoon, remove the fish to serving plates and keep warm. Boil the sauce down until it is a thick but still runny consistency. Mix in the eggs. Taste the sauce and adjust the seasoning. Spoon some sauce over each portion of fish and garnish with a sprinkle of chopped parsley.

PRIME RIB WITH YORKSHIRE PUDDING
(SERVES 6)

PRIME RIB:

The size of the roast depends on the number of servings, figuring 12 to 16 ounces of total raw weight per person. You will need a 5- to 6-pound roast for 6 people. Ask your butcher to cut through the chine bone without removing it and to tie the roast tightly. It is worth paying a bit extra for the small or loin end of a roast, which does not include the tough "litter" meat or "flap" that makes the shoulder end so large. However, if you do buy a roast from the large end, have the butcher remove the flap before tying the roast; cut the flap into stew meat for another meal.

YORKSHIRE PUDDING:
- *3 eggs*
- *1 cup milk*
- *1 cup all-purpose flour*
- *½ teaspoon salt*
- *2–3 tablespoons beef fat from pan drippings*

DO AHEAD:
When you remove the roast from the oven, leave the heat on. The puddings will need to cook at 400°F, so adjust the temperature accordingly.

Prepare the pudding batter at least an hour before you want to cook it.

Preheat the oven to 300°F.

Season the rib liberally with your favorite seasoning salt. Place in a roasting pan, bones down. Roast at 300°F for 25 to 30 minutes per pound for rare (an internal temperature of 140°F); 35 to 40 minutes per pound for medium (an internal temperature of 155°F).

After the roast is cooked, it is important to let it rest at room temperature for 20 to 30 minutes before carving so that the juices will stabilize. Carving too soon can ruin the finest roast: The juices will drain out and the meat will be dry.

You can make the pudding while the meat is roasting: Mix the eggs, milk, flour, and salt in a blender or whip them in a bowl. Refrigerate for 1 hour or longer. When ready to cook, liberally grease a muffin tin holding 8 to 10 individual molds, using the beef fat from the pan drippings. Heat until the fat sizzles. Pour the batter into the molds, place in the preheated 400°F oven, and bake for 15 minutes. Lower the heat to 375°F and continue to bake for 10 to 15 minutes, or until the tops of the puddings are crisp and brown.

NOTE: It is customary to serve the roast beef with horseradish cream. Use about 8 tablespoons drained prepared horseradish (4 tablespoons if you grate it fresh). Mix the horseradish with a splash of white wine vinegar, a dash or two of mustard powder, and a sprinkle of white pepper. Whip about ¾ cup heavy cream and fold in the horseradish mixture.

BRUSSELS SPROUTS

Wash about 1½ pounds brussels sprouts in cold water, trim the bottoms, and discard any discolored outer leaves. Bring a large pot of salted water to a boil, add the sprouts, and cook for at least 10 to 15 minutes, depending on size, or until tender all the way through. When the sprouts are done, drain them and toss immediately in a serving bowl with a good-sized lump of butter and a grind of black pepper.

WATERCRESS AND MUSHROOM SALAD

Wash and trim 1½ bunches of watercress, dry, and cut it into pieces 2 to 3 inches long. Thinly slice ½ pound of the freshest mushrooms you can find. Toss together in a salad bowl with ½ to ¾ cup of a simple vinaigrette (3 parts oil to 1 part wine vinegar seasoned with salt and pepper) and top with chopped chives and parsley.

BAGUETTE

We served a baguette with the English dinner. The recipe is on page 119.

TIPSY LADY
(SERVES 6 TO 8)

The English traditionally take leftover cake—even dried-out cake—moisten it with liqueur, sherry, or brandy (hence the name), and layer it with whipped cream and custard to make this very popular dessert. It is one of my favorites because so many flavors and textures come together in such an attractive way. Our custard recipe, thickened with egg yolks and folded into whipped cream, is based on a Bavarian cream. The simpler flour-thickened custards are more common, but this is far more elegant, and worth the little extra effort.—N.D.

BAVARIAN CREAM:
4 egg yolks
½ cup sugar
1 cup milk, scalded
1 teaspoon vanilla extract
1 cup heavy cream, whipped

TIPSY LADY:
1 sponge cake, 8 or 9 inches in diameter, or pound cake or a leftover filled and decorated cake
⅓ cup cream sherry
⅓ cup brandy
⅔ cup raspberry or strawberry jam
1 cup heavy cream, whipped
⅓ cup slivered toasted almonds

Whip the egg yolks and sugar in the top of a cold double boiler. Pour in the scalded milk, whisking all the while. Set the pot over boiling water and continue stirring until the custard starts to thicken and will coat a spoon smoothly. It will fluff up and resemble hollandaise sauce. Stir in the vanilla and pour the custard into a mixing

the procedure, using up the remaining sherry, brandy, and Bavarian cream. Place the third layer on top and cover with whipped cream. Sprinkle with the toasted almonds. (See illustration.) Refrigerate for at least 1 to 2 hours before serving so that the flavors blend and the cake moistens properly.

A Note on the Wines

The smoky-flavored finnan haddie and the creamy-textured egg sauce need a rich, full-bodied dry white wine, substantial enough to stand up to them. We poured a 1970 Sauvignon Blanc from Spring Mountain.

We decided to keep the red wine selection in the family by choosing the soft and well-balanced Spring Mountain Cabernet Sauvignon Trois Cuvées, a marriage of the vintages of 1967, 1968, and 1969. A similar French Bordeaux would be equally appropriate.

bowl. Chill in the refrigerator. When cold, whisk lightly to soften, fold in the whipped cream, and set aside.

Split the cake into 3 layers and sprinkle them with sherry and brandy. Spread 2 layers with jam. Place one of these layers in a clear glass serving bowl barely large enough to hold the whole dessert, and sprinkle it with more sherry and brandy, followed by half of the Bavarian cream. Stack the second jam-covered layer on top and repeat

Ethiopia

❖

Spiced Ground Lamb Tartare
(Kifto)
Pickled Jerusalem Artichokes

Chicken Legs in Red Pepper Sauce
Braised Okra

Injera
(Flat "Pancake" Bread)

Fresh Raspberries

Wines:
Rüdesheimer Burgweg
Monteviña White Zinfandel

In Ethiopian cooking, there is a common and frequent use of two spice bases: "berberé" and "niter kebbeh." Berberé is a smooth water paste of paprika flavored with garlic, onions, and spices. Niter kebbeh is a clarified butter flavored with most of the same spices as berberé but without paprika. In these recipes we have incorporated proportionate amounts of the appropriate spices, rather than give whole recipes for the two seasoning bases, which would leave quantities unused after your Ethiopian dinner. The final result in the flavor of each dish is precisely the same.

SPICED GROUND LAMB TARTARE
(Kifto)
(SERVES 6 TO 8 AS APPETIZER)

Somewhat like a spicy version of the Lebanese kibbeh nayyeh, kifto can also be made of beef instead of lamb, making it more like a steak tartare with an exotic flavor.

2 tablespoons butter
4 tablespoons minced onions
2 tablespoons minced green bell peppers
1–2 teaspoons minced hot chili peppers, to taste
1 teaspoon minced fresh ginger
2 cloves garlic, crushed
1 teaspoon paprika
1 teaspoon curry powder
¼ teaspoon ground cinnamon

1 pound very fresh lamb or beef, coarsely ground (meat must be totally denuded of fat and gristle before grinding)
1 tablespoon lemon juice

Melt the butter in a skillet. Add the onions, green peppers, chili peppers, ginger, and garlic and sauté gently until the onions are translucent. Immediately add the spices to the onions and cook for 1 minute to blend the flavors, then scrape with a spatula into a mixing bowl and cool.

When the onion mixture has cooled, add the ground lamb or beef and the lemon juice. Mix the ingredients well and form the mixture into a small loaf. Cover the loaf with a design of half-moon indentations made with the back of a tablespoon.

PICKLED JERUSALEM ARTICHOKES
(SERVES 6)

2 quarts Jerusalem artichokes

PICKLING MIXTURE:
2 cups white wine vinegar
1½ cups water
3 tablespoons sugar
dash or more of Tabasco sauce
1½ teaspoons salt
1 tablespoon pickling spice
6 cloves garlic, crushed

Wash and trim the Jerusalem artichokes and cut them into pieces. Place in a large bowl.

Put all of the ingredients for the pickling mixture into a saucepan and heat only to boiling. Pour the mixture over the Jerusalem artichokes. Cool. Cover and refrigerate.

NOTE: You can use this recipe to pickle other raw vegetables such as onions, carrots, squash, peppers, turnips, or cucumbers. If Jerusalem artichokes are not available, substitute any of the above for this menu.

CHICKEN LEGS IN RED PEPPER SAUCE
(SERVES 6)

In this classic recipe for one of Ethiopia's national dishes, we have given a substitution for the berberé in which curry powder replaces several of the individual spices.

> ¼ cup (½ stick) butter
> 2 large onions, chopped
> 6 chicken thighs
> 6 chicken drumsticks
> 6 cloves garlic, minced
> 2 tablespoons minced ginger
> 6 tablespoons paprika
> 2 teaspoons curry powder
> 1 teaspoon ground allspice
> 2 cups chicken broth (page 36)
> 6 eggs, hard-cooked
> 6 tablespoons plain yogurt
> 6 lemon wedges

Melt the butter in a skillet, add the onions, and sauté until they are translucent. Add the chicken pieces and cook until they are lightly browned, then remove them. Immediately add the garlic and spices, heat for 1 minute just to blend, and add the chicken broth. Cook over high heat, stirring well, until the sauce begins to bubble. Add the chicken pieces, turning them in the sauce until they are evenly coated. Lower the heat, cover the pan, and simmer the chicken for 15 minutes. Add the hard-cooked eggs and coat them well with the sauce. Cover and simmer for 10 to 15 minutes more, or until the chicken is tender.

To serve, garnish each portion with a tablespoon of plain yogurt and a wedge of lemon.

BRAISED OKRA
(SERVES 6)

> 3 tablespoons oil
> 1 large onion, thinly sliced
> 1 pound okra, stems cut off
> 3 tomatoes, peeled (see Glossary) and
>   chopped
> juice of 1 lemon
> 1 teaspoon dried basil leaves, or
>   1 tablespoon fresh
> salt and pepper

Heat the oil in a large skillet, add the onion, and sauté until it is translucent. Add the okra and stir until it is well coated with the oil. Add the tomatoes, lemon juice, basil, and salt and pepper. Cook, covered, for 5 to 10 minutes, or until the okra is just tender.

INJERA
(Flat "Pancake" Bread)

(MAKES TWENTY-FOUR 6-INCH PANCAKES OR
TWELVE 8- TO 9-INCH PANCAKES)

Injera, the national bread of Ethiopia, is
historically made of an indigenous African
grain called teff. In the United States, the
grain most similar is millet. Injera is really
a slightly chewy, thin beige pancake,
which the diner tears into small pieces to
use as a scoop, much in the way Middle
Eastern lavash or Mexican tortillas carry
food. Traditionally, one large pancake covers the serving platter with all of the foods
of the meal arranged in little piles on top.
At the end of the meal, the diners eat the
bottom pancake, by then flavored with the
various spicy gravies it has soaked up. In
the United States, injera is usually light
colored and rather bland; by comparison,
African teff pancakes have a darker color
and a slightly fermented flavor akin to
sourdough. Because of the expense of im-
porting the grain, teff is rarely used in the
United States, but the Meskerem Restaurant in Washington, D.C., serves teff injera on special request and both Narsai and
I have eaten it there.—D.M.

1½ cups all-purpose flour
½ cup rice, millet, or corn flour
4 teaspoons baking powder
½ teaspoon salt
3 cups water
2 tablespoons light salad oil
2 eggs

Mix the flours, baking powder, and salt.
Whisk in the water. Add the salad oil and
eggs and continue to whisk until smooth.
Spoon enough batter into a well-seasoned,
ungreased crêpe or omelet pan to cover the
bottom lightly, and bake over low to moderate heat. Bake on one side only. When
the top surface puffs slightly and the pancake has cooked through, gently loosen it
with a spatula and turn it out on a plate to
cool. Repeat until all the batter is used up.

To serve, fold the pancakes in quarters
and arrange on a platter.

A Note on the Wines

We suggest a cool and delicate light wine
from the Rhine, such as a Rüdesheimer
Burgweg, as a contrast to the spicy lamb
tartare.

The dark chicken meat, braised in a
pungent sauce infused with Ethiopian
spices, also goes well with a light, crisp
wine, but one with some substance. Our
choice was a blush wine, a white wine
made from red grapes, a lightly chilled
white Zinfandel made by Monteviña in
Amador County.

Finland

❖

Halibut Soup

Lamb Shanks Smothered in Onions
Baked Potato Fans
Buttered Fresh Vegetables

Leaf Lettuce with Lemon Dressing

Finnish Dark Rye Bread

Berry Compote with Walnut Cake

Wines:
Mercurey Blanc, Audiffred
Côte Rôtie, Passat

HALIBUT SOUP
(SERVES 6)

  2 pounds fish heads and trimmings
  8 cups water
  2 bay leaves
  1 stalk celery, chopped
  2 tablespoons butter
  2 medium onions, chopped
  6–8 mushrooms, sliced
  1 tablespoon flour
  1 8-ounce can tomato sauce
  6 1–1½-ounce whitefish fillets or other
     firm-fleshed fish
  6 1½-ounce halibut fillets
  2 tablespoons capers
  juice of 1 lemon
  salt and pepper
  fresh dill

DO AHEAD:

Make a fish stock by simmering the fish heads and trimmings in the water with the bay leaves and celery for 30 minutes. Strain the stock through a fine sieve and reserve.

Melt the butter in a soup pot or Dutch oven and add the onions. Sauté until the onions are translucent, then add the mushrooms. Stir in the flour until it is totally absorbed. Add the fish stock and the tomato sauce and bring to a boil. Add the fish fillets and the capers, cover the pot, and simmer until the fish is tender, about 5 to 10 minutes. Season with the lemon juice and salt and pepper. Serve in shallow soup plates with a garnish of fresh dill.

LAMB SHANKS SMOTHERED IN ONIONS
(SERVES 6)

  3 large onions, thinly sliced
  6 lamb shanks (ask the butcher to cut the
     bones in 2 or 3 places)
  salt and pepper
  ½ teaspoon whole allspice
  2–3 cups lamb or beef stock (page 23)
  1 cup white wine

Preheat the oven to 350°F.

Put the onions in a roasting pan. Season the lamb shanks with salt, pepper, and allspice and arrange them over the onions. Roast, uncovered, until the meat and the onions are well browned. Add 2 cups stock and the white wine. Cover the pan loosely with a piece of foil. Continue roasting, adding stock as needed to keep the bottom of the pan covered. Roast for a total of about 1½ hours.

Remove the meat to a serving platter and pour the sauce from the pan over the lamb.

NOTE: If the sauce is too thin, keep the lamb shanks warm and boil the sauce down rapidly until it is the consistency you desire.

BAKED POTATO FANS

Peel 1 small baking potato for each portion. Make thin slices about the thickness of a 50-cent piece, but only three-quarters of the way through the potato. Brush with melted butter and sprinkle with bread crumbs, salt, and pepper. Bake at 400°F for 1 to 1¼ hours, until the slices fan out and the potatoes are tender.

BUTTERED FRESH VEGETABLES

Select any vegetables in season for their variety of color. For the restaurant dinner we used cauliflower, carrots, peas, and green beans. Plunge each vegetable separately into boiling water and cook until tender. Turn the hot vegetables into a serving bowl, dress with pieces of butter, and sprinkle with chopped fresh parsley.

LEAF LETTUCE WITH LEMON DRESSING

This salad is seasoned with an unusual dressing. Toss washed and trimmed lettuce leaves with lemon juice, then sprinkle with salt, pepper, and sugar. Toss again. Add some lightly whipped heavy cream and toss again. (Whipping the cream only until it starts to firm up makes it easier to coat the lettuce leaves.)

FINNISH DARK RYE BREAD
(MAKES TWO 1½-POUND LOAVES)

2 cups warm water
1 package of yeast, or 1 tablespoon dry yeast
4 tablespoons molasses
1 tablespoon brown sugar
2 cups white bread or all-purpose flour
1½ cups medium rye flour
1½ cups rye meal or medium rye flour
1¼ cups whole-wheat flour
1 teaspoon cocoa powder
1 tablespoon malt powder
2½ teaspoons salt
1 teaspoon ground cardamom

Oil a bowl for the dough. Put the water in a large mixing bowl and stir in the yeast. Add the molasses and brown sugar and stir in well. Stir in all of the flours, then the cocoa powder, malt, and salt (you can measure and add the cocoa, malt, and salt directly into the flour mixture). Mix until the dough is well blended.

Knead the dough by hand or machine. If by hand, turn it out on a floured board and work it until it is smooth and elastic, approximately 10 minutes. If using a dough hook on an electric mixer, knead the dough at the slowest speed for about 5 minutes.

Pat the dough into a ball and put it in the oiled bowl. Cover the bowl with a kitchen towel and set it in a warm, draft-free place to rise until the dough has doubled in bulk, about 50 to 60 minutes. (A perfect place is a gas oven with its slight heat given off by the pilot light; an electric oven, turned on low for no more than 2 minutes, then turned off, works equally well.)

When the dough has doubled, turn it out on a floured board, punch it down, and knead it again until there is no air left in it. Shape it into 2 round loaves. Place them on the board, cover again with a towel, and let rise until almost doubled, about 30 to 40 minutes.

When the loaves have risen, cut 3 parallel arc-shaped gashes in the top of each one. (See illustration.) Cover with a towel and let rise for another 15 minutes.

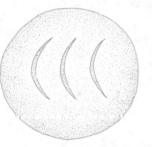

While the loaves are rising, preheat the oven to 400°F. Place a pie tin half filled with water on the bottom shelf. Position one oven rack just above the bottom rack. Flour a baking sheet or large pan.

Gently pick up the loaves and transfer them to the baking sheet or pan and place it in the oven on the rack just above the bottom rack. Bake for 50 to 60 minutes. The crust should be golden brown. Test for doneness by rapping the bottom with your knuckle. The loaf should feel firm and make a hollow sound. Cool on a wire rack.

BERRY COMPOTE WITH WALNUT CAKE
(SERVES 6)

The Finnish recipe for the berry compote calls for lingonberries instead of the cranberries listed here. If you can obtain them, lingonberries will give the dessert a more authentic flavor, but the cranberries give a similar (and excellent) result. An alternative is to use fresh currants, or a blend of any 2 or 3 kinds of berries, very slightly sweetened and warmed as described.

> 2 cups fresh cranberries and ½ cup sugar, or 1 16-ounce can whole cranberry sauce
> 2 baskets of raspberries, washed
> 1 Walnut Sponge Cake (page 179)
> 1 cup heavy cream, whipped

If you are using fresh cranberries, cook them with the sugar over moderate heat until the berries are warmed through. Remove from the heat and cool for 5 minutes. If you are using canned whole cranberry sauce, warm it enough so that it softens and is no longer gelatinous. Remove from the heat and cool for 5 minutes. Toss very gently with the raspberries. Serve immediately over a slice of the walnut sponge cake, and garnish each portion with a dollop of whipped cream.

A Note on the Wines

With the halibut soup, we selected a medium-bodied Chardonnay with the full flavor of the fruit, a Mercurey Blanc from Audiffred from the Côte d'Or in Burgundy.

Our choice to accompany the lamb shanks was a rich, earthy red typical of the wines from the Rhône, a Côte Rôtie from Passat.

France 1

❖

Beef Consommé with Madeira

Scallops and Oysters with Truffled Beurre Blanc

Roast Squabs Marinated in Raspberry Vinegar
Fried Potatoes
Mélange of Winter Vegetables

Curly Endive Salad with Lemon Vinaigrette

Baguettes, Épines, Rolls

Génoise with Strawberries and Whipped Cream

Wines:
René Manuel Clos des Bouches Chères Mersault 1974
René Manuel Clos de la Baronne Mersault 1964

BEEF CONSOMMÉ WITH MADEIRA

Heat 6 cups richly flavored beef consommé (page 23). While the soup is heating, prepare the garniture: Peel 1 small carrot and 1 celery stalk, being sure that all of the strings are removed from the celery. Cut the vegetables into very fine julienne strips about 2 inches long. Add them to the hot soup for just the last few minutes of heating. Put 1 teaspoon Madeira in each soup bowl and ladle the hot soup and julienned vegetables over it.

SCALLOPS AND OYSTERS WITH TRUFFLED BEURRE BLANC
(SERVES 6)

¾ cup dry white wine
2–3 shallots, minced
8–10 ounces tiny bay scallops or sea scallops cut into quarters
12 medium oysters, freshly shucked
½ cup (1 stick) butter, cut into small pieces
½ ounce black truffles (see Note)
salt and white pepper

Put the wine and shallots in a frying pan and simmer them for a few minutes. Add the scallops and oysters and poach until they are barely cooked through, 4 to 5 minutes. Remove the scallops and oysters with a slotted spoon to a warm serving plate.

Turn up the heat and rapidly reduce the pan juices to about ⅓ cup. Add the butter pieces, remove the pan from the heat, and whisk the mixture until the butter is well blended. Whisk in the truffles, season to taste with salt and white pepper, and spoon the sauce immediately over the scallops and oysters.

NOTE: Nothing comes close to the flavor, or cost, of truffles, but there are perfectly delicious alternatives that will give you an excellent result with a somewhat different taste. In this recipe, for example, a fine variation would be 6 to 8 medium mushrooms, cut into fine julienne, and added to the pan with the scallops and oysters.

ROAST SQUABS MARINATED IN RASPBERRY VINEGAR
(SERVES 6)

Since raspberry vinegar takes about 2 weeks to mature enough to use, start it that much ahead if you are making it for this squab recipe. The vinegar recipe given below makes 750 ml., enough to fill a standard wine bottle, a supply that should last for some time. If you do not want to make your own, raspberry vinegar is available commercially in fancy food shops and many supermarkets.

Raspberry Vinegar

½ pint fresh raspberries, or 1 defrosted
10–12-ounce package of frozen
raspberries, preferably unsweetened
2½ cups dry white wine vinegar

Gently crush the berries in a quart mason jar. Add the vinegar, cover, and leave to steep for about 2 weeks. You will be able to judge the progress by the color of the vinegar: It is ready to use almost as soon as it has taken on a rosy pink tint. Strain through a fine sieve and store in a wine bottle, as you would any vinegar.

⅓ cup raspberry vinegar
½ cup dry white wine
1 onion, coarsely chopped
3 sprigs fresh rosemary, or 1 tablespoon dried
salt and pepper
6 squabs
3 tablespoons clarified butter
1 10–12-ounce can chicken consommé
1 tablespoon beurre manié (2 tablespoons flour and 1 teaspoon soft butter, blended smooth)

DO AHEAD:

Marinate the squab for 2 to 3 hours before cooking (see instructions).

First make the marinade: Put the vinegar, wine, onion, rosemary, and salt and pepper into a blender and puree. Put the squabs in a stainless steel or glass bowl and pour the marinade over them. Marinate for 2 to 3 hours at room temperature or overnight in the refrigerator.

When the squabs are done marinating, preheat the oven to 450°F.

Wipe the squabs dry and reserve the marinade. Put the butter to heat in a large frying pan. When it is hot, brown the squabs, 2 or 3 at a time, turning them so that all sides color evenly. As the squabs brown, transfer them to a roasting pan. When all the squabs are done, roast for about 8 to 10 minutes for rare (or longer, if you prefer them more well done).

While the squabs are roasting, press the marinade through a sieve directly into the frying pan. Add the consommé and beurre manié. Simmer the sauce, whisking it gently to blend the ingredients, and cook until it is smooth and the consistency of a light pink syrup or glaze.

When the squabs have roasted, remove them from the pan and bone them if desired. (See illustrations for carving duck, page 213.)

FRIED POTATOES

These French pommes frites are a kind of homemade potato chip. Use 1 or 2 new potatoes, depending on size, for each person. Peel the potatoes and slice them paper thin. Put enough oil to cover them in a deep fryer or a deep skillet and heat it very hot. Fry the slices in batches until they are crisp and golden. Drain and serve immediately.

MÉLANGE OF WINTER VEGETABLES

For this vegetable dish, use 2 medium cucumbers; 1 bunch of fennel, bulb end only; and about ¼ pound Chinese snow peas. For preparation and cooking instructions, see the master recipe for vegetable mélange in the Perennial Favorites menu.

CURLY ENDIVE SALAD WITH LEMON VINAIGRETTE

Wash and trim 1 bunch of curly endive. Tear into pieces and place in a salad bowl. Dress with a lemony vinaigrette, using the recipe for citronnade dressing on page 308.

BAGUETTES, ÉPINES, ROLLS
(MAKES FOUR 18-INCH BAGUETTES OR ÉPINES, EIGHTEEN 4-INCH ROLLS, OR TWENTY-FOUR 3-INCH ROLLS)

- 1 package of yeast, or 1 tablespoon dry yeast
- 1½ cups warm water, plus 1 teaspoon cold water
- 1½ teaspoons sugar
- 1 tablespoon malt or molasses
- 3¾ cups or more white bread or all-purpose flour
- 1½ teaspoons salt
- 1 egg white

DO AHEAD:
Lightly oil a bowl for the dough.

Baguettes:

In a large mixing bowl dissolve the yeast in the warm water. Add the sugar and malt or molasses and mix well. Add the flour and salt and knead the mixture by hand until it comes away clean from the sides of the bowl. If the dough is too sticky, add a bit more flour. Knead for another 5 to 6 minutes by hand, or for 3 to 4 minutes in a mixer with a dough hook. The dough should be smooth and elastic. Shape the dough into a ball and put it into the oiled bowl. Cover with a towel and put it in a warm, draft-free place to rise until it has doubled, about 60 minutes.

Turn the dough out onto a floured pastry board or counter, punch it down, and knead until there is no air left in it. Make the dough into a ball and return it to the bowl. Cover, and let rise again until doubled, about 30 minutes. During the second rise, butter and flour 2 sheet pans.

When the dough has doubled, turn it out again onto a floured surface and punch it down. Divide the dough into 4 equal parts. Shape each one into a long baguette by rolling it out like a rope until it is the length of the sheet pan. Place 2 rolled-out loaves on each pan. Cover the pans loosely with a towel and put them in a warm place until the dough has doubled. While the baguettes are rising, preheat the oven to 400°F.

When ready to bake, place a pie tin half filled with water on the bottom shelf of the oven and position one rack above the center. When the baguettes have risen, slash each one 3 times diagonally with a razor blade or sharp knife. Place the loaves on the rack just above the center of the oven and bake for 25 to 30 minutes. (If your oven is not large enough to bake 4 loaves at a time, bake them in 2 batches.) Test for doneness by rapping the bottom of the loaf with your knuckle: It should feel firm and make a hollow sound.

While the baguettes are baking, whisk the egg white with the teaspoon cold water until it is frothy. When the loaves are done, remove them from the oven and instantly brush them liberally with the egg wash. Cool on a wire rack.

Épines:

Épines are baguettes shaped to resemble spines. To make them, shape the dough as for regular baguettes. With kitchen shears or a sharp, clean pair of scissors, cut the dough (see illustration), alternating each épine to the right or left. Each spiny section bakes brown and crusty and breaks off naturally from the loaf.

Rolls:

The baguette dough makes excellent rolls of any size. A 3-inch roll is the standard size for dinner, but you can shape the dough according to your preference, including making it into miniature baguettes. Rolls may bake a little faster than whole loaves.

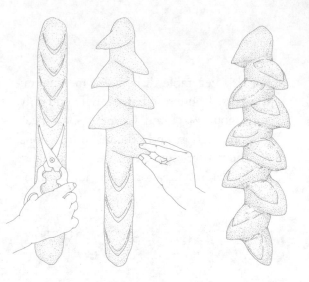

GÉNOISE WITH STRAWBERRIES AND WHIPPED CREAM
(SERVES 6)

GÉNOISE:
> 3 eggs
> 3 egg yolks
> ½ cup sugar
> 1 teaspoon vanilla extract
> 5 tablespoons butter
> ¾ cup cake flour
> 6 tablespoons cornstarch

FILLING:
> 1 pint strawberries
> 1–2 tablespoons sugar
> 1½ cups heavy cream
> 2 tablespoons Grand Marnier

DO AHEAD:
Butter and flour one 8-x-2-inch round cake pan.

Preheat the oven to 350°F.

To make the génoise, put the eggs, egg yolks, sugar, and vanilla into the top of a double boiler or the bowl of an electric mixer. Put the bowl over warm water over the heat and whisk until the mixture is a glossy golden color and somewhat warmer than lukewarm to the touch. Be careful not to allow it to become too hot and overcook. Remove the mixture immediately from the heat and whip it with an electric beater or in the mixer until it has tripled in volume and is light and fluffy in texture; this may take some time.

Melt the butter.

Sift together the cake flour and cornstarch. Gently fold them by hand into the beaten mixture. Add the hot melted butter and fold it in. Pour the batter into the cake pan. Bake for 25 to 30 minutes. Turn out onto a cooling rack.

Wash and stem the berries, saving enough of the most perfect ones for the cake top. Cut the others in half, place in a bowl, and sprinkle with the sugar, depending on the sweetness of the berries.

In a separate bowl, whip the cream until it is reasonably stiff. Add the Grand Marnier and mix it in evenly.

When the cake is thoroughly cool, cut it into 3 even, thin layers.

Place one layer of the cake upside down on a cake plate. Spread with ½ cup of the whipped cream. Set into the cream one-half of the sugared berries. Top with a second layer of cake, spread with ½ cup of cream, and set in the remaining sugared berries. Top with the third layer of cake and spread with the remaining 1½ cups of whipped cream. Arrange the reserved whole berries around the top edge in a single row.

NOTE: You can make the génoise a day in advance and refrigerate it, wrapped tight, overnight.

A Note on the Wines

The wines for this French dinner came from a very small Burgundian domain, one which both Narsai and I have visited on different occasions. The wines that proprietor René Manuel produces have a harmonious family resemblance: They are well-made, radiant, full of character and grace.

For the dish of scallops and oysters sauced with a truffled beurre blanc, we chose a white Meursault, the Clos des Bouches Chères, René Manuel 1974, a complex, full-bodied wine of great elegance.

The red wine we selected for the squab is the only red Meursault from a single estate: the velvety, finely balanced Clos de la Baronne, René Manuel 1964.—D.M.

France 2

Mushrooms Pactole

Mussels Steamed in Wine
(Moules à la Marinière)

Roast Pheasant with Calvados and Cream Sauce
Potato Balls Browned in Butter
Braised Brussels Sprouts and Roasted Chestnuts

Optional Course:
Camembert with Sliced Pears

French Bread

Soufflé Glacé au Chartreuse
(Cold Soufflé with Chartreuse)

Wines:
Mâcon-Villages, Louis Latour Chardonnay
Meursault Clos du Cromin, Monnier

MUSHROOMS PACTOLE
(SERVES 6 TO 8)

Several years ago, Jacques Manier, an innovative Parisian restaurateur, made a brilliant reputation with his Au Pactole, a small place on the Left Bank, where our family enjoyed many superb meals. The very first time we went, there was a dish of escargots that incorporated almond butter, for us a surprising new dimension. Another memorable but simple dish was one of raw mushrooms, thinly sliced, and dressed with a mixture of mayonnaise and whipped cream that was as light and delicate as any mousseline. That dish has remained one of our favorite appetizers and we have named it after that lovely restaurant.—N.D.

½ cup homemade mayonnaise made, if possible, with sherry vinegar
1 tablespoon white wine vinegar
1 tablespoon lemon juice
1 teaspoon Worcestershire sauce
1 teaspoon sherry
1 small garlic clove, crushed
2 tablespoons fresh basil leaves, or 2 teaspoons dried
1 tablespoon chopped fresh parsley
½ teaspoon salt
¼ teaspoon white pepper
½ cup heavy cream, whipped
6–8 ounces mushrooms, cleaned and sliced
6 lettuce leaves

Mix the mayonnaise with the wine vinegar, lemon, Worcestershire, sherry, garlic, basil, parsley, salt, and pepper. Fold in the whipped cream. Pour over the mushrooms and toss lightly. Serve on individual leaves of lettuce.

MUSSELS STEAMED IN WINE
(Moules à la Marinière)
(SERVES 6)

6–8 mussels per person
¼ cup (½ stick) butter, preferably sweet
3–4 shallots, minced
1–2 cloves garlic, minced
2 cups white wine
1 bay leaf
salt
freshly ground black pepper
2 tablespoons chopped fresh parsley

Scrub and beard the mussels and set aside.

Melt the butter in a large pot. Add the shallots, garlic, wine, and bay leaf and bring to a boil. Cook only a minute or two, then add the mussels and cover the pot. Cook over high heat, shaking the pot from time to time, until all the shells open, about 5 minutes. Discard any mussel that does not open.

Using a slotted spoon, divide the mussels among 6 deep bowls or soup plates. Taste the pot liquor and add salt, only if necessary (mussels are often sufficiently salty), and pepper to taste. Spoon the hot liquid over the mussels, taking care not to get any sand that may have settled to the bottom. Sprinkle generously with parsley and serve immediately.

ROAST PHEASANT WITH CALVADOS AND CREAM SAUCE

(SERVES 6)

Since pheasant drumsticks are so full of tendons that few people bother to eat them, one needs to be a bit extravagant when planning for any pheasant recipe. For this dish, ideally, the purchase of a 2-pound pheasant would provide 2 portions, each consisting of a piece of breast meat and a thigh, with the sinewy drumsticks saved to go into the soup pot with the carcasses.

3 2–3-pound pheasants
salt and white pepper
¼ teaspoon dried thyme
¼ teaspoon lavender (if available)
3 tablespoons clarified butter
1½ cups chicken broth (page 36)
3–4 shallots, minced
2 tart green apples, peeled, cored, and cut
    into 6 wedges each
⅓ cup Calvados, apple brandy, or apple
    juice
½ cup white wine
1 cup heavy cream
2 egg yolks

Preheat the oven to 375°F.

Season the pheasants lightly with salt, white pepper, thyme, and lavender. Heat the butter in a skillet and brown the pheasants, one at a time, until the skin is golden. Put the browned pheasants in a roasting pan and cook them 35 to 45 minutes for 2-pound birds, 50 to 60 minutes for 3-pound birds. The thighs should be very slightly undercooked, a timing that will also avoid the breast meat becoming dry and chewy. Test by piercing the thigh in the thickest part with a roasting fork; just as soon as the liquid runs clear, remove the pheasants to a warm serving platter. Let them rest for 20 minutes before carving.

Add the chicken broth to the roasting pan and simmer gently on the top of the stove to dissolve all the brown bits and particles. Set aside.

Add the shallots and apples to the skillet used for browning the pheasants. Sauté just until the shallots are translucent. Add the Calvados and white wine. The alcohol will evaporate with the heat whether you are using gas or electric, but be alert that it might also ignite (most likely over a gas burner) and burn for a minute or two.

Strain the juices from the roasting pan through a fine sieve into the skillet with the shallots and apples. Cook rapidly until the juices are reduced to about ¾ cup, then lower the heat to a slow simmer. Remove the apple wedges to the serving platter.

Whisk the cream and egg yolks in a small bowl. Pour the egg mixture into the sauce, stirring continuously. Simmer only long enough for the sauce to heat through, but do not let it boil. Adjust the seasoning with salt and white pepper and remove from the heat.

Carve the pheasants (see illustrations for carving duck, page 213) and arrange the slices on individual plates. Nap the slices with the sauce and garnish each portion with 2 apple wedges.

POTATO BALLS BROWNED IN BUTTER

Wash and peel about 2 pounds boiling potatoes and cut out small balls with a potato cutter. Save the potato scraps for soup. In a large skillet heat some clarified butter and brown the balls well on all sides, turning frequently to keep them from sticking. Cover and cook for about 15 minutes more, shaking the pan frequently so that they will not stick. The heat should be kept at moderate to prevent the butter from becoming too brown.

BRAISED BRUSSELS SPROUTS AND ROASTED CHESTNUTS

For this recipe you will need about 1 pound brussels sprouts and about 2 cups chestnuts (about 3 dozen). The sprouts should be parboiled in a large pot of boiling salted water until almost tender, between 6 and 8 minutes depending on size, then refreshed under cold water, and set aside.

The chestnuts should be slit down one side and roasted in a hot oven until the skins brown, the slits begin to open, and the meat becomes tender. This can also be done under the broiler. Remove the skins (the chestnuts must be hot to do this effi-

ciently, so it is best to take them out of the oven only a few at a time).

Melt clarified butter in a large skillet and braise the reserved brussels sprouts and chestnuts together for about 8 to 10 minutes, stirring frequently. Season with salt and pepper before serving.

CAMEMBERT WITH SLICED PEARS (Optional Course)

Many French meals include a cheese course or substitute it for a sweet dessert. If you want to add it to this menu, select a Camembert that is soft but still resilient, almost runny at the sides, with a sweet tangy smell. (A hint of ammonia suggests the cheese is overripe.) Divide the cheese into 6 equal wedges and place one on each dessert plate. Arrange 2 or 3 slices of unpeeled pear on each plate.

FRENCH BREAD
(Sponge Method)
(MAKES TWO 1½-POUND LOAVES)

1 package of yeast, or 1 tablespoon dry yeast
1½ cups warm water, plus 1 teaspoon cold water
2 teaspoons sugar
3¾ cups or more white bread or all-purpose flour
1 tablespoon malt or molasses
1½ teaspoons salt

DO AHEAD:

Make a sponge the night before: Mix ½ tablespoon yeast, all the warm water, 1 teaspoon sugar, and 2 cups flour. Cover the bowl with plastic wrap and leave it on the counter overnight.

The next day add the remaining ½ tablespoon yeast, 1 teaspoon sugar, 1¾ cups flour, the malt or molasses, and salt. Mix the dough until it is well blended.

Knead the dough by hand or machine. If by hand, turn it out on a floured board and work it until it is smooth and elastic, approximately 10 minutes. If using a dough hook on an electric mixer, knead the dough at the slowest speed for about 5 minutes.

Lightly oil a bowl. Pat the dough into a ball and put it in the bowl. Cover with a kitchen towel and set it in a warm, draft-free place to rise until the dough has doubled in bulk, about 50 to 60 minutes. (A perfect place is a gas oven with its slight heat given off by the pilot light; an electric oven, turned on low for no more than 2 minutes, then turned off, works equally well.)

When the dough has doubled, turn it out on a floured board, punch it down, and knead it again until there is no air left in it. Shape it into 2 long loaves. Place on the board, cover again with a towel, and let rise until almost doubled, about 30 minutes.

When the loaves have risen, cut 5 or 6 diagonal gashes with a razor across the top

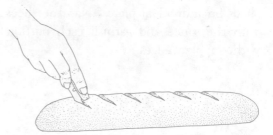

of each one. (See illustration.) Cover with a towel and let rise for another 15 minutes. Flour a baking sheet or large pan.

While the loaves are rising, preheat the oven to 400°F. Place a pie tin half filled with water on the bottom shelf. Position one oven rack just above the bottom rack.

Gently pick up the loaves and transfer to the baking sheet or pan and place it in the oven on the rack just above the bottom rack. Bake for 30 to 40 minutes. The crust should be golden brown. Test the doneness by rapping the bottom with your knuckle. The loaves should feel firm and make a hollow sound. Cool on a wire rack.

SOUFFLÉ GLACÉ AU CHARTREUSE
(Cold Soufflé with Chartreuse)
(SERVES 6)

This dessert needs at least 2 hours to chill before serving.

    4 eggs, separated
    1½ cups milk
    ¼ cup sugar

*1 tablespoon unflavored gelatin moistened
with 1 tablespoon cold water*
1 cup heavy cream, whipped
*¼ cup green Chartreuse or any favorite
liqueur*
fresh mint leaves

Put water to boil in the bottom of a double boiler.

Put the egg yolks in the top of the double boiler and beat them off the heat until they start to thicken. Stir in the milk and sugar and put the pot over the boiling water, cooking until the mixture thickens and forms a light custard. Immediately remove the top from the heat. Stir in the moistened gelatin and set the custard mixture aside to cool for about 15 minutes.

Whip the egg whites until stiff.

When the mixture has cooled, fold in the whipped egg whites, then the whipped cream, and finally the Chartreuse or liqueur.

Ladle the mixture into 6 soufflé molds or dessert glasses. Freeze until firm, a minimum of 2 hours, but better overnight.

Before serving, garnish each portion with a small cluster of fresh mint leaves.

A Note on the Wines

For the mussel dish in this French menu, we selected a crisp, light-bodied Chardonnay in the style of the Mâcon-Villages, Louis Latour.

Our choice for the pheasant in cream sauce was a rich, full-bodied Chardonnay, one with the traditional toasty scent contributed by the oak barrels used for aging. The Meursault Clos du Cromin, Monnier, typifies this style of Chardonnay. Although it is more usual to serve red wine with cheese, the rich white Meursault suggested for the pheasant will also make an especially pleasing combination with the optional course of Camembert.

France 3

❖

Clear Oxtail Soup

Smoked Trout with Horseradish Cream Sauce

Sweetbreads Sauté
Carrots Vichy
Sautéed Spinach

Endive, Watercress, and Walnut Salad

Burgundian Walnut Bread

Crêpes Soufflées Grand Marnier

Wines:
Muscadet de Sèvre-et-Maine
Château Malartic-Lagravière

CLEAR OXTAIL SOUP

Use the recipe for Oxtail Soup in the menu for England but do not return the pieces of oxtail to the broth.

SMOKED TROUT WITH HORSERADISH CREAM SAUCE

Smoked trout is available in fancy food stores, delicatessens, and many fish markets. Figure on 3 ounces per person. If the skin is still on the fish, you can serve it that way or remove it before serving. Arrange each portion on a plate with a dollop of horseradish cream sauce next to it. To make the sauce, whip ¾ cup heavy cream until stiff. Fold in 1 tablespoon grated horseradish (a little less if using fresh horseradish, which is stronger than bottled), and some coarsely ground black pepper. Garnish with a sprig of parsley or fresh dill.

SWEETBREADS SAUTÉ

(SERVES 6)

3 pounds veal sweetbreads
1 lemon
2 tablespoons pickling spice
pepper
flour
3 tablespoons clarified butter
2–3 shallots, minced
½ cup dry white wine
1½ cups veal or beef consommé (page 23)
a few sprigs parsley, minced

DO AHEAD:

Prepare the sweetbreads before sautéing (see instructions).

Wash the sweetbreads in cold water. Place them in a pot and cover them with fresh cold water. Squeeze the juice of the lemon directly into the pot and put in half of the rind. Add the pickling spice and bring the mixture to a boil. Turn down to a simmer and cook, uncovered, for 20 minutes. Remove from the heat and leave the sweetbreads in the poaching liquid for 30 minutes to cool.

Remove the sweetbreads from the liquid and trim them carefully of any membranes, skin, or fat. Cut or break them into 12 pieces. Season them with pepper and dust lightly with flour. Reserve.

Heat the butter in a large frying pan or Dutch oven. When it is hot, add the sweetbreads and brown them well on all sides. Add the shallots and cook them carefully to avoid browning them. Add the wine and consommé, bring the mixture to a boil, then lower the heat, cover, and simmer for 20 to 25 minutes, or until the sweetbreads are tender.

Remove the sweetbreads with a slotted spoon to a warm platter. Reduce the pan juices over high heat until they thicken to the consistency of heavy cream. Nap the sweetbreads with the sauce and garnish with minced parsley.

CARROTS VICHY
(SERVES 6)

Cooking vegetables in Vichy or other mineral water high in alkaline accentuates their natural color. Greens become vivid; carrots sparkle with the color of ripe oranges.

  6–8 medium carrots, peeled and sliced into
    ¼-inch rounds
  1½ cups Vichy water
  3 tablespoons butter
  salt and pepper
  3 tablespoons minced fresh parsley

Put the carrots and Vichy water into a large frying pan and cook, covered, for about 10 minutes. Remove the cover and increase the heat, cooking until any remaining water has evaporated. Add the butter and season to taste with salt and pepper. Remove from the heat, stir in the parsley, and serve immediately.

SAUTÉED SPINACH

Use the recipe for Buttered Spinach Leaves in the Czechoslovakia menu.

ENDIVE, WATERCRESS, AND WALNUT SALAD

Wash and trim 3 to 4 heads of Belgian endive, depending on size, and separate the leaves. Wash and trim 1 bunch of watercress. Dry the endive and cress well and place in a salad bowl. Add 18 to 24 walnut halves and mix lightly. Toss with a vinaigrette made of 1 cup olive oil, ⅓ cup red wine vinegar, ½ teaspoon Dijon mustard, a splash of Worcestershire sauce, salt, and pepper.

BURGUNDIAN WALNUT BREAD
(MAKES TWO 1½-POUND LOAVES)

  1 package of yeast, or 1 tablespoon dry
    yeast
  2 cups warm milk
  4 tablespoons sugar
  ¼ cup (½ stick) butter, melted and cooled
  6 cups or more white bread or all-purpose
    flour
  2 teaspoons salt
  ½ cup chopped lightly toasted walnuts

DO AHEAD:
Lightly oil a bowl for the dough.

In a large bowl mix the yeast, milk, sugar, and butter. Add the flour and salt and mix until the ingredients are well blended.
  Knead the dough by hand or machine. If by hand, turn it out on a floured board and work it until it is smooth and elastic, approximately 10 minutes. If using a dough hook on an electric mixer, knead the dough at the slowest speed for about 5 minutes. As soon as the dough is properly kneaded, work in the nuts.

Pat the dough into a ball and put it in the oiled bowl. Cover the dough with a kitchen towel and set it in a warm, draft-free place to rise until doubled in bulk, about 60 to 75 minutes. (A perfect place is a gas oven with its slight heat given off by the pilot light; an electric oven, turned on low for no more than 2 minutes, then turned off, works equally well.)

When the dough has doubled, turn it out on a floured board, punch it down, and knead it again until there is no air left in it. Shape it into 2 large round loaves. Place on the board, cover it again with a towel, and let it rise until almost doubled, about 30 minutes.

When it has risen, cut 4 gashes with a razor blade in a tic-tac-toe pattern on the top of each loaf. (See illustration.) Cover with a towel and let rise for another 15 minutes.

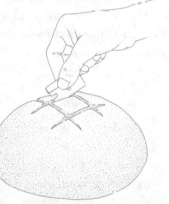

While the loaves are rising, preheat the oven to 350°F. Place a pie tin half filled with water on the bottom shelf. Position an oven rack just above the bottom rack. Flour a baking sheet or large pan.

Gently pick up the loaves and transfer them to the baking sheet or pan and place it in the oven on the rack just above the bottom rack. Bake for 50 to 60 minutes. The crust should be golden brown. Test the doneness by rapping the bottom with your knuckle. The loaf should feel firm and make a hollow sound. Cool on a wire rack.

CRÊPES SOUFFLÉES GRAND MARNIER
(SERVES 6: MAKES 15 6-INCH CRÊPES)

CRÊPES:
  2 eggs
  1/3 cup all-purpose flour
  1 tablespoon oil
  1/3 cup milk
  3 tablespoons sugar
  1/2 teaspoon vanilla extract

FILLING:
  1/4 cup (1/2 stick) butter
  1/4 cup all-purpose flour
  1/3 cup sugar
  5 eggs, separated
  6 tablespoons Grand Marnier

TOPPING:
  1 1/2 cups vanilla ice cream
  2 tablespoons brandy

To make the crêpes, whisk the eggs and flour together in a small bowl. Blend in the oil, then add the milk, sugar, and vanilla. Whip the mixture until well blended, then set aside to rest for 5 minutes.

Heat a crêpe pan or a small (6- to 8-inch) frying pan with sloping sides. (You can save time by using 2 pans simultaneously.) Wipe the pan lightly with an oiled paper towel. Pour about 1½ tablespoons of batter (about the capacity of a normal kitchen spoon) into the pan. Quickly tip the pan around to coat the bottom with the batter as thinly and evenly as possible. As soon as the edges show a bit of browning, turn the crêpe. Cook the second side for only a minute. It is important not to overcook the crêpes or they will be too dry. Continue to cook the crêpes, oiling the pan in between each one, until all of the batter is used up. Stack the crêpes on a plate as they are finished. When all are done, cover them with plastic wrap and reserve until they are needed.

To make the filling, melt the butter in a small saucepan over low heat, mix in the flour, and continue to cook, stirring, until smooth. Add the sugar and egg yolks and continue cooking until the mixture thickens to the consistency of a firm hollandaise sauce. Remove from the heat. Whisk in the Grand Marnier until well blended. Cool slightly.

While the mixture is cooling, beat the egg whites until stiff. Fold them into the cooled filling mixture.

When ready to bake the crêpes, preheat the oven to 425°F and butter a sheet pan. Take the ice cream from the freezer so that it will soften.

Arrange 3 or 4 crêpes on a work surface. Place about 2 tablespoons of the filling mixture in a line in the middle of each crêpe. Roll up the crêpe loosely and gently around the filling. Place each rolled crêpe on the sheet pan. If you arrange the crêpes in pairs, every 2 crêpes touching each other, it will simplify serving. Bake the crêpes for 6 to 7 minutes, or until they puff up like footballs.

While the crêpes are baking, add the brandy to the soft ice cream, whisking it in. When the crêpes are puffed, remove them from the oven. Working very quickly, place 2 crêpes on each plate, top each portion with ice cream, and serve immediately.

NOTES: You can make the crêpes a day or two in advance and refrigerate them until ready to use.

You can prepare the filling ahead of time, up to the point of adding the beaten egg whites. When ready to proceed, whip the reserved filling mixture again to be sure it is smooth, then fold in the beaten egg whites.

A Note on the Wines

Our preference for a wine that would go well with the smoked trout was a French Muscadet de Sèvre-et-Maine 1982, a light and delicate white from the Loire.

For the sautéed sweetbreads with their velvety glaze, we picked a rich, intense red from the Graves region, a Château Malartic-Lagravière 1966.

France 4

❋

Watercress and Lettuce Soup

Breast of Chicken, Alexis Bespaloff

Filet Farci à la Bouquetière, Sauce Bordelaise à la Minute

Dandelion Salad

Épines

Tile Tulips Filled with Three Ice Creams:
Pine Nut Brown Butter
Saffron Lemon
Double Chocolate Whammy

Wines:
Château Carbonnieux Sauvignon Blanc
Nuits-St-Georges, Clos des Forêts, Belin

The extravagance of the dishes that comprise this menu makes it particularly suitable for grand occasions.

WATERCRESS AND LETTUCE SOUP
(SERVES 6)

6 cups chicken broth (page 36)
1 onion, chopped
2 tablespoons pearl tapioca
1 bunch watercress, large stems discarded, chopped
½ head lettuce, cut into large ribbons (use any variety, such as iceberg or romaine, or the tough outer leaves only, saving the heart for salad)
salt and pepper
½ bunch spinach, chopped
1 tablespoon lemon juice

Put the chicken broth, onion, and tapioca in a soup pot or Dutch oven and simmer for about 15 minutes. Add the watercress and lettuce, season with salt and pepper, and continue to simmer until the vegetables are tender. Stir in the spinach and lemon juice and simmer for just another 2 minutes before serving. The French call this potage de santé, "health soup."

BREAST OF CHICKEN, ALEXIS BESPALOFF
(SERVES 6)

Alex is a New York wine writer whom I met at a mutual friend's house in 1972, a few months before I opened the restaurant. We became immediate friends and I invited him to lunch the next day. This is the dish I served as the main course. It was such a hit that when we opened the restaurant we put Breast of Chicken, Alex Bespaloff on our first menu. It remained on our menu, either as an entrée or an appetizer, until the restaurant closed.—N.D.

2 large or 3 medium whole chicken breasts, skinned and boned (see page 54), or skinned and boned by the butcher
salt and white pepper
½ cup all-purpose flour
3 tablespoons clarified butter
½ cup sweet Sauternes or Muscat de Frontignan
1¼ cups heavy cream
2 tablespoons finely chopped fresh parsley

Season the boned chicken lightly with salt and white pepper. Dust very lightly in the flour and shake off the excess.

Melt the butter in a large frying pan, add the chicken pieces, and sauté over moderate heat, turning frequently. As soon as the chicken turns an opaque white, remove it to a heated serving platter. (Chicken breasts become very dry if overcooked; prepared just this side of undercooked, as here, they remain very tender and delicate.)

Add the wine and cream to the pan. Boil rapidly to reduce and slightly thicken the sauce to the consistency of heavy cream. Return the chicken breasts to the pan and stir and turn gently until they are well coated with the sauce.

Arrange the coated chicken pieces on a serving platter, pour the sauce over them, and sprinkle the parsley over the top.

FILET FARCI À LA BOUQUETIÈRE, SAUCE BORDELAISE À LA MINUTE
(SERVES 6)

To avoid the farce or forcemeat "crust" breaking away during the roasting, it should be made on the same day the roast is to be cooked. The ground pork and veal must be very finely ground or pureed. Use either a grinder equipped with a disc called a fishplate, or use a food processor.

FARCE (FORCEMEAT):
1 pound pork, finely ground
1 pound veal, finely ground
½ cup pureed onion
2 teaspoons crushed garlic
⅓ cup heavy cream
4 egg yolks
1½ teaspoons salt
1 teaspoon Worcestershire sauce
1 tablespoon fresh tarragon leaves, or
*   1 teaspoon dried*
¼ teaspoon pepper

1 6–7-pound fillet of beef
2½ cups Sauce Bordelaise à la Minute
*   (page 136)*
Bouquetière (page 136)

DO AHEAD:
The beef must be trimmed of all the fat and gristle and have had the silver skin removed. Cut off the head and tail ends so that the fillet is of uniform thickness; save the trimmed ends for another meal.

By hand or machine, whip together all of the farce ingredients until they are well blended. Chill them in the refrigerator.

While the farce is chilling, cut 2 sheets of wax paper large enough to wrap around the fillet easily. Oil them lightly (use a pastry brush or a wad of paper towel dipped in oil). Remove the farce from the refrigerator and turn it out onto one of the sheets of oiled wax paper. Cover with the second sheet of waxed paper, oiled side down (against the farce). Using a rolling pin, roll out the farce between the 2 sheets of waxed paper as you would a pastry dough. Roll it to a size that will wrap amply around the fillet. Preheat the oven to 375°F.

When the farce is rolled out, remove the top sheet of paper. Place the fillet on top of the farce and carefully wrap the farce around it. Tuck in the ends carefully and smooth out the seams.

Pick up the wrapped fillet, using the bottom sheet of wax paper to help, and place the meat in a roasting pan. Pull away the wax paper very gently (slowly roll the meat and pull away the paper at the same time), being very careful to avoid tearing the farce.

Roast the fillet for 35 to 40 minutes for rare.

Meanwhile, make the sauce. Then prepare the bouquetière while the sauce simmers.

To serve, present the meat on a carving platter surrounded with the bouquetière. Put the sauce in a gravy boat to the side. To avoid masking the appearance of the meat after carving, spoon some of the sauce on each plate and arrange the slices of meat on top of the sauce. Surround the meat with a small portion of each of the vegetables making up the bouquetière.

Sauce Bordelaise à la Minute
(MAKES ABOUT 2½ CUPS)

This "instant"—à la minute—sauce came about by accident when we were catering an elaborate meal in the Napa Valley. We discovered, shortly before the meal was to begin, that we had left behind the sauce for the main course and there was no time to retrieve it. We dispatched a waiter to the nearby Oakville Grocery to find anything beef-flavored, and meanwhile set about browning garlic, parsley stems, and other aromatic vegetables in a big pot. By the time the waiter got back, we had added a bottle of good red wine, divided the sauce into two pots to help speed up the concentration, and had it boiling briskly away. Into the pot went Oakville's contribution: an assortment of beef gravy, instant beef gravy, and consommé. We strained the sauce and finished it by swirling in a few lumps of sweet butter. It was, surprisingly,

much more than adequate—almost embarrassingly delicious.

> 2 tablespoons oil
> 1 carrot, chopped
> 1 small onion, unpeeled, chopped
> 4 cloves garlic, crushed
> stems from 1 bunch parsley
> 1 bay leaf
> ½ teaspoon dried thyme
> ½ teaspoon cracked peppercorns
> 2 cups red wine
> 1 10–12-ounce can good-quality beef gravy, or 2 cups brown sauce
> salt, if necessary
> ¼ cup (½ stick) butter

Heat the oil in a sauce pot. Add the carrot, onion, garlic, parsley stems, bay leaf, thyme, and peppercorns and sauté until the vegetables are well browned. Add the red wine and canned beef gravy or brown sauce. Simmer for about 30 minutes, or until the mixture has reduced and thickened slightly. Strain the sauce through a sieve, return it to the stove, and adjust the seasoning with salt. Add the butter, remove the sauce from the heat, and whisk until all of the butter is absorbed.

Bouquetière

The bouquet surrounding the roast is an array of vegetables, selected according to season, to provide variety and color. Among the basic green vegetables that make an attractive display are asparagus, broccoli, peas, or green beans. There

should be some small oven-browned potatoes, and 1 or 2 filled vegetables: yellow
squash or mushroom caps stuffed with
creamed spinach, artichoke bottoms
stuffed with carrot puree. Very small tomato halves broiled with a dusting of bread
crumbs and a bit of Parmesan cheese add a
dash of color. The garnish should always
include a large bunch of trimmed watercress.

DANDELION SALAD

Wash and trim 2 bunches of young dandelion leaves and put them in a salad bowl.
Make a warm dressing by sautéing a few
slices of chopped bacon until brown, then
adding 2 tablespoons wine vinegar, a
squeeze of lemon juice, a tablespoon or two
of orange juice, salt, and a good grinding
of black pepper. Pour the warm dressing
over the dandelion leaves, toss well, and
serve immediately.

ÉPINES

For this French meal we suggest serving
Épines (page 119).

TILE TULIPS FILLED WITH THREE ICE CREAMS:
Pine Nut Brown Butter,
Saffron Lemon,
Double Chocolate Whammy

Tile Tulips
(MAKES 8 TO 10)

In the summer of 1984, my son Daniel
worked as a cook for Roger Vergé at Mou-
lins du Mougins in the south of France. He
came home with a taste for delicate sauces
and ethereal desserts. One of them, tuiles
(tiles), has now become one of our all-time
favorites as well. Normally, as its French
name indicates, this pastry is made in the
form of a tile, draped while still warm and
pliable over the side of a tumbler or a hor-
izontal broom handle. It can also be shaped
as a tulip, making an attractive individual
container for ice creams—as in the recipe
given here—mousses, fruits in season, or
any combination of ingredients. For special
occasions, Danny makes a giant tile about
14 inches in diameter and folds it into an
art nouveau "vase," 5 to 6 inches deep,
with gently pleated sides, then fills it with
any combination of ingredients.

To serve this dessert using all three ice
creams, make each kind at a convenient
time in advance and keep them all on hand
in the freezer.—N.D.

½ cup (1 stick) butter, at room
  temperature
8 tablespoons sugar
5 egg whites, at room temperature
½ teaspoon vanilla extract
1 cup all-purpose flour

sprigs fresh mint

DO AHEAD:
Cut 8 to 10 pieces of parchment paper into
10- to 12-inch squares.

For shaping each baked pastry into a tulip, have ready a 6-inch brioche mold or a 6-inch mixing bowl, and a tumbler large enough to fit into the mold. If you are going to bake 2 tulips at a time, have 2 molds or bowls and 2 tumblers ready.

Preheat the oven to 375°F.

Cream the butter with 5 tablespoons sugar until it is smooth and fluffy. Add 3 egg whites and the vanilla and beat until smooth. Mix in the flour, beating only until it is incorporated, scraping down the sides and the bottom of the bowl and incorporating the scrapings. Set the mixture aside.

In a separate bowl make a meringue by whipping the remaining 2 egg whites with 3 tablespoons sugar until they form high peaks but are not dry. Mix one-third of the meringue into the reserved batter, then gently fold the batter into the remaining meringue. The mixture should be quite firm rather than runny like pancake batter. Using a narrow spatula, spread the batter as thin as possible onto the parchment squares, forming 10-inch circles.

To bake, place the parchment squares, 2 at a time, on baking sheets. Place 1 or 2 sheets in the oven, baking until the tiles are almost brown, about 5 to 8 minutes. It is important to keep a close watch and remove the tiles immediately that half to one-third of the surface is browned, shaping them quickly while they are still warm and pliable.

Because the tiles cool and become crisp very quickly, work with no more than 1 or 2 at a time. As you remove them from the oven, place each tile in the brioche mold or bowl, leaving the parchment paper attached. Immediately place a tumbler in the bowl, pressing gently against the bottom and sides, so that the tile will mold into a tulip shape. As each tile cools, remove it from the bowl and gently peel off the parchment paper. Continue until all of the tiles are baked and shaped, putting 1 or 2 new ones into the oven as the previous batch is removed.

To serve, fill the tulips with ice cream (recipes below), placing 1 scoop of each kind in each tile tulip, and garnish with a sprig of fresh mint.

NOTE: If you bake tiles on a rainy day or more than a few hours before using them, keep them in a very dry place to retain their crispness.

Pine Nut Brown Butter Ice Cream
(MAKES 1 QUART)

> 3 tablespoons butter
> ⅓ cup pine nuts
> 3 cups half and half
> ½ cup sugar

Melt the butter in a small skillet. Add the pine nuts and cook until they are lightly brown. If the butter is not yet brown, remove the nuts with a slotted spoon and continue to cook until the butter browns.

Drain the excess butter from the nuts and put them aside to cool.

Put 1 cup half and half in a large saucepan. Add the sugar and cook until it dissolves. Remove from the heat and add the remaining 2 cups half and half and the brown butter. Stir in well.

Turn the mixture into the container of an ice cream machine and freeze according to the manufacturer's instructions. When the mixture starts to firm up, fold in the cooled pine nuts and continue freezing until the ice cream is done.

Saffron Lemon Ice Cream
(MAKES 1 QUART)

LEMON CURD:
>   2 egg yolks
>   zest of ½ lemon, grated
>   3 tablespoons lemon juice
>   ½ cup sugar
>   3 tablespoons sweet butter, melted

ICE CREAM:
>   ½ cup milk
>   .4 gram saffron
>   1 cup heavy cream

To make the lemon curd, set the top of a double boiler over boiling water, add the egg yolks, lemon zest, lemon juice, and sugar, and whisk until the mixture changes from a translucent yellow to a rich custardy yellow. Remove from the heat and, a little at a time, whisk in the melted butter. Set the lemon curd aside to cool to lukewarm.

While the lemon curd is cooling, heat the milk and saffron very gently, remove from the heat, and let it steep to make a pungent saffron tea. When the lemon curd has cooled and the saffron has steeped, combine them with the cream. Pour into the container of an ice cream machine and freeze according to the manufacturer's instructions until firm.

Double Chocolate Whammy Ice Cream
(MAKES 1 QUART)

>   3 ounces dark sweet chocolate
>   ¼ cup sugar
>   2 ounces caramels, or ¼ cup prepared
>   caramel sauce
>   ½ teaspoon instant coffee powder
>   1 ounce Tia Maria or other coffee liqueur
>   1 cup heavy cream
>   ½ cup milk
>   2 tablespoons shaved dark sweet chocolate

Set the top of a double boiler over boiling water. Add the 3 ounces chocolate, the sugar, and caramel. When they have melted together, remove the pan from the heat. Dissolve the coffee powder in the liqueur and stir it into the chocolate mixture. Cool to lukewarm. Whisk the cream and milk into the cooled chocolate mixture.

Pour into the container of an ice cream machine and freeze according to the manufacturer's instructions until almost firm. Fold in the chocolate shavings and continue to freeze until the ice cream is firm.

CALORIE COUNTER'S NOTE: To cut calories, make with 1½ cups milk and no cream.

A Note on the Wines

The chicken breasts cooked with sweet Sauternes and cream go well with a full-bodied dry white wine. We recommend a dry white Graves such as the Château Carbonnieux made of Sauvignon Blanc grapes, a wine with a gravelly, flinty flavor.

Our choice for the fillet of beef would be a classic, full-bodied Burgundy with the richness and complexity of a Nuits-St-Georges, Clos des Forêts, Belin.

Germany

✻

Marinated Leeks with Smoked Tongue

Lentil Soup

Rabbit Braised in Red Wine
(Hasenpfeffer)
Potato Pancakes
Broccoli with Browned Butter Sauce

Sliced Cucumbers in Sour Cream

Strass Rye Bread

Bundernuss Torte

Wines:
Schwarzhofberger, Auslese Riesling
Frick Zinfandel

MARINATED LEEKS WITH SMOKED TONGUE
(SERVES 6)

6–12 leeks
1 cup citronnade (page 308) or other
    vinaigrette dressing
1 tablespoon coarse-grained prepared
    mustard
½ cup heavy cream, whipped
10–12 ounces cooked smoked beef tongue,
    sliced ⅛ inch thick

DO AHEAD:

Prepare and marinate the leeks at least 1 hour ahead.

Trim the root end of the leeks and make a cut lengthwise from the end of the white portion through the green stalk. Wash carefully under running water, separating the green ends in order to get the sand completely rinsed out. Cut off the ends of the green stalks so that you have about equal parts white and green. Poach the leeks in ample water to cover. Test with the tip of a knife, and when they are tender throughout, remove them carefully, drain them, and put them in a bowl with the citronnade or vinaigrette dressing to marinate for 1 hour or more at room temperature.

When ready to serve, make the mustard cream by folding the mustard into the whipped cream. Arrange a portion of leeks on a salad plate. Lay the sliced tongue alongside. Spoon a dollop of the mustard cream over the leeks.

LENTIL SOUP
(SERVES 6)

3 slices of bacon, diced
1 large onion, chopped
1 stalk celery, chopped
1 carrot, finely diced
1 cup lentils, washed and drained
6 cups chicken stock (page 36)
1 tablespoon tomato paste
½ teaspoon allspice
salt and pepper
cider vinegar

Put the diced bacon and vegetables in a large soup pot and sauté them until they are lightly browned. Add the drained lentils, chicken stock, tomato paste, and allspice and stir well. Simmer for about 1 hour, or until the lentils are soft. Season with salt and pepper.

To serve, ladle the hot soup into individual bowls and pass a cruet of cider vinegar so that each diner can add some according to taste.

RABBIT BRAISED IN RED WINE
(Hasenpfeffer)
(SERVES 6)

This dish needs several hours to marinate.

3 small fryer rabbits

MARINADE:

2 cups red wine
2–4 cloves garlic, crushed

10–12 juniper berries, crushed
1 tablespoon pickling spice
1 teaspoon salt
1 onion, sliced
1 teaspoon dried marjoram

2 slices of bacon, diced
flour
1 cup chicken stock (page 36)

Cut the rabbits into quarters, reserving the bony shoulder sections for the soup pot. Disjoint the legs so that there is a leg and a portion of the saddle for each diner. (The butcher can do this for you.) If you don't mind the bonier upper portions, 2 larger fryer rabbits butchered in the same way would make 12 pieces, or 2 for each diner.

In a bowl combine the marinade ingredients and marinate the rabbit sections for 24 hours in the refrigerator or several hours at room temperature.

Remove the rabbit from the marinade and pat it dry. Strain the marinade and reserve it.

In a large frying pan or Dutch oven sauté the diced bacon until it is crisp. Remove to paper towels to absorb any excess grease, and reserve. Save the pan with the bacon fat.

Flour the rabbit. (An easy method is to put some flour in a paper bag, add a few pieces of rabbit at a time, close the top, and shake well.) Reheat the bacon fat, add the rabbit, and sauté until it is nicely browned. The rabbit will brown better if the pan is not overcrowded, so it is better to do this in batches. While the rabbit is browning, preheat the oven to 375°F.

When the rabbit has browned, add the strained marinade and the chicken stock. Cover the pot and bake for about 35 minutes, or until the rabbit is tender. When ready to serve, sprinkle the reserved crisp bacon pieces over the rabbit.

POTATO PANCAKES

For this dish, use the basic potato pancake recipe given in the Poland menu.

BROCCOLI WITH BROWNED BUTTER SAUCE

Clean and trim 1 bunch of broccoli, cutting off the tough lower stalks. In a steamer or a colander set over boiling water, steam the broccoli until it is just tender and still retains its bright green color. (You can also cook the broccoli in a large pot of boiling salted water. Drain well before proceeding.) While the broccoli is cooking, melt 2 tablespoons butter until slightly brown. Spoon it over the cooked broccoli and garnish with hard-cooked egg yolk rubbed through a sieve.

SLICED CUCUMBERS IN SOUR CREAM

Wash, peel, and cut cucumbers into thin slices. Place in a bowl or colander, sprinkle with salt, and let stand for 30 minutes. To make the dressing, mix a cup or more of sour cream with 2 or 3 tablespoons white wine vinegar, ground black pepper, and some chopped fresh chives. Squeeze the cucumbers, reserving about 2 teaspoons of the liquid to add to the dressing. Mix the cucumbers, the reserved liquid, and the sour cream dressing. Refrigerate for an hour. To serve, spoon over a bed of crisp salad greens.

STRASS RYE BREAD
(MAKES 2 ROUND LOAVES)

For many years, we were lucky enough to have as our pastry chef Joseph Maximilian Strasser from Bavaria, who had trained and apprenticed under the old school in southern Germany. He introduced this European-style bread to our bakery and over the years changed the recipe a bit, refined it a bit, marked it with his personal touch, until it became one of the most requested breads from our bakery.

> 1 package of yeast, or 1 tablespoon dry yeast
> 1 cup warm water
> 1 cup buttermilk
> 1 tablespoon molasses
> 1 egg
> 3 tablespoons salad oil
> rind of 1 orange, grated, or 1 tablespoon orange marmalade, chopped
> 1½ teaspoons fennel seeds
> 2 teaspoons salt
> 1 tablespoon malt powder or molasses
> 1 cup cracked wheat (bulgur)
> 3¼–3½ cups white bread or all-purpose flour, plus 4 teaspoons
> 2 cups medium rye flour

DO AHEAD:

Lightly oil a bowl for the dough.

Dissolve the yeast in the warm water and let it stand for a few minutes. Add the buttermilk, molasses, egg, oil, orange rind or marmalade, and fennel seeds. Mix well, then add the salt, malt or molasses, cracked wheat, 3¼ cups white flour, and the rye flour. Mix until it forms a dough. Add a little more flour if necessary.

Knead the dough by hand or machine. If by hand, turn it out on a floured board and work it until it is smooth and elastic, approximately 10 minutes. If using a dough hook on an electric mixer, knead the dough at the slowest speed for about 5 minutes.

Pat the dough into a ball and put it in the oiled bowl. Cover the dough with a kitchen towel and set it in a warm draft-free place to rise until doubled in bulk, 60 to 75 minutes. (A perfect place is a gas oven with its slight heat given off by the pilot light; an electric oven, turned on low for no more than 2 minutes, then turned off, works equally well.)

When the dough has doubled, turn it out onto a floured board, punch it down, and knead it again until there is no air left in it. Shape it into 2 round loaves. Place the loaves on the board. Cover them again with a towel, and let rise until almost doubled, 30 to 40 minutes.

While the loaves are rising, preheat the oven to 400°F. Place a pie tin half filled with water on the bottom shelf. Position an oven rack just above the bottom rack. Flour a baking sheet or large pan.

When the loaves have risen, cut 3 gashes in each direction to make a cross-hatched pattern on the top. (See illustration.) Sprinkle each loaf with 2 teaspoons flour.

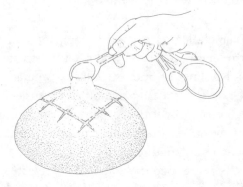

Gently pick up the loaves and transfer them to the baking sheet or pan and place it in the oven on the rack just above the bottom rack. Bake for 40 to 45 minutes. The crust should be golden brown. Test the doneness by rapping the bottom with your knuckle. The loaf should feel firm and make a hollow sound. Cool on a wire rack.

BUNDERNUSS TORTE
(SERVES 12 TO 16)

Ever since I was a child in Chicago and my mother used to buy a delicious pecan-caramel roll at Hellman's, this style of German nut cake has been one of my favorite desserts. The Germans call it Nusstorte, but it is most commonly known in the United States by its Swiss-German name, Bundernuss.—N.D.

The dough needs to be refrigerated for at least 2 hours before using.

CRUST:

½ cup (1 stick) butter
¼ cup sugar
1 egg white (reserve yolk for filling)
1 cup all-purpose flour

FRANGIPANE FILLING:

6 ounces almond paste or marzipan
1 tablespoon sugar
½ cup (1 stick) butter, softened
1 egg
1 egg yolk (reserved from crust ingredients)
2 tablespoons flour

WALNUT TOPPING:

1⅛ cups sugar
3 tablespoons corn syrup
10 tablespoons (1¼ sticks) butter, broken into small pieces
½ cup heavy cream
3 cups lightly toasted walnuts

Preheat the oven to 350°F.

For the crust, cream the butter, sugar, and egg white until smooth and fluffy. Add the flour and mix only until it is barely incorporated. Form the dough into a ball, wrap it in plastic, and refrigerate for at least 2 hours or overnight.

Roll the dough out on a lightly floured board to form a 13-inch circle. Place the dough circle carefully into an 8-inch cake pan 2 inches deep. Let the excess dough hang over the edge of the pan. Smooth out the natural pleats on the side of the pan with your fingers. Prick the bottom and sides of the dough all over with the tines of a fork. Bake until half done, about 15 minutes. Remove from the oven and allow the crust to cool in the pan. Leave the oven on.

Make the filling: Put the almond paste or marzipan, sugar, and butter in the bowl of a mixer and beat until smooth. Add the egg and the egg yolk and continue to beat until the texture is smooth and creamy. Add the flour and mix only until it is barely incorporated. Using a rubber spatula, fill the crust with the frangipane mixture. Return the pan to the 350°F oven and continue to bake for 20 to 25 minutes, or until the crust is brown and the frangipane is springy to the touch.

When the torte is done, heat the sugar and corn syrup in a 2-quart saucepan, stirring constantly with a wooden spoon, until the mixture turns a light brown caramel color. Immediately add the butter, stirring until it is completely incorporated. Remove from the heat and stir in the cream. Return the caramel mixture to the heat and boil it for 1 minute. Stir in the walnuts. Immediately pour the topping over the frangipane, smoothing it out with a knife blade or spatula.

Set the finished Bundernuss aside to cool, then refrigerate until 30 minutes before serving.

A Note on the Wines

Our choice as a good accompaniment to the marinated leeks and smoked tongue is a Riesling of intense varietal character. One such is a Schwarzhofberger Auslese, a wine of concentrated perfume and a hint of sweetness from grapes that were picked when very mature.

For the peppery rabbit, we selected a Frick, a medium-bodied Zinfandel with a good raspberrylike fruitiness in the flavor.

Greece

❖

Avgolemono with Pasta

Sautéed Prawns with a Sauce of Tomatoes, Ouzo,
Feta Cheese, and Black Olives

Sea Bass Fillet Baked with Olive Oil,
Garlic, and Oregano
Spinach and Rice

Cucumber Salad with Green Peppers, Onions,
and Yogurt-Dill Dressing

Country Bread
(Pain au Levain, Poilâne)

Fruits and Nuts

Wines:
Robert Mondavi Chardonnay
Robert Mondavi Napa Gamay

AVGOLEMONO WITH PASTA
(SERVES 6)

8 cups chicken broth (page 36)
2 ounces orzo pasta (rice- or barley-shaped
  pasta)
salt and pepper
2 eggs
juice of 2 lemons

Put the chicken broth into a large soup
kettle and bring it to a boil. Stir in the orzo
pasta and salt and pepper to taste. Simmer,
covered, until the pasta is tender, about 6
to 8 minutes. Remove the pot from the
heat. In a mixing bowl, beat the eggs
lightly until well blended. Whisk in the
lemon. This mixture is called avgolemono.

Stir a ladle of the hot chicken soup into
the avgolemono, then pour the avgolemono mixture back into the soup, stirring
continuously until a froth forms. Serve immediately before the froth subsides.

SAUTÉED PRAWNS WITH A SAUCE OF TOMATOES, OUZO, FETA CHEESE, AND BLACK OLIVES
(SERVES 6)

2 tablespoons olive oil
1 medium onion, finely chopped
2–3 cloves garlic, finely chopped
2–3 tomatoes, peeled (see Glossary) and
  chopped
salt and pepper
4–6 tablespoons ouzo or Pernod
18 large shrimp (approximately 1½
  pounds), shelled and deveined (tails may
  be left on)
approximately ¼ pound feta cheese,
  crumbled
18 black olives, pitted
1 tablespoon chopped fresh parsley

Preheat the oven to 425°F.

Heat the oil in a skillet, add the onion,
and sauté lightly until translucent. Add
the garlic, tomatoes, salt and pepper, and
ouzo or Pernod. Continue to cook until the
sauce has thickened, 5 to 10 minutes.

Divide the shrimp equally among 6 individual ramekins. Cover with the tomato
sauce and sprinkle with feta cheese, olives,
and parsley. (The dish can be prepared
ahead to this point.)

When ready to cook, place in the oven
for 10 to 15 minutes, or until heated
through and the feta has melted.

NOTE: Sometimes shrimp take on an iodinelike flavor. Soaking them in a little
milk for 30 minutes before cooking often
helps to sweeten them.

SEA BASS FILLET BAKED WITH OLIVE OIL, GARLIC, AND OREGANO
(SERVES 6)

¼ cup olive oil
6 6-ounce sea bass fillets (or substitute
  rock cod)
salt and pepper

2–3 cloves garlic, minced
1 tablespoon dried oregano
6 lemon wedges

Preheat the oven to 425°F.

Pour the olive oil into a baking dish large enough to hold the fillets. Arrange them in the dish, turning each one so that the oil coats it on both sides. Season with salt and pepper and sprinkle the garlic and oregano over the top. Bake for about 10 minutes (for a fish about 1 inch thick), or until the flesh at the thickest part has just become opaque. (To test, separate the flesh with a knife tip or with the tines of a fork.)

Garnish with lemon wedges.

SPINACH AND RICE

Wash a bunch of spinach and coarsely chop. Heat some olive oil and sauté 2 finely chopped onions until they are soft. Mix in about 1 teaspoon tomato paste and the spinach. Add about 1 cup water and bring to a boil. Season with salt, pepper, and a sprig of fresh mint, chopped. Add about ⅔ cup rice over the top of the onion-spinach mixture. Do not stir. Cover the pot and simmer until the rice is cooked, about 25 minutes. Mix before serving.

＊

CUCUMBER SALAD WITH GREEN PEPPERS, ONIONS, AND YOGURT-DILL DRESSING

Make the dressing first by combining 1½ cups plain yogurt with the juice of ½ lemon, some chopped fresh dill, and salt to taste. Chill.

Peel and thinly slice 3 or 4 cucumbers. Thinly slice 1 green pepper and ½ onion and combine with the cucumber. Mix in the yogurt dressing and serve on romaine lettuce leaves with a sprinkle of chopped fresh dill over the top.

COUNTRY BREAD
(Pain au Levain, Poilâne)

To go with these robust Greek dishes, we like a good country bread that can soak up the sauces. For the recipe, see the Basque menu.

FRUITS AND NUTS

Sweets are not the everyday dessert in Greece but are rather reserved for special occasions, holidays, or in-between-meals treats. There is also a special tradition involving hospitality and the offering of sweets to guests or travelers. When we visited friends in Greece, our hosts brought forth an elaborate tray filled with refreshments, which they parceled out onto individual trays for each member of our family:

On each was a glass of cold water, a thimble-sized glass of ouzo, a small spoon, and a little compote dish, which they filled from the large serving bowl with an extremely sweet, syrupy concoction, a fruit preserve that was almost like a honey. The procedure was to take a spoon of the sweet or a swallow of ouzo and wash it down with a sip of cold water. These offerings were meant not only to convey hospitality but to refresh the weary traveler.

In the spirit of the Greek menu, serve such fresh fruits as grapes, figs, melons, pomegranates, or whatever is in season. In Greece, the fruits usually come in a large bowl of ice water. Dried fruits such as figs and raisins are standard winter fare. And a bowl of nuts always comes along to the table.—D.M.

A Note on the Wines

A rich, oaky Chardonnay seemed a good choice to go with the sautéed prawns and their sauce of many flavors. We picked a Robert Mondavi from 1975.

The meaty sea bass with strong seasonings of garlic and oregano inspired a light to medium-bodied red wine, and we chose another Mondavi, its Napa Gamay 1974.

Holland

❖

Celery Salad with Mayonnaise and Capers

Chicken Soup with Pork Sausage

Poached Freshwater Bass with Mustard Sauce
Potato Croquettes
Green Beans

Gouda

Orange Wheat Bread

Stuffed Apples Baked in Pastry

Wines:
J. W. Morris Sauvignon Blanc
Knudsen Erath Chardonnay

CELERY SALAD WITH MAYONNAISE AND CAPERS
(SERVES 6)

1 bunch celery
Bibb lettuce leaves or small leaves of butter
*   lettuce, washed and chilled*
½ cup freshly made mayonnaise (see
*   recipes below)*
juice of 1 lemon
salt and pepper
3–4 tablespoons capers

Wash the celery and peel the stalks with a vegetable peeler to get rid of the strings. Cut the stalks into pieces 2 inches long, then into thin julienne strips. Boil the celery in salted water for 2 to 3 minutes. Rinse under cold water. Drain well and chill.

When ready to serve, arrange the lettuce leaves on salad plates. Toss the celery strips with the mayonnaise and lemon juice. Season with salt and pepper. Spoon a portion of celery over the leaves on each plate and sprinkle with capers over the top.

Whole Egg Mayonnaise (Blender Method)
(MAKES 1½ CUPS)

1 egg
1 teaspoon mustard powder
½ teaspoon salt
1 dash of Worcestershire sauce
1½ tablespoons white wine or other
*   vinegar*
1 teaspoon lemon juice
1 cup olive oil

Put all the ingredients except ¾ cup oil in a blender. Process on slow speed until the mixture is smooth. Drizzle in the remainning ¾ cup oil very rapidly, shutting off the blender and scraping down the sides with a spatula, if necessary. If you work quickly, the total blending time will not exceed 30 seconds.

Narsai's Egg White Mayonnaise
(MAKES 1½ CUPS)

2 egg whites
1 teaspoon mustard powder
1 pinch of turmeric or paprika
½ teaspoon salt
1 dash of Worcestershire sauce
1½ tablespoons white wine or other
*   vinegar*
1 teaspoon lemon juice
1 cup olive oil

Put all the ingredients except ¾ cup oil in a blender; proceed as for Whole Egg Mayonnaise, above.

CHICKEN SOUP WITH PORK SAUSAGE
(SERVES 6)

6 cups chicken stock (page 36)
2–3 cloves garlic, minced
1–2 leeks (white bulb and a little of the
*   green top), chopped*
1 bay leaf
¼ teaspoon grated nutmeg
¼ teaspoon ground ginger

6 breakfast pork link sausages, cut into ½-
    inch pieces
salt and pepper
2 tablespoons chopped fresh parsley

Put the chicken stock in a soup pot and
add the garlic, leeks, bay leaf, nutmeg, ginger, and cut-up pork sausages. Simmer for
about 30 minutes, or until the leeks are
tender. Stir in the parsley just before
serving.

POACHED FRESHWATER BASS WITH MUSTARD SAUCE
(SERVES 6)

FISH:
    1 cup water
    1 cup white wine
    1 teaspoon dillseed
    6 freshwater bass fillets
    6 sprigs parsley

MUSTARD SAUCE:
    2 tablespoons butter
    1 tablespoon flour
    1½ cups fish poaching liquid, strained
    salt and pepper
    2 tablespoons Dijon mustard
    ⅓ cup sour cream

To poach the fish, put the water and wine
in a pot large enough to hold the bass fillets, add the dillseed, and bring to a boil.
Carefully place the fish fillets in the poaching liquid, lower the heat to a moderate
simmer, and poach until the flesh is opaque
at the thickest part, about 10 minutes for a
1-inch-thick piece of fish. Remove the fish
to a serving platter and keep warm.

While the fish is cooking, start the
sauce. Melt the butter in a small saucepan.
Add the flour, whisking constantly so that
it will not lump. Cook for about 2 minutes
and reserve.

When the fish is done and removed to a
platter, add 1½ cups of the fish poaching
stock, salt, pepper, and mustard to the but-
ter-flour mixture. Boil the sauce for 3 minutes, stirring constantly. Remove from the
heat. Stir in the sour cream.

To serve, nap the fish with the mustard
sauce and garnish with sprigs of parsley.

POTATO CROQUETTES
(SERVES 6)

    1 pound baking potatoes, scrubbed
    3 eggs
    grated nutmeg
    salt
    2 tablespoons water
    bread crumbs
    oil

Boil the potatoes in their skins. Cool, then
chill them. When they are cold, peel them
and grate them into a bowl.

Separate 2 eggs and beat the whites until
stiff. Reserve 1 yolk for coating the croquettes and use the other for another purpose. Stir the remaining whole egg, a
pinch of grated nutmeg, salt, and the stiffly
beaten whites into the grated potatoes. Divide the potato mixture into 12 equal portions and roll them into balls. Coat the
balls with the beaten yolk of the reserved

egg whisked with 2 tablespoons water. Roll the balls in bread crumbs.

Preheat the oven to 200°F.

Heat the oil in a deep pot until it is moderately hot (375°F on a candy thermometer) and fry the balls, a few at a time, turning them, until they are golden brown. Remove and drain on paper towels. Put the finished croquettes on a serving platter in the oven until all are fried. Serve 2 croquettes for each portion.

GREEN BEANS

Snap the ends from 2 pounds fresh green beans and cook the beans in a large pot of boiling salted water. When they are just tender but still retain a suggestion of crunchiness, add a glass of cold water to the pot to stop the cooking, and drain the beans in a colander. Toss the beans in a skillet over moderate heat for a minute to evaporate any remaining moisture. Add salt, pepper, and 3 to 4 tablespoons butter, and toss until well heated, about 2 minutes. Add 1 teaspoon lemon juice and some minced parsley and toss again before serving. Add a sprinkle of finely chopped fresh parsley over the top.

GOUDA

A slice of well-aged Gouda cheese is a good transition between the fish course and the dessert.

ORANGE WHEAT BREAD
(MAKES TWO 1½-POUND LOAVES)

1 tablespoon dry yeast
2 cups warm water
3 tablespoons sugar
3 tablespoons butter, melted and cooled
5 cups white bread or all-purpose flour
1⅔ cups whole-wheat flour
2 teaspoons salt
rind of 2 oranges, grated, or 2 tablespoons chopped orange marmalade

DO AHEAD:
Lightly oil a bowl for the dough.

Put the yeast in a large mixing bowl, add the water, and let it stand for a few minutes until the yeast dissolves. Stir in the sugar and melted butter. Add both kinds of flour, the salt, and the orange rind, and mix well to form a dough.

Turn the mixture out on a floured board. Knead by hand or with an electric mixer with a dough hook until the dough is smooth and elastic: 8 to 10 minutes by hand, about 5 minutes by machine. Shape the dough into a ball and place it in the oiled bowl. Cover it with a towel and set it in a warm, draft-free place to rise until doubled, 45 to 60 minutes.

Turn the dough out again onto the floured board, punch it down, and knead it until there is no air left in it. Shape it into a ball, place it back in the bowl, cover it with a towel, and let it rise a second time until it has doubled, about 45 minutes.

Turn it out onto the floured board, punch it down, and knead again until there is no air left in it. Form the dough into 2 round loaves, cover them with a towel, and let them rise until almost doubled, about 30 minutes.

While the loaves are rising, flour a sheet pan, place a rack just above the center of the oven, preheat the oven to 400° F and place a pie tin half filled with water on the bottom shelf.

When the loaves have risen, use a razor blade or sharp knife to make 2 deep gashes in each direction to form a tic-tac-toe pattern on the top of each loaf (see illustration, page 131). Pick up the loaves and gently transfer them to the sheet pan.

Bake the loaves for 40 to 45 minutes. Test the doneness by rapping the bottom of the loaf with your knuckles. It should feel firm and make a hollow sound. Cool the loaves on a wire rack.

STUFFED APPLES BAKED IN PASTRY
(SERVES 6)

> 1 recipe Danish Waffle dough (page 95) or
>   your favorite pie dough
> 6 green apples, peeled and cored
> 2 tablespoons brown sugar
> 2 tablespoons butter, melted and cooled
> 1 teaspoon ground cinnamon
> 1 teaspoon dried mace
> 1/3 cup raisins
> 1 egg beaten with 1 tablespoon water
> 2 cups heavy cream

DO AHEAD:
Butter a pastry sheet.

Preheat the oven to 375°F.

Divide the dough into 6 pieces and shape into balls. Roll each one out on a floured board into a circle about 10 to 12 inches in diameter. Place an apple on each circle.

In a bowl mix the sugar, butter, cinnamon, mace, and raisins. Stuff the mixture into the apples.

Fold the dough up and over each apple. Pinch off the excess dough and crimp the loose ends firmly. Roll out the scraps of dough and make 6 circles about 2 inches across to cap the tops of the apples. Moisten one side of the circles with a pastry brush or your finger and press the caps firmly onto the tops of the apples. Place the finished pastries on the buttered pastry sheet and brush with the beaten egg. Bake for 25 to 30 minutes, or until golden brown.

Serve in a shallow bowl and pass a pitcher of heavy cream to pour around the apples.

A Note on the Wines

To begin this meal, we would pick a Sauvignon Blanc that was light, crisp, and with typical herbaceous overtones, as found in the bottling of J. W. Morris.

For the freshwater bass in a mustardy sauce, our choice is a Chardonnay of medium body and fine varietal fruit flavors such as those made by Knudsen Erath in the state of Oregon.

Hungary

❋

Mushroom Strudel

Chicken Smitaine

Stuffed Cabbage
Boiled Potatoes

Green Pepper Salad

White Bread

Dobos Torte
(Multilayered Chocolate Torte)

Wines:
Chalone Vineyards Pinot Blanc
Burgess Cellars Petite Sirah

MUSHROOM STRUDEL

(SERVES 6)

6 tablespoons butter
1 small onion, finely chopped
½ pound mushrooms, chopped
¼ teaspoon ground cinnamon
salt and pepper
4 eggs
¼ cup dry bread crumbs
4 sheets of packaged phyllo dough

DO AHEAD:

Defrost phyllo dough and return the remainder to the freezer. If a hot day, cover the sheets with wax paper and a damp cloth to keep them from drying out. Melt 4 tablespoons butter and remove from the heat.

Melt 2 tablespoons butter in a frying pan, add the onions, and sauté until they are clear and golden. Add the chopped mushrooms to the onions and cook until all the liquid has evaporated. Add the cinnamon and salt and pepper. Set the mixture aside to cool.

Beat 3 eggs lightly and mix them into the cooled mushrooms. Stir in the bread crumbs.

Preheat the oven to 375°F.

Lay out a kitchen towel or piece of foil of about the same size on the work counter. Taking one sheet at a time, stack the 4 sheets of phyllo on the towel (a phyllo sheet is about 12 x 17 inches), brushing each one with the melted butter. Using the rest of the melted butter, brush the surface of a baking pan or baking sheet wide enough to hold the rolled-up dough.

Spread the mushroom filling on the dough, leaving some space all around the edges so the filling will not ooze out during cooking. Lifting one end of the towel or foil, roll the dough and filling like a strudel or jelly roll. Roll very loosely to leave space for the eggs to swell during baking. (See illustration above.)

Place the rolled dough on the buttered pan or baking sheet and flatten slightly with the palm of the hand. Brush the top with the remaining egg, beaten lightly. Be careful that none of the egg runs onto the pan. With the tip of a sharp knife, cut slits on top 2½ inches apart. Bake for 25-30 minutes, or until crisp.

NOTE: This strudel is often made with cabbage, which we eliminated because stuffed cabbage was the main course on our menu. If you are using this recipe alone, and would like to try the cabbage version, sauté 1 cup shredded raw cabbage along with the mushrooms.

CHICKEN SMITAINE
(SERVES 6)

> 3 chicken fryer breasts (halves)
> salt and pepper
> ¼ cup (½ stick) butter
> 1 large onion, sliced
> ½ cup dry white wine
> 1 cup chicken broth (page 36)
> 1 cup sour cream
> paprika

Each half breast consists of a large muscle and a smaller, elongated section that resembles a "fillet" or "supreme." Gently remove the elongated fillet from each half. (See illustration, page 54.) Cut the remainder of each half into 3 long strips about the same size as the fillet. There will now be 12 pieces. Sprinkle them with salt and pepper. (This can be done ahead and reserved until ready to cook.)

In a large skillet, melt the butter, add the chicken pieces, and sauté them until they are barely colored, but not at all brown. Remove the chicken to a warm platter. In the same pan, sauté the onion slices until they are transparent. Add the wine and chicken broth and simmer slowly until the onions are very soft. Stir in the sour cream and boil the sauce rapidly until

it is moderately thick. Return the chicken and any juices that have accumulated on the platter to the pan. Stir gently so that the chicken pieces are well coated with the sauce. Continue to cook just long enough to heat the chicken through. Sprinkle lightly with paprika before serving.

STUFFED CABBAGE
(SERVES 6)

When I was operating the Pot Luck Restaurant in Berkeley, our two most popular entrees were Hungarian Stuffed Cabbage and Beef Stroganoff. The cabbage dish was also later very popular as an entrée for catered banquets at Narsai's. The sweet and sour flavor created by the sauerkraut seems to make even an adamant sauerkraut doubter suddenly love it.—N.D.

> 2 medium to large heads cabbage
> 2 pounds ground beef or lean ground lamb
>   or pork
> 1 onion, chopped
> ⅔ cup chopped fresh parsley
> 3–4 cloves garlic, minced
> 1½ teaspoons pepper
> 2 teaspoons salt
> 2 teaspoons dillweed
> 1 teaspoon allspice
> ⅔ cup cooked rice (or leftover pilaf)
> 2 cups tomato puree
> 2 cups sauerkraut
> 3 tablespoons brown sugar
> juice of 1 lemon

Remove the cores of the cabbage very carefully with a paring knife or short boning knife, making short back-and-forth sawing motions. Save the cores for coleslaw or another use. Parboil the prepared cabbage in a covered pot until the leaves become soft and pliable, about ten minutes. Remove the pot from the heat and chill the cabbage under cold running water. Pull off and reserve the tough outermost green leaves. Pull away 12 to 15 large leaves to use to roll around the stuffing and cut away their tough ribs, which will make rolling easier.

In a large bowl mix the ground meat, onion, parsley, garlic, pepper, salt, dillweed, allspice, rice, and ½ cup tomato puree.

Spread the deribbed cabbage leaves on a flat surface. Divide the meat mixture equally among them. Starting with the stem end, roll up each leaf around the stuffing. Leave the ends open so that the sauce can get in during cooking.

Preheat the oven to 350°F.

Rinse the sauerkraut under cold running water, drain it well, and spread it out in a 9-x-13-inch Pyrex baking pan. Arrange the stuffed cabbage rolls side by side, seam side down, on top of the sauerkraut. Mix the remaining 1½ cups tomato puree with the brown sugar and lemon juice and spread it over the top of the rolls. Cover the casserole with the reserved tough outer leaves (you can also use tough outer leaves of lettuce if necessary). Cover the pan with foil and bake for 1 hour. Remove the foil and bake for another 30 minutes.

BOILED POTATOES

Scrub and peel 6 boiling potatoes and cook them in boiling water until they are tender, 35 to 45 minutes, depending on size. Drain and serve.

GREEN PEPPER SALAD

Remove the skin of 6 large green peppers by broiling over charcoal, under the broiler, or roasting in a hot oven until they are charred all around; do not allow them to get too black or the meat under the skin will burn. Put the peppers in a brown paper bag for several minutes to loosen their skins. Peel off the skins under cold running water. After peeling, remove the stems and seeds and slice the peppers into long strips. Make a marinade of 2 parts olive oil, 2 parts wine vinegar, salt, pepper, and a pinch of sugar. Add the green peppers, mix well, and refrigerate, preferably overnight, but at least for a few hours. Remove from the refrigerator an hour before serving so that the oil will not be congealed. Serve plain or over a bed of lettuce.

WHITE BREAD

Bulgarian white bread, a type common to several neighboring European countries, is a good choice with this meal. The recipe is in the menu for Bulgaria.

DOBOS TORTE
(Multilayered Chocolate Torte)
(SERVES 10 TO 12)

CAKE:
  4 ounces almond paste
  ½ cup plus 1 tablespoon granulated sugar
  ¾ cup (1½ sticks) sweet butter, softened
  5 eggs, separated
  1 cup sifted all-purpose flour

BUTTERCREAM:
  2 eggs, separated
  ½ cup granulated sugar
  ¾ cup confectioners' sugar, sifted once
  1 cup (2 sticks) sweet butter, softened
  3 ounces dark sweet chocolate, melted and
    cooled
  1 tablespoon instant coffee powder
  1½ teaspoons vanilla extract

DO AHEAD:

Using an 8- or 9-inch cake pan bottom as a guide, draw a circle on a sheet of parchment paper and cut it out. You will need a total of 8 parchment circles. Using the first circle as a pattern, stack and cut several sheets at a time. You can also use 8- or 9-inch buttered and floured cake pans, but they are harder to work with, and not many people have 8 cake pans on hand.

Preheat the oven to 400°F.

Put the almond paste and ¼ cup sugar in the bowl of an electric mixer and blend until they are a uniform, crumbly texture. Add the butter and whip until the mixture is smooth. Add the egg yolks and continue to whip until the mixture is creamy.

While the egg yolk mixture is beating, make a meringue: Whisk the egg whites and remaining 5 tablespoons sugar in the top of a double boiler (off heat), or in a mixer bowl that will fit over the bottom of a double boiler or in a bain marie. When the egg whites are well blended, place them over the hot water in the double boiler or bain marie and continue whisking until the sugar dissolves. The egg whites should not cook, but be only lukewarm. As soon as the sugar dissolves, remove the whites from the heat for beating in the mixer.

Remove the bowl containing the egg yolk mixture from the mixer. It should be creamy enough to form a "ribbon" of the batter that falls from the beater when it is moved back and forth over the rest of the batter. Set aside.

If the lukewarm egg white mixture is not already in a mixer bowl, transfer it and immediately start to whip it at high speed, increasing until you are beating at the highest peak. Stop and set aside. The meringue should be firm but not dry.

Sprinkle the sifted flour over the reserved egg yolk mixture and fold it in gently by hand. Add a handful of the meringue and fold it in to lighten the batter. Pour the batter onto the remaining meringue and fold it in gently but thoroughly.

Arrange the 8 parchment circles on 4 baking sheets (it may be necessary to do this in batches). Divide the batter evenly among them, spreading it outward from the center of each toward the edges, using a long narrow spatula. Spread the batter as evenly and neatly as possible, particularly along the edges. Turn the spatula upright and draw it around the edge of the batter to make a smooth finish. If you have 2 ovens, bake 2 sheets at a time, one in each oven; otherwise it is probably better to control the baking by doing a sheet at a time. Bake each batch for 5 to 7 minutes. The layers should be removed as soon as they are barely done.

Invert each layer as soon as it comes from the oven onto a lightly floured work surface. Immediately peel off the paper and turn the layers over so that the original paper side is on the bottom. Cool thoroughly. Note: When all the baked layers are completely cooled, you can store them for as long as a day by stacking them with plastic wrap or wax paper between them and wrapping well with plastic wrap.

While the layers are cooling, make the buttercream. Place the 2 egg whites and granulated sugar in a stainless steel or glass mixer bowl. Set it over hot water in a frying pan over low heat and whisk until the sugar dissolves (at about 120°F on a candy thermometer). Remove immediately from the heat to the mixer and whip at the highest speed until the whites are stiff and hold their peaks. Mix in the confectioners' sugar, beating slowly until it is all absorbed. Add the butter, chocolate, instant coffee powder, and vanilla. Whip the mixture until it is creamy and fluffy, being careful to incorporate the chocolate from the sides of the bowl before it hardens.

To assemble, trim any ragged spots from the edges of the layers, using a sharp knife. They should be as uniform and even as possible. You can use the cake bottom as a guide. Dust off any residual flour.

Place the layers side by side and divide the buttercream among them, reserving about 2 portions for finishing the top and sides of the assembled cake. Place the first layer on a plate and spread the buttercream evenly over it. Put the second layer on top of the first and spread the buttercream as before. Continue until all the layers are stacked with the buttercream between them. Spread the reserved buttercream over the top and sides, making decorative swirls or patterns. If you know how to use a pastry tube, pipe some of the reserved cream into rosettes or other decorative designs.

A Note on the Wines

A full-bodied Pinot Blanc harmonizes well with the chicken breasts sautéed in onions and sour cream. Chalone Vineyards makes one in the rich, oaky style of a Chardonnay, which would be exactly right.

Our choice for the beef-stuffed cabbage is a Petite Sirah made in the style of the older Burgess wines: a complex, dark purple wine full of fruit and black pepper. (It is a wine we know intimately: The grapes for several of the vintages of the 1970s came from Doris's Howell Mountain vineyard in Napa Valley, from vines that were then over forty years old.)

Indonesia

❊

Vegetables with Spicy Peanut Dip
(Gado Gado)

Chicken Noodle Soup

Stir-Fried Prawns in Coconut Cream

Chicken Satay and Lamb Satay
Boiled Rice

Banana Fritters

Wines:
Balverne Vineyards Gewürztraminer
Louis M. Martini Zinfandel Special Selection

VEGETABLES WITH SPICY PEANUT DIP
(Gado Gado)
(SERVES 6)

2 tablespoons butter
1 large onion, sliced
3 cloves garlic, sliced
1 cup chicken consommé (page 36) (see
    Note)
2 tablespoons soy sauce
¾ cup peanut butter
1 tablespoon heavy cream
1 tablespoon grated fresh ginger
Tabasco sauce to taste
assorted raw vegetables, washed and
    trimmed

Melt the butter in a saucepan. Add the onion and garlic and sauté until they are brown. Add the consommé, soy sauce, peanut butter, cream, ginger, and Tabasco sauce and cook slowly for about 10 minutes. Purée the mixture in a blender or food processor.

The dip may be served warm or cold with an assortment of raw vegetables of your choice.

NOTE: If this dish is to be served cold, double the amount of consommé to 2 cups.

CHICKEN NOODLE SOUP
(SERVES 6)

2 tablespoons oil
3 bay leaves
1 stalk fresh lemongrass, halved
    lengthwise, or 1 tablespoon dried, tied in
    cheesecloth (see Note)
3 cloves garlic, minced
2 teaspoons minced or grated fresh ginger
a large pinch of saffron
6 cups rich chicken broth (page 36)
1 carrot, finely diced
1 ounce cellophane noodles, broken into
    2-inch lengths
salt and pepper

Heat the oil in a Dutch oven or soup pot, add the bay leaves, lemongrass, garlic, ginger, and saffron, and sauté briefly just until the spices start to sizzle. Immediately add the chicken broth to the sizzling spices and bring to a boil. (If you are using lemon juice, add it now.) Add the carrot. Lower the heat, cover the pot, and simmer the soup for 20 to 30 minutes. Add the noodles and continue simmering until they are tender. Remove and discard the bay leaves and the lemongrass. Adjust the seasoning with salt and pepper.

NOTE: If lemongrass is not available, use the juice of 1 lemon and a few scrapings of the zest. Do not add the lemon juice and zest with the other spices but wait until after the next step.

STIR- FRIED PRAWNS IN COCONUT CREAM

(SERVES 6)

> 4 tablespoons butter
> 18–24 medium prawns, peeled and
>   deveined
> ½ cup arrowroot or cornstarch
> 2–3 shallots, minced
> 1 cup coconut cream, homemade (page
>   61) or canned
> 1 tablespoon lemon juice
> a few dashes of Tabasco sauce
> salt and white pepper

Melt the butter in a large frying pan. Dip the prawns very lightly in the arrowroot or cornstarch and shake off any excess. Add them to the frying pan, along with the shallots, and sauté for 3 to 5 minutes, just enough to barely cook them through. Stir in the coconut cream, lemon juice, and Tabasco sauce. Season with salt and white pepper. Remove the prawns to a serving dish with a slotted spoon. Boil the sauce rapidly until it is smooth and thickened, and pour it over the prawns.

CHICKEN SATAY AND LAMB SATAY

(SERVES 6)

The marinade for these 2 satays is the same, but the chicken and lamb must marinate separately. The recipe for the marinade is doubled here so that you can make both satays for this menu. One-half the recipe will normally serve whenever you make only one of the dishes.

SATAY MARINADE:
> 6–8 cloves garlic, minced
> 1 onion, thinly sliced
> 3 tablespoons lemon juice
> 3 tablespoons dark brown sugar
> 3 tablespoons soy sauce
> 2 tablespoons molasses
> 2 teaspoons ground coriander
> 1 teaspoon pepper
> several dashes of Tabasco sauce
> ⅓ cup grated Brazil nuts or almonds

> 3–4 fryer chicken breast halves
> oil
> 1 pound very lean lamb, cut into ¾-inch
>   cubes (See Note)

Mix together the marinade ingredients. Divide the marinade into 2 bowls, one for the chicken, one for the lamb.

Chicken satay: Bone and skin the chicken breasts. Each half breast consists of a large muscle and a smaller, elongated section that resembles a "fillet" or a "supreme." Carefully pull the fillet away from each half. (See illustration, page 54) Cut the fillet and the remaining breast into ¾-inch squares. Thread them onto 12 small (about 6 inches long) bamboo skewers. Marinate the skewered chicken for 30 minutes at room temperature, or for 2 hours in the refrigerator. When ready to cook, brush lightly with oil. Broil until barely brown. Be careful to avoid overcooking.

Lamb satay: Be sure the lamb is free of fat and gristle. Thread the cubes onto 6-inch bamboo skewers, marinate following the same method and timing as for the chicken satay, brush with oil, and broil until just brown, so as not to overcook.

NOTE: Thick round steak cut from a leg of lamb is the easiest to use for this dish. The total trimmed weight should be between 1¼ and 1½ pounds.

BOILED RICE

Rice is a staple of Indonesian cooking. Its blandness is an excellent foil for the many highly spiced and hot dishes of that cuisine. The best way to serve it is to put a portion on each plate and surround it with the sauced or broiled foods or serve them over it.

To make a basic boiled rice, bring 2 quarts salted water to a boil, add 1 cup rice, and cook for about 25 minutes, or until the rice is tender. Pour off most of the remaining water, cover the pot, and cook briefly over the lowest heat until the rest of the moisture is absorbed. An alternative method is to add 1 cup rice to 3 cups boiling salted water, cover the pot, and cook over the lowest possible heat for 35 to 40 minutes, or until the water has been absorbed. A cup of raw rice makes about 3 cups cooked rice and will be adequate for 6 portions.

BANANA FRITTERS
(SERVES 6)

> oil
> 1 cup all-purpose flour
> 3 tablespoons brown sugar
> ½ cup milk
> 1 egg
> 4 bananas, ripe but still firm
> ground cinnamon
> freshly grated nutmeg
> confectioners' sugar

Put the oil in a French fryer with a removable basket (or use a Dutch oven and a strainer or large slotted spoon). Heat the oil to 350°F on a candy or jelly thermometer. While the oil is heating, mix the flour, brown sugar, milk, and egg until it is smooth. Peel the bananas, cut them into 1-inch pieces, dip them in the batter, and deep-fry them in the hot oil until they are nicely browned. Drain them on paper towels. Dust the fritters with cinnamon, nutmeg, and confectioners' sugar before serving.

A Note on the Wines

With the exotic and spicy Indonesian flavors, we suggest beginning with a medium-bodied white wine with distinct spiciness of its own, such as a Gewürztraminer from Balverne Vineyards.

A soft, medium-bodied Zinfandel with good varietal berrylike flavors seems the right complement to the satays—such as a Louis M. Martini Special Selection.

Iran

❊

Cold Yogurt and Cucumber Soup

Broiled Rock Cod Stuffed with Nuts

Lamb Ragout Flavored with Pomegranate Juice
Saffron Rice Pilaf
Imam Bayeldi
(Baked Eggplant with Onions and Tomatoes)

Hearts of Romaine Salad

Nani-Lavash
(Thin "Cracker" Bread)

Fresh Fruit Compote with
Orange- or Rose-Blossom Perfume

Wines:
Joseph Phelps Vineyards Sauvignon Blanc
Louis M. Martini Zinfandel

COLD YOGURT AND CUCUMBER SOUP

(SERVES 6)

3 cups plain yogurt (see Note)
1–2 cups water (see Note)
2 cucumbers, peeled, seeded, and grated,
    or 1 long "English" cucumber, peeled
    and grated.
salt
1/2 cup raisins
12 ice cubes
1/3 cup chopped fresh mint

Mix the yogurt and water to the consistency of a creamy, medium-thick soup. Add the grated cucumbers. Season with salt. To serve, ladle the soup into chilled bowls and sprinkle with raisins. Add 2 ice cubes to each bowl and garnish with chopped mint.

NOTE: Since yogurt varies considerably in consistency, the amount of water required depends on the thickness of the yogurt you use. The consistency after the water and yogurt are mixed should be that of a creamy soup. Homemade yogurt or that sold in health food stores is frequently made with whole milk and is therefore thicker and richer than most commercial yogurt. It is also generally more tangy in flavor. Try to find whole-milk yogurt for this recipe. If you are using commercial yogurt that tastes bland, add 1 or 2 teaspoons lemon juice.

BROILED ROCK COD STUFFED WITH NUTS

(SERVES 6)

2 tablespoons butter
1/4 cup chopped dates
1/4 cup chopped dried apricots
1/3 cup chopped almonds
1/3 cup pistachios or pine nuts
1/2 teaspoon pepper
1/2 teaspoon turmeric
1/2 teaspoon ground cinnamon
1/2 lime, ground with the peeling
1 tablespoon shredded orange rind
6 thick rock cod fillets, 2 1/2 ounces each
    (see Note)
1/2 cup water
juice of 1 lemon

Preheat the oven to 350°F.

Melt the butter in a skillet. Add the dates, apricots, almonds, and pistachios and sauté with the pepper, turmeric, cinnamon, lime, and orange rind. When the mixture has blended, set it aside to cool.

Slit a pocket in each fish fillet. Stuff with the cooled fruit-and-nut mixture. Arrange the fillets in a shallow baking pan or casserole. Add the water and lemon juice and bake, uncovered, for 20 to 25 minutes, or until the fish is no longer translucent in the center of the thickest part. Serve with a spoonful of the baking juices over each portion.

NOTE: In the north, on the Caspian Sea, this dish would more likely be prepared with fillets from a Beluga sturgeon.

LAMB RAGOUT FLAVORED WITH POMEGRANATE JUICE
(SERVES 6)

> 2 pounds lean boneless lamb, cut into 1-
>   ounce chunks
> 1 tablespoon oil
> 1 large onion, chopped
> 1 teaspoon turmeric
> ½ teaspoon pepper
> salt
> 1 tablespoon flour
> ½ cup ground or pulverized walnuts
> 1 cup pomegranate juice
> 1 teaspoon ground cardamom
> juice of 1 lemon

Without adding fat, brown the lamb chunks in a heavy Dutch oven. In a separate pan heat the oil and sauté the onions until they are brown, then transfer them to the Dutch oven. Sprinkle the turmeric, pepper, and salt over the meat and stir for 1 minute. Sprinkle in the flour and stir until it is absorbed. Add the walnuts, pomegranate juice, and enough water to almost cover the meat. Reduce the heat to a simmer, cover the pot, and cook until the meat is tender, 1 to 1½ hours. Add the cardamom. Squeeze in lemon juice to taste and adjust the salt. Keep warm until ready to serve.

SAFFRON RICE PILAF

Make the basic Pilaf recipe in the Perennial Favorites menu. Add a pinch of saffron threads as soon as you add the water. Stir well to get an even color.

IMAM BAYELDI
(Baked Eggplant with Onions and Tomatoes)
(SERVES 6)

The name of this dish literally means "the priest fainted." According to the legend common to many countries of the Middle East, an imam or religious leader ate so much of the delectable dish that he fell into contented sleep, a state his wife attributed, to arriving friends, to his having fainted. An equal number of versions credit the swoon to the ecstasy he experienced from the wonderful aromas and flavors.

> 2 tablespoons oil
> 2 medium onions, sliced
> 3 large tomatoes, peeled (see Glossary)
>   and chopped
> salt and pepper
> 3 cloves garlic, minced
> ¼ bunch parsley, stemmed and minced
> 2 teaspoons dried sweet basil
> 1 large eggplant

Preheat the oven to 350°F.
   Heat the oil in a skillet, add the onions,

and sauté until they are transparent. Add the tomatoes, salt and pepper, garlic, parsley, and basil and simmer for 5 to 10 minutes. Set aside.

Cut away and discard the stem of the eggplant, then cut the eggplant in half lengthwise. Cut each half into 3 wedges. Arrange the wedges skin side down in a long baking pan barely large enough to hold them. Pour the tomato-onion sauce over the eggplant. Cover with foil and bake for 20 minutes. Remove the covering and bake until the eggplant is very soft to the touch of a fork and the topping has started to brown, 15 to 20 minutes more.

HEARTS OF ROMAINE SALAD

Use only the yellow inner leaves of a head of romaine lettuce. Separate them, wash and dry well, and arrange them attractively in a bowl to be passed at the table. The traditional dipping sauce is a mixture of concentrated grape syrup and wine vinegar. A reasonably good substitute is 5 ounces of balsamic vinegar mixed with 4 to 5 tablespoons water. Provide a small amount for each guest in a bowl or cup.

NANI-LAVASH
(Thin "Cracker" Bread)

This type of bread, common throughout the Middle East, is a very thin wafer or cracker about 16 to 18 inches in diameter. Although it is usually made with white flour, a blend of wheat and white flour is sometimes used as well. The yeast-leavened dough is rolled out to barely ⅛ inch thick and baked until crisp. It will keep for many weeks in a cool, dry place.

Lavash is eaten in its crisp, cracker form, but more often is used in a soft form. To prepare it, use any packaged lavash and sprinkle as many wafers as you are going to use liberally with water. Wrap the lavash in a large, clean dish towel and let rest for a couple of hours. The lavash will absorb the water and become a soft, pliable bread, somewhat like a flour tortilla in texture. Diners tear off pieces to use as a scoop for eating. Another common use is to make a sandwich, somewhat resembling a Mexican burrito, by rolling up food inside the bread.

FRESH FRUIT COMPOTE WITH ORANGE- OR ROSE-BLOSSOM PERFUME

Use any combination of fresh summer fruit to make this compote. Cantaloupe or honeydew balls mixed with sliced peaches are particularly refreshing. Season the fruit with a sprinkle of sugar, some lemon juice, and a few splashes of rose water or orange-blossom water, along with any juice that collects in the melon shells.

A Note on the Wines

The pronounced and complex flavors of the rock cod stuffed with nuts, dried fruits, and spices need an authoritative wine, one that will add flavors in a harmonious and enriching way. Our choice is a rich Sauvignon Blanc in the style made by the Napa Valley winery of Joseph Phelps.

Lamb and Zinfandel are a perfect combination. To go with this unusual dish of lamb stewed with pomegranate juice and walnuts, we suggest a classic Zinfandel, such as an older Napa Valley Louis M. Martini.

Ireland

❖

Green Pea Soup

Fillet of Sole Sautéed with Mushrooms

Rabbit Braised with Port Wine
Potatoes Baked in Butter and Beef Stock
Broccoli

Watercress Vinaigrette

Irish Soda Bread

Lemon Curd

Wines:
J. W. Morris Winery Sauvignon Blanc
Chateau Montelena Zinfandel

GREEN PEA SOUP
(SERVES 6)

1 fresh pig's foot
2 bay leaves
8 cups water
¾ cup dried split peas
¼ cup lentils
1 medium onion, chopped
2 stalks celery, chopped
1 teaspoon dried mint
salt and pepper

Put the pig's foot and bay leaves in a heavy Dutch oven or soup pot and cover with water. Bring to a boil, then turn down to a simmer. While the pig's foot is cooking, wash the peas and lentils. After the pig's foot has simmered for 1 hour, add the peas, lentils, onion, celery, and mint and simmer for another 45 to 60 minutes. Remove the pig's foot and cool. Cut away the meat and return meat to the pot.

If the soup becomes too thick during cooking, adjust by adding water. Taste the soup when it is done, and add salt and pepper as needed.

FILLET OF SOLE SAUTÉED WITH MUSHROOMS
(SERVES 6)

6 2–3-ounce fillets of sole
salt and white pepper
4 tablespoons butter
3–4 green onions, chopped
3 cups (about 6–8 ounces) sliced mushrooms
½ cup heavy cream
½ cup white wine
1 tablespoon fresh chopped fennel or 1 teaspoon dried dillweed

Season the sole with salt and white pepper. Heat the butter in a skillet. Sauté the sole over moderately high heat until it is very lightly browned on each side. Carefully remove the sole to a heated platter. Add the green onions and mushrooms to the pan and sauté for about 5 minutes, or until they are starting to brown. Add the cream and wine and boil briskly to reduce the pan juices to a light sauce about the consistency of heavy cream. Stir in the fennel or dill and spoon the sauce over the sole fillets.

RABBIT BRAISED WITH PORT WINE
(SERVES 6)

3 small or 2 medium rabbits
1 tablespoon butter
3 slices of bacon, halved
salt and pepper
flour
1 onion, chopped
2 cups chicken broth (page 36)
¼ teaspoon ground allspice
½ teaspoon dried thyme
½ cup white wine
½ cup port
2 tablespoons chopped fresh parsley

Disjoint the rabbits, reserving the front legs for soup or a family meal. Use only the saddles and hind legs.

Melt the butter in a large frying pan or dutch oven. Add the bacon and fry until it is about half done. Season the rabbit pieces with salt and pepper and dust them very lightly with flour, shaking off any excess. Add the rabbit to the pan and brown it in the fat, turning so that all sides are well colored.

While the rabbit is still browning, add the onion. When the rabbit has browned, add the chicken broth, allspice, and thyme. Cover and simmer slowly until the rabbit is tender, about 30 minutes. Using a slotted spoon, remove the rabbit pieces to a warm serving platter. Add the white wine and port to the pan and whisk over high heat until the sauce has somewhat reduced. Pour the sauce over the rabbit and garnish the dish with a sprinkle of parsley.

POTATOES BAKED IN BUTTER AND BEEF STOCK

Wash and peel 4 large baking potatoes and slice them very thin. Put them in a shallow baking pan, dot with about 4 tablespoons butter, and cover them with 1 to 2 cups beef stock (page 23). Cover the pan with a lid or foil and bake at 350°F until the potatoes are tender, 35 to 40 minutes. Remove the foil and sprinkle the potatoes with chopped parsley and about ¼ cup dry

bread crumbs. Place under the broiler until lightly browned.

BROCCOLI

Wash and trim a bunch of broccoli, cutting away any tough ends and stems. Cut the large pieces in half. Drop the broccoli carefully into a large pot of boiling salted water. Cover the pot with a clean dishcloth or cloth napkin—one that is old enough so that it won't matter if it becomes stained —and tuck the edges down into the water to prevent its burning. The cloth will allow the natural gases to escape but keep in the steam, a trick that ensures that the broccoli will cook uniformly and retain its bright green color. As soon as the stems are barely tender, drain the broccoli as dry as possible and place it in one layer in a low casserole or baking pan. Melt about 2 tablespoons butter and mix it with about ⅓ cup heavy cream (you can prepare this ahead, while the broccoli is cooking). Pour this mixture over the broccoli and broil for just a few minutes until it starts to brown.

WATERCRESS VINAIGRETTE

Pick over 2 bunches of watercress, discarding any yellow leaves and large stem ends. Cut or break the cress into pieces about 1½ to 2 inches long. Wash, drain well, and wrap the cress in a clean dishcloth. Put in the refrigerator to chill. Mix vinegar, paprika, a little chopped onion, salt, and pepper. Whisk in about 3 parts oil to 1 part vinegar. When ready to serve, put the cress in a salad bowl and toss it with the vinaigrette dressing.

IRISH SODA BREAD

(MAKES ONE 5-x-9-INCH LOAF)

> 1 cup whole-wheat flour
> 3 cups white bread or all-purpose flour
> 1½ teaspoons salt
> 1 teaspoon baking soda
> 1 tablespoon caraway seeds
> 1¾ cups buttermilk

DO AHEAD:

Oil a standard loaf pan (about 5 x 9 inches).

Preheat the oven to 350°F.

Blend all of the dry ingredients in a large mixing bowl. Add the buttermilk and mix with the dry ingredients by machine or by hand until the sides of the bowl come clean. If kneading with a machine with a dough hook, it should take about 2 minutes; if kneading by hand, 5 to 6 minutes.

Turn the dough out onto a lightly floured board and shape it into a loaf to fit the pan. With a razor or very sharp knife, cut a gash ¼ inch deep in the center and running the full length of the loaf.

Bake the bread on a rack positioned just below the center of the oven. After 45 to 50 minutes, take the loaf out of the pan and place it directly on the oven rack. Bake for five minutes longer to brown the bottom. Cool on a wire rack.

LEMON CURD

The lemon curd used as a base for the French Saffron Lemon Ice Cream is a lovely dessert on its own. Double the recipe (page 139) and serve it alone or over a slice of Génoise (page 120) topped with a bit of raspberry puree (defrost a package of frozen raspberries, puree in a blender, and pass through a sieve to remove the seeds).

A Note on the Wines

To go with the fillet of sole and mushroom sauté, we prefer a light-bodied, perfumed, and slightly herbaceous Sauvignon Blanc made in the style of J. W. Morris.

The bacony rabbit with its dark port wine sauce seems a perfect match for a medium- to full-bodied Zinfandel, one with rich fruit flavors, such as a Chateau Montelena.

Israel

❖

Cucumber Chowder

Chicken Breasts Sautéed with Kumquats and Honey

Grilled Tournedos of Beef with Mushrooms
Baked Caraway Potatoes
Summer Squash with Tomato and Lemon Juice

Mixed Green Salad

Challah

Walnut Sponge Cake with Marinated Strawberries

Wines:
Hagafen Johannisberg Riesling
Chateau Chevalier Pinot Noir

NOTE: There was no attempt in constructing this menu to follow the established dietary rules for kosher meals.

CUCUMBER CHOWDER
(SERVES 6)

> 2 tablespoons oil
> 1 medium leek (white only), chopped
> 1 tablespoon cornstarch
> ¼ cup cold water
> 6 cups chicken broth (page 36)
> 2 cucumbers, peeled, seeded, and diced
> 1 tablespoon chopped fresh dill, or 1
>   teaspoon dried
> 2 egg yolks
> juice of 1 lemon
> salt and white pepper

Heat the oil in a soup pot or Dutch oven. Add the chopped leek and sauté until it becomes translucent. Dissolve the cornstarch in the cold water and stir it into the pot. Add the broth. Simmer for about 20 minutes. Stir in the cucumber and dill and simmer for 5 minutes more. Remove from the heat.

In a small bowl whisk together the egg yolks and lemon juice. Add a ladle of the hot soup to the egg mixture and stir well. Return the egg mixture to the soup pot and stir well. Do not reheat or the eggs may curdle. Season the soup with salt and white pepper and serve immediately.

CHICKEN BREASTS SAUTÉED WITH KUMQUATS AND HONEY
(SERVES 6)

> 2 whole chicken breasts, split into halves
> 3 tablespoons vegetable oil
> salt
> flour
> 1 cup orange juice
> ½ cup white wine
> juice of 1 lemon
> 3 tablespoons honey
> ½ teaspoon ground ginger
> Tabasco sauce or cayenne pepper
> 12 kumquats, thinly sliced

Bone and skin the 4 halves of chicken breasts (or have the butcher do it for you). Each half breast consists of a large muscle and a smaller, elongated section that resembles a "fillet" or "supreme." Carefully pull the fillet away from each half. (See illustration, page 54.) Cut the remaining breast meat into 3 or 4 strips the same size as the fillet.

Heat the oil in a skillet. While it is heating, salt the chicken pieces and dust them very lightly with flour, shaking off any excess. (A good way to do this is to put the flour in a paper bag, add several pieces of chicken at a time, close the top, and shake well.) Sauté the chicken in the hot oil only until the pieces are heated through and have turned opaque. It is important to avoid overcooking them. Transfer the chicken pieces to a warm platter.

Add the orange juice, wine, lemon juice, honey, ginger, and Tabasco sauce to taste to the pan. Whisk to dissolve all the pan drippings and cook the mixture until it reduces to a light sauce. Add the kumquats and return the chicken pieces to the pan. Stir just enough to coat the chicken lightly with the sauce. Serve immediately.

GRILLED TOURNEDOS OF BEEF WITH MUSHROOMS
(SERVES 6)

6 6-ounce tournedos of beef (center cuts of
    filet mignon), denuded of fat and gristle
    and cut 1½–2 inches thick, or 6 7–8-
    ounce rib eye steaks
salt and pepper
4 tablespoons olive oil
juice of 1 lemon
3 cloves garlic, crushed
1 large onion, thinly sliced
½ pound mushrooms, sliced
½ cup red wine

DO AHEAD:

Place the tournedos side by side in a shallow pan and sprinkle them with salt and pepper. Mix 2 tablespoons olive oil with the lemon, garlic, and onion. Rub the mixture into the tournedos. Set them aside on a plate to marinate at room temperature for 1 hour.

Heat the remaining 2 tablespoons olive oil in a large skillet over high heat. Remove the tournedos from the marinade and reserve it. With a paper towel, wipe or blot the tournedos and add them to the pan.

Cook them to the preferred degree of doneness (about 8 minutes for rare, 10 to 12 minutes for medium). Remove them to a lightly heated platter and keep them warm.

Add the marinade and mushrooms to the skillet and stir-fry until the onions and mushrooms are lightly browned. Add the red wine. Raise the heat to high to burn off the alcohol quickly. Cook until the sauce reduces to a slightly creamy consistency, then spoon it over the reserved tournedos.

BAKED CARAWAY POTATOES

Bake 6 baking potatoes for 1 hour in a hot oven. When done, cut a gash across the top of each potato, add a dab of butter, and season with salt, pepper, paprika, and a sprinkle of caraway seeds. Top with a dollop of sour cream.

SUMMER SQUASH WITH TOMATO AND LEMON JUICE

Heat about 2 tablespoons butter or oil in a skillet and sauté 1 minced onion. Add 2 tomatoes that have been peeled (see Glossary) and cut up, and 2 crookneck and 2 zucchini squash that have been cut into ½-inch slices. Cook them, covered, until the squash is just barely tender. Season with salt, pepper, and the juice of half a small lemon.

MIXED GREEN SALAD
(SERVES 6)

1 head romaine lettuce
1 bunch parsley, stemmed and chopped
1 bunch green onions, chopped
1 red bell pepper, sliced or chopped
1 green bell pepper, sliced or chopped
3–4 radishes, sliced
1 carrot, peeled and thinly sliced

DRESSING:

1 clove garlic, crushed
1 teaspoon prepared mustard
salt and pepper
¼ teaspoon paprika
juice of 1 lemon
⅓ cup olive oil
2 eggs, hard-cooked and chopped

Wash and dry the romaine lettuce and tear it into pieces. Mix all the greens and vegetables together in a salad bowl.

To make the dressing, mix the garlic with the prepared mustard, salt and pepper, paprika, and lemon juice. Whisk in the olive oil, then add the hard-cooked eggs. Add the dressing to the salad bowl and toss.

CHALLAH
(MAKES TWO 1½- POUND LOAVES)

1 package of yeast, or 1 tablespoon dry yeast
1¼ cups warm milk
6 tablespoons butter, melted and cooled
3 tablespoons sugar
5 eggs: 4 whole, 1 separated (see Note)
6¼ cups white bread or all-purpose flour
2 teaspoons salt
1 tablespoon water
2 teaspoons sesame or poppy seeds

DO AHEAD:

Lightly oil a bowl for the dough.

In a large mixing bowl mix the yeast, milk, butter, sugar, 4 eggs, and 1 egg yolk. Add the flour and salt and mix slowly with the other ingredients until well blended.

Knead the dough by hand or machine. If by hand, turn it out on a floured board and work it until it is smooth and elastic, approximately 10 minutes. If using a dough hook on an electric mixer, knead the dough at the slowest speed for about 5 minutes.

Pat the dough into a ball and put it in the oiled bowl. Cover the dough with a kitchen towel and set it in a warm, draft-free place to rise until the dough has doubled in bulk, 60 to 75 minutes. (A perfect place is a gas oven with its slight heat given off by the pilot light; an electric oven, turned on low for no more than 2 minutes, then turned off, works equally well.)

When the dough has doubled, turn it out on a floured board, punch it down, and knead it again until there is no air left in it. Divide the dough in half, then divide each half into 3 equal pieces. Roll each piece into a "rope" about 18 inches long. Pinch 3 ropes together at one end. Braid them like a pigtail and pinch together the other end. Repeat with the remaining 3 ropes to make a second loaf. Place the braided loaves on the board, cover them again with a towel, and let rise until almost doubled, 40 to 50 minutes.

While the loaves are rising, preheat the oven to 375°F. Place a pie tin half filled with water on the bottom shelf. Position an oven rack just above the bottom rack. Flour a baking sheet or large baking pan.

Beat the egg white with 1 tablespoon water. When the loaves have risen, brush them with the egg white wash and sprinkle with the sesame or poppy seeds.

Gently pick up the loaves and transfer them to the baking sheet or pan and place it in the oven on the rack just above the bottom rack. Bake for 30 to 35 minutes. The crusts should be golden brown. Test the doneness by rapping the bottom with your knuckle. The loaf should feel firm and make a hollow sound. Cool on a wire rack.

NOTE: It is really worthwhile to get very fresh eggs from ranch chickens, if at all possible. The yolks are much darker and richer than regular commercial white eggs and the bread made with them has a deeper color and flavor.

WALNUT SPONGE CAKE WITH MARINATED STRAWBERRIES
(SERVES 8 TO 10)

CAKE:
   7 eggs
   1¼ cups sugar
   1½ cups all-purpose flour
   1¼ cups finely ground walnuts
   1 tablespoon cocoa powder
   1 teaspoon ground cinnamon
   4 tablespoons butter, melted and cooled

GARNISH:
   2 baskets of strawberries, washed, hulled, and cut in halves
   ½ cup sweet kosher wine or cream sherry
   sugar to taste

Preheat the oven to 375°F.

Half-fill a large skillet with water and set it to simmer on the stove (to be used as a bain marie or water bath for warming the eggs and sugar).

Crack the eggs into a stainless steel or Pyrex bowl that fits an electric mixer. Set the bowl over the simmering water, add the sugar, and whisk constantly until the sugar dissolves and the mixture turns golden yellow. Remove the bowl from the water bath and place it in the electric mixer. Beat at high speed until the eggs and sugar more than quadruple in volume and cool down, about 5 minutes.

While the eggs are whipping, in a small bowl mix together the flour, ground nuts, cocoa, and cinnamon. Fold the flour-nut mixture gently but quickly into the egg mixture. Finally, fold in the butter.

Pour the batter into an ungreased tube pan (see Note) and bake for about 35 minutes or until a toothpick inserted in the center comes out clean. Remove the cake from the pan and set it on a rack to cool.

Meanwhile, mix together the strawberries, wine, and some sugar to taste and put in the refrigerator to macerate for 30 to 60 minutes.

To serve, slice the cake into individual portions and spoon some of the marinated strawberries over each piece.

NOTE: You can also bake this cake in 3 standard-sized pans instead of in one tube pan, yielding 3 layers.

A Note on the Wines

The delicate, fruity, medium-bodied Hagafen Johannisberg Riesling is the type of white wine that is most harmonious with the chicken breasts cooked with kumquats. Unlike most kosher wines, which are generally sweet and made from Concord grapes, Hagafen Cellars' kosher wines are made from traditional varietal wine grapes in the style of other dry table wines. The White House served a Hagafen Johannisberg Riesling at a state dinner honoring Prime Minister Menachem Begin of Israel.

A good match for the tournedos of beef with mushrooms would be a Burgundian-style, medium-bodied Pinot Noir, such as those made by Chateau Chevalier.

Italy

❊

Bagna Cauda
(Warm Spicy Garlic Dip with Raw Vegetables)

Insalata di Frutti di Mare
(Marinated Seafood)

Gnocchi Verdi or Strangolapreti
(Spinach and Ricotta "Dumplings")

Osso Buco con Gremolata
(Braised Veal Shanks with Minced Lemon Peel, Garlic, and
Anchovy)
Zucchini

Prosciutto Bread

Macedonia di Frutta (Fruit Cup)
or
Fragole all'Aceto Balsamico e Pepe
(Strawberries with Balsamic Vinegar, Sugar, and Pepper)

Wines:
Capezzana Bianco
Ghemme Riserva Caldi

Most of the recipes for this Italian dinner came from Doris's book, *A Cook's Tour of Rome* (see Bibliography). The comments are hers as well.

BAGNA CAUDA

(Warm Spicy Garlic Dip with Raw Vegetables)

The Italians at home often make a wonderful hot anchovy dip, bagna cauda, to serve as an hors d'oeuvre. Here is a popular version: Heat (but do not boil) ¼ pound butter with 6 tablespoons of the best extra-virgin olive oil. Mince as thin as possible or crush with a pestle 6 to 12 cloves garlic, depending on their size and your taste. Add them to the hot oil, keeping the temperature still below boiling, and leave for about 10 minutes. Chop about 10 anchovy fillets into fine pieces and stir into the mix. Traditionally, raw vegetables, whole or cut into strips, are dipped into the sauce: fennel, green onions, mushrooms, celery, sweet peppers, cauliflower, cucumbers, carrots, radishes, and so on. Cooked artichoke leaves and hearts and cooked asparagus are also good. If you have a chafing dish or hot tray, use it to keep the sauce warm while serving.

*

INSALATA DI FRUTTI DI MARE
(Marinated Seafood)

(SERVES 6)

This salad combines as many types of seafood as you choose to use—clams, mussels, squid, octopus, lobster, prawns, shrimp—altogether about 3 cups of cleaned and precooked seafood. If you double the recipe, you will have enough for a main course at lunch or for a light dinner.

> 2–4 squid (enough to equal 2 cups cut up)
>   (see Notes)
> 1 cup small cooked shrimp (see Notes)
> 6 large cooked prawns
> 1 heart of romaine lettuce
> 1 small firm bunch celery, or 1 celery heart

SAUCE:
> ½ cup olive oil
> ¼ cup wine vinegar
> 1 tablespoon minced anchovy fillet
> ½ teaspoon Dijon-type mustard
> 2 pinches of powdered hot red pepper
> a few drops of Worcestershire sauce
> 1 clove garlic, finely minced
> a squeeze of fresh lemon
> salt and pepper

To prepare the squid, remove the ink sacs by cutting between the tentacles and eyes, remove the bone or quill, and pull off the skin. Clean thoroughly under running water until all extraneous matter has washed away. Cut the body into 1-inch pieces but leave the tentacles whole. Boil for 3 to 5 minutes, or until just tender; do not overcook or the squid will toughen.

Mix together all of the seafood in a large bowl. Wash the romaine (there should be about 6 to 8 leaves) and break into pieces about 2 inches in size. Wash the heart of celery or several firm stalks from the bunch and cut into small pieces. Add the lettuce and celery to the seafood.

Mix together all of the ingredients for the sauce, stir well, and pour over the salad. Mix well, then refrigerate until time to serve.

NOTES: Substitute cooked clams, mussels, lobster, or octopus for some of the squid and shrimp, according to your preference.

If you use mussels or clams, scrub them well and debeard the mussels. Put them to cook with a small amount of water until the shells open. Discard any that do not open. Remove from the pan immediately and remove the meats from the shell. If you use raw prawns or lobster, cook them in a bouillon of water, celery, carrot, onion, a sprig of parsley, garlic, salt and pepper, and white wine. Remove when the shells turn a good pink color and when the lobster meat is white and opaque. Remove from the shells. Cut the lobster into pieces.

*

GNOCCHI VERDI OR STRANGOLAPRETI
(Spinach and Ricotta "Dumplings")
(SERVES 6)

There are different kinds of gnocchi in different parts of Italy. The traditional Roman gnocchi are made of potatoes and the saying is *Giovedi gnocchi, sabato trippa* —"Thursday gnocchi, Saturday tripe." Romans also are partial to gnocchi made of semolina. Perhaps the most delicious of all are the green gnocchi of the north, more commonly called ravioli verdi (green ravioli) or malfatti ("roughly made"), a comment on the homemade character of their imperfect shape. In Milan, they are familiarly called strangolapreti, "priest-chokers," and that recipe is given here.

> 2 cups cooked chopped spinach, pressed as dry as possible (approximately 2 pounds trimmed fresh spinach or 3 boxes chopped frozen)
> 2 pounds ricotta cheese
> 4–6 heaping tablespoons freshly grated Parmesan cheese
> salt
> 3 egg yolks
> 3–4 tablespoons flour

SAUCE:
> Parmesan cheese
> ½ cup (1 stick) butter, melted (or heat butter until brown)

Mix the spinach and ricotta. Add the Parmesan cheese and salt to taste. Add the egg yolks and flour, mixing until well blended. The mixture should be fairly sticky. Flour your hands well and put a small mound of flour on a board. Using your palms, shape the dough into small rolls, 1½ to 2 inches long and ¾ to 1 inch thick. Roll them in the mound of flour to make egg shapes (the size of pigeon eggs). Put each finished dumpling on a floured tray.

Bring a large pot of salted water to a boil, then lower the heat to keep it barely bubbling or the gnocchi will fall apart. Cook the gnocchi in 2 or 3 batches, depending on the size of your pot, dropping them into the water one at a time as quickly as possible. They will quickly float to the surface when cooked. As they rise, scoop them out immediately with a slotted spoon and place on a warm platter. When all the gnocchi are done, cover them with a good dusting of grated Parmesan cheese and pour the melted butter over them. The Milanese always heat the butter until it is nicely browned.

VARIATIONS: Another sauce that goes well is melted butter, a few tablespoons heavy cream, and enough grated cheese to thicken it. It is common practice to add grated nutmeg or chopped fresh basil to the ricotta mixture, but try the unadorned recipe first.

NOTE: The gnocchi can be shaped, then reserved at room temperature for 1 to 2 hours before poaching; or 2 to 4 hours if stored in the refrigerator.

OSSO BUCO CON GREMOLATA
(Braised Veal Shanks with Minced Lemon Peel, Garlic, and Anchovy)
(SERVES 6)

VEAL:
6 veal shanks with the marrow
4 tablespoons butter, plus optional 2
  tablespoons
1 tablespoon olive oil
flour
salt and pepper
½ glass dry white wine
½–1 cup water

GREMOLATA:
1 or 2 tufts parsley
zest of ½ lemon
2 cloves garlic
2 anchovy fillets
3 or 4 tablespoons broth or water
optional: ½ pound mushrooms
    1 tablespoon butter
    1 small clove garlic, minced
    salt

Select a pan with high sides, one in which the veal shanks will fit comfortably next to each other. Melt the 4 tablespoons butter with the olive oil (the added oil will raise the heating point and prevent the butter from burning). Flour the veal lightly, shake off any excess flour, and put the shanks to cook over a medium-high fire. Sprinkle the top side with salt and pepper and cook until the bottom is well browned. Turn and season again. Continue turning the meat until all the sides are browned.

Add the dry white wine to the pot and continue cooking until the sauce is well reduced. Stir in ½ to 1 cup water, enough to keep the sauce thick but prevent it from burning, cover the pot, and cook over very low heat until the veal is tender, a good hour or more.

While the veal is cooking, prepare the gremolata: Mince the parsley, lemon zest, garlic, and anchovy and mix together. Reserve. If you plan to include the optional mushrooms, prepare them now: Clean and slice the mushrooms. Melt the tablespoon butter in a small skillet. Add the mushrooms and the minced garlic and sauté until lightly browned. Add salt to taste.

About 10 minutes before serving, add the gremolata to the veal shanks, turning them gently from time to time so that they will take on the flavors. After a few minutes, carefully remove the veal to a warm serving platter. Scrape the bottom of the pot with a wooden spoon, deglazing the scrapings with several spoons of broth or water. If you want a richer, smoother gravy, add an extra 2 tablespoons butter in lumps, blending them in with the spoon. If you are using the sautéed mushrooms, add them now. Cook only long enough to heat through and pour the sauce (and mushrooms) over the meat.

NOTE: The marrow is the prize of the dish, and there are special marrow spoons to help dig it out of the bone. A demitasse or other small spoon or a seafood fork will also work quite well.

ZUCCHINI

Wash 1 large or 2 to 3 small zucchini per person. Trim off the stem ends. Cut the smaller ones in quarters, the large ones in half midway down, then each half into quarters. Heat about 2 to 3 tablespoons olive oil in a skillet. Add the zucchini pieces and cook over moderately high heat, turning frequently to prevent burning. Add 1 or 2 cloves of finely chopped garlic and continue cooking. The zucchini should brown lightly. When they are just tender (test with the tip of a knife), sprinkle with a teaspoon of oregano and season with salt and pepper.

PROSCIUTTO BREAD
(MAKES TWO 1½-POUND LOAVES)

> 2 cups warm water
> 1 package of yeast, or 1 tablespoon dry
>   yeast
> 6 tablespoons fruity olive oil
> 6¼ cups white bread flour
> 1½ teaspoons salt
> 1 tablespoon broken-up rosemary
> 4 ounces prosciutto, thinly sliced and cut
>   into ½-inch strips (see Notes)

DO AHEAD:
Lightly oil a bowl for the dough.

Put the warm water into a large bowl, add the yeast, and let it stand for a few minutes until it is dissolved. Mix in the olive oil. Add the flour and mix them in. Add the salt and rosemary and mix them in. Knead the dough for 2 to 3 minutes. Mix in the prosciutto.

Turn the dough out onto a floured board and knead it by hand for 5 to 6 minutes, or until smooth and elastic, or use a dough hook and an electric mixer and knead for about 3 minutes. Shape the dough into a ball and place it in the oiled bowl. Cover the dough with a kitchen towel and set it in a warm, draft-free place to rise until it has doubled, 45 to 60 minutes.

Turn the dough out onto a floured surface, punch it down, and knead until there is no air left in it. Return the dough to the bowl, cover it, and let it rise a second time, 20 to 30 minutes, or until it is doubled in volume.

Turn the dough out onto the floured surface. Divide it into 2 lumps. Roll each lump into a rope about 24 inches long. Bring the two ends of each rope together to form a large ring or doughnut shape, pinching the ends so that they hold together (this is sometimes easier if you let one end overlap the other). Let the loaves rise for 20 to 25 minutes, or until doubled in size.

While the loaves are rising, preheat the oven to 375°F. Place a rack just above the center of the oven. Lightly flour a baking sheet large enough to hold both loaves, or use 2 sheets (see Notes). Place a pie tin half filled with water on the bottom shelf.

Gently pick up the loaves and transfer them to the baking sheets. Place in the oven and bake for 40 to 45 minutes. Test for doneness by rapping the bottom of the loaf with your knuckle. It should feel firm and make a hollow sound. Cool on a wire rack.

NOTES: The shank end or "heel" of the prosciutto is frequently sold at a much lower price than the large center slices. If you buy the shank for this recipe, ask the butcher to remove the rind and grind the prosciutto.

If the breads do not fit on one baking sheet, it is better to use 2 baking sheets and bake in 2 ovens, or in 2 separate batches, one after the other.

MACEDONIA DI FRUTTA
(Fruit Cup)

There is really no exact recipe for this Italian improvement on the fruit cocktail. Its nature and flavor change with the fruits in season, but a good macedonia depends on 3 things: an adequate variety of mature fruit cut into large chunks and sugared well; a serving temperature that is refreshingly cool; and the addition of maraschino liqueur. Some cooks substitute Marsala or white wine, but maraschino is the traditional and characteristic ingredient. In the summer, Italians often eat macedonia with a scoop of ice cream on top.

FRAGOLE ALL'ACETO BALSAMICO E PEPE
(Strawberries with Balsamic Vinegar, Sugar, and Pepper)

The first time I saw strawberries with vinegar was on a menu at Al Moro in Rome. Of course, I thought it was a mistake or at least a euphemism, but they were absolutely serious, and I discovered that this is one of the most delicious of all ways to prepare fresh strawberries, particularly the tiny wild berries—if you are ever lucky enough to find them. Last summer, to add gilding to the lily, my waiter at Ristorante da Ivo in Venice asked if I wanted black pepper with my vinegared berries. How could I not try? The result was even more delicious. This is the recipe: Wash and cut up 1 pint of fully ripe strawberries. Add several splashes of balsamic vinegar (do not substitute) and several teaspoons sugar.

Grind on a good quantity of black pepper, a dozen twists of the pepper mill at the very least. Mix all together until well blended. The berries can repose for a few minutes or can be served immediately. Magically, no overt trace of vinegar or pepper remains, only the intensified perfume of the berries. Experiment with a small batch to work out the proportions. You may use more vinegar and pepper than you expect.

A Note on the Wines

With the marinated seafood salad, a good choice would be a light, crisp, white wine from Italy, such as a Capezzana Bianco.

Another Italian wine that would be a fitting accompaniment to the osso buco is a well-aged, mature dry red, such as a Ghemme Riserva from Caldi.

Jamaica

✻

Callaloo
(Crab and Greens Soup)

Cinderella's Coach
(Squash Filled with Shrimp, Coconut, and Rice)

Roast Pork Calypso
(Glazed Roast Pork Loin)
Cornmeal Coo-Coo
(Cornmeal and Okra Cake)
Plantains

Les Achards
(Poached Vegetables in Oil and Chili Pepper Dressing)

Rolls

Gisadas
(Custard Tarts)

Wines:
Heitz Cellars Chardonnay
Château Haut Bergey

The inspiration for the Monday Night Jamaican dinner came largely from Foods of the World, *The Cooking of the Caribbean Islands* © 1970 Time-Life Books, Inc. We adapted the recipes here, except for the salad and custard tarts, from that volume.

CALLALOO
(Crab and Greens Soup)
(SERVES 6)

In the Caribbean, callaloo is the name for the young leaves of the taro plant and for the greens also known as Chinese spinach, as well as for the lively soup made from them. Since these greens are not widely available in the United States, we have substituted spinach or any combination of spinach and chard or New Zealand spinach.

1 large or 2 small bunches spinach, or 1
  bunch spinach and 1 bunch chard or
  New Zealand spinach
3 tablespoons butter
1 small onion, finely chopped
1 clove garlic, minced
6 cups chicken stock or broth (page 36)
½ cup coconut cream, homemade (page
  61) or canned
salt and pepper
½ pound fresh crab meat
Tabasco sauce

Wash and trim the greens and cut them into shreds. Reserve.

Melt the butter in a large soup pot over moderate heat. Add the onion and garlic and cook until they become limp and translucent, but do not allow them to brown. Add the shredded greens, stirring them around with a wooden spoon until they are softened and coated with the butter and onions. Add the stock, coconut cream, and salt and pepper. Simmer the soup for about 10 minutes, or until the greens are tender. Add the crab meat and several dashes of Tabasco sauce and cook just long enough for the crab meat to heat through.

CINDERELLA'S COACH
(Squash Filled with Shrimp, Coconut, and Rice)
(SERVES 6)

This recipe, a prizewinner in the Jamaican Culinary Arts Competition a few years ago, took its name from the form in which it was presented: a half of a large pumpkin squash became the body of the coach; whole prawns became horses, drawing the coach on reins of coconut fiber; a lettuce leaf formed a seat for the prawn coachman; and 4 thick slices of tomato turned into the coach's wheels.

1 pound small or medium shrimp, shelled
½ cup fresh tomatoes, peeled (see
  Glossary), seeded, and finely chopped
4 green onions (white part only), finely
  chopped

2 tablespoons dark rum
1 tablespoon soy sauce
½ teaspoon chopped fresh chili pepper
3 large crookneck squash
2½ cups coarsely chopped fresh coconut
2½ cups hot water
salt
1 cup raw long-grain white rice
3 tablespoons butter
6 medium prawns, boiled, shelled,
  deveined, and reserved

DO AHEAD:
Marinate the shrimp-tomato mixture for 1 hour (see instructions).

Combine the shrimp with ¼ cup tomatoes, half of the green onions, 1 tablespoon rum, the soy sauce, and the chili pepper. Marinate at room temperature for an hour.

Meanwhile, cut the squash in half lengthwise. Scoop out the pulp and discard the seeds and stringy fibers. Chop the pulp (you should have about 1 cup of raw chopped squash), and reserve. Poach the hollowed-out squash shells in boiling salted water until they are barely tender but still quite firm. Remove the halves carefully, invert, and drain them until they are dry.

Prepare the coconut puree: Using a blender or food processor, puree the chopped fresh coconut, hot water, and salt until they are well blended. Empty the mixture into a large saucepan and add the reserved chopped raw squash. Bring the mixture to a boil, lower the heat, and simmer until the squash is tender, about 10 minutes, stirring frequently. Add the re-

maining ¼ cup tomatoes, the rest of the green onions, and the remaining 1 tablespoon dark rum. Bring to a boil again. Stir in the rice, cover, lower the heat, and simmer until the rice has absorbed all the liquid in the pan, about 20 to 25 minutes. Set aside.

Preheat the oven to 375°F. Butter a pan or shallow casserole.

Melt 1 tablespoon butter in a skillet. Add the marinated shrimp-tomato mixture, and sauté briefly until the shrimp turn color. Set aside.

Fill each prepared squash shell with some of the rice mixture. Top the rice with the sautéed shrimp-tomato mixture. Break the remaining 2 tablespoons butter into bits and dot the tops of the filled squash shells. Place the squash side by side in the pan or casserole. Bake until heated through and the tops take on a golden color, about 15 minutes. Remove to a serving platter or individual plates.

Decorate the neck of each squash with one of the reserved prawns held in place with a toothpick (this represents the driver of the coach).

ROAST PORK CALYPSO
(Glazed Roast Pork Loin)
(SERVES 6 TO 8)

> 1 6-pound center-cut pork loin, on the fat
>   side
> 2 cups chicken stock (page 36)

GLAZE:

> 1 cup light brown sugar
> 2 tablespoons dark rum
> 2 teaspoons finely chopped garlic
> 2 teaspoons ground ginger
> ½ teaspoon ground cloves
> 1 bay leaf, crumbled
> 1 teaspoon salt
> ¼ teaspoon pepper
>
> 2 teaspoons arrowroot combined with 1
>   tablespoon cold water until smooth
> ½ cup light rum
> 3 tablespoons strained fresh lime juice
> lime slices

Preheat the oven to 375°F.

Score the fat layer covering the pork loin in the same way you would score a ham. Roast the loin for 1 hour until it is golden brown. Skim the fat from the juices in the pan. Mix the chicken stock into the skimmed pan juices and set aside.

Mash the brown sugar with the rest of the glaze ingredients. Spread this paste evenly over the scored side of the pork. Return the meat to the oven and roast for another 30 minutes, or until the surface is crusty and brown. Remove the meat to a carving board.

Bring the pan juices and stock to a boil on the top of the stove. Stir in the mixture of arrowroot and water and cook, stirring, until the sauce thickens. Warm the rum and ignite it. When the flames recede, stir the rum into the thickened sauce. Add the strained lime juice and keep warm.

Carve the meat and spoon a bit of sauce over each portion. Garnish with fresh lime slices. Pass the remaining sauce separately.

CORNMEAL COO-COO
(Cornmeal and Okra Cake)
(SERVES 6)

> ½ pound fresh okra
> 2 cups water
> 1 teaspoon salt
> 1 cup yellow cornmeal
> 2 tablespoons butter, softened

Scrape the okra skin lightly to remove any surface fuzz. Cut off the stems and slice the okra into ¼-inch rounds. In a large saucepan combine the okra, water, and salt and bring to a boil. Lower the heat and simmer for 10 minutes, until the okra is tender but not mushy. Stirring constantly, pour the cornmeal into the okra in a slow steady stream. Continue cooking over low heat until the mixture is thick enough to leave the bottom and sides of the pan in a solid mass. This should take about 5 minutes. Turn out onto a large plate and shape the mixture into a round cake 1 inch thick and 8 inches in diameter. Spread the top with the softened butter and cut the cake into wedges for serving.

PLANTAINS

Plantains, which look like large green bananas, are related to that fruit, but because they are less sweet and must be cooked for eating, they are frequently served as a kind of vegetable.

Peel 3 ripe plantains and slice them on the diagonal into ¼-inch-thick ovals. Heat ¼ cup peanut or vegetable oil in a skillet, add the plantain slices, and fry over moderately high heat for about 4 minutes on each side so that they color evenly without burning. Drain on paper towels and serve immediately.

LES ACHARDS
(Poached Vegetables in Oil and Chili Pepper Dressing)

Wash and trim or shell 3 or 4 vegetables of your choice: peas, carrots, broccoli, string beans, cauliflower. Cut into large pieces or divide into flowerettes. Bring a large pot of water to a boil, add salt, and, one at a time, poach each kind of vegetable until it is just tender, removing the pieces in turn to a sieve or colander and refreshing under cold running water. Drain the vegetables well and turn into a large bowl.

Heat ¾ cup oil to the boiling point and turn off the fire. Add a small finely chopped onion, salt, coarsely ground black pepper, and 1 to 2 chopped fresh chili peppers or ½ teaspoon or more dried red pepper flakes. Toss the hot dressing with the poached vegetables and serve in individual lettuce cups.

ROLLS

Plain hard rolls are good with this dinner, the crust adding a nice bit of texture to a menu of mostly soft dishes. Use the recipe for Baguettes, Épines, Rolls (page 119).

GISADAS
(Custard Tarts)
(SERVES 6)

> 4 eggs
> 4 tablespoons brown sugar
> 2¼ cups evaporated milk
> 1 teaspoon vanilla extract
> 6 individual tart shells filled with any flaky pie dough or Danish Waffle dough (page 95)

Preheat the oven to 350°F.

Mix the eggs well with the sugar, milk, and vanilla.

Fill the prepared tart shells, put them on a cookie sheet, and bake for about 30 minutes, or until the crusts brown well—essential for the flakiness of the crust—and the custard is firmly set. (Test with a toothpick to the center; the custard is set when it comes out clean.)

A Note on the Wines

To carry the rather complex flavors of shrimp, coconut milk, soy sauce, rum, and chili peppers that are used for stuffing the squash for Cinderella's Coach, we suggest a rich, full, dry Chardonnay in the style made by the Heitz Napa Valley winery.

For the pork calypso, the right wine should be assertive enough to handle the glaze of rum, garlic, ginger, and brown sugar, but light enough to complement the pork without overwhelming it. An earthy red wine from a light vintage, such as a Château Haut Bergey, 1971, from the Graves region of Bordeaux, would be just the thing.

Japan

❀

Tuna Sashimi

Clear Clam Soup

Japanese Pickled Cabbage
(Tsukemono)

Duck Teriyaki
Blanched Spinach with Toasted Sesame Seeds
Steamed Rice

Hot Egg Custard with Shrimp and Chicken

Wines:
Domaine Chandon Blanc de Noirs
Stanford Hermitage

TUNA SASHIMI
(SERVES 6)

Sashimi is made from any firm-fleshed ocean fish, tuna being one of the most popular. Whatever fish is used—tuna, sea bass, swordfish, halibut—it must be absolutely fresh and odorless. Many fish dealers are accustomed to slicing fish for sashimi, but if your dealer is not, you can prepare it easily yourself.

> 3 6–8-ounce 1-inch-thick fillets of tuna, sea bass, swordfish, halibut, or other firm-fleshed ocean fish
> 6 large lettuce leaves, very finely shredded

DIPPING SAUCE:
> 2 tablespoons sake (Japanese rice wine)
> 2–3-inch piece of daikon (white Japanese radish) (see Note)
> 2 to 3 green onions
> 1/4 cup soy sauce
> juice of 1 lemon
> dash of 7-pepper spice (hichimi togarashi) (see Note)
>
> 3 teaspoons wasabi (green horseradish powder)
> water

Skin the fish fillets. Chill them before slicing. Using a very well sharpened wet knife, cut the fish evenly into pieces no thicker than 1/8 inch (about the thickness of a 50-cent piece) and approximately 2 inches long, 3 to 4 ounces per portion. Arrange the slices on each dish in a neat, overlapping pattern over a bed of the very finely shredded lettuce. Serve with individual small dishes of dipping sauce.

To make the dipping sauce (this is the recipe we used for the restaurant's Monday Night Japanese dinner), warm the sake, remove it from the heat, and ignite it. When the flame burns out, the alcohol has burned off. Pour the sake into a bowl and set aside. While it is cooling, grate enough of the daikon to make about 1/2 cup and add it to the cooled sake. Use the same type grater as for lemon rind, which will make the required fine mushy texture; or puree the daikon in a blender or food processor. Add the green onions sliced as thin as possible. Season the sake mixture with the soy sauce, the lemon juice, and, if available, a liberal dash of 7-pepper spice. Mix well.

Wasabi mixed with water to make a thick paste is often served in a small mound alongside the sashimi and added to the dipping sauce to enliven it, or is diluted with soy sauce and used directly. It is very strong, so use sparingly.

NOTES: Daikon is available at oriental markets and at many regular produce markets as well. If you cannot find it, a small mild turnip is a close substitute.

If you cannot find 7-pepper spice, use black or red pepper.

CLEAR CLAM SOUP
(SERVES 6)

> 18 clams
> 6 cups cold water
> 1 large piece (about 4 x 8 inches) of giant
>   kelp (konbu), washed
> 1 ounce dried bonita (hana-katsuo or
>   katsuobushi)
> 6 tiny sprigs watercress, 1 inch long
> 6 thin slices of lime

DO AHEAD:

Scrub the clams very carefully, then put them in a stainless steel or glass bowl. Put a Chinese cleaver in the bowl (or 2 or 3 nails, if you do not have a cleaver). Cover with cold water and set aside for about 2 hours. (The iron in the cleaver or nails causes the sand to flush out more readily into the water.)

While the clams are soaking, prepare the stock. Put the 6 cups cold water and kelp in a large soup pot or Dutch oven and heat very slowly, for 10 to 15 minutes. To prevent off-flavors, remove the kelp as soon as the water comes to a boil. Add the bonita, return to a boil, and remove immediately from the heat. Let the broth rest until the bonita settles completely to the bottom. Strain the broth and reserve the kelp and bonita for the spinach dish in this menu.

Place a sprig of watercress and a slice of lime in each soup bowl and put them at the side of the stove. Remove the clams from the soaking water and rinse them off. Bring the broth to a rapid boil, add the clams, and cook only until the shells have opened. Place 3 clams in each bowl. Carefully ladle the broth into the bowls, being careful not to stir up any sand that may have settled to the bottom of the pot. Serve immediately.

JAPANESE PICKLED CABBAGE
(Tsukemono)
(SERVES 10 TO 12)

Tsukemono means "pickled things," which traditionally are served with plain steamed rice toward the end of a meal less complicated than the one prepared here. The pickling takes several days.

> 1 small head Napa cabbage
> 1/3 cup rock salt or sea salt
> 1/2 teaspoon crushed red pepper flakes
> 2–3 cloves garlic, chopped

Wash and quarter the cabbage. Separate the leaves and remove any tough portions. In an enamel or glass bowl, layer the cabbage leaves, first shaking off any excess moisture, then sprinkling each leaf with salt, red pepper, and garlic. When all the leaves are salted, cover them with a lid that fits as tightly as possible inside the bowl. Weight the lid with a few large filled cans, a baking dish filled with water, a brick, or any other similar device. Put to marinate for 3 to 4 days in a cool place such as a garage, back porch, or unheated room.

After 3 or 4 days, remove the weights and place the covered bowl in the refrigerator.

To prepare for serving, rinse the amount you will need quickly but not thoroughly, squeeze as dry as possible, cut into ½-inch slices, and arrange in a serving dish.

DUCK TERIYAKI
(SERVES 6)

Shizuo Tsuji, the great master chef of Japanese cooking, says that duck "is generally regarded as too heavy or too overpowering in taste to be eaten often." He tells us that it is mostly eaten in one-pot meals or grilled teriyaki-style and that mainly the breast meat is used. Duck is always combined with other strong-flavored ingredients such as green onions or ginger. The recipe below is an example of a simple teriyaki preparation.

Allow time for the duck to marinate before cooking.

3 whole duck breasts, boned (page 54)
½ cup Japanese soy sauce
2 tablespoons sugar
1 cup sake or dry or medium sherry
pepper
1 2-inch piece of gingerroot, thinly sliced
12 green onions

DO AHEAD:
Some time before you are ready to cook, preheat the broiler or build a good charcoal fire.

Remove the skin of the duck breast. Cut each breast in half, then into 3 equal sections, making 18 pieces altogether. Reserve.

In a bowl large enough to hold the duck mix together the soy sauce, sugar, sake, pepper, and gingerroot. Add the duck pieces and turn them in the marinade so that they are well coated. Trim the root ends of the green onions and cut off some of the green stems, leaving about 3 inches. Add them to the duck and turn to coat them with the marinade. Place in the refrigerator to marinate for at least 30 minutes before using.

To cook, skewer pieces of duck and green onion and grill about 3 inches from the flame. Broil the duck for 3 to 4 minutes. Brush with the marinade, turn, and broil the second side until it is a good color. It should take a total of 6 to 8 minutes to broil the breasts, depending on their thickness. Take care—the meat should remain rosy in the center and not dry out. Remove the skewers and serve.

BLANCHED SPINACH WITH TOASTED SESAME SEEDS
(SERVES 6)

The Japanese make their usual stock from dried kelp and dried, shaved bonita, then use some of the cooked ingredients over again to make a weaker stock for cooking vegetables. In this recipe, the spinach is cooked in water, then dressed with the weaker stock. If you are making the complete Japanese dinner here, you can make the soup stock first, then use some of the cooked kelp and dried bonita for the second stock, niban dashi.

STOCK:

reserved cooked kelp and bonita from
Clear Clam Soup (page 196)
5 cups cold water
¼ cup dried uncooked bonita

2 bunches spinach
1 tablespoon black sesame seeds
½ teaspoon sugar
1 teaspoon Japanese soy sauce

Combine the cooked kelp and bonita with the cold water and bring to a boil. Add the dried uncooked bonita and barely simmer for 5 minutes. Rinse and squeeze out a piece of cheesecloth and set it in a fine mesh sieve. Strain the stock through the cheesecloth. You can use the stock immediately or make it as much as 2 days ahead and store it in the refrigerator.

Wash and pick over the spinach, cut off the stems, and put the leaves in a large pan with only the water that clings to them. Cover and cook over high heat. As soon as the leaves become limp, turn the spinach over and cook for another minute. The total cooking time is 2 to 4 minutes, just

enough for the spinach to become tender. Remove it immediately from the heat and drain in a colander under cold running water. Squeeze the leaves dry and cut the spinach into 1-inch ribbons. Reserve.

Toss the black sesame seeds in a hot skillet until they are toasted, being careful not to burn them. Reserve. Mix ¼ cup of the reserved stock with the sugar and soy sauce and bring just to a boil, then set aside to cool.

When ready to serve, toss the sauce with the cooked spinach leaves. Serve in individual bowls with a garnish of toasted sesame seeds over the top.

STEAMED RICE

The Japanese prefer rice that is slightly sticky. To make 6 cups, put 3 cups short-grained rice with 3½ cups water in a heavy kettle. Soak the rice for about 1 hour. Put the pot over high heat and bring to a boil, then lower the heat to low-moderate, cover the pot, and continue cooking for another 10 minutes. Turn off the heat and let the rice stand for 10 minutes. Do not lift the lid once the pot has been covered. It is normal when rice is cooked this way for the grains to clump together. If you prefer fluffy rice, use the rice recipe given with the Chinese menu.

✳

HOT EGG CUSTARD WITH SHRIMP AND CHICKEN
(SERVES 6)

½ large chicken breast, about 6–8 ounces, skinned and boned
6 medium shrimp, peeled and deveined
1 tablespoon Japanese soy sauce

CUSTARD:
6 eggs
4 cups chicken broth (page 36)
1 tablespoon sake or medium sherry

4–6 fresh water chestnuts, peeled and sliced (or use peeled, canned water chestnuts)
½ cup sliced shiitake mushrooms (or use regular mushrooms)
2 green onions, chopped
4 tablespoons fresh green peas
1 piece of gingerroot, peeled and grated (6 teaspoons)

Cut the chicken breast into ½-inch cubes, put them in a bowl, and add the shrimp. Mix in the soy sauce and marinate for 10 to 15 minutes. Drain the chicken and shrimp and reserve them in a bowl. Reserve the soy sauce separately.

To make the custard, beat the eggs in a large mixing bowl. In a second bowl mix the broth, the reserved soy sauce, and the sake or sherry. Mixing gently, incorporate the seasoned broth into the beaten eggs. Skim off any surface foam.

Divide the chicken, shrimp, water chestnuts, mushroom slices, green onions, and peas among six 8-ounce custard cups or ovenproof bowls. Ladle the custard mixture into the cups and cover each one with aluminum foil. If you have a steamer, arrange the cups on the rack, bring the water to a boil, cover, and steam for about 20 minutes, or until the custard is firm. Or put the foil-covered cups in a low baking dish, fill with water halfway up the sides of the custard cups, and bake in a hot oven (400°F) for about 30 minutes, or until the custard is firm.

To serve, remove the foil covers and garnish each portion of custard with grated ginger.

A Note on the Wines

The traditional choice to accompany a meal in Japan would be beer or warm sake. If you prefer to serve wine, as we did with all the Monday Night dinners at the restaurant, a very harmonious accompaniment to the subtle tuna and the light clam soup would be a Domaine Chandon Blanc de Noirs, a sparkling wine with a very attractive "eye of the partridge" color and a rich Pinot Noir bouquet.

To complement the richness of the duck, an intense, heavy Rhone wine such as a Stanford Hermitage would be a good choice. An alternative would be a full-bodied Zinfandel.

Lithuania

✿

Marinated Herring

Cucumbers in Sour Cream

Cheese Dumplings

Grilled Lamb Loin Marinated in Buttermilk
Grated Potato Pudding
Sautéed Beet Tops

Strass Rye Bread
White Bread

Tree Cake
(Arbata)

Wines:
Firestone Vineyard Johannisberg Riesling
Rutherford Hill Winery Merlot

MARINATED HERRING

The first course of this Lithuanian dinner presents the marinated herring and the cucumber salad on the same plate as an hors d'oeuvre. Use any good brand of commercial herring or herring sold in bulk in a good delicatessen. Arrange a portion on each plate and garnish it with chopped green onion tops. Divide the cucumber salad (recipe below) among the plates. Serve with a slice or two of Strass rye bread alongside.

CUCUMBERS IN SOUR CREAM

Peel 3 medium cucumbers, slice them paper thin, and put them in a bowl. Mix together 1 tablespoon salt, 2 tablespoons sugar, ½ teaspoon pepper, 2½ tablespoons finely minced fresh dill, and ½ cup white wine vinegar. Add the dressing mixture to the cucumbers, stir well, and marinate for 1 hour. Thoroughly drain the cucumbers, pressing out any excessive moisture, and mix them with ⅔ cup sour cream. Chill well before serving.

CHEESE DUMPLINGS
(SERVES 6)

1 cup all-purpose flour
2 eggs
½ teaspoon salt, plus more if needed

½ cup fresh goat cheese, ricotta, or baker's or farmer's cheese
3 green onions, including half the green tops, minced
1 teaspoon minced fresh mint leaves, or ½ teaspoon dried
2 tablespoons minced fresh parsley
2 tablespoons butter, melted
1 cup sour cream

DO·AHEAD:

Put the flour, eggs, and ½ teaspoon salt in a mixing bowl. Blend with an electric mixer, pastry blender, or fork until the mixture forms a dough. Shape the dough into a ball, dust it with flour, wrap it in plastic wrap, and let it rest for 30 minutes in the refrigerator.

Roll the dough on a floured pastry board into a very thin round, 18 to 20 inches in diameter. Using a cookie cutter or the rim of a drinking glass dipped in flour, cut out 24 circles about 2½ inches in diameter.

Mix the cheese, green onions, mint, and 1 tablespoon parsley. Adjust the seasoning with salt. Spoon about 1 tablespoon of cheese filling in the center of each of 12 dough circles. Moisten the edges with your finger or a pastry brush dipped in water. Cover each dough circle with another and press to crimp the edges to form small round dumplings that resemble little hats.

Cook the dumplings in a large pot of boiling salted water. Do not overcrowd or they will not rise to the surface. Boil for 8 to 10 minutes, or until tender. Using a slotted spoon, remove the dumplings to a warm platter. Toss gently with the melted butter and the remaining tablespoon parsley. Garnish with dollops of sour cream.

NOTE: If you have any dumplings left over, reheat them in a sauce made by blending 4 tablespoons sour cream into 8 tablespoons (1 stick) melted butter, without allowing it to boil.

GRILLED LAMB LOIN MARINATED IN BUTTERMILK
(SERVES 6)

MARINADE:
> 10–12 whole juniper berries
> 10–12 whole allspice
> ½ teaspoon red pepper flakes, or ¼
>   teaspoon cayenne pepper
> 1 medium onion, coarsely cut
> 3 cloves garlic
> 1 teaspoon salt
> juice of 1 lemon
> 2 cups buttermilk

> 2 lamb loins, flap removed, and fat
>   trimmed to a paper-thin layer (the
>   butcher can prepare this for you)

Puree all of the marinade ingredients in a blender.

Put the lamb loins in a stainless steel or glass bowl and pour the mixture over them. Marinate at room temperature for 3 to 4 hours or overnight in the refrigerator.

An hour or so before you are ready to cook, build a good charcoal fire (or you can cook the meat under the broiler). Remove the meat from the marinade and wipe it as dry as possible. Grill the meat to medium rare. The center should remain moist and pink.

GRATED POTATO PUDDING

Wash and peel 2 pounds boiling potatoes, then grate them into a bowl. Heat some butter in a skillet and sauté 1 chopped onion until it is nicely browned. Add it to the grated potatoes. Mix in 2 eggs, salt, white pepper, and a pinch of nutmeg.

Melt 4 tablespoons (½ stick) butter and pour it into an 8-inch round frying pan or pie tin. Turn the potatoes into the pan, smooth the top, and bake in a 400° F oven until the potatoes are browned, about 20 minutes. Remove from the oven and invert them onto a serving plate (put the plate upside down over the potatoes; using potholders, grasp the plate and pot firmly with both hands and with a firm, deliberate motion, turn the pot upside down. The potato cake should turn out onto the plate). Very carefully slide the potatoes back into the frying pan or pie tin. Continue baking in the hot oven until the top is nicely browned, approximately 20 minutes more.

SAUTÉED BEET TOPS

Wash, trim, and remove the coarse ribs from enough beet tops to make about 6 cups when chopped. Boil the tops in salted water until they are tender. Drain them well and finely chop. While the tops are cooking, chop 4 strips of bacon and sauté them until they are brown. Add 1 chopped onion to the pan, stirring over moderate heat until the onions brown lightly. Stir in 3 tablespoons flour and mix well until the onions are evenly coated. Add water, 1 tablespoon at a time, stirring in well to make a thick sauce. Add the chopped beet tops and season with salt and pepper. Lower the heat and simmer just enough to heat through.

STRASS RYE BREAD
WHITE BREAD

We suggest serving 2 breads with the Lithuanian dinner. The first, Strass Rye Bread from the Germany menu, should go along with the herring and cucumbers in sour cream. Bulgarian White Bread from the Bulgaria menu can accompany the rest of the meal.

TREE CAKE
(Arbata)

Several countries make versions of this cake, a mixture of large quantities of well-beaten eggs, sugar, and butter, drizzled slowly onto a rotating spit over an open fire. The batter cooks as it spirals, the irregular layer upon layer resembling some-

what the shape of a coniferous tree. The finished cake is about 1½ feet long. White icing laced in narrow undulating ribbons creates the effect of snow and the cake can be decorated with anything seasonal, from holly to a wreath of fresh flowers.

The Germans call the cake Baumkuchen, pyramid cake. In Sweden, where it is a specialty of Skåne, the name is spettekaka—spit cake. Those of you who have been in Paris during the Christmas season may have seen a variety of the tree cake dusted with confectioners' sugar in the windows of Fauchon, the most famous food store in Paris. These days this cake, baked for traditional or special occasions, is more and more created in the bakery than in the home.

Because the Monday Night Lithuanian dinner was a special occasion in honor of Jerry Budrick, a friend from that country and now a partner in Chez Panisse restaurant, the dessert had to be a tree cake. Although the procedure for making it is complicated for the home baker, we have tried it at home as well as at the restaurant and, although difficult, it actually does work. For the brave of heart who want to experiment, here is the recipe. Make a batter by doubling the recipe for Génoise (page 120) and then proceed as follows:

SPIT METHOD (USING AN OPEN FIRE):
Build a very hot fire in your fireplace or barbecue pit. If you have a revolving spit for barbecuing, this will work best. Otherwise you will have to rig up some kind of

rod that can be turned by hand (2 people taking turns, one dispensing the batter, the other turning the spit, and then shifting jobs when tired, will probably be better than one person working alone). Place the spit or rod over the fire so that it will be hot before you begin to bake the cake. Then, using a large spoon or a pitcher, slowly dribble the batter onto the spit, revolving it continuously over the hot fire. Move a small saucepan along under the spit to catch any batter that drips off.

Each layer should be very thin so that it will bake and brown slightly before the next layer is added. The batter should cover about 1½ feet of the length of the spit. Try to apply the batter so that the final form will be somewhat conical in shape, having fewer layers at the crown than at the base. When all of the successive layers have baked and the batter is used up, the diameter of the largest part of the cake should be about 8 inches. Remove the spit from the direct heat and allow the cake to cool. (Suspending the spit between the backs of 2 chairs protected by potholders is a safe way to do this.)

Remove the cooled cake very carefully from the spit and place it on a serving plate on its side, like a log. Drizzle any favorite white icing over the cake in lacy, undulating ribbons; or dust the cake with confectioners' sugar put through a sieve. Decorate the top with flowers or seasonal greens. Although it is not traditional, whipped cream and fresh berries served alongside pieces of unadorned cake would also make a fine combination. When the cake is cut into, the pattern of the layers will resemble the rings of a tree.

ALTERNATIVE BROILER METHOD:
If you want the flavor of the cake without undertaking the arduous procedure of making it in the traditional shape, you can build the layers by using a round cake pan and a hot broiler. Pour a very thin layer of batter into the cake pan, and place it under the broiler for 1 to 2 minutes, or until it is delicately browned. Continue until you have baked between 10 and 12 layers and used up all the batter. Cool, remove the cake carefully from the pan, and decorate to your taste. This version will result in a much moister, chewier cake, not nearly as crisp as the spit method.

A Note on the Wines

With the first courses of the Lithuanian dinner, we suggest a medium-bodied, perfumy white wine of great style and polish, such as the Johannisberg Riesling from the Santa Ynez Valley's Firestone Vineyard.

With the lamb we pair a Merlot that is soft and supple, of medium body and developing complexity, such as those made by Rutherford Hill.

Mexico

❖

Tortilla Soup

Spicy Sautéed Shrimp

Roast Kid with Adobo Sauce
Rice with Sour Cream,
Jalapeño Peppers,
and Monterey Jack Cheese
Boiled Chayote Squash

Orange, Onion, and Jicama Salad

Rolls and Tortillas

Pineapple Pudding

Wines:
Louis M. Martini Chardonnay Special Selection
Louis M. Martini Barbera

TORTILLA SOUP

Heat about ¾ cup salad oil in a deep skillet and fry 3 or 4 corn tortillas until they are crisp and light brown. Drain them on paper towels and break them into small pieces. Heat 6 cups chicken stock (page 36) in a soup pot. Add 1 large chopped onion and simmer until it is cooked through and tender. Add about ¾ cup chopped tomatoes and chili peppers to taste. Simmer until well blended. Add a heaping tablespoon chopped fresh coriander (cilantro). To serve, put some fried tortillas in the bottom of 6 deep soup bowls, ladle the hot broth over them, and top with grated Jack cheese.

SPICY SAUTÉED SHRIMP

(SERVES 6)

12–18 jumbo shrimp
½ cup pumpkin seeds (pepitas in Mexican markets)
1 small onion, cut into chunks
3 cloves garlic
½ bunch fresh coriander (cilantro), leaves only
1 large tomato, peeled (see Glossary) and cut into chunks
3–4 dry hot chilies, such as pequín, coarsely crushed, or 1–2 fresh chilies such as jalapeño or serrano, coarsely chopped (with the seeds, if you like your food hot)
1 red bell pepper, cut into chunks
½ teaspoon coriander seeds
salt and pepper
4 tablespoons olive oil
clam juice, if needed
juice of 1 lemon

Clean, peel, and devein the shrimp. Set aside.

To make the sauce, prepare the pumpkin seeds first. If they are unroasted, put them in a heavy skillet without oil or butter and toast them a few minutes until they are crackly but not browned. Put them in a food processor or blender and reduce to a fine powder. Add the onion, garlic, coriander sprigs, tomato, chilies, red bell pepper, coriander seeds, and salt and pepper, and puree until smooth.

Heat 2 tablespoons olive oil in a skillet, add the pureed pumpkin seed mixture, and cook gently for a few minutes, stirring from time to time, until it is well blended. If too thick, stir in a little clam juice; if too thin, continue to cook until it is reduced to the desired consistency.

Heat the remaining 2 tablespoons olive oil in a large skillet, add the shrimp, and sauté over moderate heat until just beginning to turn pink. Remove from the pan with a slotted spoon to a heated platter. Add the sauce to the pan. Add the lemon juice and adjust the seasoning. Return the shrimp to the pan, turning to coat them with the sauce. Serve immediately.

ROAST KID WITH ADOBO SAUCE
(SERVES 6)

According to the great Mexican cooking expert, Diana Kennedy, adobo, in the form of a thick paste, was originally used for pickling meats. It is often used as a marinade and, diluted with a bit of broth, as a sauce.

The sauce base can be made as much as a day or two ahead and refrigerated until ready to use. In any case, make it first because it will be used in roasting the meat.

SAUCE BASE:
    2 dried ancho chilies
    1 teaspoon paprika
    3 cloves garlic
    2 onions, cut into chunks
    1 teaspoon dried oregano
    1 teaspoon ground cumin
    4 tablespoons chopped fresh parsley
    2 medium tomatoes, peeled (see Glossary)
        and cut into chunks
    1 cup white wine

MEAT:
    1 large onion, sliced
    5–5½-pound saddle of kid (if unavailable,
        substitute saddle of lamb or loin of pork)
    1 cup meat (page 23) or chicken broth
        (page 36)

DO AHEAD:
Wash, seed, and devein the chilies and soak in water for 1 hour. (It is always a wise precaution to wear rubber gloves when handling hot chilies.)

To make the sauce base, combine the soaked chilies with the remaining ingredients in a food processor or blender. Puree until smooth.

To roast the meat, preheat the oven to 400°F.

Arrange the sliced onion in the bottom of a large roaster. Place the meat over the onion, and place the roaster in the oven, uncovered, for 30 minutes, or until the meat is brown. Add the broth, cover, and return to the oven. (If your roaster has no lid, use foil.) Lower the heat to 350°F and roast for 30 minutes more. If the roasting pan has become dry by the end of the second 30 minutes, moisten it with a bit of water. Add the ancho sauce base to the roaster, cover, and continue roasting for another 30 minutes, or until the meat is as tender as pot roast and the sauce base has combined with the broth and juices and formed the adobo sauce.

To serve, put the meat on a serving platter and nap with spoonfuls of the adobo sauce, passing the remaining sauce in a bowl.

VARIATIONS: If using lamb, roast at 400°F for 35 minutes to an internal temperature of 135°F; if using pork loin, roast for closer to 1 hour or more, depending on the thickness, to an internal temperature of 145°F.

RICE WITH SOUR CREAM, JALAPEÑO PEPPERS, AND MONTEREY JACK CHEESE

Preheat the oven to 350°F. Make 5 cups of cooked rice (2 cups of rice cooked with 3 cups of liquid). Season the cooked rice with salt and pepper. Butter a 2½-quart baking dish. Mix together 1 cup sour cream and a 4-ounce can of peeled, chopped green chilies. Cut ½ pound Monterey Jack cheese into strips. Layer the rice, sour cream–chili mixture, and strips of Monterey Jack cheese, starting and ending with a layer of rice. Bake for 30 minutes.

BOILED CHAYOTE SQUASH

Sometimes called vegetable pear because of its shape, the chayote is a mild-tasting squash that is often used in Mexican and Cajun cooking as a foil or base for more piquant flavorings (in Louisiana it is known as mirliton).

Peel 3 squash and cut the meat into small chunks. The large center seed is edible, but not used in this dish. Put the prepared squash in a pot with salt and enough water to cover, bring to a boil, lower the heat, and simmer for 15 to 20 minutes, or until the squash is tender. Drain and toss with melted butter. If chayote is not available, substitute any mild summer squash.

ORANGE, ONION, AND JICAMA SALAD

A single brown-skinned jicama weighs about ½ pound or more and has a crisp, mild-flavored white flesh that resembles that of the Japanese daikon radish. If you cannot obtain jicama, substitute daikon or 6 or 8 sliced red-skinned radishes. Peel the jicama and cut into small cubes. Mix with some orange segments, cucumber, onion, and red pepper. Mix ½ cup olive oil or salad oil with about 2 tablespoons wine vinegar and salt to taste. Pour over the salad, tossing until well mixed. Serve each portion on a leaf of romaine lettuce.

ROLLS AND TORTILLAS

Both rolls and tortillas go well with this dinner. Make small crusty rolls using Baguette dough (page 119). Tortillas are widely available in the frozen food section of many markets, and are always available fresh in Latin neighborhoods.

PINEAPPLE PUDDING
(SERVES 6)

2 cups finely chopped fresh pineapple or drained canned pineapple
½ cup almond paste
4 egg yolks, lightly beaten
½ cup light brown sugar

½ cup dark rum
½ teaspoon pumpkin pie spice
1 cup heavy cream, whipped

In a saucepan combine the pineapple, almond paste, egg yolks, brown sugar, rum, and pumpkin pie spice. Cook over low heat, stirring continuously, until the mixture thickens. Remove from the heat and spoon into individual dessert bowls. Put to chill in the refrigerator. When ready to serve, cover the top of each pudding with a dollop of whipped cream.

A Note on the Wines

A refreshing contrast to the spicy Mexican shrimp would be a medium-bodied Chardonnay made with a predominant fruity flavor and little oak. A Louis M. Martini Special Selection is the perfect example of this style.

The kid calls for a medium-bodied red that combines fruitiness with enough earthiness to stand up to the adobo sauce. Our choice is another Louis M. Martini wine, a Barbera, the older the better.

Nicaragua

❋

Clemente's Seviche

Meat Pies
(Nactamales)

Salmi of Duck
Sweet Potatoes

Avocado and Pineapple Salad

Rolls

Sponge Cake Roll

Wines:
Joseph Phelps Vineyards Early
Harvest Johannisberg Riesling
Joseph Phelps Vineyards Pinot Noir

CLEMENTE'S SEVICHE
(SERVES 6)

Seviche is raw fish that cooks chemically by marinating in citrus juice. The fish also takes on the oniony-peppery-citrusy flavors of the marinade and its flesh turns opaque and alabaster just like the flesh of any fish cooked over heat. Actually, both heat and lime juice transform the protein of the fish in the same way, though not by the same method.

MARINADE:

½ teaspoon dry mustard
1 teaspoon brown sugar
½ teaspoon salt
¼ teaspoon pepper
2 tablespoons chopped fresh parsley
1 chili pepper, such as serrano or jalapeño, stemmed, seeded, and minced
1–2 cloves garlic, minced
1 tablespoon white wine
1½ teaspoons Worcestershire sauce
1 tablespoon olive oil
juice and rind of 1 orange
juice of 1 lime
juice of 1 lemon

VEGETABLES:

2 tablespoons diced cucumber (from whole English cucumber, or regular cucumber, peeled and seeded)
1 small tomato, diced
½ small green bell pepper, thinly sliced
½ small red bell pepper, thinly sliced
½ small red onion, thinly sliced

12 ounces very fresh sole or other firm, white-fleshed fish, cut in ¼-x-2-inch strips
12 sprigs coriander (cilantro), leaves only

In a large stainless steel or glass bowl combine the marinade ingredients. Stir in the vegetables and the fish. Marinate for 2 to 3 hours or longer in the refrigerator. The fish should become white and opaque. Remove the orange rind and squeeze it into the fish mixture, then discard.

To serve, spoon the seviche into shallow champagne glasses or compotes and garnish with the coriander leaves.

NOTE: It is common to serve seviche over avocado halves. We have not done that here because the menu includes an avocado salad, but it is something to keep in mind for another occasion.

MEAT PIES
(Nactamales)
(SERVES 6 OR 12)

FILLING:

4 tablespoons oil
2 onions, chopped
1 red pepper, chopped
kernels from 2 ears of fresh corn
1 small plantain or very firm green banana, chopped
1 pound cooked beef, coarsely ground or minced
½ cup chopped pitted green olives
salt and pepper

CRUST:

> 1⅓ cups all-purpose flour
> ¼ cup (½ stick) butter
> ¼ teaspoon salt
> 4 eggs

Heat the oil in a heavy skillet, add the onions, and cook until they are nicely browned. Add the red pepper, corn kernels, plantain or green banana, beef, and olives and continue to cook for about 2 minutes. Season with salt and pepper and remove the mixture from the fire.

Preheat the oven to 375°F.

To make the crust, put the flour in a bowl. Cut in the butter with a pastry blender until the mixture forms into small lumps about the size of raisins. Add the salt and eggs and work the dough until it is blended. Pat the dough into a ball and turn it out onto a floured board. Knead until the dough is smooth, for 5 to 10 minutes.

Divide the dough in half and work with one-half at a time. Divide the first half into 12 equal portions and shape each one into a ball. (1) Flatten each ball into a disc, then roll out each disc on a floured board to make a circle 4 to 5 inches in diameter. Repeat with the second half of the dough. You should now have 24 circles.

(2) Cover the centers of 12 of the circles with equal amounts of the filling, leaving the edges uncovered all around. Moisten the edges lightly with water (a pastry brush or a fingertip work well). (3) Cover each circle with a circle of plain dough. Pinch the edges together tightly, then press all

around with the tines of a fork to make a pattern.

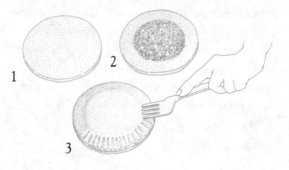

Bake the pies on an ungreased cookie sheet for 15 minutes, until the crusts are golden. Serve 1 or 2 pies per portion, depending on the rest of the menu (1 pie per portion will do for this menu, 2 pies if serving fewer courses).

SALMI OF DUCK
(SERVES 6)

> 2 4½–5-pound ducks (see Note)
> salt and pepper
> 1 unpeeled onion, chopped
> 1 carrot, cut into slices
> 1 stalk celery
> 4 cloves
> 8 whole allspice
> 1 teaspoon dried thyme
> 1 bay leaf
> ⅓ cup all-purpose flour
> 1 cup red wine
> ½ cup red wine vinegar
> ⅓ cup dark brown sugar

Preheat the oven to 450°F.

Prick the ducks here and there, particularly the fatty parts, with the tip of a sharp knife, which will help render the fat while the ducks are cooking. Season the ducks well with salt and pepper. Roast them for about 30 minutes, or until they are nicely browned. Remove to a carving board to cool. Reserve the roasting pan. Turn the oven down to 375°F.

STEP 1: *Cut away each leg and thigh.*

STEP 2: *Place leg skin side down; cut between the bones but do not disjoint completely.*

STEP 3: *Remove each half-breast with wing still attached.*

STEP 4: *Cut off the wishbone.*

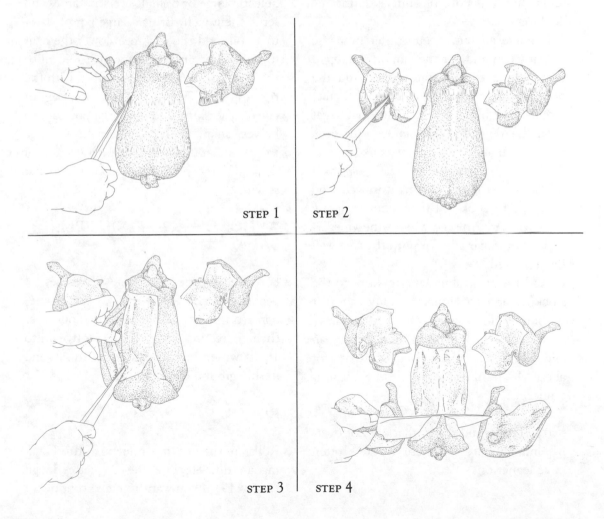

STEP 1

STEP 2

STEP 3

STEP 4

When the ducks are cool enough to handle, carve them as shown on page 213 and set aside the meat. Place the carcasses in the reserved roasting pan, return it to the oven, and continue to roast until the carcasses are very well browned.

Remove the carcasses and place them in a large stockpot. Add enough water barely to cover and bring to a boil. Lower the heat and simmer slowly, skimming off any scum that forms on the surface during the cooking.

Remove all but ½ cup of fat from the roasting pan and put the pan on the top of the stove over moderate heat. Add the onion, carrot, celery, cloves, allspice, thyme, and bay leaf and sauté in the fat until the vegetables are tender. Stir from time to time so that they cook evenly. When the vegetables are ready, sprinkle the flour over them, stirring it in well, and continue to cook until the flour is lightly browned. Add the red wine, wine vinegar, and brown sugar and stir until they are well incorporated.

Add the vegetable-wine mixture to the stockpot and continue to simmer until it becomes a glossy sauce, about 30 minutes.

Place the duck meat in the roasting pan and strain the sauce over it. Roast for about 40 minutes, or until the meat is tender.

NOTE: Try to find ducks that are not overwhelmingly fat. (Chinese markets often have leaner ones.)

SWEET POTATOES

Throughout Latin America, the whiter-fleshed, lighter-skinned boniato is the common variety of sweet potato. It is sometimes found here in the States in specialty markets, but the normal yellow-fleshed sweet potato or the golden-fleshed yam works as well for this menu.

Select 3 large or 6 small sweet potatoes and scrub them well. Bring a large pot of water to a boil, add the potatoes, lower the heat to moderate, and cook for 30 to 40 minutes, or until tender when pierced with the tip of a knife. Drain the potatoes, peel or cut off the skin, and cut large potatoes in halves, small potatoes in thirds. Arrange the potato rounds next to each portion of duck: 1 large piece or 3 small pieces per serving.

AVOCADO AND PINEAPPLE SALAD

For each portion, arrange 2 wedges of peeled avocado and 1 spear of fresh pineapple on a leaf of red lettuce. Pour over them a dressing made of 3 parts olive oil to 1 part wine vinegar seasoned with salt and freshly ground black pepper.

ROLLS

Rolls are the accompaniment to this Nicaraguan dinner. Use the Baguette dough (page 119) if you want to make your own.

SPONGE CAKE ROLL

Make a custard cream (see Gisadas, page 192), flavored during the cooking with a piece of vanilla bean or vanilla extract and a piece of cinnamon stick or a small amount of ground cinnamon. When the cream has thickened heavily, add a tablespoon of rum and set to cool.

Using the basic recipe for Génoise (page 120) or any favorite sponge cake recipe of your own, pour the dough into a buttered 10½-x-15½-inch jelly-roll pan that has been lined with buttered and floured parchment paper. Bake at 400°F for 7 to 10 minutes, or until lightly browned.

Remove the cake from the oven, turn it out onto a fresh sheet of parchment or wax paper, and carefully peel the old paper from the top of the cake. Immediately roll the warm cake into a cylinder, starting on the long edge and using the fresh wax paper to help. Allow the cake to cool.

When the cake has cooled, unroll it and spread it evenly with the cooled rum cream filling. Roll the cake into a cylinder again, dust the top and sides with confectioners' sugar, and place carefully on a serving platter.

A Note on the Wines

We would start this meal with a very light, delicate, and perfumy white wine that will be refreshing against the spicy flavors of both the seviche and the meat pies: an early harvest Johannisberg Riesling; that is, with little or no residual sugar, such as those offered by Joseph Phelps.

With the savory salmi of duck, we would pair a Pinot Noir that was rich and full-bodied, such as Joseph Phelps bottlings in this style.

Norway

❋

Spinach Soup

Large Shrimp in Cream and Dill Sauce

Roast Venison
Caraway New Potatoes
Buttered Beets

French Bread

Baked Apples

Wines:
Chateau Montelena Chardonnay 1973
Stag's Leap Wine Cellars Cabernet Sauvignon 1973

SPINACH SOUP
(SERVES 6)

This soup can be made entirely of spinach, or given a slightly different flavor and a bit more complexity by adding sorrel, as we do here. Since sorrel reduces so dramatically when cooked, it is not necessary to adjust the recipe with extra spinach if you omit sorrel.

> 1 bunch spinach, washed and trimmed, or 1 package frozen chopped spinach, defrosted
> 1–2 bunches sorrel, washed and trimmed, stems discarded
> 1 onion, chopped
> 6 cups chicken stock (page 36)
> salt and white pepper
> 1/4 teaspoon grated nutmeg
> 2 eggs, hard-cooked and chopped

Simmer the spinach, sorrel, and onion in the chicken stock. When the greens are wilted and the onions soft, strain the soup into a large bowl. Chop the solid ingredients very fine. Return them with the stock to the soup pot and put back over low heat. Season with salt, white pepper, and nutmeg and simmer for about 5 minutes longer. Before serving, garnish the soup with the hard-cooked eggs.

LARGE SHRIMP IN CREAM AND DILL SAUCE
(SERVES 6)

> 12–18 large shrimp, peeled and deveined
> flour
> 3 tablespoons clarified butter
> 1/4 cup aquavit
> 1 cup heavy cream
> 3 tablespoons chopped fresh dill, or 1 tablespoon dried
> salt and pepper

Dust the shrimp lightly with flour. Heat the butter in a large skillet until it foams. Add the shrimp and cook just long enough for them to turn color, 5 to 6 minutes (the flesh should be opaque with bright orange tinges). Remove the shrimp to a warm platter.

Add the aquavit, cream, dill and salt and pepper to the pan and whisk until well blended. Continue cooking over high heat for a minute or two, until the sauce is reduced slightly to the consistency of heavy cream. Pour the sauce over the reserved shrimp and serve immediately.

ROAST VENISON
(SERVES 6 TO 8)

> 1 4–5-pound saddle of venison
> 4 slices of bacon
> salt and pepper
> 1 cup beef stock (page 23)
> 1 cup beer
> 2 tablespoons lingonberry preserves or currant jelly

Preheat the oven to 475°F.

Tie the meat if necessary to hold its shape during roasting. Put the meat in a roasting pan. Drape the bacon slices over the top. Sear the meat in the hot oven for 20 minutes, or until it is quite brown. During the searing, remove the bacon as soon as it is well browned, and reserve it for garnishing the meat. Reduce the heat to 375°F. Sprinkle the meat very lightly with salt and pepper. Pour the stock and beer into the pan, return to the oven, and continue to cook for 1½ hours for medium/medium-rare, basting occasionally with the pan juices.

When the meat is done, remove it to a warm platter. Skim the fat from the pan juices. Adjust the sauce to make 1 cup, adding stock if there is too little, or reducing over high heat if there is too much. Whisk in the lingonberry preserves or currant jelly and blend until smooth. Taste and adjust the seasoning.

Remove the string if the roast has been tied. Carve the meat into thin slices, nap with a little sauce, and garnish with a crumble of bacon over the top. Serve the rest of the sauce on the side.

CARAWAY NEW POTATOES

If you can find tiny new potatoes, sometimes called creamers, you should prepare 20 to 24. If unavailable, use 2 or 3 small new potatoes per person. Wash and dry the potatoes but do not peel them. Put them to boil in a large pot of water. Cook until tender when pierced with the tip of a knife, anywhere from 30 to 45 minutes, depending on their size. As soon as they are cooked, drain off the water, add 4 tablespoons butter, salt and pepper, and a good sprinkle of caraway seeds. Stir together over high heat just enough to melt the butter and blend the flavors.

BUTTERED BEETS

Wash and trim 2 bunches of small, new beets. Cook in a large pot of boiling water for about 1 hour, or until tender. If you cannot find small beets, at least double the time for larger beets. Drain the cooked beets and peel or rub off the skin under cold running water. You can leave small beets whole or slice or quarter them, as you prefer. Return to the pan with a large lump of butter. Season with salt and pepper to taste. Heat until the butter is melted and the beets are hot.

FRENCH BREAD

The French bread that we used for this dinner is typical of the good solid loaves common throughout Europe. The recipe for this Country Bread is in the Basque menu.

BAKED APPLES

Scrub and core 6 large baking apples. Arrange them side by side in a baking dish. Pour over them 1 cup white wine or more, enough so that the apples are sitting in about 1 inch of liquid. Fill the centers of the apples with brown sugar and sprinkle more over the top. If you prefer a slightly richer dish, add 1 teaspoon butter to the top of each apple. Bake in a 375°F oven for 45 minutes to 1 hour, or until the apples are soft and the liquid syrupy.

While the apples are baking, put about 6 tablespoons sliced almonds in a pie tin and toast them in the oven with the apples, checking and shaking the pan frequently so that they do not burn. Remove the almonds as soon as they are golden and reserve.

Serve the apples warm or at room temperature, topped with the toasted almonds. Pass a pitcher of heavy cream on the side.

A Note on the Wines

The wines that we chose for this dinner hold a special place historically in the world's changing appreciation of California wine. Steven Spurrier, an English wine merchant, invited leading professional French growers, wine officials, restaurant owners, and writers to a series of blind tastings in Paris in 1976. When some of the California entries ranked above the French classics, it focused international attention on the high quality that California wines have achieved.

We poured the winning Chateau Montelena Chardonnay 1973 to accompany the shrimp in cream and dill sauce. It is a full-bodied, dry white wine of considerable elegance.

The red winner, the rich, complex 1973 Cabernet Sauvignon from Stag's Leap Wine Cellars, was our choice to drink with the roast of venison.

Peru

❖

Potato Soup with Avocado

Broiled Skewered Beef Heart
(Anticuchos)

Spicy Pork Stew Adobado
Boiled Sweet Potatoes
Corn on the Cob

Escarole Salad

Rolls

Fruit Compote

Wines:
Harbor Winery Zinfandel
Corti Brothers Reserve Zinfandel

POTATO SOUP WITH AVOCADO

(SERVES 6)

4 tablespoons butter
2 onions, finely chopped
2 tomatoes, peeled (see Glossary) and chopped
6 cups chicken broth (page 36)
2 potatoes, peeled and diced
a good pinch of saffron
salt
cayenne pepper
2 avocados

Melt the butter in a soup pot. Add the onions and sauté until they are tender. Add the tomatoes and cook just enough to blend in. Add the chicken broth and bring to a boil. Add the potatoes, saffron, salt, and cayenne pepper. Simmer the soup until the potatoes are tender.

Just before the soup is ready to serve, peel and seed the avocados, and cut them into thin slices. Ladle the soup into bowls and garnish each one with a few slices of avocado.

BROILED SKEWERED BEEF HEART
(Anticuchos)

(SERVES 6)

1 1-pound beef heart

MARINADE:
¼ cup red wine vinegar
¼ cup red wine
1 jalapeño pepper, cut into large pieces
2 cloves garlic
2 teaspoons cuminseed
1 teaspoon salt
1 small onion, cut into large pieces

DIPPING SAUCE:
1 tomato
½ onion
1 jalapeño pepper
several sprigs coriander (cilantro)
salt

DO AHEAD:

If using a charcoal fire for broiling the beef heart, start it 45 to 60 minutes before ready to cook. Marinate the beef heart for 1 to 2 hours (see instructions).

Trim the beef heart and cut it into ¾-inch cubes. Reserve.

Put the marinade ingredients into a blender or food processor and puree until smooth. Place the mixture in a bowl, add the cubes of beef heart, and marinate at room temperature for 1 to 2 hours. If the marinade does not cover the beef heart, add more red wine.

While the beef heart is marinating, make the dipping sauce. Finely chop the tomato, onion, pepper, and coriander and stir in the salt. You can do this by hand or in the blender or food processor (first cut the vegetables into large pieces). Reserve.

When the cubes of beef heart have marinated, remove them from the marinade and thread them on skewers. Brush with a bit of the marinade and put to broil for 3 to 4 minutes, turning so that they brown evenly on all sides. Baste once or twice with the marinade. When they are nicely browned, remove from the skewers and serve with the bowl of dipping sauce on the side.

SPICY PORK STEW ADOBADO

(SERVES 6)

1 tablespoon oil
2 pounds lean pork stewing meat, cut into
    1½-inch cubes
4–5 cloves garlic, chopped
1 onion, cut into chunks
2 tablespoons ground annatto seeds
2 teaspoons whole cuminseed
½ teaspoon ground cinnamon
salt and pepper
¼ cup mild white vinegar
½ cup dry white wine
1 cup chicken broth (page 36)
2 tablespoons orange marmalade
1 jalapeño pepper, minced, or ½ teaspoon
    red pepper flakes

Heat the oil in a heavy Dutch oven. Add the pork, garlic, and onion and sauté until the meat begins to brown. Sprinkle with the annatto, cumin, cinnamon, and salt and pepper. When the meat has browned, add the vinegar, wine, broth, marmalade, and jalapeño pepper. Cover the pot and simmer for 60 to 75 minutes, or until the pork is tender.

BOILED SWEET POTATOES

Many root vegetables are popular throughout Latin America. The familiar yellow sweet potato, and a white one called boniato, appear frequently on the menu. For our dinner, we boiled the potatoes in their jackets (it takes about the same amount of time as to boil a white potato of the same size, 30 to 40 minutes, or until tender), then peeled off the skin and served the potatoes with a dollop of sweet butter on each. About half a medium potato per portion is ample in this menu.

CORN ON THE COB

Bring a pot of water to a boil, add the husked ears of corn, and cook briefly until just tender. A good method is to add the corn to the boiling water, cover the pot, turn off the heat, and let the corn sit for a few minutes in the water until it is just tender. Cut each ear into 3-inch portions and serve steaming hot.

ESCAROLE SALAD

Wash and trim 1 head of escarole, tear it into pieces, and toss in a salad bowl with an oil and vinegar dressing made of 3 parts oil, 1 part wine vinegar, and salt and pepper to taste.

ROLLS

Small crusty rolls are a typical bread to serve with the Peruvian dinner. Use the recipe for Baguette dough (page 119).

FRUIT COMPOTE

A typical fruit compote of Peru includes dried and fresh fruits. The liquid for the syrup is traditionally made from blue or purple corn simmered for about 30 minutes, until it gives a deep purple color to the water; the corn is then discarded. Some of the fruits that are used are fresh pineapple, cherries, peaches, and dried apricots. Most people will find it difficult to obtain the corn, but a fine fruit compote can be made without it. Stew a combina-

tion of fresh and dried fruits of your choice in water to which you have added sugar, cinnamon, cloves, and the grated rind and juice of 1 lemon. The fruits should be cooked in 15 to 20 minutes. Serve warm or chilled.

A Note on the Wines

Zinfandel is generally a good choice to stand up to spicy foods, and for this Peruvian meal we would suggest, to pair with the skewered beef heart and its peppery dipping sauce, an assertive, full-bodied wine such as a Harbor Winery Zinfandel.

To go with the spicy pork stew, we recommend an intense, oaky wine, preferably an older Zinfandel that has grown more complex in flavor as it has aged, such as one of the Reserves from Corti Brothers.

Poland

❋

Cold Beet Soup with Shrimp

Turnovers Stuffed with Mushrooms, Cabbage, and Onions

Squabs Roasted Hunter's Style
Potato Pancakes

Jewish Corn Rye

Walnut Cake with Coffee Icing

Wines:
Navarro Vineyards Gewürztraminer
Sterling Vineyards Pinot Noir

COLD BEET SOUP WITH SHRIMP

This soup is a simplified version of the traditional Polish chlodnik and can be enriched by adding any of the usual ingredients included in that complex dish. To make the basic simple beet soup, cook 2 or 3 peeled beets, sliced into julienne pieces, in 6 cups water. When they are tender, 25 to 30 minutes, add about 1 tablespoon white wine vinegar (or between ¼ and ½ teaspoon citric acid, commonly called sour salt), 1 teaspoon sugar, and salt and pepper to taste. Chill. When ready to serve, stir in ¾ cup sour cream and ½ pound small cooked shrimp.

To enrich the soup, add any of the following ingredients along with the shrimp: thin slices of lemon; chopped green onions; peeled, seeded, and cubed cucumber; diced cooked veal or chicken breast; chopped hard-cooked eggs; chopped dill.

TURNOVERS STUFFED WITH MUSHROOMS, CABBAGE, AND ONIONS

(SERVES 6)

DOUGH:

6 tablespoons (¾ stick) butter, softened
4 ounces cream cheese
1 cup all-purpose flour
1 tablespoon water

FILLING:

¼ cup (½ stick) butter
1 onion, finely chopped
1 cup finely chopped mushrooms
1 cup finely shredded cabbage
salt and pepper

DO AHEAD:

Chill the dough for 1 hour (see instructions).

Put the softened butter and cream cheese in a mixing bowl and work together until blended. Add the flour and mix for a few seconds. Add the water and mix only long enough to form a smooth dough. Shape into a ball, cover with plastic wrap, and refrigerate for at least 1 hour.

To make the filling, melt the butter in a large skillet. Add the vegetables and sauté until limp and well cooked, 10 to 15 minutes. Add salt and pepper to taste. Reserve.

When ready to fill the turnovers, preheat the oven to 350°F.

Take the dough from the refrigerator and roll it out on a floured surface into a large rectangular shape about ⅛ inch thick. Cut the rectangle in half, and each half into squares, dividing the dough so that you have 12 squares. If it doesn't come out evenly, gather the odd scraps and roll them again to make the correct number.

Spoon equal amounts of filling in the center of each square. Spread filling out a bit, but leave the dough edges clean. Moisten the edges with water using a pastry brush or your fingertip. Fold over each square so that one corner meets its opposite corner, making a triangle. Press the edges with your finger, then with the tines of a fork, making a pattern and sealing at the same time. Place the filled turnovers on a baking sheet and bake for 30 minutes, until they are lightly colored. Serve 2 turnovers for each portion.

SQUABS ROASTED HUNTER'S STYLE
(SERVES 6)

6 *squabs*

MARINADE:
2 cups dry red wine
1 tablespoon juniper berries
2 bay leaves
1 teaspoon dried thyme
1 onion, coarsely chopped
3 cloves garlic
½ teaspoon salt
¼ teaspoon pepper

SAUCE:
2 cups chicken stock or consommé (page 36) (unsalted if possible)
1 ounce dehydrated mushrooms

3 tablespoons clarified butter

DO AHEAD:
Wash the squabs and pat them dry. Place them in a glass or stainless steel bowl.

Marinate the squabs for at least 3 hours (see instructions).

Make the marinade by pureeing the ingredients in a blender or food processor. Pour the marinade over the squabs, and marinate them for a minimum of 3 hours at room temperature or, preferably, overnight in the refrigerator.

When the squabs are ready, remove them from the marinade and wipe them dry. Strain the marinade into a saucepan. Add the chicken stock or consommé and the dry mushrooms (it is not necessary to presoak them). Boil the sauce mixture briskly until it reduces to a slightly syrupy consistency.

Preheat the oven to 450°F.

While the sauce is reducing, heat the clarified butter in a skillet. Brown the squabs 2 or 3 at a time, turning so that they brown evenly on all sides. Place the browned birds in a roasting pan and cook for 8 to 10 minutes for rare (or longer if you prefer them more well done).

When the squabs have roasted, remove them from the pan and bone them if desired (see illustration for carving duck, page 213). Serve them immediately with the sauce.

POTATO PANCAKES
(SERVES 6)

4 large potatoes (or enough to make 2 cups, grated)
2 eggs, lightly beaten
pinch of baking powder
salt and pepper
butter and oil

Peel, grate, and drain the potatoes briefly, enough to get rid of some excess liquid but not all of the starch. Put them in a mixing bowl and add the beaten eggs, baking powder, and salt and pepper.

Put a small lump of butter and a few drops of oil in a large skillet, just enough to grease the bottom of the pan. Spread evenly to coat the pan. When the butter is sizzling, drop the batter by spoonfuls into the pan, shaping it with the bottom of the spoon to make flat, round cakes about 3 inches in diameter. Fry about 2 minutes on each side, or until golden brown.

NOTE. Some cooks add 1 to 2 tablespoons matzoh meal or bread crumbs to bind the batter.

JEWISH CORN RYE
(MAKES TWO 1½-POUND LOAVES)

    2 cups medium rye flour
    2 cups warm water
    2 packages of yeast, or 2 tablespoons dry
        yeast
    2 tablespoons malt powder (or molasses)
    2 tablespoons salad oil
    4¼–4½ cups white bread or all-purpose
        flour
    2½ teaspoons salt
    2 tablespoons caraway seeds
    cornmeal

DO AHEAD:

To make the starter, mix 1 cup rye flour with 1 cup warm water and half of the yeast. Cover the bowl with plastic and leave it in the kitchen for 3 or 4 days. It should begin to bubble, increase in volume, and have a sour smell.

In a large mixing bowl dissolve the remaining half of the yeast in the remaining 1 cup warm water. Add the starter and stir into the yeast mixture. Add the remaining 1 cup rye flour, the malt, and the salad oil, and stir well. Add 4¼ cups of the flour, the salt, and the caraway seeds and mix in until it forms a dough. Add a little more flour if necessary.

Knead the dough by hand or machine. If by hand, turn it out on a floured board and work it until it is smooth and elastic, approximately 10 minutes. If using a dough hook on an electric mixer, knead the dough at the slowest speed for about 5 minutes. Lightly oil a bowl.

Pat the dough into a ball and put it in the oiled bowl. Cover the dough with a kitchen towel and set it in a warm, draft-free place to rise until the dough has doubled in bulk, 1 to 1¼ hours. (A perfect place is a gas oven with its slight heat given off by the pilot light; an electric oven, turned on low for no more than 2 minutes, then turned off, works equally well.)

When the dough has doubled, turn it out onto a floured board, punch it down, and knead it again until there is no air left in it. Cover it again with a towel, and let it rise until almost doubled, about 30 minutes.

When the dough has doubled again,

turn it out onto the floured board, punch it down, and knead until there is no air left in it. Divide the dough in half and shape into 2 round loaves.

To coat the loaves with cornmeal, prepare 2 bowls large enough to hold one loaf easily; fill one bowl partly with water, the other partly with cornmeal. Hold one loaf at a time gently in both hands and dip it into the water just enough to dampen it all around. Immediately set the dampened loaf in the bowl of cornmeal, jiggling the bowl until the cornmeal coats the loaf all over. Place the loaves on the counter and cover them with a towel. Let them rise until almost doubled, 15 to 30 minutes.

With a razor blade, cut 3 deep parallel gashes to make a pattern in the top of each loaf. (See illustration.) Cover the loaves with a towel and let them rise another 20 to 25 minutes.

While the loaves are rising, preheat the oven to 400°F. Place a pie tin half filled with water on the bottom shelf. Position an oven rack just above the bottom rack. Dust a baking sheet with cornmeal.

Gently pick up the loaves and transfer them to the baking sheet. Place it in the oven on the rack just above the bottom rack. Bake for 40 to 45 minutes. The crust should be golden brown. Test the doneness by rapping the bottom with your knuckle. The loaf should feel firm and make a hollow sound. Cool on a wire rack.

WALNUT CAKE WITH COFFEE ICING

Use the cake recipe for Walnut Sponge Cake in the menu for Israel.

Coffee Icing

(MAKES 1½ CUPS OR ENOUGH TO FILL AND ICE ONE CAKE)

> 2 egg yolks
> ⅔ cup powdered sugar, sifted
> 2 tablespoons instant coffee
> 1½ sticks butter, softened

Place all ingredients in a large mixing bowl. Beat until smooth, by hand or with an electric mixer, about 5 minutes. Chill until the icing has reached a spreadable consistency.

A Note on the Wines

We think a crisp, spicy, light white wine is a good choice for both the sweet and sour beet soup with shrimp and for the turnovers stuffed with mushrooms, cabbage, and onions. A Navarro Vineyards Gewürztraminer would be typical of that style.

For the squabs roasted hunter's style, we would pick a Pinot Noir that was rich, full, and intense, such as one from Sterling Vineyards.

Portugal

❖

Kale Soup
(Caldo Verde)

Salt Cod with Potatoes, Onions, and Olives
(Bacalhau à Gomes da Sá)

Braised Marinated Pork Loin
Rice, Peas, and Sweet Red Peppers

Mixed Green Salad

Rolls

Caramel Port Custard

Wines:
Vinho Verde, Lagosta Vilanova de Gaia
Dão Garrafeira S. Vicente 1965

KALE SOUP
(Caldo Verde)
(SERVES 8)

Caldo Verde is the traditional Portuguese soup of greens. Our recipe comes from Shirley Sarvis, a wonderful cook and a dear friend of both of us, and appears in *A Taste of Portugal* (see Bibliography), her definitive book on the cooking of that country. We like the flavor of kale particularly with this combination of ingredients, but as the recipe states, any greens or mixture of greens works equally well. The soup also makes an excellent lunch or light supper by doubling the quantity of each portion served.

4 large potatoes, peeled and sliced
8 quarts boiling water
about 2 teaspoons salt
about ½ teaspoon freshly ground black pepper
6 tablespoons olive oil
1 pound fresh spinach, kale, lettuce, or other greens, cut into strips as fine as possible
about 4 ounces linguiça, chouriço, or other smoked garlic sausage, cooked (simmered or slowly browned) and thinly sliced

Cook the potatoes, covered, in the boiling water with salt and pepper until tender. Remove the potatoes, coarsely mash, and return to the cooking water along with the olive oil. Bring to a boil, add the greens, and boil, uncovered, for about 3 minutes,

or just until the greens are tender but crisp. Adjust the seasoning. Ladle into soup bowls, each with a slice or two of sausage in the bottom.

SALT COD WITH POTATOES, ONIONS, AND OLIVES
(Bacalhau à Gomes da Sá)
(SERVES 6)

1 pound dried salt cod
2–3 tablespoons olive oil, plus more for dressing
1 large onion, cut into ¼-inch-thick slices
3 cloves garlic, minced
2 large potatoes, skinned and boiled, cut into ¼-inch-thick slices
coarsely ground black pepper
2 eggs, hard-cooked and sliced
12 black olives, pitted
several sprigs parsley, chopped
wine vinegar

DO AHEAD:
Soak the dried salt cod in cold water for at least 24 hours, changing the water several times during the process. The cod should become moist and soft.

Preheat the oven to 350°F.
   Put the reserved cod in a pot with enough water to cover, and simmer with the lid on for about 15 minutes, or until tender. When the fish is done, remove it to a plate to cool. When it is cool enough to handle, trim it, and remove the skin and any bones. Reserve the cod.

Heat 2 to 3 tablespoons olive oil in a large skillet. Add the onions and sauté until translucent and beginning to color. Stir in the minced garlic and sauté for only another minute or two.

Divide the potatoes, cod, and onion mixture roughly in half, and layer them in a casserole, half of each at a time: Start with a layer of potatoes and a good grind of black pepper; add a layer of the cod, broken into big pieces; add a layer of the onion and garlic mixture. Make a second layer, using up the remaining potatoes. Grind on more black pepper. Add the rest of the cod, and make a final layer of the onions and garlic.

Put the casserole in the oven to warm through. When the top has started to brown, in 10 to 15 minutes, remove the casserole from the oven and add the sliced eggs, black olives, and chopped parsley over the top. Serve immediately. It is customary to pass a cruet of olive oil and another of good wine vinegar at the table so that diners can dress their portions to taste.

BRAISED MARINATED PORK LOIN

(SERVES 6)

1 onion, chopped
2–3 cloves garlic
juice of 1 lemon
2–3 bay leaves, crushed
salt and pepper
1 4–4½-pound center-cut loin of pork

⅓ cup fruity olive oil
½ cup port
1 cup chicken broth or stock (page 36)

DO AHEAD:

Marinate the pork for 3 hours before cooking (see instructions).

In a blender or food processor puree the onion, garlic, and lemon juice. Add the bay leaves and salt and pepper. Spread this mixture over the pork loin and leave it to marinate at room temperature for 3 hours.

Heat the olive oil in a large stewpot or Dutch oven. When it is hot, add the pork and brown it on all sides. Add the port and chicken broth or stock, cover the pot, and braise the meat over low heat for about 1 hour, or until it registers at least 145°F on a meat thermometer.

To serve, remove the meat to a carving board and slice. Stir any brown scrapings in the pot into the juices. Reduce the sauce over high heat until it thickens slightly and becomes glossy. Serve the sauce alongside the sliced pork.

RICE, PEAS, AND SWEET RED PEPPERS

Make the basic Rice Pilaf in the Perennial Favorites menu. When adding the broth, also add 1 sweet red pepper that has been seeded, chopped, and sautéed in butter; and 1 cup cooked fresh, or defrosted frozen, peas. When ready to serve, sprinkle

3 or 4 tablespoons sliced toasted almonds over the top.

MIXED GREEN SALAD

Wash some Boston, Bibb, or romaine lettuce, some chicory, and a small bunch of watercress. Tear into small pieces. Toss in a salad bowl with dressing made of equal parts olive oil and lemon juice seasoned with salt and pepper. Slice 2 large tomatoes and 1 large onion. Arrange the greens on salad plates, top with the tomato and onion slices, and garnish with ripe black olives.

ROLLS

For this Portuguese meal we would suggest making small rolls from Baguette dough. (page 119.)

CARAMEL PORT CUSTARD

Flans or custards are a favorite Portuguese dessert and this one is enhanced by the addition of a bit of port wine. Use the basic custard recipe for Gisadas in the Jamaica menu, adding 2 tablespoons port along with the cream.

A Note on the Wines

To complement the kale soup and the salt cod we suggest a light, crisp, and very tart Portuguese wine such as a Vinho Verde, Lagosta Vilanova de Gaia.

The rich braised pork loin would be a good match with a medium-to heavy-bodied red wine of some complexity but still rough enough around the edges to keep it lively. An older Dão Garrafeira S. Vicente would be just right. With the restaurant dinner we served one from the 1965 vintage.

Puerto Rico

❖

Avocado Soup

Annatto Steamed Red Snapper

Rabbit Sautéed with Sherry
Buttered Sweet Potatoes
Steamed Rice

Marinated Mushrooms

Rolls

Mango Custard with Oranges

Wines:
St. Clement Vineyard Sauvignon Blanc
Stag's Leap Wine Cellars Gamay Beaujolais

AVOCADO SOUP

To make this soup, pick out 2 large avocados that are fully mature and soft to the touch, but without dark, mushy spots. Peel and seed them, then puree them in 6 cups rich chicken broth (page 36). Heat the mixture through without boiling it. Adjust the seasoning with salt and Tabasco sauce. Serve each portion garnished with some finely minced raw green pepper and a small spoonful of sour cream.

ANNATTO STEAMED RED SNAPPER

(SERVES 6)

Throughout Latin America and the Caribbean, annatto oil, produced from the annatto seed, is made at home or bought in the market to be kept on hand as a basic oil for flavoring and coloring foods. Its use is much like that of saffron and turmeric in Europe and the Middle East.

2 cups fish stock (page 113)
2–3 cloves garlic, minced
1 large onion, sliced
salt and pepper
4 tablespoons oil
2 tablespoons annatto seeds, or 2 teaspoons paprika
3 tomatoes, peeled (see Glossary) and sliced
6 2–3-ounce red snapper fillets or any other firm, white-fleshed fish fillets
2 tablespoons chopped fresh coriander leaves (cilantro)

Simmer the stock, garlic, and onion for about 10 minutes in a Dutch oven or a large skillet with a cover. Season with salt and pepper.

While the stock is simmering, heat the oil in a small saucepan. Add the annatto seeds and cook them for 2 to 3 minutes. As soon as the seeds blacken, take the pan off the heat, remove the seeds with a slotted spoon, and discard them. The oil should have a deep red-orange color and a subtle flavor. (If annatto seeds are not available, heat paprika in the oil as above.)

Mix the oil into the pot of stock. Add the tomatoes, then lay the fish fillets on top. Cover the pot and boil briskly over the highest heat for 5 to 10 minutes, or until the fish is heated through and has turned white and opaque.

Serve the fish and vegetables in shallow soup plates along with some of the broth, much as you would serve a French bourride or bouillabaisse, which it resembles. Garnish with chopped coriander leaves just before serving.

RABBIT SAUTÉED WITH SHERRY
(SERVES 6)

2–3 small-to-medium fryer rabbits
salt and pepper
flour
3 tablespoons oil
1 large onion, sliced
3–4 cloves garlic, chopped
2 red bell peppers, roasted, peeled, seeded,
    and sliced
1 hot chili pepper, seeded and deveined, or
    ¼ teaspoon red pepper flakes
1 cup sherry
1 cup chicken broth (page 36)
½ teaspoon dried thyme
2 tablespoons capers

Cut the rabbits into quarters, reserving the bony shoulders and front legs for the soup pot. Use only the saddles and hind legs. Disjoint the legs so that there is a leg and a portion of the saddle for each diner. (The butcher can do this for you.) If you don't mind using the bonier upper portions, 2 larger fryer rabbits butchered in the same way would make 12 pieces, or 2 for each diner.

Season the rabbit pieces with salt and pepper. Dust very lightly with flour and shake off the excess.

Heat the oil in a Dutch oven or a large heavy skillet with a lid. Add the rabbit and onion and sauté until they are browned. Stir in the garlic and peppers and cook until the mixture is sizzling. Add the sherry, broth, and thyme, bring to a boil,

then lower the heat to a simmer. Cook, covered, for 25 to 30 minutes, or until the rabbit is almost tender. Sprinkle on the capers and cook for an additional 10 minutes.

If the sauce has not begun to thicken by the time the capers are added, reduce it by cooking over high heat with no cover for the last 10 minutes.

BUTTERED SWEET POTATOES

Peel and cut 2 or 3 sweet potatoes into 2-inch chunks. Boil in salted water until tender. Drain and butter lightly.

STEAMED RICE

Use the recipe in the China menu.

MARINATED MUSHROOMS

Marinate about ¾ pound tiny whole button mushrooms in a basic vinaigrette or citronnade dressing (page 308). They will cool the palate at the end of this spicy meal.

ROLLS

Make small crusty rolls using the recipe for Baguette dough (page 119).

MANGO CUSTARD WITH ORANGES
(SERVES 6 TO 8)

2 mangoes, peeled and seeded
½ cup sugar
½ cup dark rum
3 tablespoons lime juice
2 eggs
1 teaspoon vanilla extract
3 oranges, peeled and divided into
  segments
1 cup heavy cream, whipped

Puree the mangoes in a blender with the sugar, rum, and lime juice. Add the eggs and blend in. Transfer the mixture to the top of a double boiler and set it over boiling water. As it cooks, whisk constantly until it becomes custardy and firms up. Pour the custard into a mixing bowl and stir in the vanilla. Chill in the refrigerator.

When ready to serve, divide the orange segments among individual sherbet glasses or dessert bowls. Stir the chilled mango custard and spoon it over the oranges. Garnish each portion with whipped cream.

A Note on the Wines

A slightly oaky, medium-bodied Sauvignon Blanc, such as made by St. Clement, would be a good match with the creamy-smooth avocado soup and the annatto steamed red snapper.

Our choice to accompany the sautéed rabbit is a fresh, fruity, light-bodied red, such as a Stag's Leap Wine Cellars Gamay Beaujolais.

Romania

✳

Cheese Pastries
(Bureks)

Fish Soup with Garlic

Grilled Beef "Hand" Sausages
Grilled Red Peppers in Oil
Kasha
(Buckwheat Groats)

White Bread

Plum Pie

Wines:
Charles Krug Winery Pinot Noir
Stag's Leap Wine Cellars Petite Sirah

CHEESE PASTRIES
(Bureks)

Use the recipe for Phyllo Pastry with Spinach-Cheese Filling in the menu for Armenia.

FISH SOUP WITH GARLIC
(SERVES 6)

The basic flavor of this Romanian ciorba, or sour soup, is reminiscent of Bulgarian tchorba or Greek avgolemono, with the addition of fish. Romanian ciorba can be made sour with pickle juice, sauerkraut, or lemon, but to our taste, lemon is the best souring agent.

> 8 cups water
> 1 pound fish trimmings (any fish but salmon)
> 2 teaspoons pickling spice
> 1 onion, chopped
> 1/2–3/4 pound fillets from any white-fleshed fish
> 1 tomato, peeled (see Glossary) and chopped
> 1 cucumber, peeled, seeded, and cut into small dice
> 2 green onions, minced
> 3–4 cloves garlic, mashed
> 2 tablespoons chopped fresh parsley
> 1/4 teaspoon cayenne pepper or Tabasco sauce
> salt
> 3 tablespoons lemon juice

Simmer the water, fish trimmings, pickling spice, and onion in a soup kettle for 30 to 40 minutes. Strain the broth into a 2- or 3-quart pot and discard the bones and onion. Skim off any fat floating on the surface.

Dice the raw fish fillets into 1/2-inch pieces and add them to the broth along with the tomato, cucumber, and green onions. Cook until the fish is done—it will turn white and opaque.

While the soup is cooking, mix together the garlic and parsley and set aside.

When the fish has cooked, season the soup with cayenne pepper or Tabasco sauce, salt, and lemon juice.

To serve, ladle the soup into bowls and immediately stir a mixture of the reserved garlic and parsley into each portion.

GRILLED BEEF "HAND" SAUSAGES
(SERVES 6)

> 1 cup beef broth (page 23)
> 2 pounds lean ground beef
> 3–4 cloves garlic, crushed
> 1 small onion, minced
> 1/2 teaspoon ground allspice
> 1/4 teaspoon fennel seed
> 2 tablespoons fresh parsley
> 1 1/2 teaspoons salt
> 1/4 teaspoon paprika
> 1/8–1/4 teaspoon cayenne pepper or Tabasco sauce

DO AHEAD:

To make a concentrated beef stock, boil down the 1 cup beef broth over high heat until it is reduced to ½ cup.

If you are going to broil the sausages over charcoal, build the fire 30 to 45 minutes before you are ready to cook.

Put the ½ cup beef stock and all the other ingredients into a large bowl. Mix with an electric mixer or beat with a wooden spoon until the mixture is very smooth and all the liquid is well incorporated.

Divide the mixture into 12 equal parts. Put a bowl of cool water at the worktable so that you can dip your hands, which helps in shaping the sausages. Wet your hands and form one portion of meat, patting it between your palms, into an oval sausage. Continue to shape the sausages until all of the meat has been used.

Grill the sausages over charcoal or under the broiler until they are medium-rare, 4 to 5 minutes on each side.

GRILLED RED PEPPERS IN OIL
(SERVES 6)

6 medium red or green peppers
2–3 cloves garlic, crushed
3 tablespoons lemon juice
3 tablespoons wine vinegar
salt and pepper
½ cup olive oil

Roast the peppers directly over a gas flame or under a broiler, until the skins are to-

tally black. As each pepper blackens, place it in a tightly covered casserole or a plastic bag and close the top tightly. Allow the peppers to "sweat" for 10 to 15 minutes. Rub or scrape off the charred skin, but avoid washing under water, as it removes the smoky flavor. Remove the stem, seeds, and veins, and slice the flesh lengthwise into strips about 1 inch wide. Arrange the pepper strips on a platter.

Mix together the garlic, lemon juice, vinegar, salt and pepper, and oil and pour over the peppers. Set aside to marinate for 30 minutes without refrigerating. Serve at room temperature.

KASHA
(Buckwheat Groats)

The kasha can be made as a pilaf, using the basic Rice Pilaf recipe in the Perennial Favorites menu or, more simply, using the same proportions, simmered with a liquid until light and tender. In either case, to obtain a light texture, mix the buckwheat kernels with an egg before adding any liquid to them. The egg coating seals the kernels and ensures their being soft and fluffy.

WHITE BREAD

Use the bread recipe in the Bulgaria menu.

PLUM PIE
(SERVES 8)

FILLING:

2½ pounds plums, halved and pitted
1 cup sugar
1 cup ground walnuts
1½ teaspoons ground cinnamon
2 tablespoons flour
grated rind and juice of 1 lemon
¼ cup butter (½ stick), melted

1½ recipes of Danish Waffle dough (page
95) or other short pastry dough (enough
to make 3 layers)

Preheat the oven to 450°F.

Mix the plums with the rest of the filling ingredients. Set aside.

Divide the prepared dough into 3 portions. Roll out one portion into a thin circle somewhat larger than a pie tin 9 inches across and 1½ inches deep. Line the bottom of the tin with the dough. The rim should be covered, but any excess dough should be trimmed off.

Spread half of the reserved plum filling over the dough in the pie tin. Roll out a second layer of pie dough the same size as the pie tin and lay it over the plums. It should just fit inside the tin and not extend over the edge or up the inside. Place the remaining half of the plum filling over the second crust. Roll out the third layer of dough the same size as the first layer. Moisten the edges of the bottom piecrust. Cover the plum filling with the third layer of dough, pressing and crimping the edges so that the bottom and top layers are sealed together. Cut vent holes and any decorations you like on the top crust.

Bake for 15 minutes, reduce the heat to 325°F, and bake for 20 to 25 minutes more, or until the crust is nicely browned.

A Note on the Wines

We recommend red wines throughout this menu, starting with a delicate, light-bodied Pinot Noir made in the style of Charles Krug, a good complement to the cheese pastries and the garlicky, lemony fish soup.

The substantial main course of grilled sausages, red peppers, and kasha would harmonize well with a robust, full-bodied wine such as a Stag's Leap Wine Cellars Petite Sirah.

Russia

Buckwheat Blini with Sour Cream,
Smoked Salmon, and Caviar

Cabbage and Beet Borscht with Sour Cream

Boned Pressed Chicken with Plum Sauce
Azerbaijan Pilaff

Pickled Mushrooms with Watercress

Buckwheat Bread

Strawberries Romanov

Wines:
Schramsberg Blanc de Blancs
Chateau Montelena Chardonnay

BUCKWHEAT BLINI WITH SOUR CREAM, SMOKED SALMON, AND CAVIAR
(SERVES 6)

At a Russian dinner, blini are generally passed still hot from the kitchen with a bowl of clarified butter to spoon liberally over them. The guests help themselves to the smoked salmon, herring, various caviars, and sour cream, set out on small plates on the table. The chosen accompaniments go on top of the blinis; the diner rolls up the blinis like jelly rolls or eats them open-faced, like an American pancake with topping. The usual Russian accompaniment is chilled vodka.

1 cup warm milk
1 tablespoon brown sugar
1 package of yeast, or 1 tablespoon dry yeast
½ cup all-purpose flour
¼ cup (½ stick) butter, softened, plus 2 tablespoons for frying
2 eggs, separated
1 cup buckwheat flour

ACCOMPANIMENTS *(increase or decrease the amounts according to taste and pocketbook):*
½ cup (1 stick) butter, melted
6 slices of smoked salmon
2–3 ounces caviar
1 cup sour cream

DO AHEAD:
The yeast needs 2 to 3 hours to rise (see instructions).

Put the warm milk into a mixing bowl and stir in the brown sugar. Dissolve the yeast in the mixture. Stir in the all-purpose flour and set the mixture aside in a warm place to rise for 2 to 3 hours. If the room is very warm, foaming may occur; if so, occasional stirring will break it down.

Cream the softened butter and incorporate the egg yolks. After the yeast mixture has had time to rise, stir in the buckwheat flour, salt, and the creamed butter and egg yolks. Stiffy beat the egg whites and fold in. Let the batter stand for 10 minutes.

Melt 1 tablespoon butter on a griddle or in a large frying pan. When it is hot and beginning to sizzle, measure out the batter with a large kitchen spoon, one spoonful for each blini, and fry in batches as you would regular pancakes, flipping them over when holes appear on the surface and the underside has begun to color. The finished blinis should be lightly browned on both sides. Use the remaining tablespoon butter to grease the griddle as needed.

To serve, put the melted butter in a serving bowl. Arrange the slices of salmon on a plate. Put the caviar in a small bowl (preferably nestled in a bed of crushed ice). Spoon the sour cream into a serving bowl. Put all of these accompaniments, 6 individual plates, and serving implements on the table. As each batch of blinis comes off the griddle, serve it immediately, cooking the next batch as the diners consume the first. Pass the accompaniments so that the diners can construct their own blinis according to taste.

CABBAGE AND BEET BORSCHT WITH SOUR CREAM

Use the recipe for Cabbage Borscht in the menu for Assyria.

BONED PRESSED CHICKEN WITH PLUM SAUCE
(SERVES 6)

This partially boned, butterflied chicken dish resembles the English spatchcock and the French crapaudine. Poussins (baby chickens) or Cornish game hens work best.

> 6 16–20-ounce Cornish hens or poussins
> salt and pepper
> ¼ cup (½ stick) butter, clarified

PLUM SAUCE:
> 12 ounces sour plums, pitted and coarsely
>   chopped
> ¾ cup water
> 2 cloves garlic, minced
> ¼ teaspoon salt
> ⅛ teaspoon cayenne pepper
> 2 tablespoons fresh lemon juice
> 3 tablespoons chopped fresh coriander
>   leaves (cilantro)

(1) Remove the backbones by cutting on either side with a sharp boning knife or poultry shears and breaking them away. (2) Cut through the cartilage behind the breastbone. (3) Remove the keel-shaped breastbones and cartilage. (4) Carefully slide a knife under the ribs and cut them away. Cut away any pieces of backbone left attached to the flesh. (Or ask your butcher to do all this for you.) (5) Starting from the skin side, cut a slit through each breast just at the position of the ribs. (6) Fold the legs under and push them through the slits in the breasts. (7) Tuck the wing tips back under the first wing joints.

Salt and pepper the chicken lightly on both sides. Melt the butter in a large frying pan. When it begins to sizzle, add 2 of the birds at a time, placing a second sauté pan on top of them to keep them flat and to ensure even and quick cooking. Turn after the first side has become golden brown, 10 to 12 minutes, and continue cooking until the second side is the same color.

Meanwhile, make the plum sauce: Simmer all the ingredients together in a saucepan for about 10 minutes or until the plums and garlic are tender. Serve the sauce warm or at room temperature.

Reserve the finished birds in a warm place until all are cooked. Serve them with the tart plum sauce on the side.

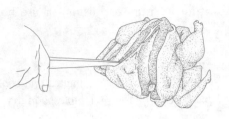

STEP 1

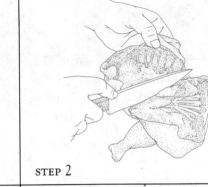

STEP 2

STEP 3

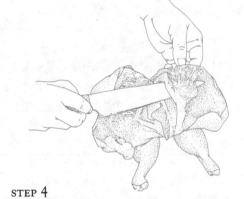

STEP 4

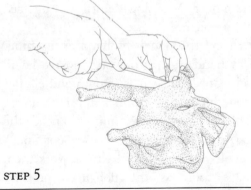

STEP 5

STEP 6

STEP 7

AZERBAIJAN PILAFF

Make the basic buttered Rice Pilaf in the Perennial Favorites menu, adding ½ cup toasted blanched almonds and 1 or 2 tablespoons toasted sesame seeds.

PICKLED MUSHROOMS WITH WATERCRESS

Select the smallest button mushrooms you can find and clean them with a dry soft brush or cloth. Cut off and discard the heavy stems and cut the remainder into pieces no more than 1½ inches long. Toss the mushrooms with a light vinaigrette (3 parts oil to 1 part wine vinegar, a little salt and pepper) and set them aside to marinate for no more than 2 to 3 hours to preserve their fresh texture. To serve, spoon the mushrooms over a bed of watercress.

BUCKWHEAT BREAD
(MAKES TWO 1½-POUND LOAVES)

For the Russian dinner we made a buckwheat bread that was really a version of our buckwheat pecan loaf, one of the most popular breads in our market. The recipe we give below is the complete recipe with the pecans; you can leave them out, as we did, for a more authentic Russian flavor, but be sure to try the loaf on other occasions with the nuts included. You can also substitute walnuts or raisins, or use both, as a variation.

> 2 cups warm milk
> ¼ cup (½ stick) butter, melted and cooled
> 1 package of yeast, or 1 tablespoon dry yeast
> 1 tablespoon sugar
> 1 tablespoon molasses
> 4¼ cups white bread or all-purpose flour
> 1½ cups buckwheat flour
> 2 teaspoons salt
> 1 tablespoon malt
> 1 teaspoon ground ginger
> ½ cup chopped toasted pecans (optional)

DO AHEAD:
Lightly oil a bowl for the dough.

Put the milk, butter, yeast, sugar, and molasses in a large mixing bowl. Add the white flour, buckwheat flour, salt, malt, and ginger. Mix slowly until well blended into a dough.

Knead the dough by hand or machine. If by hand, turn it out on a floured board and work it until it is smooth and elastic, approximately 10 minutes. If using a dough hook on an electric mixer, knead the dough at the slowest speed for about 5 minutes. If you are using the nuts, work them in as soon as the dough is properly kneaded.

Pat the dough into a ball and put it in the oiled bowl. Cover the dough with a kitchen towel and set it in a warm, draft-free place to rise until doubled in bulk, 1 to 1¼ hours. (A perfect place is a gas oven with its slight heat given off by the pilot light; an electric oven, turned on low for no more than 2 minutes, then turned off, works equally well.)

When the dough has doubled, turn it out onto a floured board, punch it down, and knead it again until there is no air left in it. Shape into 2 round loaves. Place them on the board, cover again with a towel, and let them rise until almost doubled, about 30 minutes.

When the loaves have risen, cut 3 gashes with a razor blade to make a triangular pattern on the top of each loaf. (See illustration.) Cover the loaves with a towel and let them rise for another 15 minutes.

While the loaves are rising, preheat the oven to 350°F. Place a pie tin half filled with water on the bottom rack. Position an oven rack just above the bottom rack. Flour a baking sheet or large pan.

Gently pick up the loaves and transfer them to the baking sheet or pan and place it in the oven on the rack just above the bottom rack. Bake for 50 to 60 minutes.

The crust should be golden brown. Test the doneness by rapping the bottom with your knuckle. The loaf should feel firm and make a hollow sound. Cool on a wire rack.

STRAWBERRIES ROMANOV

Wash and stem 2 pints of strawberries. Leave the small berries whole, but cut the large ones in half. Put the berries in a mixing bowl and sprinkle them with sugar to taste. Toss with ½ cup red wine and ⅓ cup Grand Marnier. Put the bowl in the refrigerator to allow the berries to macerate for 1 hour. Serve immediately in champagne or compote glasses, garnished with thread-like strips of orange zest (a tool called a zester makes this easy). An alternative is to stir 1 or 2 tablespoons orange marmalade into the red wine before adding it to the strawberries.

A Note on the Wines

The best of all choices to enhance the blini course is a sparkling wine. We would suggest a crisp, tart, Schramsberg Blanc de Blancs from Napa Valley as the perfect complement to the mixed flavors of buckwheat, sour cream, smoked salmon, and caviar.

To go with the crisp and succulent birds in a tart plum sauce, we would pick a rich, full-bodied Chardonnay such as a Chateau Montelena from Napa Valley.

Scotland

❖

Scotch Broth

Haggis Royal and Clapshot

Roast Quail with Green Grapes
Game Chips

Mixed Green Salad

Oat Bread

Poached Pears

Wines:
Gundlach-Bundschu Vineyard Co. Chardonnay Special
Selection
Stony Hill Vineyards Chardonnay

SCOTCH BROTH

(SERVES 6)

4 tablespoons barley
3 pounds lamb neck bones
6 cups water
1 small onion, chopped
1 medium carrot, diced
1 turnip, diced
½ teaspoon dried thyme
salt and pepper
2 tablespoons chopped fresh parsley

Simmer the barley and bones in the water for 1 hour. Remove the bones from the pot and set them aside to cool. When they are cool enough to handle, trim off any bits of meat, chop them coarsely, and return them to the pot. Stir in the onion, carrot, turnip, thyme, and salt and pepper. Simmer for about 30 minutes, or until the vegetables are tender. Adjust the seasoning and stir in the parsley just before serving.

HAGGIS ROYAL AND CLAPSHOT

(MAKES 2½ POUNDS SAUSAGES—TEN 4-OUNCE SAUSAGES)

The ancient Scots dish of haggis is traditionally a kind of mince or pudding made of the pluck (innards)—liver, lungs or lights, tongue, and heart—of the sheep; mixed with oatmeal toasted brown in front of an open fire; seasoned with onions and pepper; enriched with a fat such as suet; stuffed into the cleaned paunch or stomach of the sheep; and put to boil for several hours. Over the years the preparation of haggis has changed. Today it is more often made using a mixture of lamb, innards, and oatmeal, and is more likely stuffed into more traditional sausage casings. In Scotland today, butcher shops offer haggis in individual portions—actually sausages—but the dish made in the old-fashioned way, cooked in a paunch, is still the gastronomic high point of such celebrations as New Year's Eve.

It is the custom to drink Scotch whisky with haggis, whatever the occasion, and often to accompany it with clapshot, a simple mixture of yellow turnips and potatoes mashed together and seasoned with salt, pepper, and butter. You can omit it in the extensive menu below, unless you want to follow tradition completely.

This recipe is one that Narsai adapted after a trip to Campbeltown, Scotland, to taste and purchase malt whiskies from the Springbank Distillery. As a guest at lunch of William Thomsen, the director, he had his first taste of real Scots haggis.

10 1-inch natural pork casings (see Notes)
1 teaspoon vinegar
1 cup steel-cut oats (Scottish oatmeal)
¾ cup rich beef stock (page 23)
½ pound lean lamb, ground with a plate having ⅜-inch openings (see Notes)
¼ pound each lamb heart, tongue, and liver, each ground with a plate having ¼-inch openings (see Notes)

2 medium onions, chopped
½ teaspoon black pepper
2¼ teaspoons salt
1 teaspoon crushed red pepper flakes
2 tablespoons chopped fresh parsley
¼ cup red wine
a few gratings of lemon rind

DO AHEAD:

Rinse the pork casings under cold running water and soak them for 30 minutes in clean water with the teaspoon vinegar added.

Roast the oats dry on a pan, stirring occasionally, in a 350°F oven, until they are lightly browned. Turn them into a mixing bowl and stir in the beef stock. Set the mixture aside for 15 to 20 minutes, or until the liquid is absorbed into the oats.

Add the remaining ingredients to the soaked oats.

Remove the grinding plate and the blade from the grinder and attach the stuffing nozzle. Pull one end of the casings over the end of the stuffing nozzle. Tie the other end of the casings with butcher's twine or string. Slide the entire length of casing up over the end of the stuffer (it is very thin and will fit easily). If using a hand stuffer, slide the casing over the end in the same manner.

Feed the stuffing mixture into the grinder. Help to move it along by using a wooden pusher (never use your hand). As the casing fills, guide it with your other hand so that it stuffs evenly. If using a hand stuffer, feed the stuffing into the funnel end in batches by hand and proceed as above.

When the casing is filled, remove it from the nozzle of the stuffer and tie the open end securely. Holding the casing in both hands toward one end, turn and twist it over in opposite directions to make one sausage. Continue all along the casing, making a total of 10 sausages of equal size, each weighing about 4 ounces.

It is better, though not necessary, to make the sausages the day before and refrigerate them overnight still linked together. This will firm them up so that cutting apart will be easier. Once cut apart, the sausages can be cooked or reserved frozen until ready to use.

To cook the haggis, first prick the skin of each sausage a few times with the prongs of a sharp cooking fork, then boil in water like any other sausage for 20 to 30 minutes.

NOTES: The best way to grind the lamb and innards for this dish is to use a meat grinder, either hand-cranked or electric. The correct size grinding plate for each meat is given above. Do not grind everything together or you will lose the desired texture. Using a stuffing attachment is the easiest way to fill the sausages. If you do not have this equipment, ask your butcher to grind the meat and innards as specified, and use an inexpensive hand stuffer for filling the casings.

Pork casings are available in butcher supply stores and come already packaged in an amount larger than you will need for this recipe. However, they will last for a very long time if kept refrigerated and packed in the salt in which they come. Although they have already been cleaned, it is still necessary before using to wash them thoroughly in cold water to rinse away the salt, and to soak them briefly to soften them.

Clapshot
(MAKES APPROXIMATELY 2 CUPS)

  3 medium potatoes
  3 medium rutabagas
  salt and pepper
  ¼ cup (½ stick) butter, softened

Peel the potatoes and rutabagas and boil until tender. Drain them and put into a bowl. Mash until smooth, seasoning with salt and pepper to taste, and adding the butter, a bit at a time, until it is well blended in. Serve a small portion on each plate alongside the haggis.

ROAST QUAIL WITH GREEN GRAPES
(SERVES 6)

  3 cups small green grapes
  ½ cup Scotch whisky
  ½ teaspoon ground ginger

  grated zest and juice of 1 orange
  12 quail
  salt and pepper
  2 cups unsalted chicken broth (page 36) or
    soup
  3 tablespoons clarified butter

DO AHEAD:
Marinate the grapes for 1 hour in advance (see instructions).

Place the grapes in a small bowl and toss them with the whisky, ginger, orange zest, and juice. Set aside to marinate for 1 hour.

Season the quail with salt and pepper and set them aside.

Preheat the oven to 400°F.

Boil the chicken broth in a small pot until it is reduced to ½ cup. Reserve.

Heat the butter in a skillet and brown the quail a few at a time. Arrange them in a roasting pan and roast for 8 to 10 minutes, or until heated through but still pink on the bone.

Strain the liquid from the grapes into the skillet and deglaze it, scraping in all of the brownings with a wooden spoon. Pour the deglazed liquid from the skillet into the reserved chicken stock. Boil the mixture rapidly until it is syrupy and reduced to a light glaze. Adjust the seasoning. Add the grapes and continue to cook over moderate heat just enough to heat them through.

To serve, place the quail on a plate, nap them with the sauce, and arrange the grapes alongside as a garnish.

GAME CHIPS

These crunchy potatoes are the perfect accompaniment to the quail. Cut potatoes as for potato chips but at least twice as thick. Deep-fry in hot oil until they are crisp. Drain and serve.

MIXED GREEN SALAD

Use a variety of lettuces washed and trimmed and tossed with a simple vinaigrette dressing of 3 parts oil to 1 part vinegar and a little salt and coarsely ground black pepper.

OAT BREAD

(MAKES TWO 1½-POUND LOAVES)

*1 package of yeast, or 1 tablespoon dry
  yeast
2 cups warm milk
¼ cup (½ stick) butter, melted and cooled
3 tablespoons brown sugar
1 cup steel-cut oats (Scottish oatmeal)
5¼ cups white bread or all-purpose flour
2 teaspoons salt
1 teaspoon ground ginger*

DO AHEAD:
Lightly oil a bowl for the dough.

Mix the yeast, milk, butter, and brown sugar in a large mixing bowl. Add the oats, flour, salt, and ginger, and mix until well blended. Because the steel-cut oats absorb moisture slowly, the dough may seem soft or sticky; it will appear normal by the end of the first rising.

Knead the dough by hand or machine. If by hand, turn it out on a floured board and work it until it is smooth and elastic, approximately 10 minutes. If using a dough hook on an electric mixer, knead the dough at the slowest speed for about 5 minutes.

Pat the dough into a ball and put it in the oiled bowl. Cover the dough with a kitchen towel and set it in a warm, draft-free place to rise until doubled in bulk, 40 to 50 minutes. (A perfect place is a gas oven with its slight heat given off by the pilot light; an electric oven, turned on low for no more than 2 minutes, then turned off, works equally well.)

When the dough has doubled, turn it out onto a floured board, punch it down, and knead it again until there is no air left in it. Shape it into 2 round loaves. Place them on the board, cover again with a towel, and let them rise until the loaves are almost doubled, 20 to 30 minutes.

While the loaves are rising, preheat the oven to 350°F. Place a pie tin half filled with water on the bottom shelf. Position an oven rack just above the bottom rack. Flour a baking sheet or large pan.

When the loaves have risen, cut a gash with a razor completely around the circumference on the top of each loaf. (See illustration.) Cover the loaves with a towel and let them rise for another 15 minutes.

Gently pick up the loaves and transfer them to the baking sheet or pan and place

red wine and half water. Add about ½ cup brown sugar, a few cloves, and 2 or 3 pieces of lemon rind. Poach over low heat until the pears are soft but not mushy, anywhere between 30 and 40 minutes, depending on their firmness.

A Note on the Wines

it in the oven on the rack just above the bottom rack. Bake for 45 to 60 minutes. The crusts should be golden brown. Test the doneness by rapping the bottom with your knuckle. The loaf should feel firm and make a hollow sound. Cool on a wire rack.

POACHED PEARS

Peel 6 firm pears and stand them side by side in a deep pot. Cover them with half

To go with the haggis, we would select a medium-bodied white wine that is elegant and full of fruit, such as a Gundlach-Bundschu Vineyard Co. Chardonnay Special Selection of the early 1980s.

Our choice to accompany the roast quail is a rich, intense, full-bodied Chardonnay with a strong varietal flavor. A Stony Hill Vineyards would be a fine example of that style.

Spain

❄

Charcoal-Roasted Peppers and Eggplant with Garlic
Mayonnaise and Toasted Bread Crumbs
(Escalivada with Ali Oli)

Chilled Almond Soup with Melon

Lobster in Tomato-Brandy Sauce
Saffron Rice
Spinach with Pine Nuts

Curly Endive Salad

Narsai's Sweet Potato and Garlic Bread

Caramel Pears

Wines:
Gran Viña Sol Reserva, Torres
Reserva 904, Rioja Alta

CHARCOAL-ROASTED PEPPERS AND EGGPLANT WITH GARLIC MAYONNAISE AND TOASTED BREAD CRUMBS
(Escalivada with Ali Oli)

(SERVES 6)

2 red peppers
2 green or yellow peppers
3 Japanese eggplants, or 1 medium
   eggplant
½ cup fruity olive oil
salt and pepper

BREAD CRUMBS:

2–3 slices of fresh white bread, preferably
   French-type (see Note)
¼ cup olive oil

GARLIC MAYONNAISE (ALI OLI):

1 egg
1 teaspoon mustard powder
½ teaspoon salt
6–8 cloves garlic
1 tablespoon wine vinegar
1 tablespoon lemon juice
1 cup olive oil

Roast the whole peppers and eggplant over a direct flame or charcoal grill, or under the broiler, rotating so that the skins blacken evenly. As each one is charred on all sides, place it in a covered pot. The peppers and eggplant will steam in their own heat, loosening the skins. After 15 to 20 minutes, remove the skins without washing. Don't worry about a few residual flecks of black; they will only enhance the smoky flavor. (A large eggplant will take longer than the small Japanese type: rarely more than 10 to 15 minutes over a direct flame, 20 to 25 minutes under the broiler.)

Cut the peeled peppers and eggplant into strips of about the same size. Place them on a platter, drizzle with olive oil, and sprinkle with salt and pepper. Set aside for an hour or two at room temperature.

Meanwhile, mince the white bread into crumbs no larger than ⅛ to ¼ inch in size, being careful not to pulverize them into a powder. A pulsing, on-off action in a food processor does this well, and a hand meat grinder is a good second choice.

Heat the olive oil in a skillet, add the bread crumbs, and toss them in the oil. As they absorb the oil, they will get brown and crunchy. Reserve.

To make the ali oli, put the egg, mustard powder, salt, garlic cloves, vinegar, lemon juice, and ¼ cup of the oil in a blender. On slow speed, blend until the mixture becomes a smooth puree. With the blender running, drizzle in the remaining oil very rapidly. (It may be necessary to shut off the blender a time or two and to scrape down the sides with a spatula.) If you work quickly, the blending may take no more than a total of 30 seconds.

When ready to serve, sprinkle the toasted crumbs over the pepper and eggplant strips and pass garlic mayonnaise separately in a small bowl.

NOTE: You can use stale, dry bread instead, putting it in a plastic bag and mashing it with a frying pan or a rolling pin, but the results are less uniform.

CHILLED ALMOND SOUP WITH MELON
(SERVES 6)

½ cup almond butter
3 cloves garlic, chopped
½ cup white wine
1 long European cucumber, or 2 regular
    cucumbers, peeled and seeded
1 tablespoon chopped onion
4 cups chicken broth (page 36)
1 tablespoon lemon juice
salt and pepper
Tabasco sauce
18 honeydew melon balls
sour cream
2 tablespoons slivered toasted almonds
6 ice cubes
6 sprigs fresh mint

DO AHEAD:
Chill 6 soup bowls.

Heat the almond butter and 2 garlic cloves in a soup pot or Dutch oven until they just start to turn golden. Stir in the white wine and set aside to cool.

Put the cucumber, onion, remaining garlic clove, and the cooled almond-garlic mixture in a blender or food processor. Add as much of the broth as necessary to puree the ingredients. Pour the pureed mixture back into the pot. Stir in the remaining broth, lemon juice, salt and pep-

per, and Tabasco sauce. Turn the soup into a bowl and chill it in the refrigerator.

To serve, spoon the soup into the chilled bowls and garnish each portion with 3 honeydew balls, a dollop of sour cream, a sprinkle of toasted almonds, an ice cube, and a sprig of mint.

LOBSTER IN TOMATO-BRANDY SAUCE
(SERVES 6)

6 1-pound live lobsters, or 3 1½–2-pound
    live lobsters

TOMATO-BRANDY SAUCE:
¼ cup very light oil
1 large onion, minced
2–3 cloves garlic, minced
½ cup white wine
½ cup chicken broth (page 36)
¼ cup brandy
3–4 tomatoes, peeled (see Glossary),
    seeded, and chopped
2 bay leaves
½ teaspoon dried thyme
2 tablespoons chopped fresh parsley
salt and pepper

Plunge the lobsters into enough boiling salted water to cover them. Let the water come back to a boil, then time the cooking: Boil the 1- pound lobsters for 5 to 7 minutes longer, the 2-pound lobsters for 10 to 12 minutes longer.

While the lobsters are cooking, prepare

the sauce. Heat the oil in a large skillet, add the onion, and sauté until it is translucent. Add the garlic and stir until the mixture is sizzling. Add the wine, broth, brandy, tomatoes, bay leaves, thyme, and parsley. Boil rapidly, uncovered, to reduce the juices to the consistency of heavy cream. Adjust the seasoning with salt and pepper.

When the lobsters are cooked, split them in half and crack the claws. Arrange the lobsters on individual plates and pour the sauce over the exposed tail meat.

SAFFRON RICE

Make the basic Rice Pilaf found in the Perennial Favorites menu, adding a large pinch of saffron when you add the liquid.

SPINACH WITH PINE NUTS

Heat some butter in a skillet and sauté a small amount of chopped onion until it is translucent. Set aside. Blanch a bunch of spinach in boiling salted water. Drain, refresh it with cold water, and press it dry. When ready to serve, add the blanched spinach leaves to the pan of onions and toss together until the mixture is heated through. Season with salt and pepper and a squeeze of lemon. Garnish with lightly toasted pine nuts.

CURLY ENDIVE SALAD

Toss a bunch of curly endive with a very simple vinaigrette dressing (see Glossary) seasoned only with salt and pepper. The light dressing preserves the slight bitterness of the endive, which helps to cleanse the palate.

NARSAI'S SWEET POTATO AND GARLIC BREAD
(MAKES 1 LOAF)

This bread evolved out of an attempt to make an authentic Spanish bread to serve at a friend's tapas party honoring Jacques Pépin. The garlic is certainly not part of the authentic Spanish bread, but it works very well in balancing the richness of the sweet potato.

> 1 cup warm water (preferably the water
>   the sweet potatoes are boiled in)
> 1 cup mashed sweet potatoes
> 2 teaspoons sugar
> 1 package of yeast, or 1 tablespoon dry
>   yeast
> 2 small cloves garlic, crushed
> 3 cups white bread or all-purpose flour
> 1 teaspoon salt
> 2 tablespoons butter, softened, or salad oil

Place the water, sweet potatoes, sugar, and yeast in a mixing bowl. Let rest for 5 minutes. Add the garlic, flour, and salt. Mix well with a dough hook or heavy paddle. The dough will be quite soft and sticky.

Continue mixing for 2 to 3 minutes if you are using a mixing machine, 3 to 4 minutes if mixing by hand. Spread 1 tablespoon butter or oil over the dough.

Put the dough in a warm place to rise. (An ideal place is the oven. The pilot light of a gas oven provides the perfect source of heat, but an electric oven is comparable if turned on low for a minute or two, then shut off, before the dough is put in.)

When the dough has doubled in volume, anywhere between 1 and 2 hours, turn it out onto a floured surface and punch it down to get out the air that has inflated it. Kneading a few times also helps in this step. Shape the deflated dough into a ball. This is a very soft dough, so handle it gently and use plenty of flour to keep it from sticking to the board.

Butter or oil a 10-inch skillet. Put the dough in the skillet, and set aside, uncovered, until double in volume.

About halfway through the rising, preheat the oven to 400°F.

When the dough has doubled, bake for 35 to 40 minutes to brown well. Turn out onto a rack to cool.

CARAMEL PEARS
(SERVES 6)

Everyone who tastes these caramel pears agrees that they are the best they have ever eaten. Although the recipe comes from a famous French chef, our mutual friend Jacques Pépin, the flavors are classic and exactly those of the Spanish dessert of the same name.

> 6 medium pears, not too ripe (Anjou, Bosc, or Comice)
> 3–4 tablespoons granulated sugar
> 1/3 stick sweet butter, broken into bits
> 1½ cups heavy cream
> 1 tablespoon confectioners' sugar
> ¼ teaspoon vanilla extract

Preheat the oven to 425°F.

Peel and split the pears lengthwise. Remove the seeds and core. Place the pear halves, flat side down, in a gratin dish. You need a large dish in order not to have the pieces overlap. Sprinkle the granulated sugar on top, add the butter pieces, and place in the oven for 35 minutes. By this time the sugar should have caramalized and the pears should be tender when pierced with the point of a knife. If the pears are still hard, cook for another 5 or 10 minutes. Add 1 cup cream and place back in the oven. Cook for 10 to 15 minutes, basting every 5 minutes. The sauce should have reduced, be thick, and of a nice ivory color. The caramel coooking with the cream will form a rich and delicious sauce. If it reduces too much and you see that the sauce is breaking down, add 3 or 4 tablespoons water.

Whip the remaining ½ cup cream and mix in the confectioners' sugar and vanilla.

Serve the pears lukewarm. Turn each half flat side up and spoon some sauce into the hollow cavity. Bring to the table and at the last moment add 1 tablespoon cold whipped cream on top of each pear. Eat immediately, before the whipped cream melts.

A Note on the Wines

With the first part of the Spanish menu, we suggest one of the medium-bodied, light, and fruity Spanish white wines, such as a Gran Viña Sol Reserva from the Torres family.

To go with the lobster, we choose a rich, medium-bodied wine that at the same time retains an earthiness characteristic of so many Spanish wines. A good example would be a wine from the northern regions, a Reserva 904 from the Rioja Alta.

Sweden

❊

Kale Soup

Veal Timbale with Lemon Sauce

Roast Duck with Apricots and Prunes
Red Cabbage Braised in Port
Browned Potatoes

Pickled Cucumber Salad

Granny Wheat Bread

Baked Apple Halves with Almond Topping

Wines:
Vichon Chevrier (Chevrignon)
Acacia Pinot Noir

KALE SOUP

Use the recipe for Caldo Verde in the menu for Portugal, but for this menu substitute fennel or other mild-flavored sausages for the chouriços.

VEAL TIMBALE WITH LEMON SAUCE

(SERVES 6 TO 8)

TIMBALE:

bread crumbs
1 pound veal, very finely ground
¼ cup (½ stick) butter, softened
2 tablespoons flour
2 eggs, separated
1 cup heavy cream
½ cup Madeira or sherry
1 teaspoon salt
¼ teaspoon white pepper
¼ teaspoon ground ginger
¼ teaspoon ground cardamom

LEMON SAUCE:

6 tablespoons (¾ stick) butter
1 tablespoon flour
1 cup chicken or veal stock (page 36 or 23)
2 tablespoons lemon juice
salt and pepper
pinch of grated nutmeg
2 tablespoons chopped fresh parsley

DO AHEAD:

Generously grease a 4- to 5-cup loaf pan or casserole or 6 to 8 individual dariole molds. Sprinkle with bread crumbs, rotating the pan or molds so that the sides and bottom are evenly coated.

Whip the ground veal and butter by hand until smooth and well blended. In a small bowl, mix the flour, egg yolks, cream, and wine, then blend the mixture into the meat. Add the salt, white pepper, ginger, and cardamom.

Preheat the oven to 375°F.

Whip the egg whites until they are stiff. Mix one-quarter of the beaten whites into the meat mixture, then gently fold the meat mixture back into the remaining egg whites. Turn the blended meat and egg whites into the prepared baking mold or molds and cover with a lid or foil.

Set the mold or molds into a roasting pan and place in the oven. Pour boiling water into the pan to a depth of 1 inch. Bake for 1 hour. Remove the lid or foil and continue baking until the blade of a small paring knife inserted in the center comes out clean, 15 to 30 minutes more. Ten minutes before removing from the oven, make the sauce.

To make the sauce, heat 1 tablespoon butter in a saucepan, add the flour, and cook only until the flour is absorbed. Whisk in the stock and lemon juice and cook for 5 to 10 minutes, until the sauce is lightly thickened. Season with salt, pepper, and nutmeg. Add the parsley and the remaining 5 tablespoons butter, broken into small pieces. Remove the sauce from the heat and continue whisking until the butter has all been incorporated.

Unmold the timbale and serve with the lemon sauce on the side.

ROAST DUCK WITH APRICOTS AND PRUNES

(SERVES 6)

2 5–5½-pound ducks
salt and pepper
1 teaspoon dried thyme
1 teaspoon dried sage
12 dried apricot halves soaked in water for
*   30 minutes and drained*
6 pitted prunes
½ bunch parsley, with stems, coarsely
*   chopped*
1 large onion, coarsely cut
2 bay leaves
2 cups chicken broth (page 36)
½ cup white wine
1 tablespoon caraway seeds
2 tablespoons gooseberry preserves or
*   currant jelly*

Preheat the oven to 400°F.

Season the ducks inside and out with salt and pepper, thyme, and sage.

Mix the apricots, prunes, parsley, onion, and bay leaves. Divide the mixture roughly in half and stuff each duck with it. Place the ducks on a rack that fits into a roasting pan, then put them to roast. (The high temperature, which is necessary to render out the fat and brown the skin, may also produce a lot of smoke, particularly if you have an unvented electric oven.)

With a bulb baster, periodically remove the fat that renders out.

Roast the ducks for no more than 1¼ to 1½ hours if you wish the breast meat to remain pink, longer for more well done. When the ducks have roasted, remove them from the pan to a warm platter. Set them aside to rest for 15 to 20 minutes before carving.

Reserve any fat remaining in the pan for the Browned Potatoes on this menu. Add the broth, white wine, caraway seeds, and preserves, and simmer until the brown particles in the pan have all dissolved. Transfer the deglazed pan mixture to a saucepan and boil the mixture rapidly until it is reduced to about 1 cup. Strain the sauce and keep it warm.

Carve the duck (see illustration, page 213) and arrange it on the platter, using the apricots and prunes from the stuffing for the garnish. Pour the warmed sauce into a gravy boat and pass it separately.

RED CABBAGE BRAISED IN PORT

Heat some oil and butter in a skillet and sauté a small chopped onion. Add a small head of red cabbage, cored, and coarsely chopped or shredded, about 1 cup port wine, and salt and pepper. Braise, covered, for 10 to 15 minutes, or until the cabbage is tender, adding more wine or water, if needed, during the cooking.

BROWNED POTATOES

Scrub and peel 6 medium potatoes. Boil them in salted water for about 10 minutes, then drain. Put them in a pan with enough fat and drippings from the duck so that they can be turned and coated on all sides. About 45 minutes before the ducks have finished roasting, put the pan of potatoes in the same oven to complete their cooking and to brown.

PICKLED CUCUMBER SALAD

If using the traditional tough-skinned cucumber, peel and seed 2 of them; if the modern "European" type, leave both skin and seeds, as they are quite tender; one such cucumber will be sufficient. Slice the cucumbers as thin as possible so that the pieces are almost transparent. Dress them with a mixture of ¾ cup white wine vinegar, 1 tablespoon sugar, ½ teaspoon salt, ¼ teaspoon white pepper, and 2 tablespoons chopped fresh dill or 1 tablespoon dried dill weed. After marinating for 1 hour, strain off all of the liquid and garnish with a sprinkle of dill.

GRANNY WHEAT BREAD
(MAKES 2 1½-POUND LOAVES)

Our pastry chef Dennis Clews devised this recipe inspired by some English malted wheat flakes that I had brought back to the bakery from a bakers' convention. Having grown up in Australia and worked in Scotland, he was thoroughly familiar with the English product and was delighted to create a bread recipe using it. Unfortunately, the flakes are no longer imported to the United States, and so, some time ago, we adapted the original recipe to the one given here. We found that by adding malt to the dough and substituting toasted rolled wheat for the malted flakes, we could maintain the style of the original. In fact, over the last several years, it became one of the favorite breads from our bakery.

—N.D.

1 cup rolled wheat flakes (see Note)
1 cup milk
6 tablespoons (¾ stick) butter
1 cup orange juice
1 package of yeast, or 1 tablespoon dry yeast
1 tablespoon molasses
3 tablespoons honey
1 cup whole-wheat flour
2 tablespoons malt powder
2 teaspoons salt
4 cups white bread or all-purpose flour

DO AHEAD:
Toast the rolled wheat flakes by spreading them in a pan and placing them in a 350°F oven for about 5 minutes.

Lightly oil a bowl for the dough.

Heat the milk and butter gently in a saucepan until the butter has melted. Stir in the orange juice, yeast, molasses, and honey and remove from the heat.

Put the toasted wheat flakes, whole-wheat flour, malt powder, and salt in a large mixing bowl and mix well. Add the heated milk mixture and stir until all the ingredients are well blended. Mix in the bread flour.

Turn the dough out onto a floured board. Knead it by hand until it is smooth and elastic; or knead it using a dough hook and electric mixer for about 5 minutes. (The dough will be a little sticky as the liquid has not yet been absorbed by the wheat flakes.) Shape the dough into a ball and place it in the oiled bowl. Cover the dough with a kitchen towel and set it in a warm, draft-free place to rise until it has doubled—30 to 40 minutes. (A perfect place is a gas oven with its slight heat given off by the pilot light; an electric oven, turned on low for no more than 2 minutes, then turned off, works equally well.)

When the dough has risen, turn it out onto the floured board and punch it down. Knead the dough until there is no air left in it. Shape the dough into a ball, place it back into the bowl, cover it with a towel, and let it rise a second time until almost doubled—about 45 minutes.

Turn the dough out again onto a floured surface, punch it down, and knead until there is no air left in it. Form the kneaded dough into 2 round loaves. Cover the loaves with a towel, and let them rise until almost doubled—about 30 minutes.

With a razor blade, cut 4 deep gashes, making a "W" pattern on top. (See illustration.) Cover the loaves with a towel and let them rest for 25 minutes, or until doubled in size.

While the loaves are rising, dust a sheet pan with flour. Preheat the oven to 400°F. Place a pie tin half filled with water on the bottom shelf and position an oven rack just above the center.

Gently pick up the loaves and transfer them to the sheet pan. Bake for 45 to 50 minutes. Test the doneness by rapping the bottom of the loaf with your knuckle. It should feel firm and make a hollow sound. Cool on a wire rack.

NOTE: Any rolled grain—wheat, rye, or barley—will work equally well. If those rolled grains are unavailable, old-fashioned rolled oats make a good substitute.

✳

BAKED APPLE HALVES WITH ALMOND TOPPING

(SERVES 6)

1 cup white wine
6 small green apples, cored and halved
6 tablespoons sugar
3 eggs
½ cup almond paste
1 tablespoon ground cardamom
zest of 1 lemon

Preheat the oven to 350°F.

Put the white wine in a baking pan large enough to hold the apple halves side by side. Place the apple halves in the pan, cut side down, and sprinkle them with the sugar. Bake until the apples are barely tender, 30 to 40 minutes.

In a bowl mix the remaining ingredients. Spread the mixture over the apple halves. Increase the oven temperature to 400°F and continue to bake the apples until the topping is lightly browned, 15 to 20 minutes. Serve hot from the oven, or make in advance and cool to room temperature.

A Note on the Wines

A good complement to the kale soup and the timbale of veal in lemon sauce would be a flinty, crisp white wine of medium body. We suggest a Vichon Chevrier (now called Chevrignon), a blend of Semillon and Sauvignon Blanc grapes, similar to a dry white Graves.

For the duckling, we recommend a big, full-bodied, complex Pinot Noir made in Burgundian style. A good example is the Pinot Noir from Acacia, a winery in the cool southern region of the Napa Valley.

Tunisia

❖

Chicken Broth with Mint

Sea Bass with Turmeric

Couscous with Beef and Vegetables

Yogurt and Cucumber Salad

Pita Bread
(Arabic Flat Bread)

Dried Nuts, Fresh and Dried Fruits

Wines:
Saint-Véran, Les Trois Pêcheurs, Caves Prissé
Gigondas, Guigal

CHICKEN BROTH WITH MINT
(SERVES 6)

> 3 tablespoons olive oil
> 2–3 cloves garlic, chopped
> 6 cups chicken broth (page 36)
> 1 small potato, peeled and cut into ¼-inch
>   slices
> 3 tablespoons fresh mint, very coarsely
>   chopped, or 1 tablespoon dried, plus 12–
>   18 whole mint leaves
> salt
> Tabasco sauce
> 2 eggs

Heat the oil in a soup pot or Dutch oven, add the garlic, and sauté until it is translucent. Add the broth and sliced potato and simmer until the potato is tender, 20 to 25 minutes. Stir in the chopped mint and puree the mixture in a blender or food processor.

Return the soup to the pot to reheat. Adjust the seasoning with salt and Tabasco sauce. Beat the eggs in a small mixing bowl. Ladle a cup of the hot soup into the eggs, whisking continuously. Remove the soup from the heat and whisk the egg mixture back into the soup. Ladle the soup into individual bowls and float 2 or 3 mint leaves on each portion. Serve immediately.

SEA BASS WITH TURMERIC
(SERVES 6)

Since this dish is served at room temperature, make it some time in advance of serving to allow it enough time to cool.

> 1 tablespoon olive oil
> 1 large onion, sliced
> 2–3 cloves garlic, minced
> ½ teaspoon turmeric
> ½ teaspoon ground coriander (cilantro)
> 2 cups water
> juice of 1 lemon
> ¼ teaspoon crushed red pepper flakes
> salt
> 6 3-ounce pieces of sea bass or other
>   white, firm-fleshed fish
> 6 lemon wedges
> 2 tablespoons chopped fresh parsley

Heat the oil in a large skillet with a cover, or in a Dutch oven. Add the onion slices and sauté until translucent. Add the garlic, turmeric, and coriander. Stir only a minute or two, then add the water, lemon juice, and red pepper. Simmer, uncovered, for 10 to 15 minutes, or until the onions are tender. Adjust the seasoning with salt.

Arrange the pieces of fish in the pan. Cover and simmer only until heated through, 10 to 15 minutes. If the liquid in the pan does not cover the fish completely, turn the fish halfway through the cooking so that the turmeric will color it uniformly. When the fish is cooked, remove it to a serving platter to cool.

Put the skillet over a high heat. Boil down the juices until the pan is almost dry, then cool the juices and onions to room temperature.

To serve, spoon the cooled onions and remaining juices over the fish, and garnish each portion with a wedge of lemon and a sprinkle of parsley.

COUSCOUS WITH BEEF AND VEGETABLES

(SERVES 6–8)

Couscous is to North Africa what paella is to Spain. Every region, and some say every cook, has a different interpretation. The word itself describes both the grain and the complete dish with all the trimmings. Couscous even lends its name to the couscoussier, the multilayered pot in which the ingredients for a couscous traditionally cook. The moistened and swollen grain—most commonly semolina that looks like tiny bits of pasta about the size of cracked wheat, but also millet, corn, barley, or cracked wheat—is cooked in the sievelike top part of the pot in the flavorful steam rising from the stew simmering below it. The cooked grains are served surrounded by the meats and vegetables, often a large variety for an elaborate dinner, and flavored further by a hot sauce, some of which is spooned over the dish, the rest passed separately at the table. It is also traditional to eat couscous with the fingers, scooped up in soft flat bread.

Since most Western cooks do not own a couscoussier, we have simplified the cooking methods, preparing the grains and stew separately. Couscous cooked by itself can also accompany grilled or roasted meats, much like a pilaf, or be used as the basis for a stuffing for fowl.

STEW:

2 tablespoons oil
2 pounds beef stew meat, cut into 1½-inch chunks
2 onions, chopped
3–4 cloves garlic, chopped
¼ teaspoon ground allspice
½ teaspoon curry powder
½ teaspoon dried thyme
1 teaspoon dried basil
salt and pepper
6 tomatoes, peeled (see Glossary) and chopped
3–4 cups water
3 carrots, peeled and cut into 1½-inch pieces
2 medium turnips or rutabagas, peeled and quartered
½ pound whole okra, stems trimmed
½ pound string beans, cut into 1½-inch lengths
2 long green chili peppers, seeded, deveined, and cut into 1½-inch pieces, or 2 bell peppers plus ½ teaspoon crushed red pepper
2 cups cooked garbanzo beans, or 1 1-pound can, drained

Heat the oil in a large heavy pot such as a Dutch oven, add the meat, and brown it on all sides over high heat. As the moisture in the pan starts to evaporate, add the onions and continue to sauté until they are lightly browned. Add the seasonings, and stir for 2 to 3 minutes to blend in the spices. Add the tomatoes and enough water to cover and bring the pot to a boil. Reduce the heat to a slow simmer and cook for 1 hour, or until the meat is tender. Add water as necessary during the cooking to keep the meat moist. The finished stew should have a souplike, rather than a thickened saucelike, consistency. Add the vegetables and cook, uncovered, until they are tender, 25 to 30 minutes.

COUSCOUS (GRAIN):
    6 tablespoons (¾ stick) butter
    3 cups couscous
    4 cups hot water
    1 teaspoon salt

Melt the butter over low heat in a 2- to 3-quart saucepan with a lid. Pour in the couscous and stir until all the grains are coated. Add the hot water and salt. Bring to a boil, then turn down the heat to the lowest setting. Cover the pan and cook for 7 minutes, or until all the liquid is absorbed.

HOT SAUCE:
    1 8-ounce can tomato sauce
    1 teaspoon paprika
    ½ teaspoon coriander (cilantro)
    ½ teaspoon cayenne or crushed red pepper flakes
    ½ teaspoon ground cumin
    salt

Heat all the sauce ingredients in a small saucepan for a few minutes to blend the flavors. Add a few tablespoons to the sauce in the stewpot, according to taste, then pour the rest into a small bowl to pass at the table.

TO SERVE:
Mound the couscous on a large heated platter. Arrange the meats and vegetables over and around the couscous and spoon the sauce from the stew liberally over all. Pass the remaining sauce and the bowl of hot sauce at the table.

YOGURT AND CUCUMBER SALAD

Peel and seed 2 or 3 regular cucumbers (or 1 European cucumber, in which case this is not necessary). Cut the cucumbers in thin slices and toss them with plain, unflavored yogurt, salt, pepper, and chopped fresh dill. This dish is refreshing served as an accompaniment to the couscous instead of as a separate salad course.

PITA BREAD
(Arabic Flat Bread)
(MAKES 8 BREADS)

    1 recipe Assyrian Lawasha dough (page 31)

Divide the lawasha dough into 8 mounds or balls and let them rest for about 30 minutes for the final rising.

Preheat the oven to 450°F and place a sheet pan on a rack at the lowest position in the oven.

Roll the balls out onto a floured board, 2 at a time, into 8-inch rounds. Put the first 2 rounds directly onto the hot sheet pan in the oven. While they are baking, roll out the next 2 rounds. Bake each batch for 6 to 10 minutes. The dough will puff up like miniature flying saucers. As soon as each batch is lightly browned on top, remove them to a wire rack to cool. Continue the process until all the rounds are baked.

When the breads come out of the oven, they should start to collapse. If they do not, puncture their bubbly, inflated tops with a fork.

VARIATION: To make Lebanese Zahtar Bread, after the dough is rolled out into 8-inch rounds, brush each one lightly with olive oil and sprinkle with the Lebanese seasoning mixture called zahtar (predominantly thyme mixed with sumac and sesame). If zahtar is unavailable, dust the top lightly with dried thyme and sesame seeds. Bake as above.

DRIED NUTS, FRESH AND DRIED FRUITS

Make a platter of the best seasonal fruits, such as grapes, figs, apricots, loquats, and melons; add dried dates, raisins, and figs; and complete the arrangement with some walnuts and pistachios.

A Note on the Wines

For the first wine with this menu we would choose a light-bodied white wine with good fruit. Of this type, we like the Saint-Véran, Les Trois Pêcheurs, Caves Prissé, which somewhat resembles a good Mâcon.

To complement the robust main course of couscous, we would select an intensely rich, earthy red wine from the Rhone, such as a Gigondas from Guigal.

Turkey

❖

Yalandji Dolma

Cheese-Filled Phyllo Pastry
(Cigarro Burek)

Circassian Chicken
Rice Pilaf

Vegetable, Herb, and Yogurt Salad

Lavash
(Lawasha)

Fritters in Syrup
("Lips of the Beauty")

Wines:
Louis M. Martini Gewürztraminer
Beaujolais Village Joseph Drouhin et Cie

YALANDJI DOLMA

(SERVES 6)

The Turkish name Yalandji Dolma, "Pretender's Dolma," was given to this recipe because it was originally a Lenten dish made without meat, and therefore, since the proper dolma always contains a meat stuffing, considered a "pretender." Served at room temperature, this dish makes an exceptionally fine hors d'oeuvre and is wonderful picnic fare. If you make more than you need, dolmas will keep for up to a week in the refrigerator.

1 pint jar grape leaves
½ cup olive oil
3 tablespoons pine nuts or slivered
blanched almonds
1 large onion, chopped
½ cup short-grain rice
⅓ cup chopped fresh parsley
2–3 green onions, chopped, including the
green tops
3 tablespoons currants
¼ teaspoon ground allspice
⅓ teaspoon ground cinnamon
½ teaspoon salt
¼ teaspoon pepper
1 cup water
4–6 lettuce leaves
juice of 2 lemons
1 cup plain yogurt
1 tablespoon chopped fresh dill, or 1
teaspoon dried

Drain the brine from the grape leaves, put them in a bowl, cover them with cold water, and set aside.

Heat 6 tablespoons oil in a sauté pan. Add the nuts and cook over medium heat until the nuts barely turn amber. Immediately take the pan off the stove, remove the nuts with a slotted spoon, and place them in a bowl to cool. Return the pan to the heat. Add the onion and sauté slowly, until it becomes translucent but not brown. Add the rice and stir until it is coated with oil. Add the parsley, green onions, currants, allspice, cinnamon, salt and pepper, and ¾ cup water. Cover the pan and simmer the mixture until the rice absorbs the liquid, 10 to 15 minutes. Remove from the heat and stir in the reserved nuts. Set aside.

Drain the grape leaves, press out the excess water, and cut off the stems. Arrange 5 or 6 leaves, shiny side down, the stem end facing you, on a work counter. Place about 2 tablespoons of the reserved rice filling on each leaf near the stem end. Fold the stem end up and over the filling. Fold in the 2 sides, then roll up the leaf so that it resembles a short cigar. Preheat the oven to 350°F.

Line a 2- to 3-quart casserole with half of the lettuce leaves. Pack the dolmas in the casserole close to each other with the seam side down. Pour the juice of 1 lemon over them and add the remaining ¼ cup water to the casserole. Cover the dolmas with the other half of the lettuce leaves, then place the lid on the casserole and bake for 1 hour. Remove from the oven and cool to room temperature. (Note: dolmas can be refrigerated at this stage for later use.)

To serve, arrange dolmas that have reached room temperature on a large serving platter or on individual plates. Pour the juice of the second lemon over them and sprinkle with the remaining 2 tablespoons olive oil. Make the sauce by mixing the yogurt with the dill and pass it separately.

CHEESE-FILLED PHYLLO PASTRY
(Cigarro Burek)

(MAKES 40)

Throughout the Middle East, bureks are made by folding buttered, cheese-filled phyllo dough into little triangular shapes. Cigarro bureks taste the same but, as the name implies, are rolled into cylindrical shapes resembling small cigars. Bureks, frozen unbaked, can go directly from the freezer into a preheated 375°F oven to make an instant hors d'oeuvre.

6 ounces feta cheese, crumbled
4 ounces cream cheese
1 egg, beaten
2 tablespoons chopped fresh parsley
1 tablespoon chopped fresh dill, or 1 teaspoon dried
8 sheets of packaged phyllo dough
½ cup (1 stick) butter

DO AHEAD:
Defrost the phyllo dough and return the remainder to the freezer. Butter a cookie sheet. Melt the butter and remove from the heat.

Preheat the oven to 375°F.

Mix the feta and cream cheese with the egg and herbs and set aside.

Lay out one sheet of phyllo dough on a counter. (Keep the remaining dough covered with a slightly damp towel to prevent its drying out.) Brush the sheet of dough with some melted butter. Cut it the short way into 5 strips, about 3 x 10 inches each. Place 1½ teaspoons of the filling at one end of each strip. Roll the strips into cylinders about ½ inch in diameter. Continue until all of the dough has been cut, filled, and rolled.

Arrange 2 to 3 cylinders per person on the cookie sheet and brush them with more butter. (Freeze the rest of the cylinders, unbaked, for use at another time.) Bake for about 10 minutes, or until the cylinders are well browned and very flaky.

CIRCASSIAN CHICKEN
(SERVES 6)

The recipe given here is for the traditional cold dish. Since we are accompanying it with a warm rice pilaf, you may prefer to serve the chicken warm also, or at room temperature. Follow the instructions as given, eliminating the steps for cooling the chicken and sauce. When ready to serve, reheat the chicken in the sauce just long enough to warm it through.

> 3 whole chicken fryer breasts (from 3½-pound chickens)
> 2 cups chicken broth (page 36)
> 1½ cups shelled walnuts
> ½ cup chopped onions
> 3 slices of white bread
> ½ teaspoon paprika, plus more for garnish
> salt and pepper

Bone and skin the chicken: Remove the keel-shaped breastbones and cartilage, using a boning knife or poultry shears, forcing the meat away from the bone. (See illustration, page 54.) Carefully slide a knife under the breastbones and cut them away. Gently pull back the skin, using the knife to help "peel" it from the flesh. (Or ask your butcher to do this for you.) Cut each breast in half, making 6 half breasts.

Heat the broth in a frying pan. Place the chicken in the broth, cover the pan, and simmer for 10 to 15 minutes, or until the meat firms up and loses its translucent pink color. Remove the chicken with a slotted spoon and set it aside to cool. Boil down the liquid in the pan until it is reduced to 1½ cups and set it aside to cool.

In a blender or food processor puree the remaining ingredients with the reduced broth until it is smooth. When the chicken is cool, nap it with the puree and sprinkle it very lightly with paprika.

NOTE: On a hot day it may be necessary to firm up the sauce by cooling it in the refrigerator.

RICE PILAF

Use the recipe for plain Rice Pilaf in the Perennial Favorites menu, stirring in a lump of butter before serving.

VEGETABLE, HERB, AND YOGURT SALAD

This very refreshing cold vegetable and yogurt blend serves as a soup in some Middle Eastern cuisines but, as here, can make an excellent salad by increasing the proportion of vegetables to yogurt. To make the salad, peel, seed, and chop 1 or 2 cucumbers, depending on size, and put in a salad bowl. Add several chopped radishes, green onions, parsley, and fresh dill. Mix enough yogurt and lemon juice to make a dressing, season with salt and pepper, and toss with the fresh chopped vegetables.

LAVASH (LAWASHA)

The most appropriate bread for this Middle Eastern meal is the traditional lavash. For recipe and instructions on moistening, see the menu for Assyria.

FRITTERS IN SYRUP
("Lips of the Beauty")
(SERVES 6)

In traditional Turkish cooking, fritters take on very explicit shapes patterned on the human form. There are "Lips of the Beauty," "Lady's Navel," and so on. According to recent research on Mesopotamia, some of the breads and desserts in ancient Assyria took such anatomical shapes as a heart or a woman's breast as early as 1700 B.C. The fritter batter is much the same as a French pâte à chou or cream puff dough. In keeping with the Middle Eastern taste for sweets, however, fritters are traditionally saturated in syrup, much like a rum baba, as in the recipe that follows.

SYRUP:
1½ cups water
1½ cups sugar
1 teaspoon lemon juice
1 tablespoon orange-flower or rose water

FRITTERS:
1½ cups water
½ cup (1 stick) butter
1½ teaspoons sugar
1¾ cups all-purpose flour
4 eggs
light salad oil

To make the syrup, put the water, sugar, and lemon juice in a small saucepan and boil for a few minutes until the mixture becomes syrupy. Remove the syrup from the heat and cool. Stir in the orange-flower or rose water. Reserve.

To make the fritters, heat the water, butter, and sugar in a small saucepan until the butter melts and the mixture starts to boil. Add the flour all at once and stir with a wooden spoon until the mixture dries out a bit and starts to pull away clean from the sides of the pan. Remove from the heat and add the eggs, one at a time, stirring vigorously with each addition until the batter becomes smooth and glossy. Add the next egg, and continue in the same manner until all 4 eggs have been added to the batter.

Pour about 2 inches of light salad oil into a Dutch oven, a 4- to 5-quart soup kettle, or other deep pot and heat until it reaches 375°F on a candy or deep-frying thermometer. While the oil is heating, form the dough into small balls, about the size for hors d'oeuvres, dipping your hands in flour to help shape the dough. If you prefer, you can shape the dough, Turkish-style, into a fanciful design instead of into rounds.

When the oil is hot, fry 5 to 10 fritters at a time until they puff up and are nicely browned, 8 to 10 minutes. During the cooking, turn the balls in the oil so that they brown uniformly on all sides. As each batch of fritters comes out of the oil, drain them on paper towels and immediately put them to soak for 15 minutes in the reserved syrup. Serve in small bowls with a little of the syrup poured over each portion.

A Note on the Wines

The perfect match for the flaky, cheese-filled burek would be a spicy, floral, dry white Gewürztraminer, such as those made by Louis M. Martini.

The walnuts in the sauce napping the Circassian chicken suggest a red wine, but one delicate enough to allow the unaggressive flavors of the chicken to come through. A light, fruity Beaujolais Village, such as those from Joseph Drouhin, would be a good match.

United States 1:
A Shaker Menu

❖

Herb Soup

Sausage Cooked in Cider

Veal Scallops in Sour Cream
Mushrooms in Sherry Butter
Pennsylvania Dutch Filling

String Bean Salad

Biscuits

Hazelnut Cake with Rose Water Frosting

Wines:
Firestone Vineyard Johannisberg Riesling
Wente Bros. Pinot Noir

HERB SOUP

Heat 6 cups or more of rich chicken broth (page 36) and flavor it with a handful of minced assorted fresh herbs (thyme, rosemary, chervil, dill, parsley, etc.). Serve each portion over a slice of sturdy toasted bread sprinkled with grated white cheddar cheese.

SAUSAGE COOKED IN CIDER
(SERVES 6)

> 12–18 pork link sausages
> 2 green apples, peeled and cut into 6 wedges each
> 1 small onion, minced
> 1 tablespoon flour
> 1 cup cider

Pierce the sausages with a fork and place them in a frying pan. As soon as some fat renders out of the sausages, add the apple slices, and lower the heat to moderate. Cook the sausages and apple slices until they have browned, then remove them to a heated platter.

Discard all but 1 tablespoon of the fat in the pan. Add the onion and sauté just until it starts to brown. Stir in the flour. Add the cider. Mix the ingredients together well and simmer for at least 5 minutes, or until the mixture thickens and becomes shiny. Return the sausages and apple slices to the pan and simmer in the sauce for a few minutes before serving.

VEAL SCALLOPS IN SOUR CREAM
(SERVES 6)

> 1½–2 pounds veal scallops
> flour seasoned with salt and pepper
> ¼ cup (½ stick) butter
> 1 large onion, chopped
> ½ cup veal or chicken broth (page 23 or 36)
> 1 cup sour cream
> 3 tomatoes, peeled (see Glossary) and coarsely chopped
> chopped fresh parsley

DO AHEAD:

Warm a serving platter large enough to hold the veal scallops.

Dredge the veal scallops in the seasoned flour. Melt the butter in a frying pan. Add the scallops and sauté them, a few at a time, transferring them to the warm platter as they are browned.

Add the onion to the pan and simmer only until it is transparent. Stir in the broth and sour cream. Add the tomatoes and simmer until the sauce is smooth. Return the scallops and any accumulated juices to the pan. Heat through very gently. Serve sprinkled with chopped parsley.

MUSHROOMS IN SHERRY BUTTER

Heat some butter in a skillet and sauté thinly sliced fresh mushrooms quickly, deglaze the pan with sherry, and flavor with chopped fresh dill.

PENNSYLVANIA DUTCH FILLING

The original restaurant menu included potato pancakes with the veal. If you want to make them, the basic recipe is on page 226. As an alternative, this is a recipe that I first ate at my daughter-in-law Janine's house, and it is so good that we thought we should include it. It comes from Janine's Pennsylvania Dutch grandmother, who served it always on Thanksgiving with the roast turkey, as well as on other occasions, particularly with roasts and pot roasts. While it is being cooked, the house fills with a wonderful aroma of browning onions and butter. In spite of its name, this is not used to fill anything, but always as a side dish.—D.M.

There are, of course, no exact proportions, but there should be enough of the caramelized vegetables to be a very predominant flavor in the potatoes. Sauté *very slowly* 6 or 8 large chopped onions and ½ bunch of chopped celery in about 1 cup (2 sticks) butter, stirring frequently, until the vegetables become very soft and richly caramelized. It should take an hour or more. Add a few slices of broken-up French-type white bread, stale or fresh. As the bread soaks up some of the buttery juices, it will begin to brown. Stir almost continuously, scraping in the brown crusts that form on the bottom, and continue until the mixture cooks way down—to 3 or 4 cups.

While the onions and celery are cooking, boil about 6 to 8 large peeled potatoes, drain, and whip them with an electric beater with just enough milk to bind them; they should be fairly dry rather than loose and creamy. Beat in 2 eggs.

Season the caramelized onion mixture with salt and black pepper, then mix it, spoon by spoon, into the mashed potatoes. The texture shoould be thick enough to mound high on a spoon, and the color should be a deep beige-tan. When all of the onion mixture has been added, mound the potatoes in a 3-inch-deep casserole or baking dish, rounding the top. Dot with butter and bake in a 350°F oven until it poufs and browns a bit on the top, 25 to 35 minutes.

STRING BEAN SALAD

Combine shredded lettuce, cooked fresh green beans, and chopped green onions. Toss with a simple vinegar and oil dressing and garnish with fresh summer savory and, if available, nasturtium blossoms.

BISCUITS

The Shakers grew and used an abundant variety of herbs. It would be very much in keeping with their cooking to add an assorted sprinkle of some of your favorites to the basic Baking Powder Biscuit recipe in the United States Early American menu.

HAZELNUT CAKE WITH ROSE WATER FROSTING
(SERVES 8)

CAKE:
- ½ cup (1 stick) sweet butter
- 1 cup dark brown sugar
- 2 eggs
- 1½ cups all-purpose flour
- ¼ teaspoon ground allspice
- ½ teaspoon ground cinnamon
- ½ teaspoon ground ginger
- ½ teaspoon each cream of tartar and baking soda or 1¼ teaspoons baking powder
- 1 cup chopped hazelnuts

ROSE WATER FROSTING:
- ½ cup (1 stick) butter
- 1½ cups confectioners' sugar
- 1 egg
- 2 teaspoons rose water, or 1 teaspoon vanilla extract
- ½ cup heavy cream

DO AHEAD:
Butter and flour an 8-inch cake pan.

Preheat the oven to 325°F.

Beat together the sweet butter and brown sugar until they are fluffly. Add the eggs and beat until smooth, scraping down and incorporating any of the mixture that sticks to the sides of the bowl. Add the remaining cake ingredients and mix in only until blended. The batter will be very heavy, almost like cookie dough. Pour the batter into the prepared cake pan. Bake for 50 to 60 minutes. A toothpick inserted in the center of the cake should come out clean.

Turn out and cool on a rack. Cover tightly with plastic wrap and store in a cool pantry (or refrigerator, if necessary) for 2 days before using.

When the cake is ready, prepare the frosting: Cream the butter and sugar in a mixing bowl. Add the egg and beat by hand or machine until smooth. Add the rose water (or vanilla extract) and cream. Continue beating until the frosting is shiny and smooth.

To serve, slice the cake and spoon a portion of rose water frosting over each piece.

A Note on the Wines

A medium-bodied, perfumy Johannisberg Riesling, one with distinct floral aromas such as Firestone produces, is our choice to accompany the herb soup and apple-y sausages.

For the veal scallops in sour cream, we suggest a light-bodied, delicate Pinot Noir, one with good varietal character. Our choice would be a bottle from Wente Bros.

United States 2: An Early American Menu from Martha Washington's Personal Cookbook

�֎

Pease Porrage of Old Pease
(Split-Pea Soup)

Boyled Soles
(Poached Fillet of Sole with Ginger)

A Forsed Legg of Lambe
(Roast Leg of Lamb Stuffed with Herbs)
Sparragus
(Poached Asparagus with Melted Butter)

Bisket Bread
(Beaten Biscuits)

Greene Codling Tarte
(Green Apple Pie with Heavy Cream)

Wines:
Sonoma-Cutrer Vineyards Chardonnay
Harbor Winery Cabernet Sauvignon

The inspiration for this dinner came from *Martha Washington's Booke of Cookery*, a volume transcribed and annotated by Karen Hess (see Bibliography). We have interpreted and updated the original recipes to suit present tastes and supplies, but kept the spirit and flavor as close as possible to the original.

PEASE PORRAGE OF OLD PEASE
(Split-Pea Soup)
(SERVES 6)

1 cup dried (split) peas
6 cups water or chicken broth (page 36)
1 clove garlic
1 small onion, minced
1 teaspoon ground coriander (cilantro)
2 teaspoons dried mint leaves
1 teaspoon salt
pepper
4 tablespoons chopped fresh parsley
2 tablespoons butter

Pick over and wash the peas. Put them, along with the water or broth and the garlic, into a soup kettle, and simmer for 25 to 30 minutes, or until the peas are tender. Press through a sieve or puree in a blender or food processor. Return the puree to the soup pot, add the onions, coriander, mint, salt, and pepper. Simmer for another 15 to 20 minutes, or until the onions are tender. Stir in the parsley and butter just before serving.

BOYLED SOLES
(Poached Fillet of Sole with Ginger)
(SERVES 6)

1 cup dry white wine
½ cup water
1 tablespoon grated fresh ginger
6 3-ounce sole fillets
salt
6 thick slices of bread, crusts removed
¼ cup (½ stick) butter, cut into bits

Bring the wine, water, and ginger to a boil in a large frying pan. Put the fillets on a dish and sprinkle them very lightly with salt. Place them in the broth (the fish must be covered with the liquid; if not, add water), lower the heat, and poach for 5 to 10 minutes—just until opaque and cooked through.

While the fish is poaching, lightly toast the bread, then place 1 slice on each plate (in Colonial days, this was called a "sop"). Remove the fish as soon as it is cooked through and put 1 piece on each sop. Keep the plates in a warm spot.

Turn the heat to high and reduce the liquid in the pan to about 1 cup. Remove the pan from the heat and whisk in the butter, bit by bit. Pour equal amounts of sauce over the fish and serve immediately.

A FORSED LEGG OF LAMBE
(Roast Leg of Lamb Stuffed with Herbs)

(SERVES 6 TO 8)

This "Forsed Legg of Lambe" is certainly an elaborate dish. The word *forsed* comes from the French *farcir*, "to stuff." This roast is indeed stuffed, with a mixture of fresh herbs, anchovies, and capers; but that is only one part of the recipe: Its complex garnishes include sweetbreads, lamb kidneys, lamb fries, and sausages.

Martha Washington describes the fresh herb seasoning only as "sweet herbs." In several of her other recipes for lamb, however, she calls for parsley, thyme, marjoram, and rosemary, all of which are eminently sweet and excellent with lamb, and so we have used them here. As for the sausages she calls for, there are no special indications of type, but elsewhere she gives recipes for two kinds: one pork, one veal, both flavored with cloves and mace. French white wine sausages, available commercially, are the most reasonable modern-day equivalent, and we use them in our recipe. Our other departures include substituting butter for caul fat and eliminating the "little pickle of oysters" and the hard-cooked eggs that Mrs. Washington added at the end to the sauce.

STUFFING:

1 bunch parsley, stemmed and minced
4–5 anchovy fillets, minced
1 tablespoon capers, rinsed and chopped
1 teaspoon fresh thyme, or ½ teaspoon dried
1 teaspoon fresh marjoram, or ½ teaspoon dried
1 teaspoon fresh rosemary, or ½ teaspoon dried
zest of 1 lemon, grated (use zest from garnishes, see below)
¼ cup (½ stick) butter, softened
salt and pepper

LAMB:

1 6–7-pound leg of lamb, shank removed and the leg boned but left whole, not butterflied (this will give you a roast with a hole through the middle, lengthwise, to take the stuffing)
salt and pepper
grated nutmeg
1 medium onion, sliced
3–4 cloves garlic, peeled and coarsely sliced
½ cup dry white wine
1½ cups lamb or beef broth (see Note)

GARNISHES:

1½ pounds veal sweetbreads
1 tablespoon pickling spice
juice of 1 lemon (reserve zest for stuffing)
2 tablespoons butter
3–4 lamb kidneys, halved lengthwise, cleaned
3–4 lamb fries (testicles) (optional)
4 3–4-ounce French-style white wine sausages
1 bunch watercress, washed and trimmed

SAUCE:

1–2 teaspoons Worcestershire sauce
2 egg yolks

Preheat the oven to 350°F.

Mix together the stuffing ingredients. Then press the stuffing into the cavity in the lamb leg, using the handle of a wooden spoon or other tool to help push it in. Sew up both ends with white cotton thread.

Season the roast with salt, pepper, and nutmeg. Place the meat in a roasting pan and surround it with the onion and garlic. Put in the preheated oven and roast until the onion is very brown. Add the white wine and broth and continue roasting until done to your taste; it will take 1¼ to 1½ hours for medium rare (140°F on a meat thermometer).

While the lamb is roasting, prepare the garnishes. Simmer the sweetbreads for 20 minutes in water to cover, seasoned with the pickling spice and lemon juice. Remove from the heat and leave the sweetbreads in the poaching liquid for 30 minutes. Remove them and trim carefully of any membranes, skin, or fat.

Melt 2 tablespoons of butter in a skillet. When it begins to sizzle, add one garnish (except watercress) at a time: sweetbreads, kidneys, fries, and sausages, browning each batch well on all sides. Reserve.

When the lamb is done, remove it to a platter and let it rest for 20 to 30 minutes in a warm place before carving it. Transfer the pan juices and vegetables to a saucepan and put on the stove to simmer.

To make the sauce, strain the pan juices, discarding the vegetables. Return the juices to the saucepan, add the Worcestershire sauce to taste, and continue to simmer over a low flame. Skim off any surface fat. Beat the egg yolks lightly in a small bowl, whisk them rapidly into the strained juices, and remove immediately from the heat to prevent the sauce from curdling.

To serve, arrange the roast, whole or in slices, on a platter or carving board, surrounded with the browned sweetbreads, kidneys, fries, sliced sausages, and a bouquet of watercress. Pass the sauce separately.

NOTE: You can use the lamb bones and trimmings to make the broth that is called for in the roasting process. See page 23 for instructions.

SPARRAGUS
(Poached Asparagus with Melted Butter)

Wash 1 large bunch of fresh asparagus. Snap off the ends where they give naturally. If the asparagus are very large, use a vegetable peeler to remove any tough skin or fibrous pieces. In a skillet poach the stalks in rapidly boiling salted water. As soon as they are barely tender, remove from the heat and add a glass of cold water to stop the cooking. Drain well and dress with a tablespoon or two of melted butter.

BISKET BREAD
(Beaten Biscuits)

Beaten biscuits were a labor of love in the old South and there are apparently many brave souls who still make these delicious baked goods in the traditional way. Mrs. Washington's instructions called for beating the dough for a total of 4 hours, about double the amount of any other recipes we have seen. Old-fashioned beating was done with a wooden bat, a hammer, or any such heavy implement; its purpose was to tenderize the dough. Since baking powder will produce a fine, light, and tender biscuit, we suggest making a batch of standard baking powder biscuits to accompany Mrs. Washington's menu. (If you do not want to bake them yourself, the refrigerated, packaged biscuits available in all markets are a reasonable substitute.) Good biscuits can be made with packaged mixes such as Bisquick, using 2 cups mix to 1 cup milk, then following the methods for kneading, cutting, and baking given below.

Baking Powder Biscuits
(MAKES 12)

>   2 cups all-purpose flour
>   ½ teaspoon salt
>   1 tablespoon baking powder

>   ¼ cup shortening
>   ¾ cup milk

Preheat the oven to 450°F.

Mix the dry ingredients in a bowl. Cut in the shortening. When the mixture is of a mealy, coarse consistency, add the milk and mix in just enough to make a soft dough.

Turn the dough out onto a floured board and knead it no more than a dozen times. Roll out or pat out to about ½-inch thickness, then cut out into rounds with a floured cutter or the floured rim of a glass. Bake on an ungreased cookie sheet for 12 to 15 minutes. Space apart for crisp biscuits; close together to be fluffy with soft sides. Serve hot from the oven.

GREENE CODLING TARTE
(Green Apple Pie with Heavy Cream)

Codling apples are no longer available, but pippin apples work very well. Martha Washington's recipe for an open-faced apple tart was seasoned with nothing more than sugar and cinnamon and served with a pitcher of heavy cream. In those days, tarte usually meant any open-faced pie, often one made with rich dough such as French puff pastry. However, any favorite short pie dough will work well. Or use Danish Waffle dough (page 95).

Roll out the dough to about ⅛-inch thickness on a floured board. Line a deep (2-inch) tart or pie pan with the dough, doubling under any excess at the rim and fluting the edges. Fill with 6 medium pippin apples, peeled, sliced, and tossed with ½ cup sugar and a good sprinkling of cinnamon. (Although Mrs. Washington's tarte did not call for any other ingredients, 1 tablespoon tapioca sprinkled over the apples may help to keep the filling from being too liquid.) Bake the tart in a hot oven (400° to 425°F) for 35 to 45 minutes, until the fruit is tender and the crust has browned. Serve warm or at room temperature with some heavy cream or crème fraîche to pour over.

A Note on the Wines

With the gingery fillet of sole, we drank a big, rich Chardonnay of the 1982 vintage from Sonoma-Cutrer Vineyards. Any similar Chardonnay will be appropriate.

The complex leg of lamb with its stuffing of herbs, anchovies, and capers, and its many garnishes, seems to call for another big, rich wine, such as the well-balanced dry red 1975 Cabernet Sauvignon from Harbor Winery served with the original Narsai's menu.

Venezuela

❖

Onion and Tomato Soup

Braised Pork Steamed in Banana Leaves
(Hallacas)

Tripe Stew

Pineapple with Lime and Rum

Rolls

Coffee Mocha Flan

Wines:
DeLoach Vineyards Chardonnay
Joseph Phelps Heinemann Mountain Vineyards Pinot Noir

ONION AND TOMATO SOUP

Melt a little butter in a soup pot and sauté
2 or 3 sliced onions in it until they start to
brown. Add 4 cups rich chicken broth
(page 36) and 2 or 3 peeled (see Glossary)
and chopped tomatoes. Season the soup
with salt, pepper, and a pinch of oregano.
Sprinkle with fresh parsley before serving.

BRAISED PORK STEAMED IN BANANA LEAVES
(Hallacas)

(SERVES 6)

DOUGH:

1 teaspoon annatto seeds, or ½ teaspoon
   paprika
1 cup masa harina, grits, or cornmeal
1 teaspoon salt
2 tablespoons lard
¾ cup hot chicken broth (page 36)

FILLING:

1 tablespoon lard
½ pound boneless pork shoulder, defatted
   and cut into ½-inch cubes
½ small onion, chopped
1 small red pepper or pimiento, roasted,
   peeled, seeded, and chopped
2–3 cloves garlic, minced
½ cup sherry
¼ cup raisins
2 tablespoons capers
6 green olives, pitted and chopped
1 egg, hard-cooked and chopped

TURNOVERS:

2–3 banana leaves, or 12 dried corn
   husks, or 6 10-inch squares of
   parchment paper
string (optional)

DO AHEAD:

If using corn husks, prepare them 30 minutes ahead (see instructions).

To make the dough, place the annatto
seeds in a blender or food processor with ½
cup of whatever corn grain you are using,
and process until pulverized. (If you are
substituting paprika, simply mix it with the
grain.) Put the remaining ½ cup of grain
and the pulverized annatto or paprika mixture in the container of a blender. Add the
salt and lard. Mix until well blended.

Put the mixture in a bowl. Add the hot
chicken broth and stir in well. (Masa
harina or instant grits will absorb the broth
very quickly; regular grits or cornmeal will
take about 15 minutes. If using the latter,
leave the mixture in the bowl until the
liquid is absorbed, then mix again.) Set
aside.

To make the filling, heat the lard in a
skillet. Add the pork, onion, and pepper
or pimiento and sauté until browned. Add
the garlic and stir until the mixture is sizzling. Stir in the remaining ingredients.
Remove from the heat and set aside to
cool.

Meanwhile, make the turnovers. If banana leaves are available, prepare them by
cutting away the center vein with scissors,

then tearing gently along the line of the veins, and cutting into 10-inch squares. Wash gently in water.

If using dried corn husks, which work almost as well (and are easy to find in most Latin neighborhoods), moisten the husks in hot water for 30 minutes, then drain. To get a piece equivalent in size to the banana leaf, you may have to overlap 2 husks, making a finished piece of approximately 6 x 12 inches.

When the banana leaves, husks, or parchment are prepared, set them aside.

(1) Divide the dough into 6 equal parts and roll it into balls. Gently press one ball down in the center of each banana leaf, forming an oval shape about 3 x 6 inches, running diagonally across the center of the leaf.

(2) Place one-sixth of the cooled filling mixture in the center of each dough oval. (3) Fold the leaf in half diagonally so that the dough inside forms a small turnover in shape. (4) and (5) Fold in each side of the leaf and turn the top down over the sides like an envelope flap.

(6) Tie each wrapped turnover once around the middle with a piece of string or a strip of leaf or corn husk.

Set a metal colander in a deep pot. Pour in water, being careful to keep it below the bottom of the colander. If that is not possible, invert a small plate or saucer in the bottom of the colander to keep the hallacas out of the water while they cook. Place the hallacas in the colander, cover the pot, and steam for 30 minutes.

To serve, cut and remove the string, then place the hallacas on individual plates so that each diner can unfold his own.

TRIPE STEW
(SERVES 6)

*1½ pounds beef honeycomb tripe, cut into
  2-inch strips
2 large limes
1 pound veal shanks
1 veal knuckle bone
½ cup garbanzo beans
6 cloves garlic, chopped*

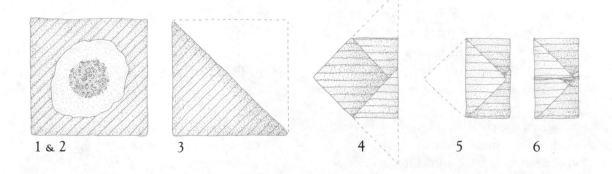

1 & 2   3   4   5   6

2 bay leaves
1 teaspoon salt
½ teaspoon white pepper
2 carrots, peeled and cut into ½-inch dice
1 pound firm yellow squash such as banana or hubbard, peeled and cut into ½-inch dice
½ small head cabbage, coarsely chopped
2 onions, coarsely chopped
3 tomatoes, peeled (see Glossary) and coarsely chopped
¼–½ teaspoon crushed red pepper flakes

DO AHEAD:

Prepare the tripe 1 hour before you are ready to start the rest of the cooking (see instructions).

Put the tripe in a glass or stainless steel bowl. Squeeze the limes over it and toss until it is well coated with the juice. Let the tripe stand for 1 hour.

Rinse the tripe under cold water and place it in a large soup pot or Dutch oven. Add the veal shanks, knuckle bone, garbanzo beans, garlic, bay leaves, salt, and white pepper. Cover the ingredients with water and bring to a boil. Lower the heat to a slow simmer. Skim the broth frequently during the cooking to keep it clear.

As soon as the shank meat is tender, remove it from the broth with a slotted spoon and place it in a bowl to cool. When the tripe is tender, remove it also to the bowl to cool.

When the shanks and tripe have cooled, remove the meat from the bones and cut the meat and tripe into bite-sized pieces.

Return them to the pot. Add the remaining ingredients. Adjust the seasoning with salt. Simmer the stew until the vegetables are tender. Serve in large soup plates.

NOTE: Depending on the wholesale butcher's method of blanching and preparing the tripe for the retail market, which varies in different regions of the country, the cooking time will vary from 2 to 2½ hours. Ask your butcher for an estimate.

PINEAPPLE WITH LIME AND RUM

Peel and halve a pineapple. Cut each half into 6 wedges. Cut away and discard the core. Squeeze fresh lime juice over the pineapple pieces and sprinkle them with dark rum. Serve 2 wedges per person with the stew.

ROLLS

Use rolls to accompany this dinner, and make them using the recipe for Baguette dough (page 119).

COFFEE MOCHA FLAN
(SERVES 6)

1 quart half and half
1 cup drip-grind Viennese or French roast coffee

½ teaspoon ground cinnamon
4 whole allspice
¾ cup brown sugar
½ ounce baking chocolate
4 eggs
2 tablespoons sherry
⅓ cup granulated sugar
1 tablespoon water
freshly grated nutmeg

Heat the half and half until it comes almost to a boil. Turn off the heat and stir in the coffee, cinnamon, and allspice. Whisk the mixture until it is well blended. Cover and set it aside to steep for 20 to 30 minutes.

Using a towel set in a colander, strain the mixture into a bowl. Stir in the brown sugar and chocolate, heating just a bit, if necessary, to dissolve the chocolate. Turn back into the bowl and cool slightly. In a separate bowl beat the eggs with the sherry and stir them into the mocha mixture. Set aside.

Preheat the oven to 350°F.

Dissolve the granulated sugar in the water in a small saucepan and heat until the sugar caramelizes. Be extremely careful, as molten sugar burns easily. Work very quickly and pour some caramel in each of 6 custard cups, turning gently to coat the bottom and sides. Pour the reserved custard mixture into the cups and set them in a roasting pan. Fill with water to half the depth of the cups. Bake for about 1 hour, or until a toothpick or thin paring knife inserted in the center comes out clean. Chill in the refrigerator.

When ready to serve, place a dessert plate over each custard cup and, holding tightly at the edges, invert the plate and cup so that the custard turns out of the cup onto the dessert plate. The caramel will now be on top. Grate a bit of fresh nutmeg over each unmolded custard.

A Note on the Wines

To accompany the soup and braised pork in banana leaves, our choice is a medium-bodied Chardonnay with a full rich nose, a style which is typical of the wines from DeLoach Vineyards.

The entrée of stewed tripe suggests a soft but rich, full-bodied Pinot Noir, such as a Joseph Phelps from the Heinemann Mountain Vineyards.

Yugoslavia

✳

Serbian Lamb Soup

Ling Cod in Tomato Sauce

Braised Veal and Pork
Buttered Egg Noodles

Cucumber and Radish Salad in Oil and Lemon Dressing

Dark Rye Bread

Slovenian Plum Pie

Wines:
Pouilly-Fuissé Domaine Corsin
Charton Bourgogne, Resèrve de la Chêvre Noire

SERBIAN LAMB SOUP

(SERVES 6)

2 pounds lamb bones and trimmings, or
    lamb neck bones
1 teaspoon pickling spice
2 quarts water
1 stalk celery, chopped
1 parsnip, peeled and diced
1 carrot, peeled and diced
1 onion, chopped
2 tablespoons rice
1 teaspoon paprika
¼ teaspoon crushed red pepper flakes
salt
2 tablespoons vinegar or lemon juice (see
    Note)
1 cup sour cream
2 egg yolks

Put the bones and pickling spice in a large soup pot or Dutch oven, cover with water, and simmer for 1½ to 2 hours. Strain the stock. Set the bones aside to cool, and return the stock to the pot. You will need 5 to 6 cups of stock; if there is more than that amount, boil briskly to reduce it. Add the vegetables, rice, paprika, and red pepper. When cool, remove the meat from the bones and add it to the soup. Simmer for about 20 minutes, or until the vegetables are tender. Adjust the seasoning with salt.

In a small bowl whisk the vinegar or lemon juice, sour cream, and egg yolks. Remove the soup from the heat. Whisk a ladle of soup into the sour cream mixture, then pour the mixture back into the soup,

stirring it in well. Serve immediately without reheating.

NOTE: Although the traditional recipes for this "national soup" all call for vinegar, as we do here, we prefer the flavor of lemon juice.

LING COD IN TOMATO SAUCE

(SERVES 6)

2 tablespoons oil
3 slices of bacon, cut into quarters
1 large onion, thinly sliced
1 teaspoon paprika
½ cup white wine
3 tomatoes, peeled (see Glossary) and
    chopped
salt and pepper
6 3-ounce fillets of ling cod (or rock cod)
6 lemon wedges
6 sprigs parsley

Heat the oil in a large frying pan or Dutch oven. Add the bacon and onion, and sauté until the onion is translucent. Sprinkle with paprika and stir until it is absorbed. Add the wine and tomatoes. Simmer for about 10 minutes, or until the onions are tender and there is very little liquid remaining. Season with salt and pepper.

Lay the fish fillets in the pan. Spoon some of the sauce over them, cover the pan, and simmer for about 5 minutes, or until the fillets are barely cooked through. Serve each portion napped with the sauce and garnished with a wedge of lemon and a sprig of parsley.

BRAISED VEAL AND PORK
(SERVES 6)

2 tablespoons oil
1 pound veal stew meat, cut into 1½-inch chunks
1 pound pork, trimmed and cut into 1½-inch chunks
2 large onions, sliced
3–4 cloves garlic, chopped
2 teaspoons paprika
2 tablespoons flour
1 cup white wine
2 cups veal or chicken broth (page 23 or 36) or water
salt and pepper
4 green bell peppers, peeled, seeded, and sliced
1 long green chili pepper, seeded, deveined, and sliced
2 cups coarsely chopped red cabbage
3 tablespoons chopped fresh parsley

Heat the oil in a heavy stew pot or Dutch oven, add the meat, and brown it on all sides over high heat. Add the onions and sauté until they are starting to brown. Add the garlic and paprika and stir the mixture for 1 to 2 minutes. Add the flour and stir until it is all absorbed. Add the wine, and the broth or water, and season with salt and pepper. Simmer, covered, for about 1 hour, or until the meat is almost tender. Add the peppers and red cabbage, cover, and simmer for another 30 minutes, or until the vegetables and meat are tender. If necessary, add more broth or water during the cooking to keep the consistency of a light sauce. Sprinkle the stew with the parsley just before serving.

BUTTERED EGG NOODLES

Cook 8 ounces egg noodles in a large pot of boiling salted water with a few drops of oil added, for 3 to 5 minutes, or until the pasta is al dente (tender but firm). Immediately pour a glass of cold water into the pot to stop the cooking. Drain the noodles in a colander, then turn them into a warmed serving bowl. Toss with several large lumps of softened butter.

CUCUMBER AND RADISH SALAD IN OIL AND LEMON DRESSING

Peel and slice 2 cucumbers and put them in a salad bowl. Wash, trim, and slice 1 bunch of radishes and add them to the cucumbers. Toss with a dressing made of 3 parts oil to 1 part lemon juice. Season with salt and a good grinding of coarse black pepper.

DARK RYE BREAD

Use the recipe for Finnish Dark Rye Bread in the Finland menu.

SLOVENIAN PLUM PIE

To make this 3-layered pie, use the recipe for Plum Pie in the menu for Romania.

A Note on the Wines

To drink with the first courses, we suggest a Pouilly-Fuissé, a medium-bodied, crisp white wine with Chardonnay character. An example would be the bottlings of the Domaine Corsin.

For the dish of braised veal and pork, we recommend a medium-bodied red, particularly one of an older vintage that has developed some elegance with age, such as a Charton Bourgogne, Resèrve de la Chêvre Noire.

Low-Calorie Dinner

❖

Quail Egg with Caviar

Skewered Lobster and Supremes of Chicken

Charcoal-Grilled Breast of Duck
Poached Asparagus with Baked Onion and Garlic Confit
Eggplant Provençal

Salade Composée

Fresh Kiwi Sorbet

The total count of this dinner is only 505 calories per person. Bread, which we did not serve, increases the total by about 85 calories a slice (simple whole wheat or French). Wine adds about 80 calories for a 3½-ounce glass of white of 12 percent alcohol, about 85 for red of the same description. As an additional diet aid, we intentionally eliminated salt, but if sodium is not a problem for you and you want to add a pinch or two, it won't increase the calories.

QUAIL EGG WITH CAVIAR

Poach 1 quail egg per person and serve it over a portion of 4 tablespoons aspic. Use the recipe for port aspic (page 306), substituting half chicken broth (page 36), half dry white wine for the port. (The calories in wine are in the alcohol, eliminated here because it dissipates in the cooking.) Spoon 1 teaspoon salmon caviar over the egg and garnish the plate with little green onion brushes.

SKEWERED LOBSTER AND SUPREMES OF CHICKEN
(SERVES 6)

*2 whole fryer chicken breasts (from 3-
    pound chickens), skinned and boned
    (see Note)*
*2 6–8-ounce lobster tails, or 6–12 shrimp,
    peeled and deveined*

*juice of 2 tangerines, or ¾ cup orange
    juice*
½ cup dry white wine
1 onion, thinly sliced
peel of ½ tangerine or orange
*1 tablespoon glace de viande (see recipe
    below), or 2 bouillon cubes*

DO AHEAD:

Marinate the chicken and lobster or shrimp for a few hours (see instructions). About 40 minutes before you are ready to cook, build a charcoal fire.

Cut the chicken breasts into bite-sized cubes. Shell the lobster by cutting it in half lengthwise through the shell. (Kitchen shears are a good tool to use.) Remove the lobster meat and cut it into pieces of the same size as the chicken. If you're using shrimp instead of lobster, leave them whole.

Put the cubes of chicken and lobster or whole shrimp in a glass or stainless-steel bowl. Pour the tangerine or orange juice and the white wine over them, add the onion slices, and mix well. Marinate in the refrigerator for a few hours or overnight.

Remove the meat from the marinade and thread it onto skewers, alternating chunks of chicken and seafood. Reserve.

To make the sauce: Pour the marinade into a saucepan, add the tangerine or orange peel and the glace de viande or bouillon cubes, and simmer until reduced by half. Strain and reserve.

Broil the skewers over hot charcoal or

297

under a high broiler, being careful not to overcook (they need only 2 or 3 minutes on each side). Brush them with the sauce while they are cooking. Serve with a bit of sauce spooned over them and the rest on the side.

NOTE: To skin and bone the chicken, remove the keel-shaped breastbone and cartilage, using a boning knife or poultry shears. Carefully slide a knife under the breastbones and cut them away. (See illustration, page 54.) Gently pull back the skin, using the knife to help "peel" it from the flesh. (Or ask your butcher to do this for you.)

Glace de Viande
(MAKES SIXTEEN 1-TABLESPOON PIECES)

6 *cups brown meat stock (page 23)*
3 *cups chicken stock (page 36)*

Strain the stock through a cloth. Place into a thick-bottom 4-quart pot. Boil rapidly to reduce. Watch carefully that it does not burn as it concentrates down. When it coats a spoon smoothly, you should have about 1 cup in volume. Transfer into a small refrigerator container, being sure to scrape all the sauce out of the pot with a spatula. Refrigerate until it jells. Cut into 4 quarters. Then cut each piece in quarters again. Wrap each of the 16 pieces in a small piece of foil. Store in the freezer.

CHARCOAL-GRILLED BREAST OF DUCK
(SERVES 6)

If you are making this complete menu, you can use the same charcoal fire to cook the chicken-lobster course before you broil the duck breasts.

3 *whole duck breasts from 4½-pound ducks*
1 *cup dry red wine*
3–4 *cloves garlic, crushed*
1 *ounce dried cepes or other dried mushrooms*
⅓ *cup Madeira or sherry*
1 *10–12-ounce can chicken broth or consommé*

DO AHEAD:
Marinate the duck breasts overnight (see instructions).

Bone the duck breasts and cut them in half (or ask the butcher to do this for you). (See illustration, page 213.) Remove pieces of fat, but leave the skin attached. Put the breasts in a glass or stainless steel bowl, add the red wine and garlic, and marinate overnight in the refrigerator.

About 40 minutes before you are ready to cook, build a charcoal fire.

When you are ready to cook, remove the duck from the marinade (reserve the marinade) and broil it over the hot charcoal, as you would a steak, until it is rare to medium-rare.

While the duck breasts are broiling,

make the sauce. Cook the dried cepes (not previously soaked) in a mixture of the Madeira or sherry, the broth or consommé, and the remaining marinade. As soon as the mushrooms are soft, take the pan from the heat. Using a slotted spoon, remove the mushrooms and reserve them in a bowl. Any sand that was trapped in the mushrooms will have settled to the bottom of the pot. Slowly decant the liquid into the bowl with the mushrooms, being careful that all the sand remains behind (the easiest way is to leave the last spoonful or two of liquid in the pot). Rinse out the pot well, return the mushrooms and liquid to the pot, and boil rapidly over a high flame until the liquid is reduced to a light, almost syrupy sauce.

Serve the duck breasts napped with a bit of the sauce.

POACHED ASPARAGUS WITH BAKED ONION AND GARLIC CONFIT
(SERVES 6)

> 1 medium onion, peeled and coarsely sliced
> 6–8 cloves garlic
> 1 cup chicken or veal stock (page 36 or 23) or water
> 18–24 asparagus spears, washed and the ends snapped off

Preheat the oven to 350°F.

Put the onion and garlic in a small ovenproof casserole and pour the stock over

them. Cover and bake until they are soft, about 30 minutes. Remove the lid and continue to bake until the onion and garlic are browned and mushy and most of the liquid has evaporated. Transfer them to a blender and puree them. Turn them into a small bowl and hold it at the side of the stove to keep warm until ready to serve.

Bring a pot of water to a rapid boil, add the asparagus, and cook uncovered to preserve the bright green color. Cook only until tender (al dente). Drain. Arrange on a serving plate and top with the warm onion and garlic confit.

EGGPLANT PROVENÇAL
(SERVES 6)

> 3 medium tomatoes, peeled (see Glossary) and seeded
> 1 small onion, chopped
> 1 teaspoon dried basil
> ¼ teaspoon dried thyme
> pepper
> 1 medium eggplant, cut into ¾-inch-thick slices
> 1 cup chicken stock (page 36)

Preheat the oven to 350°F.

Simmer the tomato pulp, onion, and herbs until they are reduced to a heavy puree. Season with pepper and set aside.

Place the eggplant slices in a baking pan and pour the chicken stock over them. Bake until they are tender and lightly browned, 25 to 30 minutes. A few minutes before the eggplant is done, rewarm the tomato sauce.

To serve, spoon 2 or 3 tablespoons of tomato sauce over each slice of eggplant.

SALADE COMPOSÉE
(SERVES 6)

1 bunch watercress
1 large head romaine lettuce, heart only
12–18 snow peas
¾ cup plain yogurt
1½ teaspoons Dijon-style mustard
1 tablespoon lemon juice
1 clove garlic, crushed
1 tablespoon chopped fresh parsley
pepper
6 thin slices of Bündnerfleisch (Swiss air-dried beef) or prosciutto
1 package of fresh snow puff mushrooms, or 6 medium mushroom caps, brushed clean and trimmed

Wash and trim the watercress and romaine (reserve the outer leaves for another use). Drain thoroughly and chop into bite-sized pieces. Chill in the refrigerator.

Pour boiling water over the stemmed and stringed snow peas, let stand for 1 minute, then drain and chill.

Make the dressing by mixing the yogurt with the mustard, lemon juice, garlic, parsley, and pepper.

Toss the chilled greens with the dressing in a large bowl. Divide the salad evenly among 6 plates. Arrange the snow peas, Bündnerfleisch or prosciutto, and mushrooms over the greens.

FRESH KIWI SORBET
(MAKES 1 QUART)

2 cups peeled, quartered kiwi fruit
juice of 1 lemon
½ cup sugar
2 tablespoons orange marmalade
1 egg white
6 large strawberries, quartered

Puree the kiwi with the lemon juice, sugar, and marmalade and set it aside in a mixing bowl. Beat the egg white until it is stiff and fold it into the puree. Freeze the mixture in an ice cream freezer. When the sorbet has frozen, remove the dasher and ripen the sorbet in the freezer of the refrigerator until it is firm, 2 to 3 hours.

To serve, for each portion put a scoop of sorbet into a champagne or compote glass, and garnish with 4 strawberry quarters pressed into the sorbet.

Annual California
Spring Festival Dinner

❖

White Bean and Pepper Salad

Poached Salmon with Ginger Sauce

Napa Valley Lamb Loins
Rice and Rye Pilaf
Steamed Asparagus with Brown Butter

Épines

Aged Teleme and California Chèvre, Apple Slices,
and California Pistachios

Wines:
Cakebread Cellars Chardonnay
Sterling Vineyards Chardonnay
Louis M. Martini Special Selection Cabernet Sauvignon
Beaulieu Vineyard Private Reserve Cabernet Sauvignon
Freemark Abbey Cabernet Sauvignon

WHITE BEAN AND PEPPER SALAD
(SERVES 6)

4 slices of thick bacon, cut into ½-inch
    pieces
2 cups cooked white Northern beans (1
    cup dry measure), or 1 15–16-ounce
    can, drained
2 small green peppers, roasted, peeled, and
    cut into 1-inch squares
2 small red peppers, roasted, peeled, and
    cut into 1-inch squares
1 small sweet red onion, thinly sliced
6–8 mushrooms, thinly sliced

VINAIGRETTE:
½ cup olive oil
2 tablespoons wine vinegar
1 teaspoon Dijon mustard
salt and freshly ground black pepper

In a skillet fry the bacon pieces until they are crisp. Drain. Mix the beans with the cooked bacon, peppers, onion, and mushrooms.

Whisk together all of the dressing ingredients. Toss the dressing with the bean mixture. Serve at room temperature or slightly chilled.

POACHED SALMON WITH GINGER SAUCE
(SERVES 6)

POACHING BOUILLON:
2 cups water
2 cups white wine
½ onion, chopped
2 bay leaves
pepper

6 2–3-ounce salmon fillets
12 spinach leaves, washed and trimmed
¼ cup (½ stick) butter
½ tablespoon shredded gingerroot (see
    Note)
salt (optional)

Put the bouillon ingredients in a pot large enough to hold the salmon pieces. Simmer for several minutes, then add the salmon pieces in one layer, cover the pot, and cook over low heat until the salmon flesh is firm and opaque all the way through. With a slotted spoon, remove the salmon to a warm plate.

Strain the poaching bouillon, return it to the pot, and boil it down over high heat until it is reduced to ½ cup. While the liquid is reducing, poach the spinach leaves in boiling salted water until they just become limp and tender, a minute or two at most. Remove them immediately and drain.

When the sauce has reduced to ½ cup, whisk in the butter and shredded ginger. Taste the sauce and add salt if necessary. Arrange 2 spinach leaves on each serving plate. Place one portion of salmon on top of the spinach and nap the fish with the finished sauce.

NOTE: If fresh gingerroot is not available, substitute 3 teaspoons capers.

NAPA VALLEY LAMB LOINS

(SERVES 6)

1 large onion, coarsely cut
2–3 cloves garlic
8–10 sprigs mustard blossoms, or 1
    teaspoon whole mustard seeds
¼ cup sherry
½ cup white wine
½ teaspoon salt
½ teaspoon pepper
2 lamb loins (see Note)
1 10–12-ounce can beef broth or
    consommé

DO AHEAD:

The lamb needs to marinate overnight (see instructions).

To make the marinade, puree the onion, garlic, mustard, sherry, white wine, salt, and pepper in a blender. Put the meat into a glass or stainless steel pan and rub well with some of the marinade. Pour the remaining marinade over the meat and refrigerate overnight.

Preheat the oven to 450°F.

Remove the meat from the pan and wipe off the excess marinade. Put the meat in a roasting pan and roast for 20 to 25 minutes for medium-rare.

While the meat is roasting, put the marinade in a saucepan, add the beef broth or consommé, and simmer for 15 minutes. Strain and return the sauce to the stove. Boil it rapidly over high heat to reduce it to the consistency of a thin syrup.

When the meat is done, remove it to a carving board and let it rest for 10 minutes. Slice into 6 portions and arrange the slices on a warm platter or individual plates. Spoon a bit of sauce around the meat and serve the rest in a sauce boat on the side.

NOTE: Ask the butcher to trim the fat very close to the meat, to remove and discard the flap, and to remove the fillets (save them for another dinner).

RICE AND RYE PILAF

See the recipe in the Perennial Favorites menu.

STEAMED ASPARAGUS WITH BROWN BUTTER

Wash and trim 1 bunch of asparagus. Snap off the ends where they break naturally. Cook the stalks uncovered in boiling salted water until they are just tender. Drain immediately and transfer to a warm serving plate.

While the asparagus is cooking, melt 1 stick of butter in a small saucepan over medium heat. Cook it, watching carefully, until it begins to color. Remove it as soon as it begins to take on a light brown color (it will continue to darken a bit after it is removed from the heat). Pour the brown butter over the asparagus. As a variation, you could add a tablespoon or two of bread crumbs or cracker meal to the melting butter and brown along with the butter.

ÉPINES

When we served this dinner, we baked épines to go along with it. Baguettes and épines are basically the same except for the final shaping. To make an épine, see page 119.

AGED TELEME AND CALIFORNIA CHÈVRE, APPLE SLICES, AND CALIFORNIA PISTACHIOS

Teleme is a type of California Jack cheese. A whole cheese is coated with rice flour and aged on an open wire rack for 90 days, forming a hard crust and developing a soft center very much like a ripe Brie. If it is not available, substitute a properly aged French Brie.

There are many excellent goat cheeses being made in California these days, a movement led by Laurie Chennel. Pick any one of the several varieties available. If you cannot obtain California cheese, substitute one made in New York State or France.

Serve the cheese on a board to pass around the table, or put individual portions on individual plates. Slice half a tart, firm apple for each person just before serving (so the slices will not brown) and finish the plate with a handful of California pistachio nuts in their shells.

A Note on the Wines

During the annual festivals, we offered between 25 and 30 wines with each dinner, available by the bottle or glass. We included several champagnes and a wide range of other types, such as late harvest Johannisberg Rieslings and California ports to go with dessert.

For this dinner, to go with the fish course we served a wide variety of full-bodied 1975 Chardonnays. The salmon with the piquant ginger sauce needed a big, rich wine such as those made by Cakebread and Sterling.

With the lamb we chose a range of classic, medium-bodied 1970 Cabernet Sauvignons, among them the Louis M. Martini Special Selection, the Beaulieu Vineyard Private Reserve, and that of Freemark Abbey.

Perennial Favorites

❖

Duck Liver Pâté with Port Aspic

Mushroom-Clam Velouté

Rack of Lamb Assyrian
Rice and Rye Pilaf
Vegetable Mélange

Romaine Hearts with Fresh Herbs
and Citronnade Dressing

Strass Rye Bread

Chocolate Decadence

Wines:
Cakebread Cellars Sauvignon Blanc
Ridge Vineyards Howell Mountain Zinfandel

Over the years, several recipes emerged as diners' favorites. We decided, one Monday Night in 1983, to put them all together for that evening's special dinner.

DUCK LIVER PÂTÉ WITH PORT ASPIC

(MAKES 1 POUND)

PÂTÉ:

- 10 tablespoons (1¼ sticks) butter
- 1 small onion, thinly sliced
- ½ small green apple, peeled and thinly sliced
- 8 ounces duck livers
- 3 tablespoons apple brandy or sherry
- 2 tablespoons heavy cream
- ½ teaspoon salt
- ½ teaspoon lemon juice

ASPIC:

- 1 teaspoon unflavored gelatin
- ½ cup port wine
- 1 tablespoon sugar
- 1 tablespoon water
- 1½ tablespoons red wine vinegar
- ¼ teaspoon dried tarragon

Heat 4 tablespoons butter in a frying pan, add the onion, and sauté until quite brown. Add the apple and continue to cook until the apple just starts to soften, 3 to 4 minutes. Turn up the heat to high and add the duck livers. Sauté until the livers are cooked but still slightly pink in the center. Transfer the mixture to a blender or food processor and set aside. Deglaze the pan with the brandy or sherry and add the deglazing to the liver mixture. Pour the cream into the livers. To avoid being burned, be sure to cover the container before starting to process the food, and to handle it with a towel or hot pad. Puree the mixture until it is smooth and set it aside to cool to lukewarm.

Put the remaining 6 tablespoons butter in a mixing bowl and whip it until it is soft. Whip the liver puree into the butter, then add the salt and lemon juice and blend in well. Pack the finished pâté in a decorative terrine or glass bowl, or for individual portions, into small ramekins, 1½- to 2-ounce capacity. Cool.

Meanwhile, soften the gelatin in the port wine and set aside. Dissolve the sugar in the water in a small saucepan and cook it rapidly until the sugar melts and begins to caramelize. Watch it carefully: Once the sugar starts to melt it will caramelize very quickly. Remove it immediately from the heat—it should be a medium caramel color—and add the port wine and gelatin. Return to low heat, add the vinegar and tarragon, and simmer for just 2 minutes. Strain through a fine sieve and set aside until it is almost cool.

Spoon over the prepared liver pâté in an ⅛-inch layer and refrigerate until ready to serve.

NOTE: If the aspic sets before you are ready to spoon it over the pâté, warm it for a minute to dissolve.

MUSHROOM-CLAM VELOUTÉ
(MAKES 8 CUPS)

> ¼ cup (½ stick) butter
> ½ cup all-purpose flour
> 4 cups clam broth
> 1½ cups water
> 1¼ cups (10 ounces) mushrooms, minced
>   by hand or chopped fairly fine in a food
>   processor
> 2 cups heavy cream
> salt and pepper

Melt the butter in a 5-quart heavy Dutch oven, add the flour, and cook slowly, stirring, until the roux has developed a hazel brown color. Add the clam broth, water, and minced mushrooms. Simmer for 10 minutes. Add the cream and simmer for 5 minutes longer. Season with salt and pepper.

RACK OF LAMB ASSYRIAN

Use the recipe for Rack of Lamb with Pomegranate Juice from the Assyrian menu.

RICE AND RYE PILAF
(SERVES 6)

Rice pilaf is basic to Assyrian cooking; to this day I have memories of my mother's rice pilaf—it remains my single favorite food. Every available variety of cereal grains can be mixed and matched in pilaf, and we cooked them all. Basically they fall into 2 categories: fast-cooking grains, generally cracked, such as cracked wheat and oats, or polished, such as white rice; and slow-cooking, whole grains with the bran covering, such as brown rice or whole wheat. Although rice and rye was our most popular combination, any mixture can be made, including 3 or 4 different grains. Any of the following grains can be substituted in this recipe.—N.D.

FAST-COOKING GRAINS	SLOW-COOKING GRAINS
white rice	rye berries
buckwheat groats (kasha)	wheat berries
cracked wheat (bulgur)	barley
steel-cut oats	brown rice
	triticale
	wild rice

> ½ cup rye berries
> ¾ cup water
> 2 tablespoons oil
> ½ small onion, chopped
> ½ cup white rice
> 1 cup chicken broth (page 36), or 1 cup
>   water and 2 bouillon cubes
> salt
> ½ teaspoon ground cumin or turmeric
>   (optional)

Put the rye berries and ¾ cup water into a pot, cover, and simmer slowly for 45 to 50 minutes, or until all of the water is absorbed. Set aside. Note: The cooked rye berries can be stored in the refrigerator for several days.

Heat the oil in a 1-quart pot with a tight-fitting lid. Add the onion and sauté until the onion begins to soften. Add the white rice. Continue cooking slowly, stirring until it starts to sizzle. Add the chicken broth or bouillon cubes and water and the previously steamed rye. Add salt to taste. Bring the grain mixture to a boil, cover the pot, and reduce to the slowest heat. Simmer for 20 minutes. Stir well from the bottom of the pot before serving.

If desired, add the ground cumin or turmeric for seasoning.

VEGETABLE MÉLANGE

This favorite came about for a fall game dinner featuring roast venison that we served to our guest, James Beard. We made a mélange of peeled broccoli stems, rutabagas, and carrots. Jim was so delighted with it that he featured it in his syndicated column as a wonderful use of the forgotten vegetable, rutabagas. We have made it often since, varying the vegetables depending on season, but always keeping a balance of color and flavor. Cut the vegetables into 3-inch-long strips, ⅛ inch thick by ½ inch wide—that is the approximate size of snow peas, which we include frequently. Cook each vegetable separately in boiling salted water until al dente (slightly under-

cooked), drain, and mix all together with a bit of butter, salt, and pepper. Almost any fresh herb or a finely minced green onion will enhance the flavor.—N.D.

ROMAINE HEARTS WITH FRESH HERBS AND CITRONNADE DRESSING

Wash and trim the romaine hearts and dry them well. Arrange on salad plates or in a large bowl and cover with citronnade dressing and a sprinkle of chopped fresh parsley, chervil, and chives, and a few small whole leaves of fresh basil. The herbs can vary according to your taste and what is available. To make the citronnade dressing, make your favorite vinaigrette (see Glossary), but substitute lemon juice for half of the vinegar. This makes a more mellow dressing, one that will not interfere with wines, so it is also an excellent choice for an extensive wine dinner.

STRASS RYE BREAD

Serve Strass Rye Bread from the Germany menu with this dinner.

✳

CHOCOLATE DECADENCE

(SERVES 12)

The cake needs to be frozen first before serving, so allow the time.

CAKE:

  1 pound semisweet chocolate, broken into
     squares
  10 tablespoons (1¼ sticks) sweet butter
  4 whole eggs
  1 tablespoon sugar
  1 tablespoon flour

TOPPING:

  1½ cups heavy cream
  1 teaspoon vanilla extract
  1 tablespoon sugar
  shaved chocolate
  1 10–12-ounce package frozen
     raspberries, defrosted

DO AHEAD:

Flour and butter an 8-inch cake pan and line it with paper.

Preheat the oven to 425°F.

Put the chocolate and butter in the top of a double boiler and heat until the chocolate is just melted. Set aside.

In the top of another double boiler, beat the eggs and sugar until the sugar dissolves and the mixture is lukewarm (do not overcook). Remove from the heat and whip until the mixture thickens and is about quadrupled in volume. Fold the flour into the thickened egg mixture. Stir a quarter of the flour-egg mixture into the melted chocolate, then fold the chocolate into the remaining egg mixture.

Pour the batter into the prepared cake pan. Shake it gently to level it. Bake for 15 minutes (the cake will still be runny in the center). Cool a bit, then freeze, preferably overnight, before removing the cake from the pan.

To unmold, carefully dip the bottom of the pan into hot water to loosen the cake. When it will move easily, unmold it onto a cake plate. Peel off the paper and discard. Whip the heavy cream, adding the vanilla and sugar as it thickens. Mask the cake with the whipped cream and decorate the top with shaved chocolate. Refrigerate until ready to serve.

Any time up to 15 minutes before serving, puree the defrosted raspberries in a blender and press through a fine sieve to remove the seeds. Spoon the raspberry puree around the cake just before serving, or spoon some of the puree around individual slices.

A Note on the Wines

This menu calls for substantial wines with distinctive character, winemakers' wines, that will add interest without competing with the food. To complement the richness of the duck pâté and port wine aspic, we would choose a generous, full- bodied Sauvignon Blanc, such as those made by Cakebread in the Napa Valley.

Winemaker Paul Draper of Ridge Vineyards makes classic claret-style Zinfandels, full of nuances and complexities. Our choice to go with another classic, the Assyrian rack of lamb, is the Ridge Howell Mountain Zinfandel (Napa Valley). The 1979, 1980, 1981, and 1982 are from the Park-Muscatine Vineyard; subsequent years combine grapes from that vineyard with those of several neighboring vineyards, with the select older grapes going into a special Ridge bottling under the Park-Muscatine label.

Narsai's Wine Card

❖

CALIFORNIA SPARKLING WINE

	Vintage
NARSAI'S CHOICE, Brut	NV
CHATEAU ST. JEAN, Blanc de Blancs	1981
S. ANDERSON, Blanc de Noir	1981
SCHRAMSBERG, Cuvee de Pinot	1979
SCHRAMSBERG, Blanc de Noir	1980
SCHRAMSBERG, Blanc de Blancs	1982
SCHRAMSBERG, Cremant Demi-Sec	1982
IRON HORSE VINEYARDS, Brut	1981
CHANDON, Napa Valley Brut	NV
CHANDON, Blanc de Noirs	NV
WEIBEL, Extra Dry	NV
LOUIS MARTINI, Moscato Amabile	NV

CALIFORNIA WHITE WINE

Chardonnay

LOUIS MARTINI, Los Vinedos Del Rio	1979
STERLING VINEYARDS	1975
SPRING MOUNTAIN VINEYARDS	1979
BURGESS CELLARS, Preston Vineyards	1977
WINE & THE PEOPLE	1975
STAGS LEAP WINE CELLARS, Napa	1976
HARBOR WINERY	1976
MAYACAMAS VINEYARDS	1979
CHALONE VINEYARDS	1980
CHATEAU MONTELENA WINERY, Napa Valley	1982
TREFETHEN VINEYARDS	1975
JOSEPH PHELPS VINEYARD	1977
HEITZ CELLARS, Lot Z-02	1970
NAVARRO VINEYARDS, Premier Reserve	1981
CUVAISON WINERY	1975
ST. CLEMENT VINEYARDS	1982

DOMAINE LAURIER	1980
CONN CREEK WINERY	1981
CHATEAU CHEVALIER WINERY	1980
GIRARD WINERY	1983
PINE RIDGE	1982
MATANZAS CREEK WINERY, Estate Bottled	1980
HAYWOOD WINERY	1980
VILLA MOUNT EDEN	1980
SONOMA CUTRER VINEYARDS, Cutrer Vineyard	1982
SAINT ANDREWS WINERY	1983
STONY HILL VINEYARD	1981
WILLIAM HILL WINERY, Gold Label	1982
WILLIAM HILL WINERY, Reserve	1982
GUNDLACH-BUNDSCHU, Special Selection	1981
FRETTER WINE CELLARS, Mountain Glenn Vineyards	1982

Johannisberg (White) Riesling

OBESTER WINERY	1982
FIELD STONE WINERY	1983
AMITY VINEYARDS (Oregon)	1982
JEKEL VINEYARDS	1982
SHOWN & SONS VINEYARDS	1981
JOSEPH PHELPS VINEYARDS, Early Harvest	1981
HEITZ CELLARS	1977
JOSEPH PHELPS SEL. Late Harvest (Sweet)	1980
BURGESS CELLARS, Late Harvest (Sweet)	1977
FELTON EMPIRE, (Sweet)	1978
LONG VINEYARDS, Late Harvest (Sweet)	1978
HAGAFEN CELLARS (Kosher)	1980

Sauvignon Blanc (Fume Blanc)

STONEGATE WINERY	1983
MAYACAMAS VINEYARDS	1982
LAKESPRING WINERY	1983
DRY CREEK VINEYARD	1983
ST. ANDREWS WINERY	1983

CHATEAU ST. JEAN, La Petite Etoile	1983
JOSEPH PHELPS VINEYARDS	1978
JOSEPH PHELPS VINEYARDS	1981
JOSEPH PHELPS VINEYARDS	1983
MONTEVINA	1976
ST. CLEMENT VINEYARDS	1982
MONTEREY VINEYARDS BOTRYTIS (Sweet)	1975
SPRING MOUNTAIN VINEYARDS	1982
ROBERT MONDAVI WINERY	1983

Other White Varietals

CHENIN BLANC, Field Stone Winery	1982
CHENIN BLANC, Girard	1983
GEWURZTRAMINER, Joseph Phelps Vineyards	1982
GEWURZTRAMINER, Navarro Vineyards	1982
GEWURZTRAMINER, Navarro Vineyards Late Harvest	1981
SEMILLON DE SOLEIL, Stony Hill Vineyard (Sweet)	1980
PINOT BLANC, Chalone Vineyards	1979

Rose

ROSE OF PETITE SIRAH, Field Stone Winery	1983

WHITE WINE FROM OTHER REGIONS

APETLONER GEWURZTRAMINER BEERENAUSLESE, Moser (Austria)	1976

CHAMPAGNE

MOET & CHANDON, Dom. Perignon	1964
MOET & CHANDON, Dom. Perignon Rose	1971

MOET & CHANDON, Dom. Perignon Magnum	1976
AYALA, CHATEAU D'AY, Extra Quality Brut	1970
TATTINGER, Blanc de Blanc, Brut	1964
TATTINGER, Brut	NV
PERRIER JOUET FLEUR DE CHAMPAGNE, Special Reserve	1975
PERRIER JOUET FLEUR DE CHAMPAGNE, Special Reserve Jeroboam	1975
SALON, LE MESNIL, Brut	1971
GOSSET, Brut Integral (Disgorged 1979)RD	1961
POL ROGER (Disgorged 1977) LD	1921
POL ROGER, Extra Cuvee	1921
POL ROGER, Chardonnay	1966
POL ROGER, Chardonnay	1971
KRUG	NV
HENRIOT, Brut	NV
HENRIOT, Brut Reserve Baron Philippe	1976
BOLLINGER, Brut Salmanazar	1973
BOLLINGER, Brut (Disgorged 1976) RD Magnum	1966
BOLLINGER, Brut (Disgorged 1977) RD	1969
BOLLINGER, Brut (Disgorged 1978) RD	1970
LOUIS ROEDERER, Brut	1929
LOUIS ROEDERER, Brut	1945
LOUIS ROEDERER, Brut Magnum	1966
LOUIS ROEDERER, Cristal Magnum	1976
LOUIS ROEDERER, Extra Dry	1955
LOUIS ROEDERER, Rose	1976
PHILIPPONNAT, Clos des Goisses (Disgorged 1981) RD	1961
PHILIPPONNAT, Clos des Goisses (Disgorged 1981) RD	1970
PHILIPPONNAT, TAILLEVANT, Blanc de Blancs	1979
LANSON Jeroboam	1947
LECHERE, Brut, Cuvee Orient Express	NV
DEUTZ, Brut, Cuvee William Deutz Magnum	1971
DEUTZ, Brut, Cuvee William Deutz (Disgorged 1978) LD	1971
DEUTZ, Brut Jeroboam	NV

FRENCH WHITE BORDEAUX

Barsac (Sweet Dessert Wine)

CHATEAU NAIRAC	1973
CHATEAU BOUSCLA	1976
CHATEAU RIEUSSEC	1975
CHATEAU LAPINESSE	1970
CHATEAU CLIMENS	1969
CHATEAU ROUMIEU	1967
CHATEAU ROUMIEU	1971
CHATEAU COUTET	1969
CHATEAU COUTET	1973
CHATEAU SUDUIRAUT	1955
CHATEAU SUDUIRAUT	1959

Sauternes (Sweet Dessert Wine)

CHATEAU D'YQUEM	1961
CHATEAU GUIRAUD	1962
CHATEAU GUIRAUD	1967
CHATEAU RAYNE VIGNEAU	1967
CHATEAU SIGALAS RABAUD	1967
CHATEAU SIGALAS RABAUD	1973

Dry White Wine

CHATEAU PIRON	1983

FRENCH WHITE BURGUNDY

MERCUREY BLANC, Audiffred	1973
CHABLIS, Domaine Laroche	1980
POUILLY VINZELLES, Cave des Grands Crus a Vinzelles	1982
POUILLY FUISSE, Rodet	1983
MEURSAULT, Domaine du Chateau de Meursault	1980
MEURSAULT GENEVRIERES, Lafon	1972
MEURSAULT, Boillot	1982
MEURSAULT, CLOS DES BOUCHES CHERES, Domaine Manuel	1963
MEURSAULT, CLOS DES BOUCHES CHERES, Domaine Manuel	1968
MEURSAULT, CLOS DES BOUCHES CHERES, Domaine Manuel	1974
MEURSAULT PORUZOT, Dom. Manuel	1967
MEURSAULT, GOUTTE D'OR, Ropiteau	1979
MEURSAULT, GOUTTE D'OR, Buisson	1978
MEURSAULT GENEVRIERES, Hospices de Beaune, Baudot	1977
MEURSAULT, BLAGNY, Cavin	1967
MEURSAULT, CLOS DU CROMIN, Monnier	1973
MEURSAULT, CLOS DU CROMIN, Monnier	1979
MEURSAULT, Morey	1977
BATARD MONTRACHET, Morey	1982
CHASSAGNE MONTRACHET, La Romanee, Laboure Roi	1982
PULIGNY MONTRACHET, Les Folatieres, Cellier de Bourgogne	1980
PULIGNY MONTRACHET Les Combettes, Carillon	1982
CORTON CHARLEMAGNE, Rodet	1981

GERMAN WHITE WINE

Rheingau & Rheinpfalz

KIEDRICHER SANDGRUB, SPATLESE, Dr. Weil	1976
RUDESHEIMER BERG ROSENECK, BEERENAUSLESE, von Sierstorpff	1976
HATTENHEIMER MANNBERG, EISWEIN AUSLESE, von Simmern	1975
NIERSTEINER REHBACH, SPATLESE, Schmitt	1982
HATTENHEIMER WISSELBRUNEN, KABINETT, Schloss Reinhartshausen	1978

ERBACHER SIEGELSBERG,
  SPATLESE, Schloss
  Reinhartshausen   1971
WACHENHEIMER
  SCHENKENBOHL,
  KABINETT, Wachtenburg-
  Luginsland   1976
SCHLOSS
  JOHANNISBERGER,
  ROSALACK, AUSLESE,
  Furst Von Metternich   1976
DEIDESHEIMER
  LIENHOELHE,
  BEERENAUSLESE, Scholl
  & Hillebrand   1976

Mosel-Saar-Ruwer
BRAUNEBERGER JUFFER,
  AUSLESE, Scholl &
  Hillebrand   1976
SCHLOSSBOCKELHEIMER
  BURWEG, AUSLESE,
  Staatlichen
  Weinbaudomanen   1976
URZIGER SCHWARZLAY,
  AUSLESE, Scholl &
  Hillebrand   1976
EITELSBACHER
  KARTHAUSERHOFBERGER,
  FEINSTE AUSLESE,
  Rautenstrauch   1959
APETLONER
  WEISSBURGUNDER,
  TROCKENBEEREN
  AUSLESE, Moser (Austria) 1976

CALIFORNIA RED WINE

Cabernet Sauvignon
STERLING VINEYARDS,
  Private Reserve   1973
STERLING VINEYARDS,
  Private Reserve   1974
CHARLES KRUG WINERY,
  Vintage Selection   1974
FROG'S LEAP WINERY   1982
CHATEAU CHEVALIER
  WINERY   1976
LOUIS MARTINI   1974
LOUIS MARTINI   1975
INGLENOOK VINEYARD   1955
JOSEPH PHELPS VINEYARD 1978
SHAFER VINEYARDS   1978

HARBOR WINERY   1975
ST. CLEMENT VINEYARDS 1978
BEAULIEU VINEYARDS,
  Private Reserve   1967
AHLGREN VINEYARD   1978
TREFETHEN VINEYARDS   1974
TREFETHEN VINEYARDS   1978
WINE & THE PEOPLE   1975
HEITZ CELLARS   1970
HEITZ CELLARS, Martha's
  Vineyard   1967
RUTHERFORD HILL
  WINERY   1978
TUDAL WINERY   1980
RIDGE VINEYARDS,
  Montebello   1975
KENWOOD VINEYARDS
  Magnum   1974

Merlot
RUTHERFORD HILL   1978
PINE RIDGE   1981
FRETTER WINE CELLARS,
  Narsai David Vineyards 1980
FRETTER WINE CELLARS,
  Narsai David Vineyards 1981
LOUIS MARTINI, Edgehill
  Selection   Magnum Blend 68/70
LOUIS MARTINI   1973
LOUIS MARTINI   1975

Zinfandel
LOUIS MARTINI   1973
LOUIS MARTINI, Special
  Selection   1974
CORTI BROTHERS
  RESERVE   1973
PELLEGRINI VINEYARD   1980
FRICK WINERY   1979
KENWOOD VINEYARDS
  Magnum   1972
SUTTER HOME, Special
  Selection   Dbl. Mag. 1974
HARBOR WINERY   1975

Pinot Noir
MONTEREY VINEYARD
  Magnum   1974
VILLA MT. EDEN   1975
CHATEAU CHEVALIER   1976
MARTIN RAY, La Montana
  #3   NV
LOUIS MARTINI   Magnum 1973

LOUIS MARTINI, Special
  Selection   1970
TREFETHEN VINEYARDS   1977
SEBASTIANI, Proprietor's
  Reserve   1973
CHARLES KRUG WINERY 1966
STERLING VINEYARDS   1973
JOSEPH PHELPS
  VINEYARDS   1976
JOSEPH PHELPS
  VINEYARDS, Heinemann
  Mountain Vineyards   1975

Petite Sirah
BURGESS CELLARS
  Magnum   1973
BURGESS CELLARS   1974
ROUDON-SMITH
  VINEYARDS   1979
FIELD STONE WINERY   1979

Other California Red Varietals
BARBERA, Louis Martini 1973
BURGUNDY, Heitz Cellars NV
BURGUNDY, Beaulieu
  Vineyards   1970
BURGUNDY, Beaulieu
  Vineyards   1971
BURGUNDY, Beaulieu
  Vineyards   Special Label 1973
MONTANARO, Montevina 1975
SYRAH, Joseph Phelps   1978

FRENCH RED BORDEAUX

Pauillac
CHATEAU LATOUR   1960
CHATEAU LATOUR   1964
CHATEAU LAFITE
  ROTHSCHILD   1952
CHATEAU LAFITE
  ROTHSCHILD   1970
CHATEAU MOUTON
  ROTHSCHILD   1970
CHATEAU BATAILLEY   1962
CHATEAU BATAILLEY   1964
CHATEAU HAUT
  BATAILLEY   1970
CHATEAU LYNCH BAGES 1960
CHATEAU LYNCH BAGES 1964
CHATEAU LYNCH BAGES 1967
CHATEAU LYNCH BAGES 1970

CHATEAU HAUT BAGES
   LIBERAL 1966
CHATEAU HAUT BAGES
   LIBERAL 1970
CHATEAU GRAND PUY
   LACOSTE 1970
CHATEAU GRAND PUY
   LACOSTE 1971

Margaux
CHATEAU MARGAUX 1953
CHATEAU LASCOMBES 1970
CHATEAU RAUZAN
   GASSIES 1966
CHATEAU RAUSAN SEGLA 1966
CHATEAU GISCOURS 1966
CHATEAU PALMER 1966
CHATEAU MARQUIS
   D'ALESME-BECKER 1964
CHATEAU MARQUIS
   D'ALESME-BECKER
   Magnum 1970
CHATEAU MARQUIS
   D'ALESME-BECKER
   Magnum 1975
CHATEAU MARQUIS
   D'ALESME-BECKER 1976

St. Julien
CHATEAU LEOVILLE LAS
   CASES 1964
CHATEAU LEOVILLE
   BARTON 1959
CHATEAU LEOVILLE
   POYFERRE 1964
CHATEAU DUCRU
   BEAUCAILLOU 1961
CHATEAU DUCRU
   BEAUCAILLOU 1964
CHATEAU GRUAUD
   LAROSE 1971
CHATEAU LANGOA
   BARTON 1970
CHATEAU GRAND SAINT
   JULIEN 1976

St. Estephe
CHATEAU CALON SEGUR 1964
CHATEAU LAFON
   ROCHET 1959
CHATEAU MONTROSE 1960
CHATEAU MONTROSE 1964

CHATEAU CAPBERN
   GASQUETON 1966
CHATEAU MEYNEY 1961

Haut Medoc
CHATEAU CANTERMERLE 1955
CHATEAU LA LAGUNE 1962
CHATEAU LA LAGUNE
   Magnum 1970
CHATEAU CISSAC
   Magnum 1970
CHATEAU CISSAC
   Magnum 1971
CHATEAU LANESSAN 1971
CHATEAU LAFLEUR
   BECADE
   Magnum 1966

Graves
CHATEAU HAUT BRION 1964
CHATEAU LA MISSION
   HAUT BRION 1967
CHATEAU HAUT BERGEY 1967
DOMAINE DE CHEVALIER 1970
CHATEAU MALARTIC
   LAGRAVIERE 1966
CHATEAU PAPE CLEMENT 1961
CHATEAU FIEUZAL 1976

Pomerol
VIEUX CHATEAU CERTAN 1967
CHATEAU LE GAY 1976
CHATEAU LA
   CONSEILLANTE 1967
CHATEAU LAFLEUR 1970
CHATEAU L'EVANGILE 1971
CHATEAU NENIN (English
   Bottled) 1959
CHATEAU NENIN 1966
CHATEAU GAZIN 1955

St. Emilion
CHATEAU CHEVAL BLANC 1967
CHATEAU TROPLONG
   MONDOT 1964
CHATEAU GRAND
   CORBIN DESPAGNE 1955
CHATEAU FONROQUE 1973
CHATEAU GRAND
   BARRAIL LAMARZELLE
   FIGEAC 1953
CHATEAU CAPET 1964

FRENCH RED BURGUNDY

Beaujolais, Chalonnais & Champenois
MOULIN A VENT, Charton 1976
FLEURIE, Charton 1976
FLEURIE, Louis Latour 1981
COTEAUX CHAMPENOIS,
   Vieilles Vignes, Bollinger 1976

Cote De Beaune
BOURGOGNE ROUGE,
   Latour 1979
COTE DE BEAUNE
   VILLAGES, Latour 1979
VOLNAY, CLOS DES
   GHENES, Domaine Du
   Chateau De Meursault 1979
AUXEY DURESSES,
   Moingeon 1978
CHASSAGNE
   MONTRACHET, Gagnard 1979
MEURSAULT, CLOS DE LA
   BARONNE, Rene Manuel 1961
MEURSAULT, CLOS DE LA
   BARONNE 1964
ST. AUBIN, Clerget 1971
BOURGOGNE, RESERVE
   DE LA CHEVRE NOIRE,
   Charton 1974
PERNAND VERGELESSES,
   LES FICHOTS, Naudin 1974
BEAUNE, CLOS DU ROY,
   Naudin 1971
BEAUNE, CLOS DU ROY,
   Naudin 1973
CORTON, Naudin 1974
ALOXE-CORTON, Naudin 1961
ALOXE-CORTON,
   Remoissenet 1970

Hospices De Beaune
These noted Burgundies are sold at auction each year to benefit the charitable Hospital of Beaune and are named for the donor.
BEAUNE, Guigone de Salins 1953
BEAUNE, Guigone de Salins 1972
BEAUNE, Maurice Drouhin
   Magnum 1972
SAVIGNY-LES-BEAUNE,
   Forneret 1971
VOLNAY, Muteau 1976
BEAUNE, Rousseau-Deslandes 1976

Cote De Nuits

LA TACHE, Domaine
  Romanee Conti   1953
LA TACHE, Domaine
  Romanee Conti   Double
  Magnum   1964
LA TACHE, Domaine
  Romanee Conti   Magnum   1970
NUITS ST. GEORGES,
  CLOS DES FORETS, Belin   1976
CLOS VOUGEOT, Jean Gros   1977
ECHEZEAUX, Domaine
  Romanee Conti   1970
GRANDS ECHEZEAUX,
  Domaine Romanee Conti   1970
MUSIGNY, Charton   1973
MUSIGNY, Faiveley   1964
MOREY ST. DENIS, Louis
  Max   1972
MAZIS CHAMBERTIN,
  Clerget   1972
GEVREY CHAMBERTIN,
  Doudet-Naudin   Jeroboam   1966

Rhone

COTE ROTIE, Passat   1967
GIGONDAS, Guigal   1976

Chateauneuf Du Pape

LES CLEFS D'OR, Deydier
  Magnum   1978
CHATEAU SAINT ANDRE,
  Rey   1979

RED WINE FROM OTHER REGIONS

Italy

BARBARESCO, Casa del
  Vino di Alba   1969

BARBARESCO, Giacomo
  Conterno   1971
TORRE QUARTO,
  CLASSICO, Cirillo Farrusi   1968
CARMIGNANO RISERVA,
  Capezzana   1969
CAREMA, Ferrando   1967
ROSSO, Col d'Orcia   1979
BAROLO, Giacomo Conterno   1968
NEBBIOLO, Giacomo
  Conterno   1971
NEBBIOLO, Giacomo
  Conterno   1974
FIORANO, Ludovisi   1970
FIORANO, Ludovisi   1974
CHIANTI CLASSICO,
  RISERVA, Antinori   1968
CHIANTI CLASSICO,
  Nittardi   1967
GHEMME, Cantina Sizzano   1961

Spain

RESERVA 904, Alta Rioja   1964

PORT

VALENTE, COSTA, Dom
  Cesar   1926
BUTLER NEPHEW   1932
SMITH WOODHOUSE,
  House Port   1947
WARRE   1947
TUKE HOLDSWORTH   1950
QUINTA DO NOVAL   1960
GRAHAM   1960
GRAHAM, Malvedos   1962
CROFT   1963
FONSECA   1963
MARTINEZ   1963
OFFLEY, BOA VISTA   1963
QUINTA DO NOVAL   1963
COCKBURN   1963

REAL VINICOLA, Quinta
  do Sibio   1963
FONSECA   1965
REBELLO VALENTE   1966
GRAHAM   1966
TAYLOR, FLADGATE   1966
COCKBURN   1967
MARTINEZ   1967
MESSIAS, Quinta do Cachao   1967
TAYLOR, FLADGATE,
  Quinta de Vargellas   1967
TAYLOR, FLADGATE,
  Camo, Finest Rich Tawny
  (bottled in 1972, older than
  40 years)   NV
SANTOS JUNIOR   Magnum   1970
TAYLOR, FLADGATE,
  LBVR   Magnum   1971
OFFLEY BOA VISTA   1972
GRAHAM, Royal Consort   NV

CALIFORNIA PORT

SUNRISE, Tinta Madeira   1965
J. W. MORRIS, Narsai's
  Special Selection Late-
  Bottled Vintage Reserve   1976
J. W. MORRIS, Founder's Port   NV
QUADY, Zinfandel Port   1975
CONTI ROYALE, Tawny Port   NV

MADEIRA

BUAL, BLANDY   1907
BUAL, VVA. ABUDARHAM   1914
MALMSEY, BLANDY
  (bottled 1962)   1871
MALMSEY, Leacock's   Solera   1863
CAMA DE LOBOS, Avery's
  Solera   1864

Glossary

❀

The glossary that follows serves several purposes. It is a small dictionary of the major terms, foreign and domestic, that occur in this book. Beyond that, it provides definitions of frequently used dishes and culinary language from an international vocabulary. And finally, it offers simple recipes, basic techniques, and hints —what the French call *trucs*, the little tricks of the trade—that make cooking easier and more understandable.

abalone: a large mollusk of the univalve type, prized for its delicate flavor. Dwindling in supply because of the incursions of man and sea otter, it commands high prices when available. Because the meat is tough, pounding is necessary to break the fibers before using, and the briefest possible cooking is necessary to prevent the meat from becoming rubbery. Also available canned, largely from Japan.

achiote: a small red seed from the annatto tree used widely as a coloring agent in the cooking of Mexico, Central America, and the Caribbean. Available as annatto seeds in Latin American markets in the United States.

agar-agar: an East Asian derivative of seaweed; used as a gelatin after cooking, it will retain its firmness at room temperature. Also used after soaking in cold water to add a crisp texture to dishes of mixed ingredients.

aioli: mayonnaise flavored with garlic. Sometimes mashed potato is added. A specialty of Provence.

ali oli: see AIOLI.

à la diable: devil-style, usually a broiled dish brushed with cayenne or other hot pepper, sometimes combined with mustard.

à la mode: in the style of; also used to mean the addition of an ice cream topping to a dessert.

albóndigas: Mexican meatballs.

al dente: cooked firm (applied to pasta, rice, or vegetables).

alla diavola: Italian-style grilled or broiled chicken.

almond powder: used in Chinese cooking.

almonds, toasted: place on a cookie sheet or pie tin in a single layer and bake at 150°F for 5 to 10 minutes, or until barely colored. Immediately transfer to a cool container.

amandine: sliced almonds browned in butter and used to garnish fish and such vegetables as green beans.

andouille: French, tripe sausages; Cajun, hot smoky pork sausages.

angelica: an herb, the stems of which are candied in strips for use in decorating desserts.

anise: a plant yielding licorice-flavored seeds that are used dried or ground in baking and cooking. *Anise oil* is also used as a flavoring agent in baking. See also STAR ANISE.

annatto: see ACHIOTE.

arrowroot: a thickening agent that can be sprinkled directly (as on the raw apples of a pie filling) or dissolved in cold water and added to hot liquids such as sauces or gravies. Can be used for thickening in equal amounts as a substitute for cornstarch, or in half the amount in place of flour.

arugula (rocket plant, roquette): a highly flavored green used in salads.

ascorbic acid (vitamin C): used in pickling and preserving to prevent fruit from browning. Sometimes sold as ascorbic acid mixture.

asparagus: to prepare asparagus for cooking, snap off the stem end where it normally gives way (rather than cutting), which will leave all of the edible stalk. For very large stalks, peeling with a vegetable peeler will eliminate some of the heavier "tufts" and also give a more brilliant color after cooking. Asparagus can be cooked in a flat layer in a large skillet in boiling salted water or steamed in an appropriate cooker, but should be removed immediately when it is just tender (test with the tip of a paring knife), refreshed under cold water, and drained. If it is to be used immediately after cooking, stop the cooking as soon as it is done by adding a cup of cold water; drain, and serve. If you wrap it in a towel or napkin for serving, it will stay warm for a longer period.

aspic: stock that has been reduced enough to turn to a jelly when refrigerated. Adding gelatin to stock without further reducing it will give the same result, although the flavor will be less concentrated.

au gratin: topped with bread crumbs and butter and/or cheese, and baked or put under the broiler until golden.

au jus: meat served with its natural juices.

baba: a yeast pastry baked in a small cylindrical or cup-shaped mold, then saturated with sugar syrup and rum. (See also SAVARIN.)

baba ghanouj or baba ghanoush: a Middle Eastern salad made of broiled chopped eggplant mixed with sesame paste, garlic, olive oil, lemon juice, and chopped parsley.

bain marie: double boiler; a receptacle containing hot water into which a smaller receptacle is put to ensure that its contents cook evenly; used for such foods as custards and sauces.

bake: to cook in a gas, electric, or clay oven using dry heat.

baker's stone: a flat stone designed to fit home ovens, used to simulate the floor of the baker's traditional brick oven. (See also QUARRY TILES.)

baking powder: a leavening agent used in baking. Commercial baking powder is double-acting and works partly upon being added to liquid, partly upon being exposed to heat. Homemade baking powder, a mixture of one-third cream of tartar and two-thirds baking soda, is single-acting and the batter to which it is added must be baked immediately.

baking soda: sodium bicarbonate, an alkaline powder. When used as a leavening agent in baking, it must be mixed with an acid ingredient, such as cream of tartar, to produce the chemical reaction that releases the gas that makes dough rise. Some fruits, such as persimmon, have such high natural acidity that a persimmon pudding, for example, would not require any cream of tartar.

ballottine: meat or fowl that is boned, stuffed, rolled up, and tied into a package or bundle, then braised or roasted (similar to GALANTINE); generally served warm, in slices, but can be served cold.

bamboo shoots: in Asian cooking, used to add texture and contrast to other dishes; they are available canned and, in some areas, fresh in the spring. They should be rinsed thoroughly and kept under water in the refrigerator.

banana leaves: used to wrap other foods, much in the way that corn husks are used. Available fresh in many Asian markets in refrigerated packages.

barbecue: to cook on a grill or a spit over coals of wood or charcoal (or mesquite, which is currently very popular). Also, foods cooked in this manner are called barbecue, particularly if marinated and basted in highly seasoned sauces. Hickory wood or chips added to the fire give a smoky flavor; applewood, grapevine cuttings, dried fennel, and other aromatics each impart a distinctive character.

bard: to add a layer of fat over lean meat or poultry to compensate for the lack of its own. The butcher will usually do this on request.

baste: to keep what is cooking from drying out by moistening frequently with natural juices, added liquid, or a marinade. Basting also helps the skin of poultry to become crisp and golden.

bastilla: a Moroccan pigeon pie made with flaky pastry, nuts, eggs, and a mixture of spices such as cinnamon, ginger, turmeric, saffron, and sugar. Among the many alternate spellings are pastilla, bysteeya, bisteeya.

beans (fresh): these include *green beans* (string beans or snap beans); *wax beans* (yellow); *Italian or Romano beans,* flat and meatier in texture; *French haricots verts,* tiny green beens slightly thicker than matchsticks; *Chinese long beans,* about the same thickness as haricots verts but between 12 and 18 inches long; *fava beans* (broad beans), which must be shelled before cooking (and if large and more mature, the outer shell of the individual bean must be removed as well); *lima* and *baby lima beans,* which must be shelled; *black-eyed peas,* which must be shelled; and *soybeans,* which may be cooked in the pod and popped out for eating. *To cook:* Bring a large pot of salted water to the boil, add the beans, and cook only until just tender. Add cold water immediately to unshelled beans to stop the cooking, and drain well. (Some cooks prefer to refresh the beans by running cold water into the pot slowly, or running cold water over the beans in a colander.) If not using immediately, undercook the beans and when ready to use finish by reheating in oil or butter with whatever seasonings are called for. Blanched beans tossed with a vinaigrette dressing also make a good cold salad.

beans and legumes (dried): among the varieties available are *pink beans* or *pinto beans,* used widely in Mexican cooking; *black beans,* often used in Latin American cooking and in the islands of the Caribbean, and frequently combined with rice; *red beans* or *kidney beans; garbanzo beans* or *chick-peas,* widely used in Mexico and in the Middle East, where, pureed and mixed with ground sesame seeds, lemon juice, and garlic, they are a favorite appetizer called hummus; *lima beans* and *baby lima beans; Great Northern beans* (white beans) and *navy beans* (small white beans) can be used in place of dried French *flageolets* in cassoulets and to accompany lamb, and are the right type for minestrone; *soybeans; mung beans; split peas* (available in both yellow and green varieties); *lentils;* and *black-eyed peas. To cook:* Wash and pick over carefully for small stones and other matter. Put the beans in a pot in 3 times their volume of water, bring to a boil over high heat, and cook for exactly 2 minutes. Remove from the heat, cover, and let stand for exactly 1 hour. Drain the beans and discard the soaking liquid (it now contains about 80 percent of the water-soluble elements responsible for flatulence). Add enough fresh water to cover the beans, bring to a boil, then lower to a simmer, and cook until the beans are tender, usually 1½ to 2 hours, or according to the recipe. Some cooks believe that you should add salt after the beans are cooked to avoid making them tough. Use any excess liquid for soups or sauces. Dried beans in a closed container will keep for about one year.

bean sauce: a strong Chinese flavoring ingredient made of fermented soybeans preserved in salt.

bean sprouts: most commonly, mung bean sprouts, but others, such as soybean sprouts, are on the market and easy to get.

béarnaise sauce: basically a hollandaise sauce made with vinegar in place of lemon juice, and flavored with tarragon, chervil, shallots, and cayenne pepper.

beat: the same as to whip, a process of incorporating air into the basic mixture either by hand or machine.

beaten biscuits: a Southern specialty made of dough beaten constantly with a hammer or other implement for about 30 minutes, or until it is light and smooth. Traditionally served with thin slices of Smithfield ham.

béchamel sauce: white sauce; made by melting butter, whisking in an equal amount of flour, and adding warm milk while stirring constantly to avoid lumps. The amount of butter and flour determines the thickness of the sauce: 1½ tablespoons butter and 1½ tablespoons flour to 2 cups milk will make a thin sauce; 2 to 2½ tablespoons, a medium sauce; 3 tablespoons, a thick sauce.

berberé: hot, spicy seasoning paste used in Ethiopian cooking.

Bercy sauce: a reduction of butter, shallots, white wine, and fish stock thickened with a blend of flour and butter (beurre manié) and combined with chopped parsley that results in a sauce for fish. Some cooks add lemon juice.

beurre blanc: a reduction of white wine, wine vinegar, and shallots into which butter is whisked until the sauce reaches a light mayonnaiselike consistency.

beurre manié: equal amounts of flour and softened butter worked together into a smooth paste, used to thicken sauces and gravies.

beurre noir: butter cooked until it is a deep brown; used as a simple sauce, frequently with the addition of capers or vinegar, for such dishes as sautéed brains.

bird's nest: a rare and expensive Chinese delicacy, most often simmered in soup, this small, gelatinous nestlike substance is actually hardened translucent "saliva" of swifts, formed by the predigestion of seaweed.

bisque: traditionally, a rich shellfish soup made by sautéing shellfish, such as lobster or crayfish, in the shells; then simmering with wine, seasonings, and vegetables; pureeing; and enriching with stock, heavy cream, shellfish butter, and Cognac. Commonly any velvety smooth, creamed, pureed soup.

bitter melon: a southeast Asian squashlike vegetable with a bitter flavor and a corrugated skin.

black beans (fermented): used as a condiment in Chinese cooking.

black mushrooms, dried: Chinese and Japanese mushrooms of the shiitake type, of a more intense flavor than the fresh.

blanche: to immerse briefly in boiling water.

blend: to mix ingredients thoroughly.

blood orange: a deep red–fleshed orange, called tarocco in Italy, where it is widely available. Imported to the United States and recently also grown here.

blood pudding or sausages (boudins noirs): black sausages made of pork blood, cereal, and spices (but in France of an onion-cream-fat mixture instead of grain); usually served with cooked apples.

boil: to bring liquid to a cooking temperature of 212°F or more, at which stage it should be bubbling rapidly. *Full rolling boil:* the stage at which the entire pot is bubbling vigorously; *steady boil:* a moderate, continuous bubbling.

bok choy: see CHINESE CABBAGE.

bombe: frozen molded dessert, often combining several colors and flavors.

bonito or bonita: in Japanese cooking, a fish used in its dried and shaved form; also known as hana katsuo or katsuobushi.

bonne femme: in French cooking, a dish generally incorporating sliced mushrooms.

Bordelaise sauce: brown sauce with the addition of shallots, red wine, and poached beef marrow (although the marrow is often omitted nowadays).

bouillabaisse: a rich Mediterranean fish soup, usually served as a main course.

bouillon: a soup made of clarified stock. See also BROTH; CONSOMMÉ; STOCK.

bouillon cubes: bouillon to which seasonings have been added, reduced to a concentrated form. Used as a substitute for stock or glace de viande (reduced stock). One cube dissolved in 1 cup of boiling water gives 1 cup of bouillon.

bouquet garni: a flavoring mixture of herbs and aromatics tied together for easy removal from the pot in which it cooks. Usually parsley, celery leaves, bay leaves, and thyme.

(sauce) Bourguignonne: a combination of red Burgundy wine and rich brown sauce or stock.

bourride: a Provençal fish stew, usually served with a garlic mayonnaise (aioli) or a red garlic mayonnaise (rouille).

brains: calf's brains, a perishable delicacy, must be soaked in several changes of acidulated water for several hours, then trimmed of their filament and white solids before using. Some cooks also blanch them, then weight them to firm them and make slicing easier.

braise: to sauté meats or vegetables quickly

in a small amount of fat over high heat, then to add a small quantity of liquid and simmer, covered, on the top of the stove or in a slow oven until tender.

brochette: skewer. *En brochette:* any food broiled and served on a skewer.

broil: to cook under an oven flame or electric element, or over direct heat, such as on a grill or barbecue; to *pan-broil* is to cook over high heat on the stove top using a minimum of fat, more akin to frying.

broth: a clear soup.

brown: to give good color to a food and often, as with a steak, to seal in its juices. Foods browned in fat should first be patted dry, and cooked in small enough batches so that they are never crowded.

bruise: a method used to smash foods lightly, just enough to release their flavors; usually done with the flat side of a knife or cleaver.

bruschetta: Italian grilled, country-style bread, rubbed with garlic and seasoned with green virgin olive oil after toasting.

bûche de Noël: Christmas cake in the shape of a Yule log.

bulgur wheat: parboiled, cracked red wheat, also called ala, used for pilaf, stuffing, cereal, and other dishes.

Bundernusse (Torte): the Swiss name for a German type of nut cake.

Bündnerfleisch: air-dried beef from Switzerland, sliced thin like prosciutto.

burrito: a wheat-flour taco.

butter: *beurre manié:* equal amounts of soft butter and flour worked together until smooth. Used as a thickening agent. *Clarified:* butter heated until the milk solids settle to the bottom and the clear (clarified) liquid on the top can be poured off; has a higher heating temperature before reaching a burning point than unclarified butter. *Compound (flavored):* butter that is softened and flavored by such additions as herbs or purees of shellfish shells or toasted peppers, then shaped into a roll, refrigerated, and sliced off as needed to top meats, fish, or vegetables, or to enrich soups or sauces. *Cube:* ¼ pound. *Salted:* longer lasting because the salt acts as a preservative, but less delicate in flavor. *Sauce:* see MAÎTRE D'HÔTEL BUTTER (lemon-parsley butter) and BEURRE BLANC (white butter sauce). *Stick:* ¼ pound. *Sweet butter:* the best-flavored, freshest butter. In the recipes in this book that specify only butter, sweet butter is generally preferable, although salt butter is perfectly acceptable. *Whipped:* aerated to make it light and fluffy by beating to incorporate air.

calabaza: the Caribbean name for calabash, green pumpkin or squash.

callaloo or calalu: the greens of the taro plant, used in the Caribbean to make a soup, also called callaloo. The oriental greens, Chinese spinach, are also called callaloo in Latin America, and are often one of the ingredients in the soup.

calzone: a large turnover made of pizza dough or flaky pastry, stuffed with cheese and some combination of minced ham, chicken, meat, fish, or vegetables, herbs, and spices.

canapés: small open-faced sandwiches usually served with drinks before meals or during receptions.

capon: a male chicken that has been castrated, resulting in a large bird with very tender flesh suitable for roasting.

caponata: an Italian cooked mixture of eggplant, peppers, garlic, onions, and tomatoes, much like the French ratatouille, but with the addition of capers, vinegar, and sugar. Usually served cold as an hors d'oeuvre.

caramel: a syrup made by melting sugar in water until the water evaporates and the sugar browns; *to caramelize* is to cook sugar or other food until it takes on a golden-brown color. To caramelize a mold in which a custard is to bake is to pour in enough caramel syrup to cover the bottom, and rotate the mold so that the syrup covers the bottom evenly. To make *caramel sauce:* thin caramel syrup with cream over low heat. See also CRÈME CARAMEL and CRÈME BRULÉE.

cardoons: stalks of an artichokelike plant that is a member of the thistle family; somewhat bitter in flavor.

carob: generally used as a chocolate substitute, the brown powder is made from seed pods of the carob tree; also known as St.-John's-bread.

casing: the flushed intestines of pork, beef, or lamb, used for stuffing sausages. Synthetic casing is sometimes used commercially.

cassoulet: a French dish of beans, baked with sausage, goose, duck, or pork, depending on the region.

caul fat (crépine): the membrane that surrounds pigs' stomachs, used to enclose various terrines and pâtés, the most famous of which are called crépinettes. Sometimes called lace fat because of the lacy interweaving of fat in the membrane.

caviar: the lightly salted roe of various fish. In the United States, only the roe of sturgeon can be called caviar; all other roe needs the name of the fish as well—whitefish caviar, salmon caviar, flying fish caviar, and so on. The finest caviar is from the beluga, osetra, or sevruga sturgeons of the Caspian Sea. When sold fresh, it is salted to about 3 percent and called malossal, meaning "little salt" in Russian. The sterilized caviar packed in jars and stored without refrigeration is frequently salted up to 10 percent to stabilize it for longer shelf life.

celeriac: celery root.

celery cabbage: same as Napa cabbage; see CHINESE CABBAGE.

celery root: celeriac.

cellophane noodles or Chinese vermicelli or bean threads: translucent noodles made of mung bean flour, used in the cooking of China and southeast Asia.

cepes or cèpes: see PORCINI.

challah: Jewish egg bread in the shape of a twist.

chanterelles or chantarelles (*Cantharellus cibarius*): delicate orange-colored wild mushrooms, also known as girolles and Pfifferling

Chantilly or crème à la Chantilly: French heavy cream (CRÈME FRAÎCHE), whipped. Use whipping cream, which has the same butterfat content but not quite the tang of the slightly fermented French cream.

chapati: baked whole-wheat Indian bread, flat like lavash and tortillas.

charcuterie: originally, prepared pork products such as sausages, hams, and pâtés, but now including a wide range of other prepared meats, fish, and fowl, as well as salads, olives, pickles, mayonnaise, and other dishes. Also the shop in which the products are sold.

charlotte: a molded dessert combining fruits and cake or ladyfingers, usually served warm, or cake or ladyfingers combined with flavored creams or custards, served cold.

chartreuse: a mold of chopped foods.

chasseur sauce (hunter's sauce): brown sauce to which tomato sauce, wine, and mushrooms have been added.

chaudfroid: a mayonnaise with gelatin added, used to coat and decorate foods such as chicken or fish.

chayote squash: a pear-shaped squash known also as mirliton or vegetable pear.

chestnuts: the best chestnuts are firm and plump. To peel fresh chestnuts, cut a slit from top to bottom on the flat side; place a small number at a time in a pan under the broiler, or on a grill over charcoal, until the skins begin to brown. They will peel easily while hot; if they cool, return to the heat for a minute. Some cooks prefer to boil them, but toasting adds to the flavor. Available canned whole, plain, or in syrup, and pureed.

chèvre: the name used for goat cheese.

(sauce) chevreul: a game sauce made by combining a poivrade sauce with small bits of game and red wine.

chicharrones: in Latin America and the Caribbean, pork CRACKLINGS.

chick-peas: garbanzo beans.

chiffonade: thinly julienned leafy vegetables such as sorrel, spinach, or basil, cooked with, or used to garnish, a dish.

chili oil: a very hot red oil made by steeping chili peppers in vegetable oil. Available commercially.

chili peppers: see PEPPERS.

Chinese cabbage: includes several different vegetables of the choy family, primarily *Napa cabbage* (or celery cabbage), which most resembles Western cabbage in flavor, but is more tender and resembles romaine in shape; *bok choy*, a leafy green vegetable with white stalks somewhat resembling chard, which grows and is marketed in bunches like celery.

Chinese chives: a flat, grasslike vegetable of the lily family with a garlicky flavor, used in Chinese cooking. Sometimes called garlic chives.

Chinese dried shrimp: an essential seasoning ingredient in Chinese cooking, these tiny pink shrimp must be soaked in water for at least 30 minutes before cooking.

Chinese ham: see SMITHFIELD HAM.

Chinese parsley: see CORIANDER.

Chinese roasted salt-pepper: a ground condiment made by roasting together, then crushing, salt with a small amount of Sichuan peppercorns. A ubiquitous "dip" in China, particularly used for deep-fried foods.

chitterlings or chitlins: the entrails or small intestines of hogs. In Italy, where they are called pagliata, they are a favorite ingredient in a sauce for pasta and are braised as an entrée, particularly in areas near the slaughterhouses.

chocolate: a product obtained from roasted and ground cocoa beans. *Chocolate liquor:* also called *unsweetened* or *baking* chocolate, the basic chocolate with no sugar or other additives, used for baking and cooking, and sold in solid bars divided into 1-ounce sections; *semisweet chocolate:* chocolate mixed with sugar and sometimes other additives; *sweet chocolate:* chocolate mixed with more sugar than semisweet and with additional cocoa butter; *milk chocolate:* sweet chocolate to which milk has been added; *white chocolate:* pure cocoa butter with milk and sugar added but no brown chocolate liquor; *chocolate chips:* small semisweet chocolate bits used in baking. *To melt chocolate:* Heat bits or broken pieces in the top of a double boiler over simmering water until they liquefy; or place in an ovenproof bowl in a slow oven. The white bloom that sometimes appears on stored chocolate is cocoa butter, and not harmful. See also COCOA and CAROB.

chorizo or chouriço: spicy Spanish or Mexican pork sausage.

Choron sauce: béarnaise sauce combined with tomato paste or puree.

chutney: a hot, spicy Indian relish made of large chunks of fruit flavored with sugar, vinegar, spices, and usually chili peppers.

cilantro: see CORIANDER.

citron: a citrus fruit, the peel of which is candied and used in baked goods.

citronella: see LEMONGRASS.

clarified butter: see BUTTER; CLARIFY.

clarify: to remove solids from butter or stock. *To clarify butter:* Put in a saucepan (or ovenproof container) and heat over low heat on the stove top (or in a very slow oven) until all of the milklike solids settle to the bottom. Pour off the clear liquid on the top, which is the clarified butter, and conserve in the refrigerator. This butter will heat to a much higher temperature than unclarified butter before burning. *To clarify stock:* Be sure that all fat has been removed from the stock (overnight in the refrigerator will solidify the fat on the top, making removal easy). For a pot of stock, whip several egg whites to a loose stiffness. Fold them into about 2 cups of stock, then fold the mixture into the full pot of hot stock. Mix in, turn to low heat, enough to keep the pot at a slow bubble. Solids will combine with the egg whites forming a dense "scum." Continue to simmer for 20 to 25 minutes, then spoon out and strain through a damp dish towel placed in a colander over a large bowl. The clear liquid will pour through, leaving the scummy residue behind.

cobbler: a type of deep-dish pie made with biscuit dough and fruit.

cocoa: the powder that remains after the cocoa bean is roasted and ground and the cocoa butter is removed. Very small amounts of cocoa butter are occasionally left in. *Dutch process cocoa* is treated by an alkaline process to neutralize some of the bitter flavor.

coconut: available fresh or, with sugar added, in packaged form. *Coconut milk (or cream):* Pour 2 cups boiling water over the shredded meat of 1 coconut. Let stand for 30 minutes. Press the mixture through a sieve, discarding the shreds. Let the liquid stand until the water settles to the bottom. Skim off the rich "cream" on top. Makes about ½ cup. Also available canned.

conch: a large mollusk, the meat of which is used in chowders and other dishes. It must be pounded like octopus to tenderize it. It most closely resembles abalone in flavor and texture. In the Caribbean, it is commonly served raw, or barely blanched, in seviche. Pronounced "conk" in many areas.

confit: usually duck or goose, cooked in, and preserved under, its own fat.

consommé: clarified stock served as a soup. When chilled, it becomes jellied. See also BROTH, STOCK.

coquilles: shells or shell-shaped baking dishes. *En coquilles:* food served cooked in shells or shell-shaped dishes.

coriander: the fresh, pungent leaves used in Mexican, Chinese, Indian, and other Asian cuisines; also known as cilantro, Chinese parsley, or Mexican parsley; *seeds:* the dried seeds are used in spice mixtures and marinades; *ground:* the dried ground seeds are often an ingredient in curries.

cornichons: see PICKLES.

cornstarch: a powder used to thicken sauces or gravies by mixing with cold water until thoroughly dissolved, then adding in small amounts to the hot liquid. Also used as an ingredient to thicken pie fillings and puddings. It can be used in equal amounts as a thickener in place of arrowroot, and in half the amount, in place of flour.

coulibiac (koulebiaka): a many-layered dish usually of salmon, crêpes, rice, mushrooms, onions, hard-cooked eggs, sour cream, dill, parsley, and other seasonings, enclosed and baked in a pastry crust. Originally the dish was made with cabbage, with salmon sometimes served on the side. It came into the Parisian repertoire from Russia. The traditional accompaniment is a cup of hot consommé.

coulis: originally, natural meat sauces (juices), but more recently used to mean thick purees, often of vegetables.

coupe: usually a dessert of ice cream. Also used for dishes whose sides are rounded.

court-bouillon: a seasoned poaching liquid for fish, meat, or poultry.

couscous: the finely cracked semolina used widely in North Africa and the Middle East. The grain is often cooked by steaming it over a stew of meats and vegetables, then served with the cooked ingredients over it, and the sauce, usually seasoned with hot peppers and spices, served to the side.

cracklings: pork fatback, cut into small bits and rendered until crisp. See also CHICHARRONES.

cream: *coffee cream (light cream):* cream with less butterfat than whipping cream; *half and half:* half cream, half whole milk, often used in place of light cream; *heavy cream (whipping cream):* cream that contains the most butter fat and the only cream that will whip; *sour cream:* cultured cream that has been thickened. See also CRÈME FRAÎCHE; CHANTILLY. *To cream:* Work shortening or butter until it is smooth and the consistency of mayonnaise or thickly whipped cream.

cream of tartar: made from the lees or residue left after the fermentation of wine. An acid medium, it is added in beating egg whites to stabilize them and is an ingredient in single-acting or homemade baking powder: one-third cream of tartar to two-thirds baking soda.

cream puff dough: a cooked mixture of water and butter into which flour is mixed and eggs added to make a thick, shiny dough; used for making cream puffs, éclairs, and other similar pastries.

cream sauce: BÉCHAMEL or white sauce with cream added.

crème á la Chantilly: see CHANTILLY.

crème anglaise: a vanilla-flavored custard sauce made of milk, egg yolks, and sugar.

crème brulée: custard with a hard, crackly, caramelized topping made by spreading the cold baked custard with brown sugar and running it under the broiler until the sugar liquefies.

crème caramel: custard with a syrupy caramel topping.

crème fraîche: French heavy cream of a high butterfat content, thickened slightly by a mild natural fermentation, used in cooking, and as a topping for desserts. Can be whipped to make crème à la Chantilly. *To make crème fraîche:* Pour 2 cups heavy (whipping) cream in a jar or bowl, add 6 to 7 teaspoons buttermilk or a little more of sour cream, mix, cover, and leave at room temperature for 24 hours. Stir and refrigerate. Makes about 2 cups. Will keep for at least 2 weeks. Note: It is important to use real whipping cream; any cream with additives or sterilants will not ferment properly.

crème patissière: see PASTRY CREAM.

crêpes: thin pancakes.

crêpinettes: see CAUL FAT (CRÉPINE).

croquettes: mashed or chopped foods mixed with eggs, sauce, or other binding agents; formed into patties; breaded; and fried until golden and crisp.

crostini: in Italian cooking, croutons or toasts. In Florence, the name given to small pieces of toasted bread topped with a warm, coarse puree of chicken livers, anchovies, and capers; in Rome, toasts often covered with melted provatura cheese and anchovies.

(en) croute: enclosed and baked in a pastry crust, such as pâté en croute or salmon en croute.

croutons: bread cut into small ovals or squares and sautéed in oil or butter (or a mixture of both) until golden brown on both sides. Croutons can also be made by toasting or broiling in the oven. *To make garlic croutons:* Rub the bread before toasting it with a raw clove of garlic. Also available packaged, but not as good as freshly made.

curry: an Indian blend of pungent spices differing according to the dish that is to be cooked. Turmeric, a common ingredient of curry powder, gives it its intensely deep yellow-ochre color. Also the name of a dish cooked in such a mixture of spices.

custard sauce: see CRÈME ANGLAISE.

cut in: to incorporate firm butter or shortening into flour by working with a knife or pastry blender until the mixture is granular and in small lumps about the size of peas.

dacquoise: crisp meringue and hazelnut cake.

daikon: Japanese long white radish; substitute turnips.

dal: in Indian cuisine, dried legumes such as peas, beans, and lentils. Also the cooked, pureed dishes made from them, served as an accompaniment at most meals.

dashi: in Japanese cooking, basic fish stock. (Substitute chicken stock.)

decant: to pour off the clear liquid from any sediment or settled deposits, as in decanting old wines. Can also be used in pouring off liquid that can be used for stock, such as after soaking mushrooms or steaming clams or mussels, but care must be taken to keep any sand from getting into the liquid.

deep-dish pie: a pie baked in a baking dish and made without a bottom crust.

deglaze: to add liquid to the brown drippings left in a pan in which food has been sautéed or roasted, scraping and incorporating them to make a natural sauce or gravy.

degrease: to skim off any fat. For soups and sauces, this is most easily accomplished by refrigerating overnight until the fat solidifies on top.

demiglace: espagnole sauce (rich, thickened meat stock combined with tomato sauce) further reduced and flavored with Madeira or sherry.

dolma or dolmeh: stuffed grape leaves. Also stuffed mixed vegetables such as peppers, cabbage leaves, squash, and tomatoes.

drawn butter: see BUTTER; CLARIFIED.

dredge: to coat with flour. An easy method is to put a small amount of flour in a paper bag, add the food to be dredged in small quantities, close the bag, and shake well. The food will be evenly dusted.

duchess potatoes (pommes duchesse): a mixture of mashed potatoes and cream puff pastry, or mashed potatoes and butter, cream, and egg yolks, used to make borders and other garnishes.

duxelles: finely chopped mushrooms sautéed in butter with chopped shallots until all the liquid has evaporated. *Duxelles sauce* is made by sautéing mushrooms as above and adding stock or gravy.

eggplant: Western eggplant is usually larger, with tougher skin, less succulent flesh, and more seeds than the smaller thin varieties from Asia and the Middle East. Japanese eggplant is the small variety most often found in U.S. markets.

eggs: when eggs are called for, use large Grade A or AA, which contain about 2 tablespoons of white and 1 of yolk. *To hard-cook eggs:* Bring water to a boil, add the eggs with a slotted spoon, boil gently for 12 minutes, then refresh under cold running water. Some people make a small hole in one end with a straight pin before cooking. *Egg whites can be frozen* and later defrosted, the quantity needed poured off, and the rest refrozen. *To measure only a portion of an egg:* Beat the egg, then pour off the amount needed, reserving the rest for another use. *To beat egg whites:* A copper bowl is the best utensil, but any material except plastic will work.

enchilada: a filled tortilla served in a sauce.

enoki or enokidaki mushrooms: tiny white-stemmed button mushrooms available packaged in bunches in plastic envelopes. The lower strawlike parts of the stems must be cut off.

epazote: an herb of strong flavor used widely in Mexican cooking. Available in the United States in Mexican markets.

escalope: meat, fish, or poultry cut into small, thin slices (about ¼ inch thick), sometimes pounded to flatten them further, and usually quickly sautéed.

escargot butter: see SNAIL BUTTER.

espagnole sauce: rich meat stock thickened and combined with tomato sauce.

étuvé: braised (étoufée in New Orleans).

farce: see FORCEMEAT.

fats: see individual names.

fennel: a licorice-flavored plant eaten raw, much like celery, and cooked as a vegetable. The seeds are used in baking, and dried fennel stalks added to a charcoal fire contribute an aromatic smoky flavor to the food being grilled. The raw vegetable is sometimes called sweet anise, which it strongly resembles.

feuilletage: see PUFF PASTRY.

fillet: a piece of meat, fish, or poultry from which all the bones, skin, and gristle have been removed. *To fillet* is to bone a piece of meat, fish, or fowl.

fines herbe: a mixture of herbs generally including parsley, chervil, chives, and tarragon or thyme.

finnan haddie: golden, smoked haddock, a specialty of Scotland. Usually split and filleted but also sold in chunks. In the United States, large Atlantic cod is often used in place of true haddock. The golden color is artificially added.

fish sauce: an extract based on fermented fish, used widely as a condiment in the sauces and cooking of southeast Asia.

5-spice powder: a Chinese seasoning actually containing 5 to 7 spices including ground cinnamon, cloves, star anise, fennel seed, ginger, and Sichuan peppercorns.

flake: to shred coarsely or break into flake-like pieces.

flambé: to flame, usually in rum, Cognac, or other liquors. Also a dish prepared in that fashion. Warming the alcohol first ensures a good flame.

flan: custard.

floating islands (oeufs à la neige): poached meringues served on a bed of vanilla custard cream and garnished with threads of caramel.

flour: the three major kinds of flour are *all-purpose flour*, a blend of hard-wheat and soft, which works well for most kinds of baking and cooking; *bread flour*, sometimes called *hard-wheat* or *high-gluten* flour, which makes a more chewy and crusty loaf; and *cake flour*, soft-wheat, low-protein, high-starch flour, best for cakes because it produces a finer texture and more tender product than high-gluten flour. Other types of flours include *rye flour*, low in gluten, which produces a dense product unless blended with wheat flour in large proportions, and of which there are four kinds—white rye, medium rye (straight rye flour), dark rye (with bran particles added), and rye meal or pumpernickel (with bran particles added). *Bleached flour* is chemically treated to whiten it; *unbleached flour*, slightly less white, has had no whitening agents added. *Enriched flour* has had vitamins and minerals replaced or added. *Gluten flour*, very high in protein and relatively starch-free, is often used as an additive to flours for pasta and bread. *Pumpernickel* (see rye). *Rice flour* is used unblended by people with allergies to wheat, and in Chinese cooking for noodles and baked goods; produces a heavy product unless blended with wheat flour. *Potato flour* is used as a thickening agent and in bread making. *Instant flour* is processed so that it can be added to liquids without forming lumps, but is not generally satisfactory for baking. *Self-rising flour* has salt and baking powder added. *Chestnut flour* is used in Chinese cooking. *Whole-wheat flour* is made of the entire wheat kernel, making it more nutritious as well as more perishable. *Pastry flour* is the same as cake flour. *Triticale* is a hybrid of wheat and rye grains. *Graham flour* is interchangeable with whole-wheat flour. *Stone-ground flour* is milled using old-style stone grinders in place of newer metal ones, which produce more heat and destroy more nutrients. *Semolina* is made from hard durham wheat and is used for high-quality pasta and some kinds of gnocchi. *Soy flour*, made from soybeans and rich in protein but lacking gluten, must be combined with wheat flour for baking. *Buckwheat flour*, made from buck-wheat seeds, is used for crêpes, pasta, and some breadstuffs, after mixing with regular flour. *Barley flour* is nutritious but low in protein. Unless otherwise noted, the recipes in this book call for unbleached, enriched, all-purpose white flour.

focaccia or fogaccia: pizza dough or crust, baked flat like a bread, sometimes with simple toppings such as olive oil, garlic, or anchovies.

fold in: to incorporate a lighter ingredient, such as whipped cream or egg whites, into a heavier one, such as batter or pudding, in order to lighten it. By using a scooping-under and folding-over motion, just enough to incorporate the lighter ingredient, a minimum of beaten air is lost.

forcemeat: finely chopped or ground foods used to stuff other food. Also called farce or stuffing.

frangipane: a thick mixture based on almond paste or marzipan.

French dressing: see VINAIGRETTE.

fricassee: a stew, usually of poultry.

fries: calf or lamb testicles (French animelles).

fry: to cook foods in hot fat over high heat. Deep-frying is done in a deep pan in 2 or 3 inches of hot fat, often using an insertable mesh basket that can be removed to drain the foods of excess fat. The best oils for frying are those with little fla-

vor and a high burning point, such as peanut or vegetable oil.

fumé: smoked.

galangal or galingale: rhizomes related to
ginger, much favored in medieval cookery
for their pungent aroma. Widely used in
Asian medicine and cooking, less frequently in the cooking of the Middle East,
in some areas of Africa, and in parts of
India. In the United States, available in
southeast Asian and Indian markets, most
commonly in dried form, both powdered
and sliced, and very occasionally fresh.
Known also as Laos powder or Indian ginger. The name galingale is sometimes used
for the roots of the sedge, also called chufas
or rush nuts.

galantine: classically, a specific preparation
of poultry, but now used more generally for
any meat or fowl that is boned, stuffed,
tied, and poached in broth. Served cold,
in slices, with the natural aspic. The term
is nowadays used interchangeably with
BALLOTTINE.

ganache: a thick, glossy mixture of sweetened chocolate and heavy cream used as a
cake filling or icing, or for the centers of
chocolate truffles.

garam masala: a mixture of ground spices
widely used in Indian cooking, containing
dried coriander seeds, cloves, black pepper,
cardamom seeds, cumin, and cinnamon.
Available already mixed.

garbanzo beans: same as CHICK-PEAS.

garlic: for most purposes, fresh is preferable
to dried or powdered. If using prepared
garlic, the *granulated* form is preferable to
garlic salt. *Garlic powder* has a strong, concentrated flavor and should be used in
smaller quantities than other dried forms.
To peel fresh garlic: Tap the clove sharply
with the flat side of a knife or cleaver,
which will break the skin and allow the
clove to slip out easily. The best advice for
getting rid of pungent *garlic odor* left on
your hands is Jacqueline Mallorca's: Rub
your fingers thoroughly with the bowl of a
stainless steel spoon under cold running
water, then wash hands with soap and
water. It never fails.

garni: garnished.

gazpacho: a cold Spanish soup based on
pureed tomatoes, peppers, and bread to
which vinegar and other seasonings, and
finely chopped vegetables such as tomatoes, peppers, onions, and cucumbers, are
added. Often served with a garnish of
chopped hard-cooked eggs and sometimes
with an ice cube to keep it cold.

gelatin: a protein derived from bones and
tendons, packaged as a colorless, unflavored granular powder that is used to set
up liquids for making aspics, cold jellied
soups, and wine and other flavored jellies;
and to stabilize and solidify whipped cream
and custard desserts such as Bavarian
creams. *To use:* Dissolve 1 packet (1 tablespoon) in a small amount of cold liquid
until it softens and becomes viscous, 4 to 5
minutes, then add to the stock or other
food. If the mixture needs further cooking,

heat gently, but do not boil, until well blended and free of granules. One package or 1 tablespoon of gelatin will gel 2 to 3 cups of liquid, depending on the degree of firmness desired and the other ingredients included. French gelatin comes in sheets, 4 of which equal 1 packet of U.S. gelatin.

gelato: Italian ice cream of more dense texture than American or French ice cream.

génoise: sponge cake.

ghee: Indian clarified butter, with a higher heating temperature than untreated butter. See also CLARIFY.

gherkins: see PICKLES.

giblets: the offal, or the hearts, livers, and gizzards of fowl.

ginger: *root:* the many-sectioned knobby, bulblike part of the plant, used to add a pungent, often hot, flavor to the foods with which it is mixed or cooked. *Young ginger,* the white fresh root with thin skin and lavender tinges, is more delicate and less fibrous, but available only a few months of the year. Some cooks feel that mature brown-skinned gingerroot needs to be peeled before using, but others think it is wasteful and unnecessary. Sliced, chopped, or grated ginger is widely used in the cooking of Central and South America, India, Africa, Asia, and the Middle East. The root can be frozen whole and cut off or grated as needed. *Dried:* has a less potent flavor and is not a good substitute for the fresh root. In powdered or ground form, it contributes flavor to baked goods, such as gingerbread and gingersnaps, to spice mixtures, and to pâtés and sausages. *Candied:* various types of sugared ginger are used largely in desserts—*stem (immature) ginger* in syrup; *glazed ginger; crystallized ginger;* and *Chinese preserved ginger* cooked with sugar and spices. *Beverages:* Ginger is used to flavor such drinks as ginger ale or ginger beer.

ginkgo nuts: the pits of the plant, used in Asian cooking, particularly Japanese and Chinese. Sometimes available fresh in the United States in Asian markets, more generally found canned in brine. The fresh variety has a hard shell resembling a pistachio, which must be cracked and peeled before the white-fleshed nut is usable.

ginseng: a root used in the Orient for its medicinal properties; often made into tea and used in cooked dishes.

glace de viande: the reduction of stock to a highly concentrated, syrupy form; see also GLAZE.

glaze: the reduction of stock to a highly concentrated form, used as a base or added in small quantities to enrich sauces or soups. Also called GLACE DE VIANDE. *Glazes* for desserts are made of currant jelly or strained apricot jam (used to glaze fruit tarts); or sugar syrup (to coat fruits). Aspic is also sometimes thinned and used as a glaze. *To deglaze* is to make a gravy of the concentrated pan drippings after roasting or sautéing, by scraping and blending them into added liquid.

gluten: a component of wheat flour that, when mixed with liquid and kneaded, forms an elastic dough essential to making leavened breads.

gnocchi: Italian "dumplings" made of semolina, potatoes, cornmeal, or ricotta and spinach, blended with eggs, grated cheese, and seasonings, and poached or baked.

gougère: a baked savory made of cream puff pastry mixed with grated cheese.

(sauce) grand veneur: a rich sauce for game made by combining a poivrade sauce with currant jelly and heavy cream, sometimes with the addition of black truffles.

granita: Italian water ice of a slightly crystalline texture, flavored with such essences as coffee or lemon, or with fruit such as crushed strawberries. Called granité in France.

grape leaves: popular throughout the Middle East, stuffed and cooked in a variety of fashions. In the United States the leaves are packed in brine and sold in jars. See also DOLMA.

gravlax: Scandinavian raw, boned salmon cured in sugar, salt, and dill.

green sauce (sauce verte): in French cooking, a mayonnaise to which parsley, watercress, and spinach are added. In Italian cooking (salsa verde), a puree of parsley, capers, garlic, anchovies, and olive oil.

grenadin: originally an escalope of fillet of veal, but now applied to other meats or fowl cut in similar fashion.

grenadine: a red flavoring syrup made of pomegranate juice and sugar.

gribiche: a mayonnaise to which minced shallots, chopped hard-cooked eggs, gherkins or pickles, capers, and herbs such as parsley, chives, and tarragon have been added.

grill: to broil over a live fire; also the apparatus used for such cooking or the single open metal rack on which the foods are cooked.

grissini: bread sticks.

grits: coarsely ground hominy eaten as a thick boiled mush or cut into squares and fried.

guacamole: mashed avocado dip or topping, usually combined with chopped hot chilies, onions, tomatoes, and cilantro leaves, and sometimes lime juice. Keeping the pit in the finished mixture is supposed to help keep it from browning.

gumbo: a thick Cajun-style seafood, chicken, or vegetable soup, often with the addition of ham, sausages, or other meat, highly seasoned, thickened with okra or gumbo filé, and served over rice.

gumbo filé: a powder made from sassafras leaves, used as a thickening agent and to add flavor in certain New Orleans recipes.

haggis: a Scottish puddinglike dish made of steel-cut oats and onions mixed with the liver, lungs, and heart of a sheep, then stuffed into the stomach paunch and boiled. Nowadays also stuffed into hog casing to make an individual portion much like a sausage.

head cheese: the cooked meat of the pig's head cut into pieces and set in aspic or jelly made from the stock. Served cold in slices.

hearts of palm: small shoots from the crown of the palm tree, generally served as a salad. Sometimes available fresh, but more often canned.

herbs: fresh and dried herbs are interchangeable in most cases (but fresh basil, for example, is essential in making pesto), but you need more of a fresh herb, approximately 1 tablespoon fresh to 1 teaspoon dried. Crushing herbs gently helps to release their flavors. Replace dried herbs often since they tend to lose their pungency quickly. Crumbled herbs are better than finely ground, for most purposes.

hochepot: a stew of several kinds of meat, pigs' feet, sausages, vegetables, including cabbage, and herbs and spices.

hoecakes: Southern cornmeal patties, usually fried in bacon fat and served with syrup.

hoisin sauce: a thick pastelike condiment made of soybeans and spices, used in Chinese cooking.

hollandaise sauce: a warm mixture of egg yolks, butter, and lemon juice, cooked until thickened.

hominy: whole kernels of corn leached in a solution of boiling water and lye, then washed and hulled. Available dried or canned.

hopping John: a Southern dish of black-eyed peas cooked with rice.

horseradish: fresh horseradish root is intensely strong; use care when grating. Mix with white vinegar and store in the refrigerator, just as with prepared horseradish. The red variety of prepared horseradish is colored with beets. Also see WASABI (Japanese horseradish).

hummus: a Middle Eastern puree of garbanzo beans, olive oil, sesame seeds, lemon juice, and garlic.

hush puppies: deep-fried corn-bread balls, traditionally served with fried fish.

ice cream: a flavored mixture based on custard and cream, on sugar syrup and cream, or on sweetened fruit pulp, egg whites, and cream.

ice milk: "ice cream" made with milk and additional emulsifiers.

injera: Ethiopian pancake bread made of teff, a milletlike grain, and cooked on a griddle or in a skillet.

innards: see GIBLETS.

Italian parsley: broad-leafed and more flavorful than the curly-leafed types. Although it resembles coriander or Chinese parsley in appearance, it has no similarity in flavor.

Italian sauce: see TOMATO SAUCE.

jambalaya: a Louisiana rice dish made with various combinations of meat, chicken, ham, sausages, seafood, and lively, hot seasonings.

jardinière: a mixture of vegetables.

jicama: a brown-skinned, white-fleshed vegetable, usually peeled, sliced, and eaten raw or added to salads. The texture is crisp and the flavor mild and sweet.

julienne: food cut into matchstick-sized pieces; also the verb meaning to cut foods into that shape.

kabob or kebab: small chunks of meat, fish, fowl, or shellfish—sometimes with vegetables—broiled, often on a skewer. Some kabobs are made of ground meats shaped into balls. In Indian cooking, kabobs are sometimes sautéed or cooked in a tandoor clay oven. See also SHASHLIK.

kasha: toasted buckwheat groats.

kelp: dried kelp, called konbu, used frequently in Japanese cooking. See also NORI and SEAWEED.

kimchi or kimchee: a Korean peppery hot dish of pickled cabbage and other vegetables, generally served as a relish.

kirsch: cherry liqueur.

knead: the process of working dough until the gluten develops and the texture becomes smooth and somewhat elastic; done by hand, by using a mixer with a dough hook, or in a food processor with a metal or plastic blade attachment.

kofta: in Indian and Middle Eastern cooking, balls of ground meat browned by sautéing or broiling, then simmered in sauce.

konbu or kombu: processed, dried kelp used to flavor the rice for Japanese sushi and other dishes.

korma: braised dishes in Indian cooking.

lard: to add strips of fat to lean cuts of meat by threading the fat through the meat with a larding needle; also used to add flavor, such as a bacony taste to a pot roast. Butchers will lard meat on request. Also rendered pork fat, sometimes with additives, in solid form, is used in cooking and pastry making. Fresh pork fatback is a good substitute in cooking.

lawasha: the Assyrian name for lavash, the common bread in the Middle East.

legumes: see BEANS.

lemongrass: an aromatic grass that adds a lemonlike flavor to dishes in which it is cooked. Popular in southeast Asia. Also called citronella.

lights: the edible lungs of animals.

lotus root: used raw or cooked, this vegetable root adds a crisp texture and subtle flavor as well as an unusual appearance, because of the shot-hole pattern of its slices.

lumpia: a Philippine pancake stuffed with crisp, stir-fried vegetables and usually dipped in a pungent sauce.

lyonnaise: cooked with onions.

macédoine: a mixture of cut-up fruits or vegetables.

macerate: to soften or break down a food into small parts by soaking in a liquid; also to soak in a flavored liquid so that some of the flavor will be absorbed. Generally used for fruits. See also MARINATE.

mâche: corn salad; a small green leaf used in salads; also called lamb's lettuce.

Madeira sauce: rich brown sauce or demi-glace to which Madeira is added.

maître d'hôtel butter (beurre maître d'hôtel): an uncooked mixture of butter, lemon juice, chopped parsley, salt, and pepper; used to garnish hot meats, fish, or vegetables.

maltaise sauce: hollandaise sauce combined with the juice and some of the grated rind of an orange.

mango: a tropical fruit with an exotic perfumelike flavor and juicy flesh.

manioc: also called cassava or yucca; a tropical plant whose roots are used widely in Latin American cooking, most commonly as ground and toasted meal, sometimes with added seasonings or butter, to accompany feijoada and other dishes; also boiled as an alternative to potatoes; and sliced and deep fried for chips. It is the common source of TAPIOCA.

margarine: vegetable fat in solid form, colored and flavored to resemble butter. Used as a butter substitute in low-cholesterol diets.

marinade: a liquid mixture used to tenderize and impart flavors to foods immersed in it for several hours or longer.

marinate: to place foods in a marinade to tenderize them and add flavor. Generally applied to meats, fish, fowl, and vegetables, whereas the term *macerate* is usually applied to fruits.

marrow: the substance contained in the bones of animals; poached beef marrow from the leg is generally the type used in cooking, sometimes spread on toasts as an hors d'oeuvre, or as an addition to sauces such as Bordelaise; *marrow bones:* in Italian cooking, osso buco, veal shins with marrow, braised and served as an entrée.

masa harina: cornmeal made of leached kernels, used in making tortillas, and in other Mexican cooking.

Mascarpone or Mascherpone: a fresh Italian cream cheese, often mixed with sugar, coffee, liqueurs, or brandy and eaten as a dessert.

mask: to nap or frost with a sauce, such as mayonnaise.

mayonnaise: a thick sauce of egg yolks, oil, Dijon mustard, vinegar or lemon, salt, and white pepper. In French cooking, when a food such as chicken is combined with mayonnaise, it is referred to as a mayonnaise (of chicken).

mein: Chinese egg noodles.

melt or melts: the spleen of an animal. Also the gonads of male fish (also spelled milt) fried in butter like the female roe.

menudo: a rich Mexican tripe soup.

meringue: egg whites beaten stiff with the addition of sugar. *Italian meringue:* egg whites beaten stiff and folded into a boiled sugar syrup.

mesclun: a mixture of the leaves of young lettuces and aromatic plants such as arugula, dandelion, or chervil, used for salad.

mesquite: a family of shrubs and trees that grows extensively in the arid regions of Mexico and the Southwest, harvested and made into charcoal. Its popularity over other types of charcoal is owing largely to the high heat it generates, which seals in the juices.

meunière: browned butter to which lemon juice and parsley are added; generally served with fish.

Mexican parsley: see CORIANDER.

mille-feuilles: Napoléons, a dessert made of puff pastry, custard filling, and icing.

minestrone: a thick Italian vegetable soup with beans and pasta or rice.

mint sauce: chopped mint leaves cooked with sugar and vinegar.

mirepoix: finely minced carrot, celery, and onion sautéed in butter, usually with a small amount of finely diced ham; used as the base for sauces and roasts.

mirin: a sweetened sake used frequently in Japanese cooking.

mirliton: the common name in Louisiana for chayote squash or vegetable pear.

miso: fermented soybean paste used in Japanese cooking. The white or light variety is milder than the red.

mocha: a flavoring combining chocolate and coffee.

mole: a Mexican sauce that includes chocolate, chilies, and pungent seasonings.

monosodium glutamate (MSG): a standard additive in much Asian cooking, widely used for its flavor-enhancing properties. Not used in any recipes in this book because many people have allergic reactions to it ("MSG syndrome"). Note: MSG is often an ingredient in bottled or canned products, so check labels if you are sensitive to it.

morel or morille: *Morchella esculenta, Morchella vulgaris):* highly esteemed, dark brown to black spongelike, pocked wild mushroom.

Mornay sauce: béchamel sauce to which cream, egg yolks, and grated cheese are added.

mousse: a cold dessert incorporating beaten heavy cream or egg whites, which lighten it; or a pâté or pureed food into which whipped cream or egg whites have been incorporated.

mousseline: hollandaise sauce to which whipped cream has been added.

MSG: see MONOSODIUM GLUTAMATE.

mushrooms: see particular kind or preparation. *To clean fresh mushrooms:* Use a mushroom brush or a damp cloth, but avoid washing in water because the spongelike properties of the mushroom will soak it up. Do not peel. *Dried mushrooms:* Soak for 20 to 30 minutes, or until plump and softened. The flavor is generally stronger than the fresh equivalent and will therefore give a different taste to dishes in which they are substituted. The liquid used for soaking can be strained and added to soups and gravies.

mustard: a family of plants, some of which are valuable for their seeds, which are ground and used as a condiment; and others for their leaves, which are cooked and used as a vegetable. *Ground mustards,* available in dry, powdered form (English, Chinese), are reconstituted by mixing with water and are generally hot. *Prepared mustards* differ according to texture and to additives such as wine or spices, and vary from mild to hot. *Creole and German mustards* are coarse ground and dark in color; *French and U.S. mustards* are smooth; *Dijon mustard* has white wine or the juice of unripened grapes (verjuice) added.

mutton: older mature lamb, more popular in Europe than in the United States.

naan: Indian oven-baked, leavened flat breads.

(sauce) nantua: béchamel sauce mixed with shellfish butter (butter cooked with the crushed shells of shellfish, then strained).

Napa or Nappa cabbage: also called Chinese or celery cabbage, this rather mild-flavored vegetable adds a crisp texture when used raw and a gentle flavor when cooked. Used throughout east Asia. See also CHINESE CABBAGE.

niter kebbeh: in Ethiopia, a cooking butter containing the flavors of garlic, onion, gingerroot, and a rich mixture of spices.

nopales (nopal), nopalitos: prickly pear cactus, used in cooking and salads; the spines must first be removed and the pieces boiled.

nori: seaweed (laver), available in dried sheets, widely used in Japanese cooking, and also in many Chinese dishes. Its flavor is greatly enhanced by frying or quick-toasting. It is the covering in many varieties of sushi.

nougat: a confection of nuts, sugar, butter, and other ingredients, sometimes chewy, sometimes crunchy.

Nusstorte: German nut cake. (See also BUNDERNUSSE.)

offal: see GIBLETS.

oil: the liquid obtained by pressing olives, kernels, nuts, and seeds. Used for salad dressings, in cooking, and sometimes to dress vegetables or other foods. *Olive oil* comes in various qualities, the best of which is green, extra-virgin; *sesame oil, Chinese style,* is concentrated in taste and is used largely to add flavor; other lighter *sesame oils* are used as other vegetable oils; *walnut oil* adds a distinctive flavor to salads and vegetables; *hazelnut oil* is similarly used for salads and to dress vegetables; *peanut oil,* often used in Chinese cooking, is good for deep-frying and other cooking; *vegetable oils* include *coconut, corn, palm, soybean,* and *safflower oil,* and are widely used for frying and sautéing. *Shortening,* made of solidified vegetable oil, is multipurpose and generally much better for baking than liquid oil. *Chili pepper oil,* oil in which hot, dried, red peppers have been steeped, is commonly used in Asian cooking.

onions: to peel boiling onions, cut a cross with a sharp knife into the stem end, drop in boiling water for a minute or two, remove, cool under cold running water, and slip off the skin.

osso buco: an Italian dish of braised marrow bone (veal shin).

oven temperatures: the recipes in this book have been tested on a gas range. If you are using electric, set all oven temperatures approximately 15° to 25°F lower than specified.

oyster mushroom (*Pleurotus ostreatus*): oyster-shaped mushroom that grows in overlapping clusters or colonies on dead or dying trees.

oyster sauce: a strong oyster-based sauce used in Chinese cooking.

paella: a Spanish dish based on rice, shellfish, chicken, sausages, meats, vegetables, and saffron, the mixture differing by region. Also the name of the two-handled pan used for cooking the dish.

paillard: very thin slices of meat, often pounded before cooking.

panaché: a mixture of two different kinds, such as vegetables, salad, or ice cream.

panade or panada: a thick pastelike mixture of milk or water cooked with butter, to which flour has been added.

panbroil: to cook over high heat on the

stove top using a minimum of fat; more akin to frying.

pancetta: Italian bacon, seasoned with salt and pepper, but not smoked.

panettone: a not very sweet, Italian briochelike cake studded with candied fruit peel.

panné: to coat a food lightly in flour, dip it in egg, then in bread crumbs, and sauté in fat until golden.

papadum: Indian wafer-bread cooked in oil to make it puffy and crispy.

(en) papillote: food baked in parchment or foil.

paratha: flaky, Indian whole-wheat bread cooked ("fried") on a griddle. Sometimes stuffed.

parboil: to cook briefly in boiling water.

parsley: curly-leafed is the most common variety. See also CORIANDER (the same as cilantro, Chinese parsley, Mexican parsley); and ITALIAN PARSLEY.

pastry cream (crème patissière): a soft custard used as a filling in cakes and éclairs and in combination with fruits in tarts. Often flavored with liqueurs or chocolate.

pâté: baked, seasoned, ground meat, fish, or vegetables, usually served cold; sometimes baked in a pastry crust (en croute).

pâte à choux: see CREAM PUFF DOUGH.

pâte brisée: French tart dough.

pâte feuilletée: see PUFF PASTRY.

peas: *English-style peas* must be shelled before cooking. *Petits pois,* tiny French peas, are seldom found fresh in the United States but are available frozen and canned. *Chinese pea pods* or *sugar peas* are eaten with the pod and are best when small and tender, before the seeds are too developed. *Sugar snap peas,* also eaten pod and all, are a cross between a type of green bean and a Chinese pea pod. See also "split peas," under BEANS.

peel: to remove the skin of fruits or vegetables; also the skin itself. Some foods, such as tomatoes, peel more easily if blanched first for 1 minute in boiling water. Small onions, with a cross cut through the root end, will slip out of their skins easily after blanching. Also, a wooden paddle with an elongated handle, used to transfer loaves of unbaked bread to the oven. A bread board or a baking sheet makes a satisfactory substitute.

pepper: the seeds or pods of various pepper plants used whole or ground as a condiment, including *black, white,* and *green peppercorns; ground black, white,* and *red pepper* (*cayenne, paprika, chili powder*); and *red pepper flakes. Hungarian-style paprikas* vary in their degree of hotness. *Sansho,* Japanese pepper, is a principal ingredient in pepper seasoning mixes such as 7-spices seasoning. *Sichuan peppercorns,* from the Chinese fagara or wild pepper plant, are not related to the black peppercorn; they are best toasted and ground. *Red peppercorns* are mild in flavor and not of the capsicum pepper family. See also PEPPERS.

peppers: *sweet peppers* include *green* bell peppers, which ripen to *red; yellow* bell peppers; *purple* bell peppers; and *pimientos,* mild red peppers pointed at the tip, and available more frequently canned than fresh. Sweet peppers are good raw or cooked. *To peel:* Char the skin all around over charcoal or under the broiler or directly over a gas burner. Place in a brown paper bag for a few minutes, then peel, when cool enough to handle. The steam from the cooking loosens the skin and makes peeling easier, and the toasting adds an excellent flavor. *Chili peppers:* hot peppers of varying degrees, depending on type, but also varying within the same kind, unpredictably. The seeds and ribs are the hottest part, and can be left or removed, depending on the degree of heat desired. Chili peppers are available fresh, canned, dried, in flakes, ground, and powdered. Among the most widely available fresh chilies are the small, somewhat pointed, green *serranos;* the slightly plumper, slightly larger, more round-ended green *jalapeños;* and the green *chilies poblanos,* usually at least finger length or longer, tapering toward the bottom and of varying heat, used for chilies rellenos (stuffed chilies). Dried chili poblano is called *chili ancho;* dried *chili chilpotle* or *chipotle* is a jalapeño. Serranos are the hot kind that come pickled in cans. Small Italian green peppers, *peperoncini,* are mildly hot and generally pickled, although in Italy they are available fresh and are delicious fried. *Cayenne peppers* are sometimes available in their green form fresh, but more frequently matured, dried, and powdered. Toasting fresh chilies brings out their flavor. *Tabasco peppers* are used only in the making of the fiery *Tabasco sauce,* which should be used cautiously. Handle all hot chilies carefully, especially avoiding touching your eyes. Washing does not always remove the "hot" from your fingers, so it is a good precaution to use rubber gloves.

Périgord sauce (sauce Périgueux): a rich brown sauce to which Madeira and chopped black truffles have been added.

pesto: a puree of fresh basil leaves, olive oil, garlic, and Parmesan cheese, often with the addition of pine nuts or walnuts. Used as a sauce for pasta, as an addition to soups such as minestrone, and as a garnish for vegetables.

pickles: members of the cucumber family prepared by curing in brine, various seasonings, and often vinegar. *Cornichons:* tiny pickles, traditionally used to garnish pâtés; *dill:* seasoned with dill; *gherkins:* same as cornichons, but in America generally sweet; *kosher-style:* seasoned with garlic and dill; the best are made without vinegar. See also TSUKEMONO.

pilaf: a basic Middle Eastern dish of rice (often combined with other grains), cooked lightly in butter before adding seasonings and stock (or other liquid), covering, and cooking gently until tender. Often chopped onions are sautéed in the butter before the rice is added and currants, raisins, pine nuts, or other flavoring agents are stirred in at the end of cooking.

pimiento: sweet red pepper, usually found canned.

pine nuts: the edible kernels found in the cones of some varieties of pines. The piñon pines of the Southwest yield a rounder nut with a more pronounced flavor than the more commonly available pignoli. Also known as Indian pine nuts, after the Indians who are the principal harvesters, the piñon kernels are found generally unshelled, while the pignoli nuts have been shelled and blanched.

pita bread: a flat, double pancakelike bread that pulls apart to form a pocket for stuffing; also called pocket bread. Popular throughout the Middle East.

plantain: a green bananalike fruit that is always cooked before eating.

pluck: see GIBLETS.

plum sauce: a thick, pungent Chinese sauce of pureed plums, hot chilies, sugar, and other piquant condiments; used as a dip or as a spread on pancakes in which other food will be placed.

poach: to cook immersed in simmering liquid.

poivrade sauce: a rich brown sauce (or game stock) to which red wine, vinegar, and crushed black peppercorns are added.

polenta: cornmeal.

(sauce) Polonaise: bread crumbs sautéed in butter until brown, used as a sauce for asparagus and cauliflower, sometimes with the addition of chopped hard-cooked egg.

pomelo: the very large and thick-skinned original grapefruit, often with tough membranes dividing the fruit, and many seeds. Found in China and the Caribbean; available in the United States in Chinese markets and some produce stores.

pooris: Indian breads that crisp and puff up dramatically when deep-fried.

porcini (*Boletus edulis*): large brown-capped wild mushrooms. Called cèpes in French.

posol, posole, or pozole: a Mexican soup made of hominy, pork, chili peppers, onions, and seasonings, accompanied by limes, raw vegetables such as radishes, green onions, and shredded lettuce, and hot pepper sauce. Also an early California settlers' dish of whole wheat berries and beans topped with brown sauce.

potato flour: see FLOUR.

potatoes: see names of individual dishes.

praline: a candy made of nuts, butter, sugar, and cream.

preserved lemons: salted and spiced lemon sections used in Moroccan cooking.

profiteroles: small cream puffs, usually filled with vanilla ice cream and served with chocolate sauce.

proof: to test a small amount of yeast to make sure it is still effective.

prosciutto: Italian ham; usually prosciutto crudo, cured ham, in the United States. Prosciutto crudo is pressed until very dry and sliced paper thin.

puff pastry (pâte feuilletée): a multilayered dough of flour and water alternating with butter, which puffs into many crisp, thin leaves in baking.

pumate: Italian sun-dried tomatoes, usually sold in the United States packed in olive oil.

puree: to reduce to a thick concentrated state by sieving, mashing by hand or in a mill, or by blending in a food processor or blender. Also, the food as so prepared.

quarry tiles: square unglazed tiles that can be placed on the rack of a home oven to simulate the brick floor of a baker's oven. (See also BAKER'S STONE.)

quenelles: small dumplings, generally of finely ground meat or fish lightened with cream and egg whites (quenelles mousseline); sometimes with the addition of a panade of cooked milk and flour (quenelles lyonnaise). The mixture is poached and sauced, or added to other dishes, as well as being used as a garnish.

quesadilla: a lightly fried, crisp turnover made from a tortilla, usually filled with cheese and sometimes peppers and tomatoes.

radicchio: a red-leafed salad plant resembling a small red cabbage in appearance but with more of a bitter-lettuce or chicory flavor.

radish: a white-fleshed pungent root vegetable most commonly having a red skin; there are also black-skinned varieties and all-white icicle radishes. The French often serve radishes topped with a dab of sweet butter. See also DAIKON.

raita: an Indian salad of yogurt mixed with raw or cooked vegetables and spices.

ramekin: a baking dish, such as a custard cup.

ramen: instant-cooking Japanese egg noodles, generally served in a small amount of broth.

ravigote sauce: vinaigrette with the addition of capers, onion, and herbs, and sometimes hard-cooked egg.

reduce: to cook slowly to evaporate liquid and concentrate flavors, as in a sauce.

refresh: a process to immediately stop the cooking of foods such as vegetables, fruits, or eggs by running cold water over them, incidentally preserving the original brightness of color.

remoulade: mayonnaise combined with herbs such as tarragon, parsley, and chervil; chopped capers, gherkins, or pickles; Dijon-style mustard; and mashed anchovies.

render: to melt out the fat by cooking slowly.

rice: *white rice::* polished grains that have the outer layer removed, along with much of the nutritional value of the vitamin B it contains; *brown rice:* unpolished, that is, retaining the bran, and therefore of higher nutritional value; *short-grain white rice:* when cooked, a starchier, gummier rice than long-grain; *long-grain white rice:* when cooked retains the individual grains; *converted rice:* long-grain white rice processed to remove some of the starch and to restore the nutrients lost in milling; *instant rice:* precooked, dehydrated rice that cooks rapidly but has a less desirable texture than regular rice; *glutinous or sweet rice:* short-grain sticky rice often used in certain Asian dishes, particularly desserts; *Arborio rice:* Italian short-grain rice, especially suited to the making of risotto; *wild rice:* nutty brown kernels that look like rice but are actually the seeds of a wild grass that grows around lakes in Canada, Minnesota, and Wisconsin, and now cultivated to a degree in California; *gohan:* Japanese cooked white rice; *basmati:* a common rice used in the cooking of India; *domsia:* Persian rice. *Pilaf:* the basic Middle Eastern rice dish, often mixed with other grains. *Risotto:* the Italian word for rice, but also a dish in which rice is the basic ingredient. *To rice:* to press food through a ricer or sieve to make it the consistency of rice.

rice flour or rice powder: in Japanese cooking, called mochiko; also used in making Chinese pastries and noodles, and in Indian cooking.

rice wine: *Chinese rice wine* (Shaoxing, Shao Hsing, or Hsao Shing) is made from fermented, short-grain, glutinous rice and aged for several years before using. It is now fairly widely available in Chinese markets, but dry sherry is an acceptable substitute. *Japanese sake,* usually drunk warm, can be replaced with dry white wine for cooking purposes, although the flavor is not comparable. *Mirin,* another Japanese rice wine, has a sweeter taste; use sherry as a substitute.

ricotta: Italian cottage cheese, somewhat like baker's or farmer's cheese.

rillettes: cooked, shredded meat, usually pork, served as an alternative to pâté.

rind: the outer skin of citrus fruits and melons. When using citrus rind in cooking, remove any of the white pith still attached, to avoid a bitter flavor. A knife-shaped vegetable peeler is useful in removing thin strips of rind without pith. Watermelon rind is a favorite for pickling.

risotto: Italian for rice. Also a dish based on rice, usually served as an alternative to pasta for the first course.

rijsttafel: rice table, an elaborate meal developed by the Dutch colonials in Indonesia, consisting of rice eaten with an enormous succession of foods of varying kinds and seasonings.

roast: to cook in an oven in dry heat; used for meats and poultry. The same process used for pastries, breads, vegetables, casseroles, custards, puddings, and fish is termed "to bake." To roast in moist heat, such as for a pot roast, is called "to braise."

(sauce) Robert: brown sauce combined with onions, tomato sauce, white wine, mustard, and sometimes chopped pickles and vinegar.

rocket plant: see ARUGULA.

Rocky Mountain oysters or mountain oysters or prairie oysters: beef testicles (French animelles).

roquette: see ARUGULA.

rouille: a Provençal sauce to accompany fish stew, usually based on a garlic mayonnaise with tomato concentrate or red pepper added to give it the rusty color from which it takes its name. Some cooks also add anchovy.

roux: a cooked blend of equal amounts of butter and flour used to thicken sauces. A *white roux* is cooked briefly so that it does not color; a *brown roux* is cooked until it takes on a rich brown color.

Russian dressing: mayonnaise combined with chili sauce.

sabayon or zabaglione: a dessert made by beating egg yolks, sugar, and Marsala over low heat until they thicken to the consistency of a fluffy mayonnaise. Sometimes used as a sauce.

saffron: The stigma of a variety of crocus, available as threads or powder, used to add a distinctive flavor as well as color to the foods with which it is cooked. Extremely expensive. Pungent, so use sparingly.

sake: Japanese rice wine (substitute dry white wine). See also RICE WINE.

salt (sodium chloride): available in various forms, the most common of which is table salt in iodized or uniodized form. *Sea salt*, which has a slightly saltier flavor, is available coarsely ground or in larger crystals that can be used in a mill. *Kosher salt* comes in coarse crystalline form and is slightly less salty than sea salt or table salt. *Rock salt* comes in large crystals and, mixed with ice, is used as a refrigerant in making ice cream; mixed with mustard as a coating for beef, it forms a solid crust when broiled or roasted that seals in the juices and can be cracked off before serving. Salt sprinkled on raw cucumbers or eggplant will leach out some of the bitter fluids. In cooking soups, stocks, stews, sauces, or gravies, add salt sparingly and adjust at the end of the cooking, because as the liquid evaporates the salt becomes more concentrated. *Salt substitutes* (usually potassium chloride) are available for people who must avoid sodium salt.

salt cod: semidehydrated dried cod, cured by salting, the basis for such dishes as Spanish bacalao with green sauce, French brandade de morue, Portuguese bacalhau à Gomes de Sá, and Italian stuffed baccalà, Venetian-style. Salt cod must be soaked overnight or up to 24 hours in several changes of cold water, or under continuously running cold water, before cooking.

salsa verde: see GREEN SAUCE.

sambal: a relish containing hot chili pepper paste, used largely as a condiment in southeast Asia.

samosa: small stuffed pastries served as an appetizer in Indian cooking.

sansho pepper: a Japanese spice of much fragrance, always included in the mixture called 7-SPICE SEASONING.

sashimi: Japanese raw fish thinly sliced and usually served with WASABI, a hot horseradish paste.

satay: marinated strips of meat, fish, or chicken threaded on skewers and broiled, served in Malaysia as an appetizer or main course.

sauces: see individual kinds.

sauté: to fry on the top of the stove using a small amount of fat, then moistening (deglazing) with a liquid such as wine or broth, and simmering in the concentrated juices, which make a natural sauce.

savarin: a ring-shaped pastry made with the same dough as a baba, then saturated with sugar syrup and kirsch (rather than rum, as with a baba). The center of the ring is usually filled with some combination of whipped cream, custard, and fresh fruit. (See also BABA.)

scald: to immerse in boiling water briefly; to bring a liquid such as milk to the boiling point.

scallop: see ESCALOPE; also a shellfish (coquilles St. Jacques).

scalloped potatoes (gratin dauphinois or pommes dauphinois): a mixture of sliced potatoes, garlic, milk, butter, and Gruyère cheese baked until browned.

score: to make a pattern of incisions in meat or fish either by cutting or grilling.

scrapple: the trimmings and scraps of pork mixed with cornmeal and spices; a specialty of the Pennsylvania Dutch.

sea urchin: a round, spiny, shelled sea animal ranging from about 2 to 10 inches across, prized for its roe. Both the male gonads ("white roe") and the female ovaries are eaten.

sear: to cook food quickly over high heat to form a brown coating and seal in the juices.

seaweed: marine plants or algae, most frequently used in Asian cooking. See also KONBU and NORI.

semi-freddo: an Italian frozen mousse or pudding.

sesame oil: see OIL.

sesame paste: a thick Chinese seasoning sauce made of toasted sesame seeds. See also TAHINI.

sesame seeds: to toast: Put in a pie tin and bake at 400°F until just beginning to brown, 3 to 4 minutes, shaking the pan from time to time. Remove at once to a cool bowl.

7-spice seasoning (shichimi): a spicy Japanese blend of crushed red and sansho peppers and other spices. Substitute red or black pepper.

shallots (échalotes): small bulbs of the onion family combining a mild hint of garlic in their flavor.

Shao Hsing: see RICE WINE.

shark fins: a Chinese delicacy, especially valued as an ingredient in soup, to which they add a fine gelatinous quality.

shashlik: Russian-style shish kabob of marinated meat chunks threaded on a skewer and broiled.

she-crabs: female crabs with roe, used in the South to make she-crab soup. If unavailable, male crabs and hard-cooked egg yolks will give a similar result.

sherbet: an American version of the French sorbet or water ice—fruit juices or purees mixed with sugar and sometimes egg whites, and frozen—with milk or cream added.

shiitake mushrooms (*Lentinus edodes*): a tasty brown mushroom cultivated on logs, popular in China and Japan and now grown commercially in the United States. Also available dried.

shortening: solidified vegetable oil.

Sichuan or Szechuan peppercorns: a fragrant spice that resembles peppercorns in appearance, used in Chinese cooking.

simmer: to cook a food gently at a point just below a boil.

skewer: a metal or bamboo tool on which foods are threaded for broiling. Also used to close the opening of poultry, etc.

smitane: cooked with sour cream or a sour cream sauce.

Smithfield ham: an intensely salty, heavily smoked ham particularly popular in the Southeast United States. Its preparation should first include several soakings to remove excess saltiness. It is the closest approximation in the United States to Chinese ham and can be used in all recipes calling for that ingredient.

smoking: fish is smoked by either cold- or hot-smoking. Hot-smoking takes less time and produces a firm, cooked texture and a fish that keeps for a shorter period. Cold-smoking is done at low heat over a long period of time, up to a week or more. In either method the fish must first be cured by soaking in a brine solution or packing in a dry salt mixture. Meats, fish, and fowl can be smoked in closed barbecue ovens. Various woods and aromatic chips determine the type of smoky flavor.

smorgasbord: a Swedish selection of hot and cold dishes of great variety including hors d'oeuvre and light entrées.

smørrebrød: Danish open-faced sandwiches, often constituting a whole meal.

snail butter: a blend of creamed butter, minced garlic, shallots, parsley, salt, and pepper. Used to stuff snail shells or ramekins when baking snails.

soba: Japanese buckwheat noodles; *cha-soba* are buckwheat noodles flavored with green tea.

soffritto: a base for or addition to soups, stews, meats, sauces, and vegetables, made by sautéing a mince of onion, celery, parsley, carrot, garlic, and sometimes prosciutto, in olive oil. Similar to a piccolo tritato, which contains lemon peel and sometimes anchovies.

soft-shell crabs: young growing crabs in the stage of molting or casting off their shells. They can be eaten in their entirety. *Blue crabs* are the type most often available in the United States.

sorbet: fruit juices or purees, wines, liqueurs, or herbs mixed with sugar or sugar syrup and frozen. Sometimes beaten egg whites are added to produce a smoother texture. Also called ice or water ice.

soubise: a béchamel sauce thickened with a puree of cooked onions.

soufflé: a baked dish made of any food incorporated into a base of white sauce and egg yolks and lightened with stiffly beaten egg whites. Used as an appetizer, main course, or dessert.

sour cream: see CREAM.

soybean curd: TOFU.

soy sauce: a liquid mixture of fermented soybeans, yeast, wheat, salt, and sugar. Japanese and Chinese soy sauces have somewhat different flavors and the Japanese is much less salty. Chinese soy sauce is available in two styles—*dark or black soy* contains molasses; *thin soy* is lighter and saltier.

spices: ground spices lose their pungency as they age so it is best to replenish them frequently or as soon as they show signs of losing aroma, flavor, or color. Whole spices can be ground as you need them. Whole spices such as cloves can be stuck into an onion, if one is called for, then easily removed after imparting their flavor. Similarly, whole spices can be tied inside a cheesecloth packet, then removed after cooking. To grind whole spices, use a mortar and pestle, a blender, or a food processor, taking care to avoid overgrinding or powdering unless that is called for.

spoon bread: a Southern bread made of cornmeal, eggs, milk, and butter, spooned from the dish in which it is baked.

star anise: a star-shaped spice with a licorice flavor used widely in Chinese cooking.

steam: to cook a food in the steam generated by a boiling liquid below it.

steep: to soak a substance in boiling water or other liquid so that the essence blossoms and flavors the liquid; for example, to steep tea leaves in water to make tea, or hot chili peppers in oil to make chili oil.

stew: a dish of meat, fish, poultry, or vegetables cooked slowly for a long period of time in a flavored sauce. To stew is to prepare food in that fashion.

stir-fry: to toss small pieces of food in a wok in very little oil over very high heat to sear in the juices, then add liquids and seasonings and cook briefly, just enough to finish the preparation.

stock: meat, fish, or fowl cooked slowly with bones and trimmings, aromatic vegetables, herbs, and seasonings in a large amount of water. For brown stock, the bones and vegetables are browned first in the oven to give a richer flavor and deeper color. The finished broth may be eaten as a simple soup or clarified to use as a consommé or the basis of an aspic. Strained and defatted stock is the base of soups and sauces and may be frozen for future use. Stock may be reduced by half to a DEMI-GLACE or rich brown sauce, or further, to a concentrated, rich, syrupy glaze, GLACE DE VIANDE. Stock can be made also entirely of vegetables. Canned bouillon and bouillon cubes are satisfactory substitutes, but never as good as the real thing. Canned consommé is usually too sweet to use as a substitute.

straw mushroom (*Volvariella volvocea*): a highly prized Chinese mushroom, available in the United States canned or dried. The popular name comes from the ancient practice of growing the mushrooms on palettes of straw.

stuffing: see FORCEMEAT.

suckling lamb or pig: an animal slaughtered when 2 to 6 weeks old.

sugar: its several forms include *granulated sugar,* the common table and all-purpose cooking sugar; *superfine granulated sugar,* sometimes called frosting sugar, more finely ground, and therefore quicker to dissolve and to blend, good for bar sugar, iced drinks, icings, and for making meringues; *confectioners'* or *powdered sugar,* good for uncooked icings, for baking, and for dusting; *brown sugar,* dark or light, interchangeable unless the type is specified; *vanilla sugar,* made by burying a vanilla bean in a container of sugar so that its flavor will permeate the sugar. *To caramelize sugar:* Melt the sugar in a saucepan, swirling from time to time, until it liquefies and takes on a caramel color. Remove immediately from the heat as soon as it starts to caramelize since it will continue to cook and to darken and can easily burn and become acrid in flavor. *To spin a thread:* Cook a syrup of sugar and water until it reaches 238°F on a candy thermometer, at which stage the sugar will spin threads if a utensil is dipped in the syrup, then removed and gently waved to and fro in the air.

suimono: basic Japanese chicken broth with various garnishes.

sumac: the sour berries of a nonpoisonous variety of the sumac bush, dehydrated and coarsely ground, used in Middle Eastern cooking.

supreme: boned and skinned breast of chicken.

sushi: Japanese vinegar rice combined with raw fish and other foods and served in finger-sized portions.

sweetbreads: two kinds are found in the market, the long thymus gland or throat sweetbread and the rounded irregular lobe, called the heart or belly sweetbread (pancreas). The thymus gland, from calves and lambs, atrophies as the animal grows, whereas the small belly sweetbread, choice when from a young animal, enlarges and toughens as the animal matures. Calf sweetbreads are the most desirable, lamb sweetbreads next. Before cooking, sweetbreads must be soaked in ice water (or water acidulated with vinegar or lemon juice) for at least 30 minutes. Most cooks then blanch the sweetbreads, although some people prefer to eliminate this step because some flavor may be sacrificed. Blanching helps to firm up the sweetbreads and facilitate the removal of the filament or membrane and the connective tubes. After blanching, the sweetbreads should be refreshed immediately in cold water, then trimmed. All of this can be done ahead of the final cooking, even the day before. If the sweetbreads are to be sliced, weighting them lightly will make it easier. If the sweetbreads are to be braised, add any of the trimmings to the sauce.

syllabub: frothy Elizabethan dessert made by whipping sweetened citrus juice, sherry or brandy, and cream, then folding the mixture into beaten egg whites and chilling.

Tabasco sauce: a very hot liquid seasoning made from Tabasco peppers and vinegar and aged for 3 years. Tabasco is a trademark owned by the McIlhenny family.

tabbouleh: a Middle Eastern salad made of parsley, bulgur wheat, chopped onions, garlic, tomato, lemon juice, and olive oil.

taco: a filled tortilla, often fried crispy.

tahini: a Middle Eastern paste made of ground sesame seeds.

tamarind: a fruit common to southeast Asia, available as a dried brown pod, the acid pulp of which is steeped to obtain a sourish liquor used for flavoring drinks, preserves, and other dishes. The pulp is also available compressed and packaged.

tandoori: the Indian process of cooking in a clay oven called a tandoor. The fire in the bottom produces extremely hot coals and high temperatures. Thin bread doughs are cooked by slapping them on the walls, where they puff and take on shape, other foods by threading and suspending them on long skewers. Tandoori foods are first marinated in yogurt and spices to which a red dye is added, giving them a characteristic bright red finish, then basted during cooking with clarified butter (GHEE), which smokes and adds to the flavor.

tapas: a very wide variety of hors d'oeuvre

served in bars in Spain as a premeal appetizer.

tarama: (Greek) the roe of fish, commonly mullet, cod, or carp, used fresh, smoked, or preserved in brine. The base of the appetizer taramasalata.

taramasalata or taramosalata: a Greek appetizer made of pureed fish roe, onions, garlic, bread, lemon juice, and olive oil.

taro: a starchy, edible root used in Japanese and other Asian cooking and in Latin America and the Caribbean. The young leaves of the plant, called callaloo or calalu, are the base of a soup popular throughout the Caribbean islands.

tartar sauce: mayonnaise combined with chopped pickles, parsley, chervil, and chives. Sometimes chopped olives are added.

tarte Tatin: "upside down" caramelized apple tart.

tasso: smoky, spicy Cajun-style ham.

temperatures: temperatures are measured in degrees Fahrenheit (F) or Celsius, also called Centigrade (C). To convert Fahrenheit to Centigrade, subtract 32 from the Fahrenheit temperature, multiply the result by 5, then divide by 9. To convert Centigrade to Fahrenheit, multiply the Centigrade temperature by 9, divide the result by 5, then add 32. The *boiling point of water* is 212°F, or 100°C. *Low oven temperatures* range from 225° to 325°F; *medium* from 325° to 390°F; *hot* from 400° to 450°F;

and *very hot* over 450°F. The temperatures in this book are given in degrees Fahrenheit.

tempura: Japanese foods, including seafood, shellfish, and vegetables, that are coated in a very light batter, deep-fried, and served with a sauce for dipping.

teriyaki: traditionally a Japanese dish of meat, chicken, or seafood glazed with a rich soy sauce mixture toward the completion of grilling or pan-frying, but more frequently in the United States, such a dish marinated in, and basted with, a soy-based sauce.

terrine: a clay or ceramic baking dish, generally used for cooking pâtés; also the name given to pâtés cooked in a terrine.

timbale: traditionally a mold used for preparing various dishes cooked in a crust; also dishes prepared in that fashion; also dishes, the filling of which is cooked apart and served in the baked and molded crust. In modern usage, timbales are custards mixed with other foods and baked in a mold without a crust.

tofu: soybean curd.

tomato: *fresh tomatoes* come in a variety of types: *cherry tomatoes*, small tomatoes most frequently used as hors d'oeuvre and garnishes, but also excellent cooked, and often of fuller flavor than larger sizes; *salad tomatoes*, of various dimensions, the largest and meatiest of which is *beefsteak*, and all of which can also be used for cooking; *saladette*, *plum*, or *Italian tomatoes*, small plum or pear-shaped tomatoes with more intense flavor, firmer pulp, and fewer seeds, making them excellent for cooking, especially of sauces, but can also be used raw. *Canned tomatoes* come as *puree;* as *solid pack,* whole peeled tomatoes; as a thick concentrated *paste;* and as a *sauce.* Tomato paste in a tube is easier to use because it can be measured in the small amount usually called for without having a great deal left over. *Sun-dried tomatoes* or *pumate,* prepared from Italian tomatoes, have an intense flavor and come in dried form or under oil. *Tomato concassé* is peeled, seeded, and lightly pressed tomato, coarsely chopped; cooked in butter, it becomes *tomato fondue. To peel a tomato:* Blanch it in boiling water; the skin will slip off easily. *To seed a tomato:* Cut it in half and squeeze each half gently; the seeds will be forced out, leaving the pulp.

tomato sauce: basically a seasoned puree of lightly sautéed onions and tomatoes, which can be made more complex by the addition of stock and vegetables.

tortilla: Mexican pancake of wheat or corn flour used as the base for many filled and rolled dishes, as well as the breadstuff accompanying meals.

tostada: a fried tortilla presented like an open-faced sandwich covered with fillings.

trifle: an English dessert of cake variously combined with custard, whipped cream, liquor or sherry, and fruit.

tripe: the stomach of an animal, most commonly beef tripe. *Honeycomb tripe* comes from the second stomach, *flat tripe* from the paunch or first stomach. Broadly used, tripe includes also the intestines.

tripes à la mode de caen: tripe cooked very slowly in a tightly covered pot with stock, vegetables, seasonings, and Calvados.

trotters: pigs' or other animals' feet, often pickled; or boiled, breaded, and broiled.

truffle: an edible fungus that grows underground. The finest are from Italy and France. Black truffles, coal black in color, range in size up to that of a golf ball or larger. White truffles, more highly prized and expensive ($300 or more a pound), have an even more intensely pungent aroma, described as earthy or smoky.

truss: tying poultry for cooking so that the legs and wings are secured against the body.

tsukemono: Japanese pickled vegetables, usually served at the beginning of the meal.

udon: a Japanese wheat noodle.

vacherin: a large meringue shell, generally filled with ice cream and fruit.

veal: *Dutch-process* and *milk-fed* veal are the same; Provimi is a trademarked brand name for Dutch-process; *kip* is baby beef, more reddish than white or pink in color, and more like beef than veal; *drop calf* is meat from an animal butchered at 2 weeks of age, containing little fat or mature configuration and therefore best braised or stewed.

vegetable pear: see MIRLITON.

velouté: thickened stock used as the base for a sauce or a soup.

verjuice: the juice of green (unripened) grapes.

veronique: a preparation garnished with grapes, most frequently fillet of sole.

vichyssoise: a cold cream soup based on leeks and potatoes.

vinaigrette: same as French dressing or oil-and-vinegar dressing. To make a basic vinaigrette, combine 2 to 3 parts oil (preferably olive) to 1 part wine vinegar and season with salt and pepper. The dressing can be varied by using different oils and vinegars and by the addition of Dijon-type mustard and herbs.

vinegar: the product of acetic fermentation of any alcoholic liquid such as wine or cider, used for pickling or preserving, in salad dressings, sauces, and marinades, and as a seasoning. *White vinegar* is strong and multipurpose; *red and white wine vinegars* are milder and preferable for salad dressings, sauces, and marinades; *cider vinegar* is golden, sharp, and useful in pickling; *herb and fruit vinegars* are made by adding the desired herb or fruit to the vinegar and leaving it for a period of time, then draining off the infusion; *rice vinegar*, a mild white vinegar, is used in Chinese and Japanese cooking; *aceto balsamico* (balsamic vinegar) is an Italian vinegar made by curing the vinegar over several years in a series of casks made of mulberry, chestnut, juni-

per, oak, and other woods. The very best quality vinegar may have been in casks for as long as 100 years. Aceto balsamico is used in salad dressings, to season boiled and fried vegetables and other foods just before serving, and mixed sparingly with sugar to bring out the essence of fresh strawberries.

vol-au-vent: a large patty shell made of puff pastry dough.

wasabi: a very strong Japanese horseradish; usually available in green powdered form, and mixed with water to form a paste.

water chestnuts: used in Asian cooking to add a crisp, crunchy texture and mildly sweet flavor. Available canned, but often found fresh (unpeeled) in Asian markets.

water ice: see SORBET.

Welsh rarebit: toasts covered with a mixture of melted cheese, beer, mustard, and egg yolks.

white bait: very young fish of several varieties including herring, silverside, and anchovy, floured and deep-fried whole.

white pudding or sausages (boudins blancs): delicate sausages made of the white meat of pork or chicken mixed with eggs, cream, onions, and a filler of rice or bread crumbs.

white sauce: see BÉCHAMEL.

wine: wine in cooking is used for marinating, poaching, deglazing, making sauces, and adding flavor. Dry table wine is most frequently used in Western cooking, although many dishes, particularly some desserts, require the sweeter or more pronounced flavors of vermouth, sherry, Marsala, port, and Madeira. The Chinese and Japanese use RICE WINES such as Shaoxing and mirin. The alcohol in wine burns off completely in cooking. When choosing wine for cooking, keep in mind that its flavor will become concentrated as it reduces so that it should at least be something good enough to drink; the better it is, the finer the result will be.

winter melon: a large squashlike Chinese vegetable sold in wedges of varying sizes to be cut up into soup; also often used whole —the top cut off and replaced as a lid, the seeds and fibers removed—as a receptacle for the broth and other flavorful ingredients that steam inside as it cooks. A scoop of the tender melon flesh is served in each bowl along with the soup.

wok: the traditional round-bottomed iron cooking utensil of the Chinese, used for stir-frying, deep-fat frying, and steaming. *To season* a wok before using it the first time, clean out the oil that comes on it by scouring well, heat over the burner until very hot, then rub with an oil-soaked cloth or paper towel until the oil smokes and the wok begins to darken in the center. Cool and wipe clean. You may need to repeat this process 2 or 3 times until the wok has soaked up enough oil to protect its surface from rusting. As the wok is used, it will develop a patina or coating that should never be cleaned off with soup or by scouring. In China they say that the best chefs cook food that takes on the smoky flavor of their woks. If a wok loses its patina or gets gummy, you can reseason it. There are rings in which to set the wok over an electric burner and also flat-bottomed woks for electric stoves.

yeast: a minute fungus which acts as a leaven in dough by fermenting the sugar, creating carbon dioxide gas that expands the gluten and makes the bread rise. The heat of baking kills the yeast, stopping the action. Yeast comes packaged in dry, granular form or in compressed cakes that are short-lived, even under refrigeration. *To proof yeast:* Mix a small amount of sugar with about ¼ cup tepid water and sprinkle the contents of 1 packet of yeast (or 1 cake of compressed yeast, crumbled) over the mixture, stir in, and let stand for several minutes. If the yeast is active, the mixture should begin to bubble. Wild yeast is the basis of sourdough breads; the starter is perpetuated by putting a bit from one batch into a new batch before using up the old.

yogurt: milk thickened by fermentation.

zabaglione (Italian): same as SABAYON.

zahtar: a Lebanese seasoning mixture made predominantly of thyme mixed with sumac and sesame.

zakuska or zakuski: Russian hors d'oeuvre.

zest: the very thin, colored, outer peel of oranges, lemons, or other citrus fruits, not including the white pithy layer underneath, used for flavoring.

Bibliography

❖

Over the ten years of working out the Monday Night dinners at Narsai's, we drew on many books to provide the background, context, and inspiration for what eventually numbered more than 500 special menus. The select bibliography that follows includes all of those resources as well as additional titles for readers who are encouraged to find out more about any one of the ethnic cuisines or special menus in this book.

AFRICA (EAST)
Eldon, Kathy, and Eamon Mullan. *Tastes of Kenya*. Nairobi, Kenya: Kenway Publications, 1981.
Van derPost, Laurens, and the Eds. of Time-Life Books. *African Cooking*. Foods of the World series. New York: Time-Life Books, 1970.

AFRICA (WEST)
Wilson, Ellen Gibson. *A West African Cook Book*. New York: M. Evans, 1971.

ARMENIA
Hogrogian, Rachel. *The Armenian Cookbook*. New York: Atheneum, 1978.
Papashvily, Helen and George, and the Eds. of Time-Life Books. *Russian Cooking*. Foods of the World series. New York: Time-Life Books, 1969.

ASSYRIA (see MIDDLE EAST)

AUSTRALIA
Steinberg, Rafael, and the Eds. of Time-Life Books. *Pacific and Southeast Asian Cooking*. Foods of the World series. New York: Time-Life Books, 1970.

AUSTRIA
Beer, Gretel. *Austrain Cooking and Baking*. New York: Dover Publications, 1975. Originally published as *Austrian Cooking* by Andre Deutsch, 1954.
Langseth-Christensen, Lillian. *Gourmet's Old Vienna Cookbook*. New York: Gourmet Books, 1959.
Wechsberg, Joseph, and the Eds. of Time-Life Books. *The Cooking of Vienna's Empire*. Foods of the World series. New York: Time-Life Books, 1968.

BARBECUE (see also GRILLING)
Waldron, Maggie. *Barbecue and Smoke Cookery*. San Francisco: 101 Productions, 1983.

BASQUE (French)
Fisher, M.F.K., and the Eds. of Time-Life Books. *The Cooking of Provincial France*.

Foods of the World series. New York: Time-Life Books, 1968.

BASQUE (Spanish) (see SPAIN)

BELGIUM

Field, Michael and Frances, and the Eds. of Time-Life Books. *A Quintet of Cuisines.* Foods of the World series. New York: Time-Life Books, 1970.

Hazelton, Nika. *The Belgian Cookbook.* New York: Atheneum, 1970.

BRAZIL

Leonard, Jonathan Norton, and the Eds. of Time-Life Books. *Latin American Cooking.* Foods of the World series. New York: Time-Life Books, 1968.

BREAD (see also DESSERTS)

Beard, James, *Beard on Bread.* New York: Alfred A. Knopf, 1973.

Bread. The Good Cook series. Alexandria, Virginia: Time-Life Books, 1981.

Brown, Edward E. *The Tassajara Bread Book.* Boulder, Colorado: Shambhala Publications, 1970.

Casella, Dolores. *A World of Breads.* New York: David White, 1966.

Clayton, Bernard, Jr. *The Breads of France.* Indianapolis: Bobbs-Merrill, 1978.

———. *The Complete Book of Breads.* New York: Simon and Schuster, 1974.

David, Elizabeth. *English Bread and Yeast Cookery.* New York: Viking Press, 1980.

Jones, Judith and Evan. *The Book of Bread.* New York: Harper & Row, 1982.

BULGARIA

Field, Michael and Frances, and the Eds. of Time-Life Books. *A Quintet of Cuisines.* Foods of the World series. New York: Time-Life Books, 1970.

CARIBBEAN ISLANDS (see also individual countries; LATIN AMERICA)

Ortiz, Elisabeth Lambert. *Complete Book of Caribbean Cooking.* New York: M. Evans, 1983.

Wolfe, Linda, and the Eds. of Time-Life books. *The Cooking of the Caribbean Islands.* Foods of the World series. New York: Time-Life Books, 1970.

CHARCUTERIE (see PÂTÉS)

CHEESE

Jones, Evan. *The World of Cheese.* New York: Alfred A. Knopf, 1978.

Marquis, Vivienne, and Patricia Haskell. *The Cheese Book.* New York: Simon and Schuster, 1985.

CHILE (see BRAZIL)

CHINA

Chao, Buwei Yang. *How to Cook and Eat in Chinese.* New York: John Day, 1949.

Chiang, Cecilia Sun Yun. *The Mandarin Way.* Boston: Atlantic Monthly Press Book, 1974.

Claiborne, Craig, and Virginia Lee. *The Chinese Cookbook.* Philadelphia and New York: J. B. Lippincott, 1972.

Hom, Ken. *Chinese Technique.* New York: Simon and Schuster, 1981.

———. *Ken Hom's Chinese Cookery.* New York: Harper & Row, 1986. Originally published in London by British Broadcasting Corporation, 1984.

Kuo, Irene. *The Key to Chinese Cooking.* New York: Alfred A. Knopf, 1977.

Miller, Gloria Bley. *The Thousand Recipe Chinese Cookbook.* New York: Grosset & Dunlap, 1970.

Perkins, David W., ed. *Hong Kong & China Gas Chinese Cookbook.* Hong Kong: Hong Kong & China Gas Co., 1978.

Sakamoto, Nobuko. *The People's Republic of*

China Cookbook. New York: Random House, 1977.

Tiger, Lionel. *China's Food*. New York: Friendly Press, n.d.

Tropp, Barbara. *The Modern Art of Chinese Cooking*. New York: William Morrow, 1982.

CREOLE AND CAJUN COOKING

Collin, Rima and Richard. *The New Orleans Cookbook*. New York: Alfred A. Knopf, 1975.

Feibleman, Peter S., and the Eds. of Time-Life Books. *American Cooking: Creole and Acadian*. Foods of the World series. New York: Time-Life Books, 1971.

Hearn, Lafcadio. *Creole Cooke Book*. New Orleans: Pelican Publishing House, 1967. Originally published in 1885.

The Original Picayune Creole Cook Book. New Orleans: Times-Picayune Publishing, 1947.

Prudhomme, Paul. *Chef Paul Prudhomme's Louisiana Kitchen*. New York: William Morrow, 1984.

CUBA (see caribbean islands)

CZECHOSLOVAKIA

Rosický, Marie. *Bohemian-American Cook Book*. Omaha: Automatic Printing Co., 1947.

Shenton, James P., Angelo M. Pellegrini, Dale Brown, Israel Shenker, Peter Wood, and the Eds. of Time-Life Books. *American Cooking: The Melting Pot*. Foods of the World series. New York: Time-Life Books, 1971.

DENMARK

Jensen, Bodil. *Take a Silver Dish . . .* Copenhagen: Høst and Søns Forlag, 1962.

Brown, Dale, and the Eds. of Time-Life Books. *The Cooking of Scandinavia*. Foods of the World series. New York: Time-Life Books, 1968.

DESSERTS, PASTRIES, SAVORIES, BREADS

Braker, Flo. *The Simple Art of Perfect Baking*. New York: William Morrow, 1985.

Clayton, Bernard, Jr. *The Complete Book of Pastry*. New York: Simon and Schuster, 1981.

Cunningham, Marion. *The Fannie Farmer Baking Book*. New York: Alfred A. Knopf, 1984.

Dodge, Jim, and Gayle Wilson. *Dessert at the Stanford Court*. New York: Simon and Schuster, 1986.

Field, Carol. *The Italian Baker*. New York: Harper & Row, 1986.

Heatter, Maida. *Book of Great Desserts*. New York: Alfred A. Knopf, 1979.

———. *Maida Heatter's Book of Great Chocolate Desserts*. New York: Alfred A. Knopf, 1980.

———. *Maida Heatter's New Book of Great Desserts*. New York: Alfred A. Knopf, 1982.

Lenôtre, Gaston. *Lenôtre's Desserts and Pastries*. Rev. and adapted by Philip and Mary Hyman. Woodbury, New York: Barron's, 1977.

Peck, Paula. *The Art of Fine Baking*. New York: Simon and Schuster, 1961.

Shere, Lindsey Remolif. *Chez Panisse Desserts*. New York: Random House, 1985.

Sousanis, Marti. *The Art of Filo Cookbook*. Berkeley: Aris Books, 1983.

EAST (Far East and Middle East, India, Bali, Japan, and China—see also individual countries)

Jaffrey, Madhur. *Madhur Jaffrey's World-of-the-East Vegetarian Cooking*. New York: Alfred A. Knopf, 1981.

ECUADOR (see brazil)

ENGLAND

Bailey, Adrian, and the Eds. of Time-Life Books. *The Cooking of the British Isles*. Foods of the World series. New York: Time-Life Books, 1969.

Chamberlain, Samuel. *British Bouquet*. New York: Gourmet Distributing Corp.; London: Hamish Hamilton, 1963.

ETHIOPIA (see EAST AFRICA)

FINLAND (see also DENMARK)

Djakangas, Beatrice A. *The Finnish Cookbook*. New York: Crown, 1964.

FISH

Cameron, Angus, and Judith Jones. *The L. L. Bean Game & Fish Cookbook*. New York: Random House, 1983.

Cronin, Isaac. *The International Squid Cookbook*. Berkeley: Aris Books, 1981.

Cronin, Isaac, Jay Harlow, and Paul Johnson. *The California Seafood Cookbook*. Berkeley: Aris Books, 1983.

McClane, A. J. *The Encyclopedia of Fish Cookery*. New York: Holt, Rinehart & Winston, 1977.

———. *McClane's North American Fish Cookery*. New York: Holt, Rinehart & Winston, 1981.

Walker, Charlotte. *Fish & Shellfish*. Tucson: HP Books, 1984.

FRANCE (see also BASQUE, FRENCH)

Beck, Simone. *Simca's Cuisine*. New York. Alfred A. Knopf, 1972.

———. *New Menus from Simca's Cuisine*. New York: Harcourt Brace Jovanovich, 1979.

Beck, Simone, Louisette Bertholle, and Julia Child. *Mastering the Art of French Cooking*. Vol 1. New York: Alfred A. Knopf, 1961.

Chamberlain, Samuel. *Bouquet de France*. New York: Gourmet Distributing Corp., 1957.

Chamberlain, Samuel and Narcissa. *The Flavor of France*. New York: Hastings House, 1978.

Child, Julia, and Simone Beck. *Mastering the Art of French Cooking*. Vol. 2. New York: Alfred A. Knopf, 1970.

Claiborne, Craig, Pierre Franey, and the Eds. of Time-Life Books. *Classic French Cooking*. Foods of the World series. New York: Time-Life Books, 1970.

David, Elizabeth. *French Provincial Cooking*. New York: Harper & Row, 1962.

Diat, Louis. *Sauces, French and Famous*. New York and Toronto: Rinehart & Co., 1951.

Escoffier, Auguste. *The Escoffier Cookbook*. New York: Crown, 1941.

———. *Le Guide Culinaire*. Trans. by H. L. Cracknell and R. J. Kaufmann. New York: Mayflower Books, 1921.

———. *Ma Cuisine*. New York: A & W Publishers, 1978.

Fisher, M.F.K., and the Eds. of Time-Life Books. *The Cooking of Provincial France*. Foods of the World series. New York: Time-Life Books, 1968.

Lach, Alma. *Hows and Whys of French Cooking*. Chicago and London: University of Chicago Press, 1970.

Lucas, Dione, and Marion Gorman. *The Dione Lucas Book of French Cooking*. U.S. and Canada: Little, Brown, 1973.

Mapie, the Countess de Toulouse Lautrec. *La Cuisine de France*. Ed. and trans. by Charlotte Turgeon. New York: Orion Press, 1964.

Moutagne, Prosper. *Larousse Gastronomique*. New York. Crown, 1961.

Olney, Richard. *The French Menu Cookbook*. New York: Simon and Schuster, 1970.

———. *Simple French Food*. New York: Atheneum, 1974.

Pellaprat, Henri-Paul. *Modern French Culinary Art*. Cleveland and New York: World Publishing, 1966. Rev. ed. by John Fuller, ed., Boston: CBI Publishing, 1974.

Pépin, Jacques. *Everyday Cooking with Jacques Pépin*. New York: Harper & Row, 1982.

————. *A French Chef Cooks at Home*. New York: Simon and Schuster, 1975.

————. *La Methode*. New York: Times Books, 1979.

————. *La Technique*. New York: Quadrangle/ New York Times Book Co., 1976.

Root, Waverley. *The Food of France*. New York: Alfred A. Knopf, 1958.

Sokolov, Raymond. *The Saucier's Apprentice*. New York: Alfred A. Knopf, 1976.

Willan, Anne. *French Regional Cooking*. New York: William Morrow, 1981.

GAME

Beard, James. *James Beard's Fowl and Game Cookery*. New York: Harcourt Brace Jovanovich, 1979.

Cameron, Angus, and Judith Jones. *The L. L. Bean Game & Fish Cookbook*. New York: Random House, 1983.

GENERAL

Andrews, Jean. *Peppers: The Domesticated Capsicums*. Austin: University of Texas Press, 1984.

Beard, James. *Beard on Food*. New York: Alfred A. Knopf, 1974.

————. *James Beard's Theory and Practice of Good Cooking*. New York: Alfred A. Knopf, 1977.

————. *The New James Beard*. New York: Alfred A. Knopf, 1981.

Beck, Bruce. *Produce*. New York: Friendly Press, 1984.

Better Homes and Gardens Kitchen Appliance Cook Book. Des Moines: Meredith, 1982.

Carcione, Joe. *The Greengrocer Cookbook*. Millbrae, California: Celestial Arts, 1975.

Claiborne, Craig, ed. *The New York Times Cookbook*. New York: Harper & Row, 1961.

The Fannie Farmer Cookbook, 12th ed. Rev. by Marion Cunningham with Jeri Laber. New York: Alfred A. Knopf, 1979.

Farmer, Fannie Merritt. *The Boston Cooking-School Cook Book*. Boston: Little, Brown, 1946. Originally published in Boston, 1896.

Freiman, Jan Salzfass. *The Art of Food Processor Cooking*. Chicago: Contemporary Books, 1980.

Given, Meta. *Meta Given's Modern Encyclopedia of Cooking*. Chicago: J. G. Ferguson and Associates, 1954.

Grigson, Jane. *The Mushroom Feast*. New York: Alfred A. Knopf, 1975.

Harris, Lloyd. *The Book of Garlic*. San Francisco: Panjandrum Press, 1974.

Kafka, Barbara, James Beard, Milton Glaser, and Burton Richard Wolfe, eds. *The Cook's Catalogue*. New York: Harper & Row, 1975.

Kander, Mrs. Simon. *The Settlement Cook Book*. Rev. ed. New York: Simon and Schuster, 1965.

Klein, Maggie Blyth. *The Feast of the Olive*. Berkeley: Aris Books, 1983.

Lirio, Jack. *Cooking with Jack Lirio*. New York: William Morrow, 1982.

Renggli, Seppi, with Susan Grodnick. *The Four Seasons Spa Cuisine*. New York: Simon and Schuster, 1986.

Rombauer, Irma S., and Marion Rombauer Becker. *Joy of Cooking*. Indianapolis and New York: Bobbs-Merrill, 1975.

GERMANY

Hazelton, Nika Standen, and the Eds. of Time-Life Books. *The Cooking of Germany*. Foods of the World series. New York: Time-Life Books, 1969.

Mitchell, Jan. *Lüchow's German Cookbook*. Garden City, New York: Doubleday, 1967.

Sheraton, Mimi. *The German Cookbook*. New York: Random House, 1965.

Wason, Betty. *The Art of German Cookery.* Garden City, New York: Doubleday, 1967.

GREECE

Marketos, Olympia. *Athens à la Carte.* Chicago, New York, San Francisco: Rand McNally, 1963.

Nickles, Harry G., and the Eds. of Time-Life Books. *Middle Eastern Cooking.* Foods of the World series. New York: Time-Life books, 1969.

Skouna, Sophia. *The Greek Cookbook.* New York: Crown, 1974.

Tselementes, Nicholas. *Greek Cookery.* New York: D.C. Divry, 1952.

The Women of St. Paul's Greek Orthodox Church. *The Art of Greek Cookery.* Garden City, New York: Doubleday, 1963.

Yianilos, Theresa Karas. *The Complete Greek Cookbook.* New York: Avenel Books, 1970.

GRILLING (see also BARBECUE)

Sinnes, A. Cort, and Jay Harlow. *The Grilling Book.* Berkeley: Aris Books, 1985.

HOLLAND (The Netherlands)

Field, Michael and Frances, and the Eds. of Time-Life Books. *A Quintet of Cuisines.* Foods of the World series. New York: Time-Life Books, 1970.

HUNGARY

Biro, Charlotte. *Flavors of Hungary.* San Francisco: 101 Productions, 1973.

Lang, George. *The Cuisine of Hungary.* New York: Bonanza Books, 1971.

Shenton, James P., Angelo M. Pellegrini, Dale Brown, Israel Shenker, Peter Wood, and the Eds. of Time-Life Books. *American Cooking; The Melting Pot.* Foods of the World series. New York: Time-Life Books, 1971.

Weiss, Edward, with Ruth Buchan. *The Papri-kás Weiss Hungarian Cookbook.* New York: Gramercy Publishing, 1983. Originally published by William Morrow, 1979.

INDIA

Chowdhary, Savitri. *Indian Cooking.* London: Andre Deutsch, 1959.

Jaffrey, Madhur. *Invitation to Indian Cooking.* New York: Vintage, 1975.

Rau, Santha Rama, and the Eds. of Time-Life Books. *The Cooking of India.* Foods of the World series. New York: Time-Life Books, 1969.

Sahni, Julie. *Classic Indian Cooking.* New York: William Morrow, 1980.

Singh, Dharam Jit. *Classic Cooking from India.* London: Arco Publications, 1958.

INDONESIA (see also AUSTRALIA)

Marks, Copeland, with Mintari Soeharjo. *The Indonesian Kitchen.* New York: Atheneum, 1981.

INTERNATIONAL

Baker, Charles H., Jr. *The Gentleman's Companion.* New York: Crown, 1946.

Campbell, Elizabeth. *Encyclopedia of World Cookery.* London: Spring Books, n.d.

The Complete Book of World Cookery. New York: Crescent, 1972.

The Gourmet Cookbook. Vols. 1 and 2. New York: Gourmet Books, 1965.

Hering, Richard. *Hering's Dictionary of Classical and Modern Cookery.* Giessen, Germany: Fachbuchuerlag Dr. Pfanneberg, 1958.

Margittai, Tom, and Paul Kovi. *The Four Seasons.* New York: Simon and Schuster, 1980.

Metzelthin, Pearl V. *The New World Wide Cook Book.* New York: Bramhall House, 1951.

Morphy, Countess. *Recipes of All Nations.* New York: William H. Wise, 1935.

Muscatine, Doris. *A Cook's Tour of San Francisco.* New York: Charles Scribner's Sons, 1963; rev. ed., 1969.

Shenton, James P., Angelo M. Pellegrini, Dale Brown, Israel Shenker, Peter Wood, and the Eds. of Time-Life Books. *American Cooking: The Melting Pot.* Foods of the World series. New York: Time-Life Books, 1971.

Simon, André L. *Guide to Good Food and Wines: A Concise Encyclopedia of Gastronomy, Complete and Unabridged.* London and Glasgow: Collins, 1960.

Soper, Musia. *Encyclopedia of European Cooking.* London: Spring Books, 1962.

IRAN

Nickles, Harry G., and the Eds. of Time-Life Books. *Middle Eastern Cooking.* Foods of the World series. New York: Time-Life Books, 1969.

IRELAND

Bailey, Adrian, and the Eds. of Time-Life Books. *The Cooking of the British Isles.* Foods of the World series. New York: Time-Life Books, 1969.

Cole, Rosalind. *Of Soda Bread and Guinness.* Indianapolis and New York: Bobbs-Merrill, 1973.

Sheridan, Monica. *The Art of Irish Cooking.* New York: Crown by arrangement with Doubleday, 1965.

ISRAEL (see IRAN)

ITALY (see also PASTA)

Boni, Ada. *Italian Regional Cooking.* Trans. by Maria Langdale and Ursula Whyte. New York: E. P. Dutton, 1969.

———. *Talisman Italian Cookbook.* New York: Crown, 1972.

Bugialli, Giuliano. *The Fine Art of Italian Cook-*
ing. New York: Quandrangle/The New York Times Book Co., 1977.

———. *Giuliano Bugialli's Classic Techniques of Italian Cooking.* New York: Simon and Schuster, 1982.

———. *Giuliano Bugialli's Foods of Italy.* New York: Stewart, Tabori & Chang, 1984.

Caggiano, Biba. *Northern Italian Cooking.* Tucson: HP Books, 1981.

Chamberlain, Samuel. *Italian Bouquet.* New York: Gourmet Distributing Corp., 1958; London: Hamish Hamilton, 1958.

David, Elizabeth. *Italian Food.* New York: Alfred A. Knopf, 1958; New York and London: Penguin, 1970.

Hazan, Marcella. *The Classic Italian Cookbook.* New York: Alfred A. Knopf, 1976.

———. *More Classic Italian Cooking.* New York: Alfred A. Knopf, 1978.

Martini, Anna. *The Mondadori Regional Italian Cookbook.* New York: Crown, 1983.

Middione, Carlo. *The Food of Southern Italy.* New York: William Morrow, 1986.

Muscatine, Doris. *A Cook's Tour of Rome.* New York: Charles Scribner's Sons, 1964.

Root, Waverley. *The Food of Italy.* New York: Atheneum, 1977.

Root, Waverley, and the Eds. of Time-Life Books. *The Cooking of Italy.* Foods of the World series. New York: Time-Life Books, 1968.

JAMAICA (see CARIBBEAN ISLANDS)

JAPAN

Andoh, Elizabeth. *At Home with Japanese Cooking.* New York: Alfred A. Knopf, 1980.

Steinberg, Rafael, and the Eds. of Time-Life Books. *The Cooking of Japan.* Foods of the World series. New York: Time-Life Books, 1969.

Tsuji, Shizuo. *Japanese Cooking: A Simple Art.*

Tokyo, New York, San Francisco: Kodansha International, 1980.

KENYA (see AFRICA)

LATIN AMERICA

Baker, Charles H., Jr. *The South American Gentleman's Companion.* New York: Crown, 1951.

Food of Latin America, Mexico and the Caribbean. Round the World Cooking Library series. New York: Drake Publishers, 1973, 1974.

Ortiz, Elisabeth Lambert. *The Book of Latin American Cooking.* New York: Alfred A. Knopf, 1979.

LITHUANIA

Dauzvardis, Josephine J. *Popular Lithuanian Recipes.* Chicago: Lithuanian Catholic Press, 1974.

Papashvily, Helen and George, and the Eds. of Time-Life Books. *Russian Cooking.* Foods of the World series. New York: Time-Life Books, 1969.

MEAT

Allen, Jana, and Margaret Gin. *Innards and Other Variety Meats.* San Francisco: 101 Productions, 1974.

Ellis, Merle. *Cutting-up in the Kitchen.* San Francisco: Chronicle Books, 1975.

MEXICO (see also BRAZIL; LATIN AMERICA)

Hansen, Barbara. *Mexican Cookery.* Tucson: HP Books, 1980.

Kennedy, Diana. *The Cuisines of Mexico.* New York: Harper & Row, 1972.

————. *The Tortilla Book.* New York: Harper & Row, 1975.

————. *Recipes from the Regional Cooks of Mexico.* New York: Harper & Row, 1978.

Ortiz, Elisabeth Lambert. *The Complete Book of Mexican Cooking.* New York: M. Evans, 1980.

MIDDLE EAST (see also IRAN)

Bhatti, A. Nisa. *Modern Muslim Cooking of Indo-Pakistan.* Lahore, India: Indus Publishing House, 1964.

Dosti, Rose. *Middle Eastern Cooking.* Tucson: HP Books, 1982.

Mallos, Tess. *The Complete Middle East Cookbook.* New York: McGraw-Hill, 1979, 1980.

Najor, Julia. *Babylonian Cuisine: Chaldeau Cookbook From the Middle East.* New York: Vantage, 1981.

Roden, Claudia. *A Book of Middle Eastern Food.* New York: Alfred A. Knopf, 1972.

Seranne, Ann, and Eileen Gaden. *The Best of Near Eastern Cookery.* Garden City, New York: Doubleday, 1964.

MOROCCO

Wolfert, Paula. *Couscous and Other Good Food from Morocco.* New York: Harper & Row, 1973.

NICARAGUA (see BRAZIL)

NORWAY (see DENMARK)

PASTA (see also ITALY)

Beard, James. *Beard on Pasta.* New York: Alfred A. Knopf, 1983.

Buonassisi, Vincenzo. *Pasta.* Trans. by Elizabeth Evans. Wilton, Connecticut: Lyceum Books, 1976.

Burum, Linda. *Asian Pasta.* Berkeley: Aris Books, 1985.

Middione, Carlo. *Pasta! Cooking It, Loving It.* New York: Irena Chalmers, 1982.

Pasta. The Good Cook series. Alexandria, Virginia: Time-Life Books, 1981.

Waters, Alice, Patricia Curtan, and Martine

Labro. *Chez Panisse Pasta, Pizza, & Calzone.* New York: Random House, 1984.

PASTRIES (see DESSERTS)

PÂTÉS AND CHARCUTERIE

Grigson, Jane. *The Art of Charcuterie.* New York: Alfred A. Knopf, 1968.

Iribe, Maybelle, and Barbara Wilder. *Pâtés for Kings and Commoners.* New York: Hawthorn Books, 1977.

Wise, Victoria. *American Charcuterie.* New York: Viking, 1986.

PERSIA

Hekmat, Forough. *The Art of Persian Cooking.* Garden City, New York: Doubleday, 1961.

PERU (see BRAZIL)

POLAND

Field, Michael and Frances, and the Eds. of Time-Life Books. *A Quintet of Cuisines.* Foods of the World series. New York: Time-Life Books, 1970.

Ochorowicz-Monatowa, Marja. *Polish Cookery: The Universal Cookbook.* New York: Crown, 1975.

Rysia. *Old Warsaw Cook Book.* New York: Gramercy Publishing, 1958.

PORTUGAL (see also BASQUE, SPANISH)

Domeneck, Alejandro. *Spanish and Portuguese Cooking: Favorite Recipes from the Iberian Peninsula.* Round the World Cooking Library series. New York: Drake Publishers, 1973, 1974.

Sarvis, Shirley. *A Taste of Portugal.* New York: Charles Scribner's Sons, 1967.

Vaz, August Mark, and Elizabeth S. Vaz. *Cooking with a Portuguese Flavor.* San Francisco: Filmer Brothers Press, Taylor & Taylor, 1979.

PUERTO RICO (see CARIBBEAN ISLANDS)

ROMANIA

Field, Michael and Frances, and the Eds. of Time-Life Books. *A Quintet of Cuisines.* Foods of the World series. New York: Time-Life Books, 1970.

Stan, Anisoara. *The Romanian Cook Book.* Secaucus: Castle, 1951.

RUSSIA

Markevitch, Marie Alexandre. *The Epicure in Imperial Russia.* San Francisco: Colt Press, 1941.

Papashvily, Helen and George, and the Eds. of Time-Life Books. *Russian Cooking.* New York: Time-Life Books, 1969.

Petrovskaya, Kyra. *Kyra's Secrets of Russian Cooking.* Englewood Cliffs, New Jersey: Prentice-Hall, 1961.

Selivanova, Nina Nikolaevna. *Dining and Wining in Old Russia.* New York: E. P. Dutton, 1933.

SALADS

Salads. The Good Cook series. Alexandria, Virginia: Time-Life Books, 1980.

SCANDINAVIA

Bonekamp, Gunnevi. *Scandinavian Cooking.* Round the World Cooking Library series. New York: Drake Publishers, 1973.

Sarvis, Shirley, and Barbara Scott O'Neil. *Cooking Scandinavian.* Garden City, New York: Doubleday, 1963.

SCOTLAND

Bailey, Adrian, and the Eds. of Time-Life Books. *The Cooking of the British Isles.* Foods of the World series. New York: Time-Life Books, 1969.

McNeill, F. Marian. *The Scots Kitchen.* London, Toronto, Sydney, New York: Granada, 1981.

Walker, Sara Macleod. *The Highland Fling Cookbook*. New York: Atheneum, 1971.

SPAIN

Casas, Penelope. *Tapas*. New York: Alfred A. Knopf, 1985.

Domeneck, Alejandro. *Spanish and Portuguese Cooking: Favorite Recipes from the Iberian Peninsula*. Round the World Cooking Library series. New York: Drake Publishers, 1973, 1974.

Emery, William H. *The Flavor of Spain*. Boston: CBI Publishing, 1983.

Feibleman, Peter S., and the Eds. of Time-Life Books. *The Cooking of Spain and Portugul*. Foods of the World series. New York: Time-Life Books, 1969.

Norman, Barbara. *The Spanish Cookbook*. New York: Bantam Books, 1971.

SPICES AND HERBS

Cost, Bruce. *Ginger East to West*. Berkeley: Aris Books, 1984.

Day, Avanelle, and Lilllie Stuckey. *The Spice Cook Book*. New York: David White, 1964.

Hayes, Elizabeth S. *Spices and Herbs Around the World*. New York: Doubleday, 1961.

Stobart, Tom. *Herbs, Spices and Flavorings*. Woodstock, New York: Overlook Press, 1982.

SWEDEN (see DENMARK)

SWITZERLAND

Field, Michael and Frances, and the Eds. of Time-Life Books. *A Quintet of Cuisines*. Foods of the World series. New York: Time-Life Books, 1970.

THAILAND (see AUSTRALIA)

TUNISIA (North Africa)

Field, Michael and Frances, and the Eds. of Time-Life Books. *A Quintet of Cuisines*. Foods of the World series. New York: Time-Life Books, 1970.

TURKEY (see IRAN)

UNITED STATES

The American Heritage Cookbook. New York: American Heritage/Bonanza Books, 1982.

Beard, James. *James Beard's American Cookery*. Boston: Little, Brown, 1972.

Booth, Letha. *The Williamsburg Cookbook*. Williamsburg, Virginia: The Colonial Williamsburg Foundation, 1971.

Brown, Dale, and the Eds. of Time-Life Books. *American Cooking*. Foods of the World series. New York: Time-Life Books, 1968.

———. *American Cooking: The Northwest*. Foods of the World series. New York: Time-Life Books, 1970.

Ferrary, Jeanette, and Louise Fiszer. *The California-American Cookbook*. New York: Simon and Schuster, 1985.

Hess, Karen. *Martha Washington's Booke of Cookery*. New York: Columbia University Press, 1981.

Hutchison, Ruth. *The New Pennsylvania Dutch Cook Book*. New York: Harper & Row, 1958.

Idone, Christopher. *Glorious American Food*. New York: Random House, 1985.

Jones, Evan. *American Food*, 2nd ed. New York: Random House, 1981.

Leonard, Jonathan Norton, and the Eds. of Time-Life Books. *American Cooking: New England*. Foods of the World series. New York: Time-Life Books, 1970.

———. *American Cooking: The Great West*. Foods of the World series. New York: Time-Life Books, 1971.

The Los Angeles Times California Cookbook. New York: Harry N. Abrams, 1981.

Muscatine, Doris. *A Cook's Tour of San Francisco.* New York: Charles Scribner's Sons, 1963; rev. ed. 1969.

Shenton, James P., Angelo M. Pellegrini, Dale Brown, Israel Shenker, Peter Wood, and the Eds. of Time-Life Books. *American Cooking: The Melting Pot.* Foods of the World series. New York: Time-Life Books, 1971.

Walter, Eugene, and the Eds. of Time-Life Books. *American Cooking: Southern Style.* Foods of the World series. New York: Time-Life Books, 1971.

Waters, Alice. *Chez Panisse Menu Cookbook.* New York: Random House, 1982.

Wilson, José, and the Eds. of Time-Life Books. *American Cooking: The Eastern Heartland.* Foods of the World series. New York: Time-Life Books, 1971.

Wolcott, Imogene. *The New England Yankee Cook Book.* New York: Coward-McCann, 1939; repr. Louisville, Kentucky: Cookbook Collectors Library, n.d.

VENEZUELA (see BRAZIL)

VIETNAM (see also AUSTRALIA)

Ngô, Bach, and Gloria Zimmerman. *The Classic Cuisine of Vietnam.* Woodbury, New York: Barron's, 1979.

WINE

Adams, Leon. *The Wines of America*, 3rd ed. New York: McGraw-Hill, 1985.

Asher, Gerald. *On Wine.* New York: Random House, 1982.

Broadbent, Michael. *The Great Vintage Wine Book.* New York: Alfred A. Knopf, 1980.

Chroman, Nathan. *The Treasury of American Wines.* New York: Rutledge-Crown Publishers, 1973.

Ensrud, Barbara. *Wine with Food.* New York: Congdon & Weed, 1984.

Grossman, Harold J. *Grossman's Guide to Wines, Spirits, and Beers,* 6th ed. Rev. by Harriet Lembeck. New York: Charles Scribner's Sons, 1977.

Halász, Zoltán. *The Book of Hungarian Wines.* Trans. by Zsuzsa. Rev. by Elizabeth West. Budapest: Corvina Kiadó, 1981.

Hallgarten, S. F. *Alsace and Its Wine Gardens.* London: André Deutsch, 1957.

Hazan, Victor. *Italian Wine.* New York: Alfred A. Knopf, 1982.

Johnson, Hugh. *Wine.* New York: Simon and Schuster, 1974.

———. *Modern Encyclopedia of Wine.* New York: Simon and Schuster, 1985.

Kafka, Barbara. *American Food & California Wine.* New York: Harper & Row, 1981.

Langenbach, Alfred. *German Wines and Vines.* London: Vista Books, 1962.

Lichine, Alexis. *Wines of France,* New York: Alfred A. Knopf, 1969.

———. *Alexis Lichine's New Encyclopedia of Wines & Spirits,* 3rd ed. New York: Alfred A. Knopf, 1981.

Muscatine, Doris, Maynard Amerine, and Bob Thompson. *The University of California/Sotheby Book of California Wine.* Berkeley and Los Angeles: University of California Press; London: Philip Wilson, 1984.

Olken, Charles, Earl Singer, and Norman Roby. *The Connoisseurs' Handbook of California Wines,* 2nd ed. New York: Alfred A. Knopf, 1982.

Quimme, Peter (pseud.). *The Signet Book of American Wine,* 3rd ed. New York: New American Library, 1980.

Schoonmaker, Frank. *Frank Schoonmaker's Encyclopedia of Wine,* 6th ed. New York: Hastings House, 1978.

Simon, André L., ed. *Wines of the World,* 2nd ed. Rev. by Serena Sutcliff. New York: McGraw-Hill, 1981.

Thompson, Bob. *California Wine,* 2nd ed. Menlo Park, California: Lane, 1977.

————. *The Pocket Encyclopedia of California Wines*. New York: Simon and Schuster, 1985.

Thompson, Bob, and Hugh Johnson. *The California Wine Book*. New York: William Morrow, 1976.

Thompson, Bob, and the Eds. of Sunset Books and Sunset Magazine, *Guide to California's Wine Country*, 3rd ed. Menlo Park, California: Lane, 1982.

Waugh, Alec, and the Eds. of Time-Life Books. *Wines and Spirits*. Foods of the World series. New York: Time-Life Books, 1968.

YUGOSLAVIA

Shenton, James P., Angelo M. Pellegrini, Dale Brown, Israel Shenker, Peter Wood, and the Eds. of Time-Life Books. *American Cooking: The Melting Pot*. Foods of the World series. New York: Time-Life Books, 1971.

Index

About the Authors

For ten years Narsai David was the owner and chef of the legendary Berkeley restaurant Narsai's, and for seven years, the television chef on the national PBS program *Over Easy*. At present, he is the host of the popular radio show *Narsai & Company* on KCBS in San Francisco and is energetically involved in the development of products for the *Narsai's* line of specialty foods. He lives with his wife, Venus, and son, Daniel, in Berkeley, California.

Doris Muscatine is a food, wine, and cultural history writer based in Berkeley, California. She owns a vineyard with her husband, Charles, and writes regularly for such publications as *House & Garden, Bon Appetit,* and *Image Magazine* of *The San Francisco Examiner*. She is the author of *A Cook's Tour of San Francisco, A Cook's Tour of Rome,* and *Old San Francisco—the Biography of a City,* and an editor of *The University of California/Sotheby Book of California Wine.*